BHAGAVAD GĪTĀ REVEALED

Terri Stokes

Śrī Śrī Krishna-Arjuna

Michael Beloved/ Madhvācārya dās

Original Sanskrit text :

- Chapters 23 -40 Bhishma Parva, Mahābhārata--granted and permitted by John Smith-University of Cambridge, Bhandarkar Oriental Research Institute.

Numbered, four-lined, formatted: Marcia & Michael Beloved
Devanagari script: Sanskrit 2003 Font
Transliteration: URW Palladio ITU font/ ITranslator
Word-for-Word typeset: Bernard Adjodha/Michael Beloved
Format assistant: Marcia K. Beloved
Cover Art- Universal Form: Terri Stokes-Pineda
Ist Edition Cover Layout: Sir Paul Castagna
This Edition Cover Layout: Author
Sri Sri Krishna-Arjuna Line Art: Terri Stokes-Pineda
Cover Paths/Color Application: Author

Correspondence:

Michael Beloved
3703 Foster Ave
Brooklyn NY 11203
USA

Paul Castagna
P.O. Box 150
Iron Belt WI 54536
USA

Email:
axisnexus@gmail.com

2nd. Edition 2010

ISBN
978-0-9793916-2-0
LCCN
2008906318

Bhagavad Gītā Revealed

Sanskrit Text

ENGLISH
Transliteration, Word-for-Word Meaning,
TRANSLATION

Edited/ Translated
Michael Beloved/ Madhvācārya dās

Scheme of Pronunciation

Consonants

Gutturals:	क	ख	ग	घ	ङ	
	ka	kha	ga	gha	ṅa	
Palatals:	च	छ	ज	झ	ञ	
	ca	cha	ja	jha	ña	
Cerebrals:	ट	ठ	ड	ढ	ण	
	ṭa	ṭha	ḍa	ḍha	ṇa	
Dentals:	त	थ	द	ध	न	
	ta	tha	da	dha	na	
Labials:		प	फ	ब	भ	म
	pa	pha	ba	bha	ma	

Semivowels:

य	र	ल	व
ya	ra	la	va

Numbers:

० १ २ ३ ४ ५ ६ ७ ८ ९

0 1 2 3 4 5 6 7 8 9

Sibilants:	श	ष	स
	śa	ṣa	sa

Aspirate: ह

ha

Vowels:

अ	आ	इ	ई	उ	ऊ	ऋ	ॠ
a	ā	i	ī	u	ū	ṛ	ṝ
ए	औ	ओ	औ	ळ	ॡ	<	:
e	ai	o	au	lṛ	lṝ	ṁ	ḥ

Apostrophe ऽ

Table of Contents

Introduction

This translation, using the Bhagavad-Gītā as well as the Mahābhārata from which the text was extracted, gives a view of the cultural and social conditions in which Arjuna queried and Sri Krishna answered. This translation was motivated by a desire to show that Sri Krishna's ideas were mostly centered on yoga practice as it could be applied to cultural life. That is karma yoga, which is karma and yoga, or cultural activities and the practice of ashtanga yoga.

We are told by devotional authorities in India, that the Gītā concerns only bhakti yoga, which is usually defined as a loving feeling applied to Sri Krishna along certain scripturally-approved guidelines in a particular disciple succession which originated from Sri Krishna.

Other religious and moral authorities explained that the Gītā really concerns not bhakti yoga but karma yoga, which they define as cultural activities which are done with detachment as explained by Sri Krishna.

This translation shows that karma yoga means karma and yoga. Bhakti yoga means bhakti and yoga. As far as the Gītā is concerned, any unbiased reader of the Sanskrit will find that the stress is on karma yoga. Bhakti yoga is mentioned rarely but Arjuna's dearness to Sri Krishna is highlighted throughout the text. The stress however is on karma yoga. But karma yoga in the Gītā is more than cultural activities with detachment applied. It is rather, cultural activities with yoga expertise applied. Yoga is a psychological discipline. Cultural activities is the social lifestyle. When the two are used together, that is karma yoga. Sri Krishna identified this karma yoga as His own discipline, His own yoga.

If the exponents of bhakti yoga are saying that this type of karma yoga is itself bhakti yoga, then we have no difference of opinion with them. Readers should always keep in mind that this discourse took place under military conditions and not under a religious ceremonial atmosphere. Today the Bhagavad-Gītā is used mostly in temples and it is considered a religious text, but it was delivered to a battle commander on a warfield.

I encourage all readers of the Gītā to make the progression to the Mahābhārata from which the Gītā was extracted from the Bhishma Parva. If one can understand the social setting of the discourse one would be more apt to understand its application to our culture.

How to use this book:

Make a casual reading of the English translation which is in bold print.

Make a second reading of the English translation pausing at verses of interest.

Make a third reading of the English translation, checking the word-for-word meanings at verses of interest.

Finally, make an indepth study of the entire text.

A note on the diacritical marks and pronounciation:

Names like Krishna and Arjuna are accepted in common English usage. Their English spellings occur in the translation without diacritical marks.

There is a pronunciation guide on page 4.

***Here are some hints** on how to use the diacritical marks for near-exact pronunciation:*

*Letters with a **dot** under them, should be pronounced while the tongue touches and is released curling slightly at the top of palate.*

*The s sound for ś carries an h with it and is said as the **sh** sound in **she**.*

*The s sound for ṣ carries an h with it and is said as the **sh** sound in **shun**.*

The h sound for ḥ carries an echoing sound of the vowel before it, such that oḥ is actually **oho** *and **aḥ** is actually **aha**.*

*In many Sanskrit words the **y** sound is said as an **i** sound, especially when the y sound preceeds an a. For instance, prāṇāyāma should be praa-**nai**-aa-muh, rather than praa-naa-**yaa**-muh.*

*The a sound is more like **uh** in English, while the **ā** sound is like the a sound in **far**.*

*The **ṛ** sound is like the **ri** sound in **ridge**.*

*The **ph** sound is never reduced to an f sound as in English. The **p sound** is maintained.*

*Whenever **h** occurs after a consonant, its integrity is maintained as an air forced sound.*

*If the h sound occurs after a vowel and a consonant, one should let the consonant remain with the vowel which preceeds it and allow the h sound to carry with the vowel after it, such that Duryodhana is pronounced with the d consonant allied to the o before it and the h sound manages the a after it.Say Dur-**yod-ha**-na or Dur-**yod-han**. Do not say Dur-yo-**dha**-na. Separate the d and h sounds to make them distinct. In words where you have no choice and must combine the d and h sound, as in the word dharma. Make sure that the **h sound** is heard as an **air sound pushed out from the throat**. Dharma should never be mistaken for darma. But adharma should be **ad-har**-ma.*

*The **c** sound is **ch**, and the **ch** sound is **ch-h.***

CHAPTER 1

Arjuna's Discouragement*

धृतराष्ट्र उवाच
धर्मक्षेत्रे कुरुक्षेत्रे
समवेता युयुत्सवः ।
मामकाः पाण्डवाश्चैव
किमकुर्वत संजय ॥ १.१ ॥

dhṛtarāṣṭra uvāca
dharmakṣetre kurukṣetre
samavetā yuyutsavaḥ
māmakāḥ pāṇḍavāścaiva
kimakurvata saṁjaya (1.1)

dhṛtarāṣṭra — Dhritarashtra; uvāca — said; dharmakṣetre — at the place for settling political affairs; kurukṣetre — at Kurukshetra, a small plain in Punjab, India; samavetā — meeting together; yuyutsavaḥ — being possessed with battle spirit; māmakāḥ — my sons; pāṇḍavāś — the sons of Pandu; caiva — and indeed; kim — what; akurvata — did so; saṁjaya — Sanjaya

Dhṛtarāṣṭra said: O Sanjaya, being possessed with battle spirit and meeting together, what did my sons and the sons of Pandu do at Kurukṣetra, the place for settling political affairs? (1.1)

संजय उवाच
दृष्ट्वा तु पाण्डवानीकं
व्यूढं दुर्योधनस्तदा ।
आचार्यमुपसंगम्य
राजा वचनमब्रवीत् ॥ १.२ ॥

saṁjaya uvāca
dṛṣṭvā tu pāṇḍavānīkaṁ
vyūḍhaṁ duryodhanastadā
ācāryamupasaṁgamya
rājā vacanamabravīt (1.2)

saṁjaya uvāca — Sanjaya said; dṛṣṭvā — after observing; tu — indeed; pāṇḍavānīkaṁ — Pandava army; vyūḍhaṁ — which was set in battle formation; duryodhanas — Duryodhana, the eldest son of Dhrtarashtra, the crown prince of the Kurus; tadā — at that time; ācāryam — military teacher; upasaṁgamya — approaching; rājā — crown prince; vacanam — remark; abravīt — said

Sanjaya said: Indeed, after observing the Pandava army which was set in a battle formation, the Crown Prince Duryodhana, while approaching the Military Teacher, said this remark: (1.2)

**The Mahābhārata contains no chapter headings. This title was assigned by the translator on the basis of verse 27 of this chapter.*

पश्यैतां पाण्डुपुत्राणाम्
आचार्य महतीं चमूम् ।
व्यूढां द्रुपदपुत्रेण
तव शिष्येण धीमता ॥१.३॥

paśyaitāṁ pāṇḍuputrāṇām
ācārya mahatīṁ camūm
vyūḍhāṁ drupadaputreṇa
tava śiṣyeṇa dhīmatā (1.3)

paśyaitāṁ = see this; pāṇḍuputrāṇām — of the sons of Pandu; ācārya — sir; mahatīm — great; camūm — army; vyūḍhāṁ — which is set for combat; drupada putreṇa — by the son of Drupada; tava — your; śiṣyeṇa — by a student; dhīmatā — by perceptive

Sir, see this great army of the sons of Pandu, which is set for combat by your perceptive student, the son of Drupada. (1.3)

अत्र शूरा महेष्वासा
भीमार्जुनसमा युधि ।
युयुधानो विराटश्च
द्रुपदश्च महारथः ॥१.४॥

atra śūrā maheṣvāsā
bhīmārjunasamā yudhi
yuyudhāno virāṭaśca
drupadaśca mahārathaḥ (1.4)

atra — here; śūrā — heroes; maheṣvāsā — great bow men; bhīmārjunasamā — equal to Bhima and Arjuna; yudhi — in battle; yuyudhāno — Yuyudhana; virāṭaś — Virata; ca — and; drupadaś — Drupada; ca — and; mahārathaḥ — the great chariot fighter

Here are heroes, great bowmen, who are equal in battle to Bhima and Arjuna. There is Yuyudhāna, Virāṭa, and Drupada, the great chariot fighter. (1.4)

धृष्टकेतुश्चेकितानः
काशिराजश्च वीर्यवान् ।
पुरुजित्कुन्तिभोजश्च
शैब्यश्च नरपुंगवः ॥१.५॥

dhṛṣṭaketuścekitānaḥ
kāśirājaśca vīryavān
purujitkuntibhojaśca
śaibyaśca narapuṁgavaḥ (1.5)

dhṛṣṭaketuś — Dhṛṣṭaketu; cekitānaḥ — Cekitāna; kāśirājaś — the king of Kāśi; ca — and; vīryavān — valiant man; purujit — Purujit; kuntibhojaś — Kuntibhoja; ca — and; śaibyaś — Śaibya; ca — and; narapuṅgavaḥ — bull among men

There is Dhṛṣṭaketu, Cekitāna, and the Kāśi ruler, that valiant man. There is Purujit and Kuntibhoja and Śaibya, the bull-bodied man. (1.5)

युधामन्युश्च विक्रान्त
उत्तमौजाश्च वीर्यवान् ।
सौभद्रो द्रौपदेयाश्च
सर्व एव महारथाः ॥१.६॥

yudhāmanyuśca vikrānta
uttamaujāśca vīryavān
saubhadro draupadeyāśca
sarva eva mahārathāḥ (1.6)

yudhāmanyuś — Yudhāmanyu; ca — and; vikrānta — valiant; uttamaujāś — Uttamauja; ca — and; vīryavān — heroic; saubhadro — the son of Subhadrā; drāupadeyāś — the sons of Draupadī; ca — and; sarve — all; eva — indeed; mahārathāḥ — champions of chariot warfare

There is the valiant Yudhāmanyu and the heroic Uttamauja. There are the son of Subhadrā and the sons of Draupadī, who indeed, are all champions of chariot warfare. (1.6)

अस्माकं तु विशिष्टा ये
तान्निबोध द्विजोत्तम ।
नायका मम सैन्यस्य
संज्ञार्थं तान्ब्रवीमि ते ॥१.७॥

asmākaṁ tu viśiṣṭā ye
tānnibodha dvijottama
nāyakā mama sainyasya
saṁjñārthaṁ tānbravīmi te (1.7)

asmākaṁ — our men; tu — but; viśiṣṭā — distinguished; ye — who; tān — them; nibodha — be informed; dvijottama — O best of the initiates; nāyakā — commanders; mama — of my; sainyasya — of the army; saṁjñārthaṁ — for the sake of giving information; tān — them; bravīmi — I mention; te — to you

But, O best of the initiates, be informed of our men who are distinguished. For the sake of giving information to you, I mention the leaders of my army. (1.7)

भवान्भीष्मश्च कर्णश्च
कृपश्च समितिंजयः ।
अश्वत्थामा विकर्णश्च
सौमदत्तिस्तथैव च ॥१.८॥

bhavānbhīṣmaśca karṇaśca
kṛpaśca samitiṁjayaḥ
aśvatthāmā vikarṇaśca
saumadattistathaiva ca (1.8)

bhavān — your qualified self; bhīṣmaś — Bhishma; ca — and; karṇaśca — Karṇa; kṛpaś — Kṛpa; ca — and; samitiṁjayaḥ — victorious in battle; aśvatthāmā — Aśvatthāmā; vikarṇaś — Vikarṇa; ca — and; saumadattis — the son of Somadatta; tathaiva — as well; ca — and

There is your qualified self, and Bhishma, Karṇa and Kṛpa who are victorious in battle. There is also Aśvatthāmā, Vikarṇa and the son of Somadatta. (1.8)

अन्ये च बहवः शूरा
मदर्थे त्यक्तजीविताः ।
नानाशस्त्रप्रहरणाः
सर्वे युद्धविशारदाः ॥१.९॥

anye ca bahavaḥ śūrā
madarthe tyaktajīvitāḥ
nānāśastrapraharaṇāḥ
sarve yuddhaviśāradāḥ (1.9)

anye — other; ca — and; bahavaḥ — many; śūrā — heroes; madarthe — for my sake; tyakta jīvitāḥ — would give their lives; nānā śastra praharaṇāḥ — wielding various weapons; sarve — all; yuddha viśāradāḥ — being experts in warfare

And many other heroes wielding various weapons, being experts in warfare, would give their lives for my sake. (1.9)

अपर्याप्तं तदस्माकं	aparyāptaṁ tadasmākaṁ
बलं भीष्माभिरक्षितम् ।	balaṁ bhīṣmābhirakṣitam
पर्याप्तं त्विदमेतेषां	paryāptaṁ tvidameteṣāṁ
बलं भीमाभिरक्षितम् ॥ १.१० ॥	balaṁ bhīmābhirakṣitam (1.10)

aparyāptaṁ— inadequate; tad — this; asmākaṁ — of ours; balaṁ — military force; bhīṣmābhi rakṣitam — supervised by Bhishma; paryāptaṁ — sufficient; tvidam = tu — however + idam — this; eteṣām — of these; balam — military power; bhīmābhirakṣitam — protected by Bhīma

Inadequate is this military force of ours which is supervised by Bhishma. Sufficient, however, is their military power which is protected by Bhīma. (1.10)

अयनेषु च सर्वेषु	ayaneṣu ca sarveṣu
यथाभागमवस्थिताः।	yathābhāgamavasthitāḥ
भीष्ममेवाभिरक्षन्तु	bhīṣmamevābhirakṣantu
भवन्तः सर्व एव हि ॥ १.११ ॥	bhavantaḥ sarva eva hi (1.11)

ayaneṣu — in maneuvers; ca — and; sarveṣu — in all; yathā bhāgam — as by assignment; avasthitāḥ — positioned; bhīṣmam — Bhishma; evābhirakṣantu= eva — definitely + abhirakṣantu — protect; bhavantaḥ — your honorable master; sarve — all; eva – indeed; hi — certainly

And in all maneuvers, as positioned by assignment, all you honorable masters should definitely protect Bhishma. (1.11)

तस्य संजनयन्हर्षं	tasya saṁjanayanharṣaṁ
कुरुवृद्धः पितामहः ।	kuruvṛddhaḥ pitāmahaḥ
सिंहनादं विनद्योच्चैः	siṁhanādaṁ vinadyoccaiḥ
शङ्खं दध्मौ प्रतापवान् ॥ १.१२ ॥	śaṅkhaṁ dadhmau pratāpavān (1.12)

tasya — of him (Duryodhana); saṁjanayan — producing; harṣaṁ — happiness; kuruvṛddhaḥ — the eldest Kuru; pitāmahaḥ — the grandfather; siṁha nādaṁ — a lion-like roar; vinadyo ccaiḥ — sounding a loud; śaṅkhaṁ — conchshell; dadhmau — blew; pratāpavān — voluminously

The eldest Kuru, the grandfather, voluminously blew his conchshell, sounding a loud lion-like roar, thus producing great happiness for Duryodhana. (1.12)

ततः शङ्खाश्च भेर्यश्च
पणवानकगोमुखाः ।
सहसैवाभ्यहन्यन्त
स शब्दस्तुमुलोऽभवत् ॥ १.१३ ॥

tataḥ śaṅkhāśca bheryaśca
paṇavānakagomukhāḥ
sahasaivābhyahanyanta
sa śabdastumulo'bhavat (1.13)

tataḥ — then; śaṅkhāś — conches; ca — and; bheryaś — kettledrums; ca — and; paṇavānaka gomukhāḥ — cymbals, drums and trumpets; sahasaivābhyahanyanta = sahasā — simultaneously + eva indeed + abhyahanyanta — were sounded; sa — that; śabdas — sound; tumulo — tumultuous; 'bhavat (abhavat) — was

And then the conches and kettledrums, the cymbals, drums and trumpets, were simultaneously sounded. That sound was tumultuous. (1.13)

ततः श्वेतैर्हयैर्युक्ते
महतिस्यन्दने स्थितौ ।
माधवः पाण्डवश्चैव
दिव्यौ शङ्खौ प्रदध्मतुः ॥ १.१४ ॥

tataḥ śvetairhayairyukte
mahatisyandane sthitau
mādhavaḥ pāṇḍavaścaiva
divyau śaṅkhau pradadhmatuḥ (1.14)

tataḥ — then; śvetair — with white; hayair — with horses; yukte — harnessed; mahati — in a magnificent; syandane — swift-moving chariot; sthitau — standing; mādhavaḥ — the descendant of Madhu; pāṇḍavaś caiva — and indeed the son of Pandu; divyau — supernatural; śaṅkhau — two conches; pradadhmatuḥ — blew

Then, standing in a magnificent, swift-moving chariot with white horses harnessed, the descendant of Madhu and the son of Pandu blew two supernatural conchshells. (1.14)

पाञ्चजन्यं हृषीकेशो
देवदत्तं धनंजयः ।
पौण्ड्रं दध्मौ महाशङ्खं
भीमकर्मा वृकोदरः ॥ १.१५ ॥

pāñcajanyaṁ hṛṣīkeśo
devadattaṁ dhanaṁjayaḥ
pauṇḍraṁ dadhmau mahāśaṅkha
bhīmakarmā vṛkodaraḥ (1.15)

pāñcajanyaṁ — the conch named Pāñcajanya; hṛṣīkeśo — Krishna; devadattaṁ — a conch named Devadatta; dhanaṁjayaḥ — conqueror of wealthy countries; pauṇḍraṁ — conch named Paundra; dadhmau — blew; mahāśaṅkha — great conch; bhīma karmā — one whose actions are terrible; vṛkodaraḥ — wolf-bellied man

The conchshell named Pāñcajanya was blown by Hṛṣīkeśa, Krishna. The Devadatta conch was sounded by the conqueror of wealthy countries, Arjuna. Bhīma, the wolf-bellied man whose actions are terrible, blew the great conch named Paundra. (1.15)

अनन्तविजयं राजा
कुन्तीपुत्रो युधिष्ठिरः ।
नकुलः सहदेवश्च
सुघोषमणिपुष्पकौ ॥१.१६॥

anantavijayaṁ rājā
kuntīputro yudhiṣṭhiraḥ
nakulaḥ sahadevaśca
sughoṣamaṇipuṣpakau (1.16)

anantavijayaṁ — name of a conchshell; rājā — king; kuntī putro — son of Kuntī ; yudhiṣṭhiraḥ — Yudhishthira; nakulaḥ — Nakula; sahadevaś — Sahadeva; ca — and; sughoṣa maṇipuṣpakau — names of two conchshells: Sughosha and Manipushpaka

The King, Kuntī's son, Yudhishthira, blew the Anantavijayam. Nakula and Sahadeva blew the Sughosha and Manipushpaka respectively. (1.16)

काश्यश्च परमेष्वासः
शिखण्डी च महारथः ।
धृष्टद्युम्नो विराटश्च
सात्यकिश्चापराजितः ॥१.१७॥

kāśyaśca parameṣvāsaḥ
śikhaṇḍī ca mahārathaḥ
dhṛṣṭadyumno virāṭaśca
sātyakiścāparājitaḥ (1.17)

kāśyaś — King of Kāśi; ca — and; parameṣvāsaḥ — superior bowman; śikhaṇḍī — Śikhandī; ca — and; mahā rathaḥ — great chariot fighter; dhṛṣṭadyumno — Dhṛṣṭadyumna; virāṭaś — Virata; ca — and; sātyakiś cā 'parājitaḥ = sātyakiś — Satyaki + ca — and + aparājitas — unconquered one

The King of Kāśi, the superior bowman, and Śikhandī, the great chariot fighter, Dhṛṣṭadyumna and Virata and Sātyaki, the unconquered one, (1.17)

द्रुपदो द्रौपदेयाश्च
सर्वशः पृथिवीपते ।
सौभद्रश्च महाबाहुः
शङ्खान्दध्मुः पृथक्पृथक् ॥१.१८॥

drupado draupadeyāśca
sarvaśaḥ pṛthivīpate
saubhadraśca mahābāhuḥ
śaṅkhāndadhmuḥ pṛthakpṛthak (1.18)

drupado — Drupada; draupadeyāś — sons of Draupadi; ca — and; sarvaśaḥ — all together, being grouped together; pṛthivī pate — O King of the province; saubhadraś — son of Subhadra; ca — and; mahābāhuḥ — strong-armed; śaṅkhān — conchshells; dadhmuḥ — blew; pṛthak pṛthak — one by one

...O king of the province, Drupada and the sons of Draupadi, being grouped together, and the strong-armed son of Subhadra, blew conchshells in series. (1.18)

स घोषो धार्तराष्ट्राणां
हृदयानि व्यदारयत् ।
नभश्च पृथिवीं चैव
तुमुलो व्यनुनादयन् ॥१.१९॥

sa ghoṣo dhārtarāṣṭrāṇāṁ
hṛdayāni vyadārayat
nabhaśca pṛthivīṁ caiva
tumulo vyanunādayan (1.19)

sa — the; ghoṣo (ghoṣaḥ) — noise; dhārtarāṣṭrāṇāṁ — the men of Dhṛtarāṣṭra; hṛdayāni — emotions; vyadārayat — disrupted; nabhaś — the sky; ca — and; pṛthivīṁ — the earth; caiva — and indeed; tumulo — vibrating sound; vyanunādayan — cause to resonate

The noise disrupted the emotions of the sons of Dhṛtarāṣṭra, and the vibrating sound caused the sky and earth to resonate. (1.19)

अथ व्यवस्थितान्दृष्ट्वा धार्तराष्ट्रान्कपिध्वजः । प्रवृत्ते शस्त्रसंपाते धनुरुद्यम्य पाण्डवः ॥१.२०॥	atha vyavasthitāndṛṣṭvā dhārtarāṣṭrānkapidhvajaḥ pravṛtte śastrasaṁpāte dhanurudyamya pāṇḍavaḥ (1.20)

atha — then; vyavasthitān — in battle formation; dṛṣṭvā — after observing; dhārtarāṣṭrān — the sons of Dhṛtarāṣṭra; kapidhvajaḥ — the man with a monkey insignia; pravṛtte — in the challenge; śastrasaṁpāte — in the clash of weapons; dhanur — bow; udyamya — raising; pāṇḍavaḥ — son of Pāṇḍu

Then after observing the sons of Dhṛtarāṣṭra in battle formation, the man with a monkey insignia, that son of Pandu, raised his bow in the challenge of the clash of weapons. (1.20)

हृषीकेशं तदा वाक्यम् इदमाह महीपते । सेनयोरुभयोर्मध्ये रथं स्थापय मेऽच्युत ॥१.२१॥	hṛṣīkeśaṁ tadā vākyam idamāha mahīpate senayorubhayormadhye rathaṁ sthāpaya me'cyuta (1.21)

hṛṣīkeśaṁ — Hṛṣīkeśa, Krishna; tadā — then; vākyam — request; idam — this; āha — he spoke; mahīpate — O Lord of the earth; senayoḥ — of the two armies; ubhayoḥ — of the two; madhye — in the midst; rathaṁ — chariot; sthāpaya — cause to be parked; me — my; 'cyuta = acyuta — unaffected

Then he spoke this request to Hṛṣīkeśa, Krishna: O Lord of the earth, cause my chariot to be parked in the midst of the two armies, O unaffected one, (1.21)

यावदेतान्निरीक्षेऽहं योद्धुकामानवस्थितान् । कैर्मया सह योद्धव्यम् अस्मिन्रणसमुद्यमे ॥१.२२॥	yāvadetānnirīkṣe'haṁ yoddhukāmānavasthitān kairmayā saha yoddhavyam asminraṇasamudyame (1.22)

yāvad — so that; etān — these; nirīkṣe — I can see; 'ham = aham — I; yoddhu-kāmān — battle hungry; avasthitān — armed warriors; kair — with whom; mayā — with myself; saha — with; yoddhavyam — should be fought; asmin — in this; raṇasamudyame — in the battle engagement

...so that I can see these battle-hungry, armed warriors, with whom I should fight in this battle engagement. (1.22)

योत्स्यमानानवेक्षेऽहं य एतेऽत्र समागताः । धार्तराष्ट्रस्य दुर्बुद्धेर् युद्धे प्रियचिकीर्षवः ॥१.२३॥	yotsyamānānavekṣe'haṁ ya ete'tra samāgatāḥ dhārtarāṣṭrasya durbuddher yuddhe priyacikīrṣavaḥ (1.23)

yotsyamānān — those who are about to fight; avekṣe — I wish to observe; 'ham = aham — I; ya — who; ete — these; 'tra = atra — here; samāgatāḥ — assembled together; dhārtarāṣṭrasya — of the son of Dhṛtarāṣṭra; durbuddher — of the evil-minded; yuddhe — in battle; priyacikīrṣavaḥ — desiring to please

I wish to observe those who are to fight, who assembled here desiring to please the evil-minded son of King Dhṛtarāṣṭra, in battle. (1.23)

संजय उवाच एवमुक्तो हृषीकेशो गुडाकेशेन भारत । सेनयोरुभयोर्मध्ये स्थापयित्वा रथोत्तमम् ॥१.२४॥	saṁjaya uvāca evamukto hṛṣīkeśo guḍākeśena bhārata senayorubhayormadhye sthāpayitvā rathottamam (1.24)

saṁjaya – Sanjaya; uvāca — said; evam — thus; ukto — being addressed; hṛṣīkeśo — Hrisikesa; guḍākeśena — by the thick-haired baron; bhārata — O descendant of Bharata; senayor — of the two armies; ubhayor — of the two; madhye — in the middle; sthāpayitvā — caused to be positioned; rathottamam — best of the chariots

Sanjaya said: O descendant of Bharata, thus being addressed by Arjuna, the thick-haired baron, Krishna, who is known as Hṛṣīkeśa, caused the best of the chariots to be positioned in the midst of the two armies. (1.24)

भीष्मद्रोणप्रमुखतः सर्वेषां च महीक्षिताम् । उवाच पार्थ पश्यैतान् समवेतान्कुरूनिति ॥१.२५॥	bhīṣmadroṇapramukhataḥ sarveṣāṁ ca mahīkṣitām uvāca pārtha paśyaitān samavetānkurūniti (1.25)

bhīṣma droṇa pramukhataḥ — in the presence of Bhisma, Droṇa; sarveṣām — of all these; ca — and; mahīkṣitām — rulers of the earth; uvāca — (Krishna) said; pārtha — O son of Pṛthā; paśyai 'etān — behold them; samavetān — are assembled together; kurūn — Kurus; iti — thus

In the presence of Bhishma, Droṇa and all those rulers of the earth, Krishna said: O son of Pṛthā, behold these Kurus who are assembled here together. (1.25)

तत्रापश्यत्स्थितान्पार्थः
पितॄनथ पितामहान् ।
आचार्यान्मातुलान्भ्रातॄन्
पुत्रान्पौत्रान्सखींस्तथा ।
श्वशुरान्सुहृदश्चैव
सेनयोरुभयोरपि ॥ १.२६ ॥

tatrāpaśyatsthitānpārthaḥ
pitṝnatha pitāmahān
ācāryānmātulānbhrātṝn
putrānpautrānsakhīṁstathā
śvaśurānsuhṛdaścaiva
senayorubhayorapi (1.26)

tatrā apaśyat — there he saw; sthitān — standing; pārthaḥ — the son of Pṛthā; pitṝn — fathers; atha — then; pitāmahān — grandfathers; ācāryān — revered teachers; mātulān — maternal uncles; bhrātṝn — brothers; putrān — sons; pautrān — grandsons; sakhīṁs — friends; tathā — as well as; śvaśurān — fathers-in-law; suhṛdaś = suhṛdaḥ — well-wishing men; caiva – and indeed; senayoḥ — in the two armies; ubhayoḥ — in the both; api — also

The son of Pṛthā saw men who were fathers, grandfathers, revered teachers, maternal uncles, brothers, sons, grandsons, as well as friends, fathers-in-law and well-wishing friends, standing there in both armies. (1.26)

तान्समीक्ष्य स कौन्तेयः
सर्वान्बन्धूनवस्थितान् ।
कृपया परयाविष्टो
विषीदन्निदमब्रवीत् ॥ १.२७ ॥

tānsamīkṣya sa kaunteyaḥ
sarvānbandhūnavasthitān
kṛpayā parayāviṣṭo
viṣīdannidamabravīt (1.27)

tān — them; samīkṣya — observing; sa — he; kaunteyaḥ — son of Kuntī; sarvān — all; bandhūn — relatives; avasthitān — armored; kṛpayā — with compassion; parayāviṣṭaḥ — overwhelmed by deep; viṣīdann — feeling discouraged; idam — this; abravīt — he said

Observing all his relatives in the armored state, that son of Kuntī was overwhelmed by deep compassion. Feeling discouraged, he spoke this: (1.27)

दृष्ट्वेमान्स्वजनान्कृष्ण
युयुत्सून्समवस्थितान् ।
सीदन्ति मम गात्राणि
मुखं च परिशुष्यति ॥ १.२८ ॥

dṛṣṭvemānsvajanānkṛṣṇa
yuyutsūnsamavasthitān
sīdanti mama gātrāṇi
mukhaṁ ca pariśuṣyati (1.28)

dṛṣṭvemaṁ — having seen this; svajanān — my people; kṛṣṇa — Krishna; yuyutsūṁ — eager for combat; samavasthitān — standing near; sīdanti — collapse; mama — my; gātrāṇi — legs; mukhaṁ — mouth; ca — and; pariśuṣyati — dries up

Having seen this situation of my own people, standing near, eager for combat, my legs collapse and my mouth dries up. (1.28)

वेपथुश्च शरीरे मे
रोमहर्षश्च जायते ।
गाण्डीवं स्रंसते हस्तात्
त्वक् चैव परिदह्यते ॥ १.२९ ॥

vepathuśca śarīre me
romaharṣaśca jāyate
gāṇḍīvaṁ sraṁsate hastāt
tvak caiva paridahyate (1.29)

vepathuś — trembling; ca — and; śarīre — in the body; me — my; romaharṣaś — bristling of hair; ca — and; jāyate — takes place; gāṇḍīvaṁ — Gāṇḍīva bow; sraṁsate — falls; hastāt — from the hand; tvak — skin; caiva — and indeed; paridahyate — burns

A trembling is in my body and a bristling of my hairs takes place. The Gāṇḍīva bow falls from my hand. Indeed, my skin burns. (1.29)

न च शक्नोम्यवस्थातुं
भ्रमतीव च मे मनः ।
निमित्तानि च पश्यामि
विपरीतानि केशव ॥ १.३० ॥

na ca śaknomyavasthātuṁ
bhramatīva ca me manaḥ
nimittāni ca paśyāmi
viparītāni keśava (1.30)

na — not; ca — and; śaknomy — I can; avasthātuṁ — to remain standing; bhramatīva — as if it wanders; ca — and; me — my; manaḥ — the mind; nimittāni — indications; ca — and; paśyāmi — I perceive; viparītāni — bad; keśava — beautiful-haired one

I cannot remain standing. My mind feels as if it wavers. I perceive bad indications, O beautiful-haired one. (1.30)

न च श्रेयोऽनुपश्यामि
हत्वा स्वजनमाहवे ।
न काङ्क्षे विजयं कृष्ण
न च राज्यं सुखानि च ॥ १.३१ ॥

na ca śreyo'nupaśyāmi
hatvā svajanamāhave
na kāṅkṣe vijayaṁ kṛṣṇa
na ca rājyaṁ sukhāni ca (1.31)

na — no; ca — and; śreyaḥ — benefit; 'nupaśyāmi = anupaśyāmi — I can imagine; hatvā — killing; svajanam — my folks; āhave — in battle; na — nor; kāṅkṣe — desired; vijayaṁ — victory; kṛṣṇa — O Krishna; na — nor; ca — and; rājyaṁ — political power; sukhāni — good feelings; ca — and

And I can imagine no benefit in killing off my kinfolk in battle. I do not desire victory, O Krishna, or political power, or good feelings. (1.31)

किं नो राज्येन गोविन्द
किं भोगैर्जीवितेन वा ।
येषामर्थे काङ्क्षितं नो
राज्यं भोगाः सुखानि च ॥ १.३२ ॥

kiṁ no rājyena govinda
kiṁ bhogairjīvitena vā
yeṣāmarthe kāṅkṣitaṁ no
rājyaṁ bhogāḥ sukhāni ca (1.32)

kiṁ — what value would there be; no — to us; rājyena — with political control of a nation; govinda — Chief of the cowherds; kiṁ — what use would there be?; bhogair — with enjoyments; jīvitena — with life; vā — or; yeṣām — whose; arthe — in the interest; kāṅkṣitaṁ — was desired; no — of us; rājyaṁ — political control; bhogāḥ — enjoyable aspects; sukhāni — pleasures; ca — and

What value to us would there be with political control of a nation, O Chief of the cowherds? What use would there be with the enjoyable aspects or with life? Those in whose interest, the political control, the enjoyments and pleasures, were desired by us, (1.32)

त इमेऽवस्थिता युद्धे
प्राणांस्त्यक्त्वा धनानि च ।
आचार्याः पितरः पुत्रास्
तथैव च पितामहाः ॥१.३३॥

ta ime'vasthitā yuddhe
prāṇāṁstyaktvā dhanāni ca
ācāryāḥ pitaraḥ putrās
tathaiva ca pitāmahāḥ (1.33)

ta — they; ime — these; 'vasthitā = avasthitā — are armored; yuddhe — in battle formation; prāṇāṁs — lives; tyaktvā — having left aside; dhanāni — financial assets; ca — and; ācāryāḥ — revered teachers; pitaraḥ — fathers; putrās — sons; tathaiva — also; ca — and; pitāmahāḥ — grandfathers

...(they) are armed in battle formation, having left aside their lives and financial assets. These are revered teachers, fathers, sons and also grandfathers, (1.33)

मातुलाः श्वशुराः पौत्राः
स्यालाः संबन्धिनस्तथा ।
एतान्न हन्तुमिच्छामि
घ्नतोऽपि मधुसूदन ॥१.३४॥

mātulāḥ śvaśurāḥ pautrāḥ
syālāḥ saṁbandhinastathā
etānna hantumicchāmi
ghnato'pi madhusūdana (1.34)

mātulāḥ — brothers of mothers; śvaśurāḥ — fathers of wives; pautrāḥ — grandsons; śyālāḥ — brothers-in-law; saṁbandhinas — relatives; tathā — also; etān — them; na — not; hantum — to kill; icchāmi — I desire; ghnato — those who are intent on killing; 'pi = api — even though; madhusūdana — slayer of Madhu

...brothers of our mothers, fathers of our wives, grandsons, brothers-in-law, and also their relatives. O slayer of Madhu, I do not desire to slay them even though they are intent on killing, (1.34)

अपि त्रैलोक्यराज्यस्य
हेतोः किं नु महीकृते ।
निहत्य धार्तराष्ट्रान्नः
का प्रीतिः स्याज्जनार्दन ॥१.३५॥

api trailokyarājyasya
hetoḥ kiṁ nu mahīkṛte
nihatya dhārtarāṣṭrānnaḥ
kā prītiḥ syājjanārdana (1.35)

api — even; trailokya — of the three sectors, of the universe; rājyasya — political control; hetoḥ — on account of; kiṁ - what; nu — then; mahīkṛte —

for the sake of the earth; nihatya — killing; dhārtarāṣṭrān — the sons of Dhṛtarāṣṭra; naḥ — to us; kā — what; prītiḥ — joy; syāj — might it be; janārdana — O motivator of people

...even for political control of the three sectors of the universe, how then for the earth? O motivator of people, what joy should be had by killing the sons of Dhṛtarāṣṭra? (1.35)

पापमेवाश्रयेदस्मान्
हत्वैतानाततायिनः ।
तस्मान्नार्हा वयं हन्तुं
धार्तराष्ट्रान्स्वबान्धवान् ।
स्वजनं हि कथं हत्वा
सुखिनः स्याम माधव ॥ १.३६ ॥

pāpamevāśrayedasmān
hatvaitānātatāyinaḥ
tasmānnārhā vayaṁ hantuṁ
dhārtarāṣṭrānsvabāndhavān
svajanaṁ hi kathaṁ hatvā
sukhinaḥ syāma mādhava (1.36)

pāpam — sin; evāśrayed = eva — even + āśrayed — should take hold; asmān — to us; hatvaitān = hatvā — having killed + etān — these; ātatāyinaḥ — offenders; tasmān — therefore; nārhā — unjustified; vayaṁ — we; hantuṁ — to kill; dhārtarāṣṭrān — sons of Dhṛtarāṣṭra; svabāndhavān — our relatives; svajanaṁ — our own people; hi — indeed; kathaṁ — how; hatvā — having killed; sukhinaḥ — happiness; syāma — should be; mādhava — descendant of Madhu

Having killed the offenders, sin will take hold of us. Therefore we are not justified to kill the sons of Dhṛtarāṣṭra, our relatives. Having killed our own people, how should we be happy, O descendant of Madhu? (1.36)

यद्यप्येते न पश्यन्ति
लोभोपहतचेतसः ।
कुलक्षयकृतं दोषं
मित्रद्रोहे च पातकम् ॥ १.३७ ॥

yadyapyete na paśyanti
lobhopahatacetasaḥ
kulakṣayakṛtaṁ doṣaṁ
mitradrohe ca pātakam (1.37)

yadyapyete = yadi — if + api — even + ete — these; na — not; paśyanti — see; lobhopahata cetasaḥ = lobha — greed + upahata — possessed by + cetasaḥ — thoughts; kulakṣayakṛtaṁ = kula — clan + ksaya — destruction + kṛtaṁ — caused; doṣaṁ — fault; mitradrohe = mitra — friend + drohe — harm; ca — and; pātakam — crime

Even if these persons, their minds being possessed by greed, do not see the fault caused by the destruction of the clan and the crime of hurting a friend, (1.37)

कथं न ज्ञेयमस्माभिः
पापादस्मान्निवर्तितुम् ।
कुलक्षयकृतं दोषं
प्रपश्यद्भिर्जनार्दन ॥ १.३८ ॥

kathaṁ na jñeyamasmābhiḥ
pāpādasmānnivartitum
kulakṣayakṛtaṁ doṣaṁ
prapaśyadbhirjanārdana (1.38)

kathaṁ — how; na — not; jñeyam — to be understood; asmābhiḥ — by us; pāpād — from sin; asmān — from this; nivartitum — turn away; kulakṣaya = kula — clan + kṣaya — destruction; kṛtaṁ — caused; doṣaṁ — crime; prapaśyadbhiḥ — by due reason; janārdana — O motivator of human beings

...O motivator of human beings, why, by due reason, should we not understand that we should turn away from this sin, the crime caused by the destruction of the clan? (1.38)

कुलक्षये प्रणश्यन्ति
कुलधर्माः सनातनाः ।
धर्मे नष्टे कुलं कृत्स्नम्
अधर्मोऽभिभवत्युत ॥ १.३९ ॥

kulakṣaye praṇaśyanti
kuladharmāḥ sanātanāḥ
dharme naṣṭe kulaṁ kṛtsnam
adharmo'bhibhavatyuta (1.39)

kulakṣaye — in destruction of the family clan; praṇaśyanti — vanish; kuladharmāḥ — family traditions; sanātanāḥ — ancient; dharme — in the traditional values; naṣṭe — in the removal; kulaṁ — clan; kṛtsnam — whole; adharmo — lawlessness; 'bhibhavatyuta = abhibhavati — it overpowers + uta — even

In the destruction of the clan, the ancient family traditions vanish. In the removal of the traditional values, the entire clan is overpowered by lawlessness. (1.39)

अधर्माभिभवात्कृष्ण
प्रदुष्यन्ति कुलस्त्रियः ।
स्त्रीषु दुष्टासु वार्ष्णेय
जायते वर्णसंकरः ॥ १.४० ॥

adharmābhibhavātkṛṣṇa
praduṣyanti kulastriyaḥ
strīṣu duṣṭāsu vārṣṇeya
jāyate varṇasaṁkaraḥ (1.40)

adharmābhibhavāt = adharma — lawlessness + abhibhavāt — from predominant; kṛṣṇa — O Krishna; praduṣyanti — are degraded; kulastriyaḥ — the women of the clan; strīṣu — in women; duṣṭāsu — degraded; vārṣṇeya — O clansman of the Vṛṣṇis; jāyate — there arises; varṇasaṁkaraḥ — sexual intermixture of the classes

Due to the predominance of lawlessness, the women of the clan are degraded. In such women, O clansman of the Vṛṣṇis, there arises the sexual intermixture of the classes. (1.40)

संकरो नरकायैव
कुलघ्नानां कुलस्य च ।
पतन्ति पितरो ह्येषां
लुप्तपिण्डोदकक्रियाः ॥ १.४१ ॥

saṁkaro narakāyaiva
kulaghnānāṁ kulasya ca
patanti pitaro hyeṣāṁ
luptapiṇḍodakakriyāḥ (1.41)

saṁkaraḥ — sexual intermixture; narakāyaiva = narakāya — to hell + eva — indeed; kulaghnānāṁ = kula — clan + ghnānāṁ — destroyers; kulasya — of the clan; ca — and; patanti — are degraded; pitaro — the departed ancestors; hyeṣāṁ = hi — indeed + eṣām — of these; luptapiṇḍodakakriyāḥ = lupta — deprived of + piṇḍa — psychic cakes + udaka — psychic water + kriyāḥ — ceremonial rites

Indeed, the sexual intermixture causes the destroyers of the clan and the clan itself to go to hell. The departed ancestors of those clansmen, being deprived of the psychic cakes and water which are offered ceremonially, are degraded. (1.41)

दोषैरेतैः कुलघ्नानां
वर्णसंकरकारकैः ।
उत्साद्यन्ते जातिधर्माः
कुलधर्माश्च शाश्वताः ॥ १.४२ ॥

doṣairetaiḥ kulaghnānāṁ
varṇasaṁkarakārakaiḥ
utsādyante jātidharmāḥ
kuladharmāśca śāśvatāḥ (1.42)

doṣair — with sins; etaiḥ — by these; kulaghnānāṁ — of the family destroyers; varṇasaṁkarakārakaiḥ = varṇasaṁkara — sexual intermixture of classes + kārakaiḥ — by producing; utsādyante — disappeared; jātidharmāḥ — individual skills; kuladharmāś — family duties; ca — and; śāśvatāḥ — long-standing, traditional

By the sins of the family destroyers and by the sexual intermixture of the classes, individual skills and traditional family duties disappear. (1.42)

उत्सन्नकुलधर्माणां
मनुष्याणां जनार्दन ।
नरके ऽनियतं वासो
भवतीत्यनुशुश्रुम ॥ १.४३ ॥

utsannakuladharmāṇāṁ
manuṣyāṇāṁ janārdana
narake 'niyataṁ vāso
bhavatītyanuśuśruma (1.43)

utsanna kula dharmāṇāṁ = utsanna — destroyed + kuladharmāṇāṁ — of family customs; manuṣyāṇām — of men; janārdana — O Kṛṣṇa; narake — in hell; 'niyataṁ = aniyatam — indefinitely; vāso — dwelling; bhavatītyanuśuśruma = bhavati — it is + iti — was developed + anuśuśruma — we heard repeatedly

O Krishna, those who destroy the family customs dwell in hell indefinitely. This was declared repeatedly. (1.43)

अहो बत महत्पापं
कर्तुं व्यवसिता वयम् ।
यद्राज्यसुखलोभेन
हन्तुं स्वजनमुद्यताः ॥ १.४४ ॥

aho bata mahatpāpaṁ
kartuṁ vyavasitā vayam
yadrājyasukhalobhena
hantuṁ svajanamudyatāḥ (1.44)

aho — O!; bata — what a wonder!; mahat — great; pāpaṁ — sin; kartuṁ — to perform; vyavasitā — committed to; vayam — we; yad — which; rājyasukhalobhena = rājya — aristocratic + sukha — pleasure + lobhena — with greed; hantuṁ — to kill; svajanam — own folks; udyatāḥ — eager for

O! What a wonder! We are committed to perform a great sin, being eager to kill our kinfolk, through greed for aristocratic pleasures. (1.44)

यदि मामप्रतीकारम्
अशस्त्रं शस्त्रपाणयः ।
धार्तराष्ट्रा रणे हन्युस्
तन्मे क्षेमतरं भवेत् ॥ १.४५ ॥

yadi māmapratīkāram
aśastraṁ śastrapāṇayaḥ
dhārtarāṣṭrā raṇe hanyus
tanme kṣemataraṁ bhavet (1.45)

yadi — if; mām — me; apratīkāram — unresisting; aśastraṁ — without weapons, unarmed bearing; śastrapāṇayaḥ — those weapons, unarmed bearing; dhārtarāṣṭrā — sons Dhṛtarāṣṭra; raṇe — in battle; hanyuḥ — they may kill; tan — this; me — to me; kṣemataraṁ — greater happiness; bhavet — would be

If the weapon-bearing sons of Dhṛtarāṣṭra should kill me in battle, while I was unresisting, and unarmed, this to me would be greater pleasure. (1.45)

एवमुक्त्वार्जुनः संख्ये
रथोपस्थ उपाविशत् ।
विसृज्य सशरं चापं
शोकसंविग्नमानसः ॥ १.४६ ॥

evamuktvārjunaḥ saṁkhye
rathopastha upāviśat
visṛjya saśaraṁ cāpaṁ
śokasaṁvignamānasaḥ (1.46)

evam — thus; uktvā — having spoken; 'rjunaḥ - Arjuna; saṁkhye — in the conflict; rathopastha = ratha — chariot + upastha — seat; upāviśat — sat down; visṛjya — casting aside; saśaraṁ — together with arrow; cāpaṁ — bow; śokasaṁvignamānasaḥ = śoka — sorrow + saṁvigna — overwhelmed + mānasaḥ — heart

Having spoken, Arjuna, who was in the midst of the conflict, sat down on his chariot. Casting aside his arrow and bow, he was overwhelmed with sorrow. (1.46)

CHAPTER 2

The Divine State*

संजय उवाच
तं तथा कृपयाविष्टम्
अश्रुपूर्णाकुलेक्षणम् ।
विषीदन्तमिदं वाक्यम्
उवाच मधुसूदनः ॥२.१॥

saṁjaya uvāca
taṁ tathā kṛpayāviṣṭam
aśrupūrṇākulekṣaṇam
viṣīdantamidaṁ vākyam
uvāca madhusūdanaḥ (2.1)

saṁjaya — Sanjaya; uvāca — said; taṁ — to him; tathā — in this way; kṛpayāviṣṭam — overcome with pity; aśrupūrṇākulekṣaṇam = aśru — tear + pūrṇa — filled + ākula — perplexed + īkṣaṇam — eyes; viṣīdantam — saddened with hopelessness; idaṁ — this; vākyam — response; uvāca — spoke; madhusūdanaḥ — killer of Madhu

Sanjaya said: To him who was overcome with pity, whose eyes were filled with tears, who was perplexed and saddened with hopelessness, the killer of Madhu spoke this response: (2.1)

श्रीभगवानुवाच
कुतस्त्वा कश्मलमिदं
विषमे समुपस्थितम् ।
अनार्यजुष्टमस्वर्ग्यम्
अकीर्तिकरमर्जुन ॥२.२॥

śrībhagavānuvāca
kutastvā kaśmalamidaṁ
viṣame samupasthitam
anāryajuṣṭamasvargyam
akīrtikaramarjuna (2.2)

śrī bhagavān — the Blessed Lord; uvāca — said; kutastvā = kutas — how + tvā — to you; kaśmalam — sickly emotion; idaṁ — this; viṣame — at a crucial time; samupasthitam — come; anāryajuṣṭam — not suitable for a cultured man; asvargyam — not facilitating heaven in the hereafter; akīrtikaram — causing disgrace; arjuna — O Arjuna

The Blessed Lord said: How has this sickly emotion come to you at a crucial time? It is not suitable for a cultured man. It does not facilitate heaven in the hereafter. It causes disgrace, O Arjuna. (2.2)

**The Mahābhārata contains no chapter headings .This title was assigned by the translator on the basis of verse 27 of this chapter.*

क्लैब्यं मा स्म गमः पार्थ
नैतत्त्वय्युपपद्यते ।
क्षुद्रं हृदयदौर्बल्यं
त्यक्त्वोत्तिष्ठ परंतप ॥२.३॥

klaibyaṁ mā sma gamaḥ pārtha
naitattvayyupapadyate
kṣudraṁ hṛdayadaurbalyaṁ
tyaktvottiṣṭha paraṁtapa (2.3)

klaibyaṁ — cowardly behavior; mā — not; sma — in fact; gamaḥ — should entertain; pārtha — O son of Patha; naitat — not this; tvayyupapadyate = tvayi — in your + upapadyate — is suitable; kṣudraṁ — degrading; hṛdayadaurbalyaṁ — emotional weakness; tyaktvottiṣṭha = tyaktva — give up + uttiṣṭha — stand up; paraṁtapa — scorcher of the enemy

O son of Pṛthā, you should not entertain cowardly behavior. This is not suitable for you. Give up this degrading emotional weakness. Stand, O scorcher of the enemy. (2.3)

अर्जुन उवाच
कथं भीष्ममहं संख्ये
द्रोणं च मधुसूदन ।
इषुभिः प्रतियोत्स्यामि
पूजार्हावरिसूदन ॥२.४॥

arjuna uvāca
kathaṁ bhīṣmamahaṁ saṁkhye
droṇaṁ ca madhusūdana
iṣubhiḥ pratiyotsyāmi
pūjārhāvarisūdana (2.4)

arjuna — Arjuna; uvāca — said; kathaṁ — how; bhīṣmam — Bhisma; ahaṁ — I; saṁkhye — in battle; droṇaṁ — Droṇa; ca — and; madhusūdana — O killer of Madhu; iṣubhiḥ — with arrows; pratiyotsyāmi — I will attack; pūjārhāv arisūdana = pūjārhāu — worthy of reverence + arisūdana — killer of the enemy, Krishna

Arjuna said: How will I attack in battle, Bhishma and Droṇa, who are worthy of reverence, O Krishna? (2.4)

गुरूनहत्वा हि महानुभावान्
श्रेयो भोक्तुं भैक्ष्यमपीह लोके
हत्वार्थकामांस्तु गुरूनिहैव
भुञ्जीय भोगान्रुधिरप्रदिग्धान् ॥२.५॥

gurūnahatvā hi mahānubhāvān
śreyo bhoktuṁ bhaikṣyam apīha loke
hatvārthakāmāṁstu gurūnihaiva
bhuñjīya bhogān rudhira-pradigdhān (2.5)

gurūn — the revered teachers; ahatvā — not killing; hi — in fact; mahānubhāvān — great-natured; śreyo — better; bhoktuṁ — to eat; bhaikṣyamapīha = bhaikṣyam — begging + api — also + iha — here; loke — on earth; hatvārthakāmāṅs = hatvā — having killed + artha — on the basis of + kāmān — impulsive desires; tu — but; gurūn — revered teachers; ihaiva = iha — here + eva — indeed; bhuñjīya — I would enjoy; bhogān — luxuries; rudhirapradigdhān = rudhira — bloody + pradigdhān — stained

In fact, it is better to eat by begging in this world than by killing the revered teachers who are great-natured. But having slain the venerable teachers on the basis of impulsive desires, I would enjoy blood-stained luxuries here on earth. (2.5)

न चैतद्विद्मः कतरन्नो गरीयो
यद्वा जयेम यदि वा नो जयेयुः ।
यानेव हत्वा न जिजीविषामस्
तेऽवस्थिताः प्रमुखे धार्तराष्ट्राः ॥२.६॥

na caitadvidmaḥ kataranno garīyo
yadvā jayema yadi vā no jayeyuḥ
yāneva hatvā na jijīviṣāmas
te'vasthitāḥ pramukhe dhārtarāṣṭrāḥ (2.6)

na — not; caitad — and this; vidmaḥ — we know; kataran — which of the alternatives; no = nah — for us; garīyo — is better; yad — which; vā — other; jayema — we should conquer; yadi — if; vā — or; no = naḥ — to us; jayeyuḥ — they should triumph over; yān — who; eva — indeed; hatvā — having killed; na — us; jijīviṣāmas — we desire to outlive; te — they; 'vasthitāḥ = avasthitāḥ — stand armed; pramukhe — before us; dhārtarāṣṭrāḥ — the sons of Dhṛtarāṣṭra

And this we do not know, which of the alternatives is better; whether we should conquer or if they should triumph over us. It concerns these sons of Dhṛtarāṣṭra who stand armed before us, and whom we would not desire to outlive, if they are killed. (2.6)

कार्पण्यदोषोपहतस्वभावः
पृच्छामि त्वां धर्मसंमूढचेताः
यच्छ्रेयः स्यान्निश्चितं ब्रूहि तन्मे
शिष्यस्तेऽहं शाधि मां त्वां प्रपन्नम्
॥२.७॥

kārpaṇyadoṣopahata-svabhāvaḥ
pṛcchāmi tvāṁ dharma-saṁmūḍhacetāḥ
yacchreyaḥ syānniścitaṁ brūhi tanme
śiṣyaste'haṁ śādhi māṁ tvāṁ prapannam
(2.7)

kārpaṇyadoṣopahatasvabhāvaḥ = kārpaṇya — mercy-prone + doṣa — faulty weakness + upahata — overcome + svabhāvaḥ — my feelings (a person being afflicted with inappropriate mercy, a compulsive mercy-prone man); pṛcchāmi — I ask; tvāṁ — you; dharmasaṁmūḍhacetāḥ = dharma — sense of duty + saṁmūḍha — clouded by confusion + cetāḥ — mind (one whose sense of duty is clouded by confusion of mind); yacchreyaḥ = yac (yad) — which + chreyaḥ (śreyah) — is better; syān — it should be; niścitaṁ — for certain; brūhi — tell; tan — this; me — to me; śiṣyas — student; te — of yours; 'haṁ = aham — I; śādhi — instruct; mām — me; tvāṁ — you; prapannam — submission

As a mercy prone man, overcome by these feelings of pity, with my sense of duty clouded by mental confusion, I ask You to tell me with certainty, what is preferable. I am a student of Yours. Instruct me, who am submitted to You. (2.7)

न हि प्रपश्यामि ममापनुद्याद्
यच्छोकमुच्छोषणमिन्द्रियाणाम् ।
अवाप्य भूमावसपत्नमृद्धं
राज्यं सुराणामपि चाधिपत्यम् ॥२.८॥

na hi prapaśyāmi mamāpanudyād
yacchokamucchoṣaṇam indriyāṇām
avāpya bhūmāvasapatnam ṛddhaṁ
rājyaṁ surāṇāmapi cādhipatyam (2.8)

na- not; hi- in fact; prapaśyām- I see; mamāpanudyād = mama- of me + apanudyāt --should remove; yacchokam = yac (yad) — which + chokam (śokam) — sadness; ucchoṣaṇam — absorbs; indriyāṇām — sensual enthusiasm; avāpya — acquiring; bhūmāvasapatnam = bhūmau — on earth + asapatnam — unrivaled; ṛddham — prosperity; rājyaṁ — rulership; surāṇām— of the angelic kingdom; api — also; cādhipatyam = ca — and + adhipatyam — sovereignty

In fact, I do not see, what would remove the sadness that absorbs my enthusiasm, even unrivaled rulership and prosperity on earth or sovereignty over the angelic kingdom. (2.8)

संजय उवाच
एवमुक्त्वा हृषीकेशं
गुडाकेशः परंतप ।
न योत्स्य इति गोविन्दम्
उक्त्वा तूष्णीं बभूव ह ॥२.९॥

saṁjaya uvāca
evamuktvā hṛṣīkeśaṁ
guḍākeśaḥ paraṁtapa
na yotsya iti govindam
uktvā tūṣṇīṁ babhūva ha (2.9)

saṁjaya — Sanjaya; uvāca — said; evam — thus; uktvā — having appealed to; hṛṣīkeśaṁ — Kṛṣṇa; guḍākeśaḥ — Arjuna; paraṁtapa — scorcher of enemies; na — not; yotsya — I will fight; iti — thus; govindam — chief of the cowherds; uktvā — having spoken; tūṣṇīṁ — silently; babhūva — became; ha — indeed

Sanjaya said: O Dhṛtarāṣṭra, scorcher of enemies, after appealing to Krishna, Arjuna said to Govinda, the chief of cowherds, "I will not fight." Having said this, he became silent. (2.9)

तमुवाच हृषीकेशः
प्रहसन्निव भारत ।
सेनयोरुभयोर्मध्ये
विषीदन्तमिदं वचः ॥२.१०॥

tamuvāca hṛṣīkeśaḥ
prahasanniva bhārata
senayorubhayormadhye
viṣīdantamidaṁ vacaḥ (2.10)

tam — to him; uvāca — spoke; hṛṣīkeśaḥ — Kṛṣṇa; prahasan — smiling; iva — like; bhārata — O descendant of Bharata; senayoḥ — of the two armies; ubhayoḥ — of both; madhye — in the middle; viṣīdantam — dejected; idaṁ — this; vacaḥ — speech

Then, in the middle of both armies, Krishna, who was smiling, spoke this speech to the dejected Arjuna. (2.10)

श्रीभगवानुवाच
अशोच्यानन्वशोचस्त्वं
प्रज्ञावादांश्च भाषसे ।
गतासूनगतासूंश्च
नानुशोचन्ति पण्डिताः ॥२.११॥

śrībhagavānuvāca
aśocyānanvaśocastvaṁ
prajñāvādāṁśca bhāṣase
gatāsūnagatāsūṁśca
nānuśocanti paṇḍitāḥ (2.11)

śrī-bhagavān — the Blessed Lord; uvāca — said; aśocyān — that which should be regretted; anvaśocas — mourned; tvaṁ — you; prajñāvādāṁś — intelligent statements; ca — and; bhāṣase — you express; gatāsūn — departed souls; agatāsūṁś — those not departed; ca — and; nānuśocanti = na — not + anuśocanti — mourn; paṇḍitāḥ — educated men

The Blessed Lord said: You mourned for that which should not be regretted. And you expressed intelligent statements, but the educated persons mourn neither for the embodied or departed souls. (2.11)

न त्वेवाहं जातु नासं
न त्वं नेमे जनाधिपाः ।
न चैव न भविष्यामः
सर्वे वयमतः परम् ॥२.१२॥

na tvevāhaṁ jātu nāsaṁ
na tvaṁ neme janādhipāḥ
na caiva na bhaviṣyāmaḥ
sarve vayamataḥ param (2.12)

na — no; tv (tu) — in fact; eva — alone; aham — I; jātu — ever; na — not; āsam — I did exist; na — nor; tvaṁ — you; neme = na — nor + ime — these; jana-adhipāḥ — rulers of the people; na — not; caiva — and indeed; na — nor; bhaviṣyāmaḥ — we will exist; sarve — all; vayam — we; ataḥ - from now; param — onwards

There was never a time when I did not exist, nor you nor these rulers of the people. Nor will we cease to exist from now onwards. (2.12)

देहिनोऽस्मिन्यथा देहे
कौमारं यौवनं जरा ।
तथा देहान्तरप्राप्तिर्
धीरस्तत्र न मुह्यति ॥२.१३॥

dehino'sminyathā dehe
kaumāraṁ yauvanaṁ jarā
tathā dehāntaraprāptir
dhīrastatra na muhyati (2.13)

dehinaḥ — of the embodied soul; asmin — in this; yathā — as; dehe — in the body; kaumāraṁ — in childhood; yauvanam — in youth; jarā — in old age; tathā — so in sequence; deha — body; antara — another; prāptiḥ — acquirement; dhīraḥ — wise person; tatra — on this topic; na — not; muhyati — is confused

As the embodied soul endures childhood, youth and old age, so another body is acquired in sequence. The wise person is not confused on this topic. (2.13)

मात्रास्पर्शास्तु कौन्तेय
शीतोष्णसुखदुःखदाः ।
आगमापायिनोऽनित्यास्
तांस्तितिक्षस्व भारत ॥२.१४॥

mātrāsparśāstu kaunteya
śītoṣṇasukhaduḥkhadāḥ
āgamāpāyino'nityās
tāṁstitikṣasva bhārata (2.14)

mātrāsparśāḥ — mundane sensations; tu — but; kaunteya — O son of Kuntī; śītoṣṇasukhaduḥkhadāḥ = śīta — cold + usna — heat + sukha — pleasure + duḥkha — pain + dāḥ — causing; āgamāpāyino = āgama — coming + apāyinaḥ — going; 'nityās = anityāḥ — not manifested continually; tāṁs — them; titikṣasva — you should cope; bhārata — O man of the Bharata family

O son of Kuntī, mundane sensations which cause cold and heat, pleasure and pain, do come and go. Cope with them, O man of the Bharata family. (2.14)

यं हि न व्यथयन्त्येते
पुरुषं पुरुषर्षभ ।
समदुःखसुखं धीरं
सोऽमृतत्वाय कल्पते ॥२.१५॥

yaṁ hi na vyathayantyete
puruṣaṁ puruṣarṣabha
samaduḥkhasukhaṁ dhīraṁ
so'mṛtatvāya kalpate (2.15)

yaṁ.- whosoever; hi — indeed; na — not; vyathayantyete = vyathayanti — afflict + ete — these mundane sensations; puruṣaṁ — that person; puruṣarṣabha — O bull among men; samaduḥkhasukhaṁ — steady in miserable and enjoyable conditions; dhīraṁ — wise man; so — he; 'mṛta tvāya = amṛtatvāya — to immortality; kalpate — is fit

O bull among men, these mundane sensations do not afflict the wise man who is steady in miserable or enjoyable conditions. That person is fit for immortality. (2.15)

नासतो विद्यते भावो
नाभावो विद्यते सतः ।
उभयोरपि दृष्टोऽन्तस्
त्वनयोस्तत्त्वदर्शिभिः ॥२.१६॥

nāsato vidyate bhāvo
nābhāvo vidyate sataḥ
ubhayorapi dṛṣṭo'ntas
tvanayostattvadarśibhiḥ (2.16)

nāsato = na- no + asatas - of the non-substantial things; vidyate- there is; bhāvo- enduring existence; nābhāvo = na — no + abhāvaḥ — lack of existence; vidyate — there is; sataḥ — substantial things; ubhayoḥ — of the two; api — also; dṛṣṭaḥ — perceived; 'ntas = antaḥ — certainty; tvanayos = tu — but + anayoḥ — of these two; tattvadarśibhiḥ = tattva — reality + darśibhiḥ — by mystic powers

Of the non-substantial things, there is no enduring existence. Of the substantial things, there is no lack of existence. These two truths were perceived with certainty by the mystic seers of reality. (2.16)

अविनाशि तु तद्विद्धि
येन सर्वमिदं ततम् ।
विनाशमव्ययस्यास्य
न कश्चित्कर्तुमर्हति ॥२.१७॥

avināśi tu tadviddhi
yena sarvamidaṁ tatam
vināśamavyayasyāsya
na kaścitkartumarhati (2.17)

avināśi — indestructible; tu — indeed; tad — that factor; viddhi — know; yena — by which; sarvam — all; idaṁ — this world; tatam — is pervaded; vināśam — destructible; avyayasyāsya — of the everlasting principle; na — no; kaścit — anyone; kartum - to accomplish; arhati — can

Know that indestructible factor by which all this world is pervaded. No one can accomplish the destruction of that everlasting principle. (2.17)

अन्तवन्त इमे देहा
नित्यस्योक्ताः शरीरिणः ।
अनाशिनोऽप्रमेयस्य
तस्माद्युध्यस्व भारत ॥२.१८॥

antavanta ime dehā
nityasyoktāḥ śarīriṇaḥ
anāśino'prameyasya
tasmādyudhyasva bhārata (2.18)

antavanta — terminal; ime — these; dehā — bodies; nityasyoktāḥ = nityasya — of the eternal + uktāḥ — it is declared; śarīriṇaḥ — of the embodied soul; anāśinaḥ — of the indestructible; 'prameyasya = aprameyasya — of the immeasurable; tasmāt — therefore; yudhyasva — fight; bhārata — O descendant of Bharata

It is declared that the bodies of the eternal, indestructible, immeasurable embodied soul are terminal. Therefore fight, descendant of the Bharatas. (2.18)

य एनं वेत्ति हन्तारं
यश्चैनं मन्यते हतम् ।
उभौ तौ न विजानीतो
नायं हन्ति न हन्यते ॥२.१९॥

ya enaṁ vetti hantāraṁ
yaścainaṁ manyate hatam
ubhau tau na vijānīto
nāyaṁ hanti na hanyate (2.19)

ya — who; enaṁ — this embodied soul; vetti — concludes; hantāraṁ — the killer; yaścainaṁ = yas — who + ca — and + inam — this embodied soul; manyate — thinks; hatam — is killed; ubhau — both; tau — two viewers; na- not; vijānītaḥ- understood; nāyaṁ = na — not + ayam — this embodied soul; hanti — kill; na — nor; hanyate — can be killed

Both viewers do not understand, namely: He who concludes that the embodied soul is the killer and he who thinks that the embodied soul is killed. The embodied soul does not kill nor can he be killed. (2.19)

न जायते म्रियते वा कदा चिन्
नायं भूत्वा भविता वा न भूयः ।
अजो नित्यः शाश्वतोऽयं पुराणो
न हन्यते हन्यमाने शरीरे ॥२.२०

na jāyate mriyate vā kadā cin
nāyaṁ bhūtvā bhavitā vā na bhūyaḥ
ajo nityaḥ śāśvato'yaṁ purāṇo
na hanyate hanyamāne śarīre (2.20)

na — not; jāyate — is born; mriyate — dies; vā — either; kadācin — at any time; nāyaṁ = na — nor + ayam — this embodied soul; bhūtvā — having been; bhavitā — will be; vā — or; na — not; bhūyaḥ — again; ajo — birthless; nityaḥ — perpetual; śāśvataḥ — eternal; 'yaṁ = ayam- this; purāṇaḥ — primeval; na- not; hanyate — is killed; hanyamāne — in the act of killing; śarīre — in the body

This embodied soul is not born, nor does it die at any time, nor having existed will it not be. Being birthless, eternal, perpetual and primeval, it is not slain in the act of killing the body. (2.20)

वेदाविनाशिनं नित्यं
य एनमजमव्ययम् ।
कथं स पुरुषः पार्थ
कं घातयति हन्ति कम् ॥२.२१॥

vedāvināśinaṁ nityaṁ
ya enamajamavyayam
kathaṁ sa puruṣaḥ pārtha
kaṁ ghātayati hanti kam (2.21)

vedāvināśinaṁ = veda — knows + avināśinam — indestructible; nityaṁ — eternal; ya = yaḥ — who; enam — this; ajam — not born, birthless; avyayam — imperishable; kathaṁ — how; sa = saḥ — he; puruṣaḥ — person; pārtha — O son of Partha; kaṁ — whom; ghātayati — causes to kill; hanti — kills (directly); kam — whom

O son of Pṛthā, how can the person who knows this indestructible, eternal, birthless and imperishable principle, cause someone to be killed or even kill someone directly? (2.21)

वासांसि जीर्णानि यथा विहाय
नवानि गृह्णाति नरोऽपराणि ।
तथा शरीराणि विहाय जीर्णा;न्य्
अन्यानि संयाति नवानि देही ॥२.२२॥

vāsāṁsi jīrṇāni yathā vihāya
navāni gṛhṇāti naro'parāṇi
tathā śarīrāṇi vihāya jīrṇāny
anyāni saṁyāti navāni dehī
(2.22)

vāsāṁsi — clothing; jīrṇāni — worn out; yathā — as when; vihāya — discarded; navāni — new; gṛhṇāti — takes; naro = naraḥ — person; 'parāṇi = aparāṇi — others; tathā — so; śarīrāṇi — bodies; vihāya — abandoned; jirṇāny = worn-out; anyāni — others; saṁyāti — encounters; navāni — new; dehī — the embodied soul

As when discarding old clothing, a person takes new garments, so the embodied soul abandons old bodies taking new ones. (2.22)

नैनं छिन्दन्ति शस्त्राणि
नैनं दहति पावकः ।
न चैनं क्लेदयन्त्यापो
न शोषयति मारुतः ॥२.२३॥

nainaṁ chindanti śastrāṇi
nainaṁ dahati pāvakaḥ
na cainaṁ kledayantyāpo
na śoṣayati mārutaḥ (2.23)

nainaṁ = na — not + enam — this; chindanti — pierce; śastrāṇi — weapons; nainaṁ = na — not + enam — this; dahati — burns; pāvakaḥ — fire; na — not; cainaṁ = ca — and + enam — this; kledayantyāpo = kledayanti — soak + āpo = āpaḥ — water; na — nor; śoṣayati — dry out; mārutaḥ — the wind

Weapons do not pierce, fire does not burn, and water does not wet, nor does the wind dry that embodied soul. (2.23)

अच्छेद्योऽयमदाह्योऽयम्
अक्लेद्योऽशोष्य एव च ।
नित्यः सर्वगतः स्थाणुर्
अचलोऽयं सनातनः ॥२.२४॥

acchedyo'yamadāhyo'yam
akledyo'śoṣya eva ca
nityaḥ sarvagataḥ sthāṇur
acalo'yaṁ sanātanaḥ (2.24)

acchedyaḥ — not to be pierced; 'yam = ayam — this; adāhyo = adāhyaḥ — not to be burnt; 'yam = ayam — this; akledyo = akledyaḥ — not to be moistened; 'śoṣya = aśoṣya — not to be dried; eva — indeed; ca — and; nityaḥ — eternal; sarvagataḥ — penetrant of all things; sthāṇuḥ — a permanent principle; acalo = acalaḥ — unmoving; 'yaṁ = ayam — this; sanātanaḥ — primeval

This embodied soul cannot be pierced, cannot be burnt, cannot be moistened and cannot be dried. And indeed, this soul is eternal. It can penetrate all things. It is a permanent principle and is stable and primeval. (2.24)

अव्यक्तोऽयमचिन्त्योऽयम्
अविकार्योऽयमुच्यते ।
तस्मादेवं विदित्वैनं
नानुशोचितुमर्हसि ॥२.२५॥

avyakto'yamacintyo'yam
avikāryo'yamucyate
tasmādevaṁ viditvainaṁ
nānuśocitumarhasi (2.25)

avyakto = avyaktaḥ — undisplayed; 'yam = ayam — this; acintyo = acintyah — unimaginable; 'yam = ayam — this; avikāryo = avikāryaḥ — unchanging; 'yam = ayam — this; ucyate — it is declared; tasmāt — therefore; evaṁ — thus; viditvainaṁ = viditva — knowing + enam — this; nānuśocitum = na — not + anuśocitum — to lament; arhasi — you should

This embodied soul is undisplayed, unimaginable, and unchanging. Therefore knowing this, you should not lament. (2.25)

अथ चैनं नित्यजातं
नित्यं वा मन्यसे मृतम् ।
तथापि त्वं महाबाहो
नैनं शोचितुमर्हसि ॥२.२६॥

atha cainaṁ nityajātaṁ
nityaṁ vā manyase mṛtam
tathāpi tvaṁ mahābāho
nainaṁ śocitumarhasi (2.26)

atha — furthermore; cainaṁ = ca — and + enam — this; nityajātaṁ = nitya — continually + jātam — being born; nityam — continually; vā — or; manyase — you think; mṛtam — dying; tathā 'pi = tathā — so + api — also; tvam — you; mahābāho — strong-armed man; nainaṁ = na — not + enam — this; śocitum arhasi = śocitum — to mourn + arhasi — you can

And furthermore if you think that this embodied soul is continually being born or continually dying, even so, O strong-armed man, you should not lament. (2.26)

जातस्य हि ध्रुवो मृत्युर्
ध्रुवं जन्म मृतस्य च ।
तस्मादपरिहार्येऽर्थे
न त्वं शोचितुमर्हसि ॥२.२७॥

jātasya hi dhruvo mṛtyur
dhruvaṁ janma mṛtasya ca
tasmādaparihārye'rthe
na tvaṁ śocitumarhasi
(2.27)

jātasya — of that which is born; hi — infact; dhruvo = dhruvaḥ — certain; mṛtyur = mṛtyuḥ — death; dhruvaṁ — certain; janma — birth; mṛtasya — of that which is dead; ca — and; tasmādaparihārye = tasmāt — therefore + aparihārye — in what is unavoidable; 'rthe = arthe — in the assessment; na — not; tvaṁ — you; śocitum — to lament + arhasi — you should

In fact, of that which is born, death is certain; of that which is dead, birth is certain. Therefore in assessing what is unavoidable, you should not lament. (2.27)

अव्यक्तादीनि भूतानि
व्यक्तमध्यानि भारत ।
अव्यक्तनिधनान्येव
तत्र का परिदेवना ॥२.२८॥

avyaktādīni bhūtāni
vyaktamadhyāni bhārata
avyaktanidhanānyeva
tatra kā paridevanā (2.28)

avyaktādīni = avyakta — undetected + ādīni- beginnings of a manifestation; bhūtāni — living beings; vyakta madhyāni = vyakta — visible + madhyāni — interim states; bhārata — O descendant of Bharata; avyakta nidhanāny eva = avyakta — undetected + nidhanāni — ends of a manifestation + eva — again; tatra — there; kā — what; paridevanā — complaint

The living beings are undetected in the beginning of a manifestation, visible in the interim stages, and are again undetected at the end of a manifestation. What is the complaint? (2.28)

आश्चर्यवत्पश्यति कश्चिदेनम्
आश्चर्यवद्वदति तथैव चान्यः ।
आश्चर्यवच्चैनमन्यः श्रृणोति
श्रुत्वाप्येनं वेद न चैव कश्चित् ॥२.२९॥

āścaryavatpaśyati kaścidenam
āścaryavadvadati tathaiva cānyaḥ
āścaryavaccainamanyaḥ śṛṇoti
śrutvāpyenaṁ veda na caiva kaścit
(2.29)

āścaryavat — wonderful; paśyati — perceives; kaścidenam = kaścid — someone + enam — this; āścaryavad — fantastic; vadati — describes; tathai 'va = tathā — so + eva — indeed; cānyaḥ = ca — and + anyah — another person; āścaryavaccainam = āścaryavat — amazing + ca — and + enam — this; anyaḥ — another; śṛṇoti — hears; śrutvāpyenaṁ = srutva — having heard + api — also + enam — this; veda — knows; na — not; caiva = ca — and + eva — in fact; kaścit — anyone

Someone perceives this embodied soul as being wonderful. Another person describes it as amazing. Another hears of it as being fantastic. And even after hearing this, no one knows this embodied soul in fact. (2.29)

देही नित्यमवध्योऽयं
देहे सर्वस्य भारत ।
तस्मात्सर्वाणि भूतानि
न त्वं शोचितुमर्हसि ॥२.३०॥

dehī nityamavadhyo'yaṁ
dehe sarvasya bhārata
tasmātsarvāṇi bhūtāni
na tvaṁ śocitumarhasi (2.30)

dehī — embodied soul; nityam — eternally; avadhyo = avadhyaḥ — non-killable; 'yaṁ = ayam — this; dehe — in the body; sarvasya — of all, in all cases; bhārata — O descendant of Bharata; tasmāt — therefore; sarvāṇi — all; bhūtāni — beings; na — no; tvaṁ — you; śocitumarhasi = śocitum — to mourn + arhasi — should

In the body, in all cases, this embodied soul is always non-killable, O descendant of Bharata. Therefore you should not mourn for any of these beings. (2.30)

स्वधर्ममपि चावेक्ष्य
न विकम्पितुमर्हसि ।
धर्म्याद्धि युद्धाच्छ्रेयोऽन्यत्
क्षत्रियस्य न विद्यते ॥२.३१॥

svadharmamapi cāvekṣya
na vikampitumarhasi
dharmyāddhi
yuddhācchreyo'nyat
kṣatriyasya na vidyate (2.31)

svadharmam — your assigned duty; api — also; cāvekṣya = ca — and + avekṣya — looking, mentally considering; na — no; vikampitum — to consider alternatives; arhasi — you should; dharmyād = dharmyāt — from righteousness; dhi = hi — indeed; yuddhācchreyo = yuddhāt — from battle + chreyo = śreyas — better; 'nyat = anyat — other; kṣatriyasya — of the son of a king; na — no; vidyate — there is

And considering your assigned duty, you should not look for alternatives. In fact, for the son of a king, there is no other duty which is better than a righteous battle. (2.31)

यदृच्छया चोपपन्नं स्वर्गद्वारमपावृतम् । सुखिनः क्षत्रियाः पार्थ लभन्ते युद्धमीदृशम् ॥२.३२॥	yadṛcchayā copapannaṁ svargadvāramapāvṛtam sukhinaḥ kṣatriyāḥ pārtha labhante yuddhamīdṛśam (2.32)

yadṛcchayā — by a stroke of luck; copapannaṁ = ca — and + upapannam — made available; svargadvāram = svarga — heaven + dvāram — gate; apāvṛtam — is open; sukhinaḥ — thrilled, happy; kṣatriyāḥ — warriors; pārtha — O son of Pṛthā; labhante — get; yuddham — battle opportunity; īdṛśam — such

And by a stroke of luck, the gate of heaven is opened. Thrilled are the warriors who get such a battle opportunity, O son of Pṛthā. (2.32)

अथ चेत्त्वमिमं धर्म्यं संग्रामं न करिष्यसि । ततः स्वधर्मं कीर्तिं च हित्वा पापमवाप्स्यसि ॥२.३३॥	atha cettvamimaṁ dharmyaṁ saṁgrāmaṁ na kariṣyasi tataḥ svadharmaṁ kīrtiṁ ca hitvā pāpamavāpsyasi (2.33)

atha — now; cet — if; tvam — you; imaṁ — this; dharmyaṁ — appropriate duty; saṁgrāmaṁ — warfare; na — not; kariṣyasi — will conduct; tataḥ — then; svadharmaṁ — own duty; kīrtiṁca = kīrtiṁ — reputation + ca — and; hitvā — having neglected; pāpam — sin, fault; avāpsyasi — will acquire

Now if you do not conduct this righteous war, then, by neglecting your duty and reputation, you will acquire a fault. (2.33)

अकीर्तिं चापि भूतानि कथयिष्यन्ति तेऽव्ययाम् । संभावितस्य चाकीर्तिर् मरणादतिरिच्यते ॥२.३४॥	akīrtiṁ cāpi bhūtāni kathayiṣyanti te'vyayām saṁbhāvitasya cākīrtir maraṇādatiricyate (2.34)

akīrtiṁ — downfall; cāpi = ca — and + api — also; bhūtāni — the people; kathayiṣyanti — will speak; te — of you; 'vyayām = avyayām — continually; saṁbhāvitasya — for an honored man; cākīrtir = ca — and + akīrtiḥ — loss of reputation; maraṇād = maraṇāt — than the loss of body; atiricyate — is harder to bear

The people will speak of your downfall continually. And for an honored man, the loss of reputation is harder to bear than the loss of his body. (2.34)

भयाद्रणादुपरतं
मंस्यन्ते त्वां महारथाः ।
येषां च त्वं बहुमतो
भूत्वा यास्यसि लाघवम् ॥२.३५॥

bhayādraṇāduparataṁ
maṁsyante tvāṁ mahārathāḥ
yeṣāṁ ca tvaṁ bahumato
bhūtvā yāsyasi lāghavam (2.35)

bhayād = bhayāt — because of fear; raṇād = raṇāt — from the excitement of battle; uparataṁ — withdraw from; maṁsyante — they think; tvāṁ — you; mahārathāḥ — great warriors; yeṣāṁ — of whom; ca — and; tvaṁ — you; bahumato = bahumataḥ — high opinion; bhūtvā — had; yāsyasi — you will come; lāghavam — insignificance

The great warriors will think that because of fear, you withdrew from battle. And to those who held a big opinion, you will appear to be insignificant. (2.35)

अवाच्यवादांश्च बहून्
वदिष्यन्ति तवाहिताः ।
निन्दन्तस्तव सामर्थ्यं
ततो दुःखतरं नु किम् ॥२.३६॥

avācyavādāṁśca bahūn
vadiṣyanti tavāhitāḥ
nindantastava sāmarthyaṁ
tato duḥkhataraṁ nu kim (2.36)

avācyavādāṁśca = avācya — not to be said, slurred + vādān — words, saying + ca — and; bahūn — many; vadiṣyanti — will speak; tavāhitāḥ = tava — about you + ahitāḥ — enemies; nindantas — laughed at; tava — of you; sāmarthyaṁ — capability; tato = tataḥ — from that; duḥkhataraṁ — greater grief; nu — but; kim — what

The enemies will say many slurs about you, thus laughing at your capability. But, what would be a greater grief than this? (2.36)

हतो वा प्राप्स्यसि स्वर्गं
जित्वा वा भोक्ष्यसे महीम् ।
तस्मादुत्तिष्ठ कौन्तेय
युद्धाय कृतनिश्चयः ॥२.३७॥

hato vā prāpsyasi svargaṁ
jitvā vā bhokṣyase mahīm
tasmāduttiṣṭha kaunteya
yuddhāya kṛtaniścayaḥ (2.37)

hato = hataḥ — be killed; vā — either; prāpsyasi — you will achieve; svargaṁ — angelic world; jitvā — having conquered; vā — or; bhokṣyase — you will enjoy; mahīm — the nation; tasmād = tasmāt — therefore; uttiṣṭha — stand up; kaunteya — O son of Kunti; yuddhāya — to battle; kṛtaniścayaḥ — be decisive

Either be killed and achieve the angelic world or having conquered, enjoy the nation. Therefore stand up and be decisive, O son of Kuntī. (2.37)

सुखदुःखे समे कृत्वा
लाभालाभौ जयाजयौ ।
ततो युद्धाय युज्यस्व
नैवं पापमवाप्स्यसि ॥२.३८॥

sukhaduḥkhe same kṛtvā
lābhālābhau jayājayau
tato yuddhāya yujyasva
naivaṁ pāpamavāpsyasi (2.38)

sukhaduḥkhe = sukha — happiness + duḥkhe — in distress; same — in the same emotions; kṛtvā — having regard; lābhālābhau — gains or losses; jayājayau — victory or defeat; tato = tataḥ — them; yuddhāya — to battle; yujyasva — apply yourself; naivaṁ = na — not + evam — thus; pāpam — sin,demerit; avāpsyasi — you will get

Having regarded happiness, distress, gains, losses, victory and defeat, as the same emotions, apply yourself to battle. Thus you will get no demerit. (2.38)

एषा तेऽभिहिता सांख्ये
बुद्धिर्योगे त्विमां शृणु ।
बुद्ध्या युक्तो यया पार्थ
कर्मबन्धं प्रहास्यसि ॥२.३९॥

eṣā te'bhihitā sāṁkhye
buddhiryoge tvimāṁ śṛṇu
buddhyā yukto yayā pārtha
karmabandhaṁ prahāsyasi (2.39)

eṣā — this; te — to you; bhihitā = abhihitā — stated; sāṁkhye — in Sāṁkhya philosophy; buddhir = buddhiḥ — insight; yoge — in yoga discipline; tvimām = tu — but + imāṁ — this; śṛṇu — hear; buddhyā — with the insight; yukto = yuktaḥ — yoked; yayā — by which; pārtha — O son of Pṛthā; karmabandhaṁ — complication of action; prahāsyasi — you will avoid

As explained in the Sāṁkhya philosophy, this vision is the insight, but hear of its application in yoga practice. Yoked with this insight, O son of Pṛthā, you will avoid the complication of action. (2.39)

नेहाभिक्रमनाशोऽस्ति
प्रत्यवायो न विद्यते ।
स्वल्पमप्यस्य धर्मस्य
त्रायते महतो भयात् ॥२.४०॥

nehābhikramanāśo'sti
pratyavāyo na vidyate
svalpamapyasya dharmasya
trāyate mahato bhayāt (2.40)

nehābhikramanāśo = na — not + iha — in this insight + abhikrama — endeavor + nāśo (nāśaḥ) — loss; 'sti = asti — it is; pratyavāyo = pratyavāyaḥ — reversal; na — not; vidyate — there is; svalpam — a little; apy = api — even; asya — of this; dharmasya — of righteous practice; trāyate — protects; mahato = mahataḥ — from the great; bhayāt — from danger

In this insight, no endeavor is lost nor is there any reversal. Even a little of this righteous practice protects from the great danger. (2.40)

व्यवसायात्मिका बुद्धिर्
एकेह कुरुनन्दन ।
बहुशाखा ह्यनन्ताश्च
बुद्धयोऽव्यवसायिनाम् ॥२.४१॥

vyavasāyātmikā buddhir
ekeha kurunandana
bahuśākhā hyanantāśca
buddhayo'vyavasāyinām (2.41)

vyavasāyātmikā — intentional determination; buddhir = buddhih — technical insight; ekeha = eka — one view + iha — in this instance; kurunandana — O dear man of the Kuru family; bahuśākhā — many offshoots; hyanantāś = hi — in fact + anantāś — endless; ca — and; buddhayo = buddhayaḥ — views; 'vyavasāyinām = avyavasāyinām — of the person with many hopes

When a person's intentional determination is guided by technical insight, he experiences one view, O dear man of the Kuru family. But the views of a person with many hopes are diverse and endless. (2.41)

यामिमां पुष्पितां वाचं
प्रवदन्त्यविपश्चितः ।
वेदवादरताः पार्थ
नान्यदस्तीति वादिनः ॥२.४२॥

yāmimāṁ puṣpitāṁ vācaṁ
pravadantyavipaścitaḥ
vedavādaratāḥ pārtha
nānyadastīti vādinaḥ (2.42)

yām — which; imām — this; puṣpitāṁ — poetic; vācaṁ — quotation; pravadantyavipaścitaḥ = pravadanti — they proclaim + avipaścitaḥ — ignorant reciters; vedavādaratāḥ — enjoying Vedic Sanskrit poetry; pārtha — O son of Pṛthā; nānyad = na — not + anyat — anything; astīti = asti — it is + iti — thus; vādinaḥ — saying

This is poetic quotation which the ignorant reciters proclaim, O son of Pṛthā. Enjoying the Vedic verses, they say there is no other written authority. (2.42)

कामात्मानः स्वर्गपरा
जन्मकर्मफलप्रदाम् ।
क्रियाविशेषबहुलां
भोगैश्वर्यगतिं प्रति ॥२.४३॥

kāmātmānaḥ svargaparā
janmakarmaphalapradām
kriyāviśeṣabahulāṁ
bhogaiśvaryagatiṁ prati (2.43)

kāmātmānaḥ — people of a sensuous nature; svargaparā — people intent on going to the swarga (angelic) world; janmakarmaphalapradām = janma — rebirth + karma — cultural act + phala — pay-off + pradām — offering; kriyāviśeṣabahulāṁ = kriyā — ceremonial rites + viśeṣa — specific + bahulām — various; bhogaiśvaryagatiṁ = bhoga — enjoyment + aiśvarya — political power + gatiṁ — aim; prati — toward

Those reciters, being people of a sensuous nature, being intent on going to the Svarga angelic world, offering such rebirth as payoff for cultural activities, make themselves busy in various specific ceremonial rites, and focus on enjoyment and political power. (2.43)

भोगैश्वर्यप्रसक्तानां
तयापहृतचेतसाम् ।
व्यवसायात्मिका बुद्धिः
समाधौ न विधीयते ॥ २.४४ ॥

bhogaiśvaryaprasaktānāṁ
tayāpahṛtacetasām
vyavasāyātmikā buddhiḥ
samādhau na vidhīyate (2.44)

bhogaiśvaryaprasaktānāṁ = bhoga — pleasure + aiśvarya — power + prasaktānāṁ — of the attached, of the prone; tayāpahṛtacetasām = tayā — by this + apahṛta — captivated + cetasām — idea; vyavasāyātmikā = vyavasāya — focused determination + ātmikā — self; buddhiḥ — intellect; samādhau — in meditation; na — not; vidhīyate — is experience

Being absorbed by this way of life, pleasure-prone and power-seeking people, are captivated by this idea. Thus in meditation, the self-focused intellect is not experienced by them. (2.44)

त्रैगुण्यविषया वेदा
निस्त्रैगुण्यो भवार्जुन ।
निर्द्वंद्वो नित्यसत्त्वस्थो
निर्योगक्षेम आत्मवान् ॥ २.४५ ॥

traiguṇyaviṣayā vedā
nistraiguṇyo bhavārjuna
nirdvaṁdvo nityasattvastho
niryogakṣema ātmavān (2.45)

traiguṇya — three mood; viṣayā — phases; vedā — Vedas; nistraiguṇyo = nistraiguṇyaḥ — without the three moody phases; bhavārjuna = bhava — be + arjuna — Arjuna; nirdvandvo = nirdvandvaḥ — without fluctuation; nityasattvastho = nityasattvasthaḥ = nitya — always + sattva — reality + sthaḥ — fixed; niryogakṣema — without grasping and possessiveness; ātmavān — soul-situated

Three moody phases are offered by the Vedas. Be without the three moods, O Arjuna. Be without the moody fluctuations. Be always anchored to reality. Be free from grasping and possessiveness. (2.45)

यावानर्थ उदपाने
सर्वतः संप्लुतोदके ।
तावान्सर्वेषु वेदेषु
ब्राह्मणस्य विजानतः ॥ २.४६ ॥

yāvānartha udapāne
sarvataḥ saṁplutodake
tāvānsarveṣu vedeṣu
brāhmaṇasya vijānataḥ (2.46)

yāvān — as much; artha — importance; udapāne — in a well; sarvataḥ — in all directions; saṁplutodake = saṁpluta — flowing + udake — in water; tāvān — so much; sarveṣu — in the entire; vedeṣu — in the Vedas; brāhmaṇasya — of a brahmin; vijānataḥ — perceptive

For as much importance as there is in a well when suitable water flows in all directions, so much worth is in the entire Vedas for a perceptive brahmin. (2.46)

कर्मण्येवाधिकारस्ते
मा फलेषु कदाचन ।
मा कर्मफलहेतुर्भूर्
मा ते सङ्गोऽस्त्वकर्मणि ॥ २.४७ ॥

karmaṇyevādhikāraste
mā phaleṣu kadācana
mā karmaphalaheturbhūr
mā te saṅgo'stvakarmaṇi (2.47)

karmaṇyevādhikāraste = karmaṇi — in performance + eva — alone + adhikāraḥ — command, privilege + te — your; mā — not; phaleṣu — in the aftermath of consequences; kadācana — at any time; mā — not; karmaphalahetur = karmaphala — a result + hetur (hetuh) — motivation; bhūr = bhūḥ — be; mā — not; te — your; saṅgo = sangah — attachment; 'stv = astu — should be; akarmaṇi — non-action, idleness

The command is yours while performing, but not at any time in the aftermath of consequences. Do not be motivated by a result, nor harbor an attachment to idleness. (2.47)

योगस्थः कुरु कर्माणि
सङ्गं त्यक्त्वा धनंजय ।
सिद्ध्यसिद्ध्योः समो भूत्वा
समत्वं योग उच्यते ॥ २.४८ ॥

yogasthaḥ kuru karmāṇi
saṅgaṁ tyaktvā dhanaṁjaya
siddhyasiddhyoḥ samo bhūtvā
samatvaṁ yoga ucyate (2.48)

yogasthaḥ- in yoga attitude; kuru — do perform; karmāṇi — actions; saṅgaṁ — attachment to crippling emotions; tyaktvā — having abandoned; dhanaṁjaya — conqueror of wealthy countries; siddhyasiddhyoḥ — to success or failure; samo = samaḥ — attitude of indifference; bhūtvā — be; samatvaṁ — indifference; yoga — yogic practice; ucyate — it is said

So perform actions in the yoga mood. Attachment to crippling emotions should be abandoned, O conqueror of wealthy countries. Be indifferent to success or failure. It is said that indifference denotes yoga. (2.48)

दूरेण ह्यवरं कर्म
बुद्धियोगाद्धनंजय।
बुद्धौ शरणमन्विच्छ
कृपणाः फलहेतवः ॥ २.४९ ॥

dūreṇa hyavaraṁ karma
buddhiyogāddhanaṁjaya
buddhau śaraṇamanviccha
kṛpaṇāḥ phalahetavaḥ (2.49)

dūreṇa — by far; hyavaraṁ = hi — surely + avaraṁ — inferior + karma — cultural action; buddhiyogād = buddhiyogāt — intellectual discipline through yoga; dhanaṁjaya — victor of wealthy countries; buddhau — mystic insight; śaraṇam — location of confidence; anviccha — put; kṛpaṇāḥ — low and pathetic; phalahetavaḥ — people motivated for a result

Surely, cultural action is by far inferior to intellectual discipline through yoga. O victor of wealthy countries. One should take shelter in mystic insight, for how pathetic are those who are motivated by the promise of results. (2.49)

बुद्धियुक्तो जहातीह
उभे सुकृतदुष्कृते ।
तस्माद्योगाय युज्यस्व
योगः कर्मसु कौशलम् ॥२.५०॥

buddhiyukto jahātīha
ubhe sukṛtaduṣkṛte
tasmādyogāya yujyasva
yogaḥ karmasu kauśalam (2.50)

buddhiyukto = buddhiyuktaḥ — a person disciplined by the reality-piercing insight; jahātīha = jahāti — he discards + iha — here; ubhe — both; sukṛtaduṣkṛte — pleasant and unpleasant work; tasmād = tasmāt — therefore; yogāya — to yoga; yujyasva — take yourself to; yogaḥ — yogic mood; karmasu — in performance; kauśalam — skill

A person who is disciplined by the reality-piercing insight discards in each life both pleasant and unpleasant work. Therefore take to the yogic mood. Yoga gives skill in performance. (2.50)

कर्मजं बुद्धियुक्ता हि
फलं त्यक्त्वा मनीषिणः।
जन्मबन्धविनिर्मुक्ताः
पदं गच्छन्त्यनामयम् ॥२.५१॥

karmajaṁ buddhiyuktā hi
phalaṁ tyaktvā manīṣiṇaḥ
janmabandhavinirmuktāḥ
padaṁ gacchantyanāmayam (2.51)

karmajaṁ — produced by actions; buddhiyuktā — disciplined mystic seers; hi — indeed; phalaṁ — result; tyaktvā — having abandoned; manīṣiṇaḥ — wise people; janmabandhavinirmuktāḥ = janma — rebirth + bandha — bondage + vinirmuktāḥ — freed from; padaṁ — place; gacchanty = gacchanti — go; anāmayam — misery-free

Having abandoned the results which are produced by actions, and being freed from the bondage of rebirth, those wise people, the disciplined mystic seers, go to the misery-free place. (2.51)

यदा ते मोहकलिलं
बुद्धिर्व्यतितरिष्यति ।
तदा गन्तासि निर्वेदं
श्रोतव्यस्य श्रुतस्य च ॥२.५२॥

yadā te mohakalilaṁ
buddhirvyatitariṣyati
tadā gantāsi nirvedaṁ
śrotavyasya śrutasya ca (2.52)

yadā — when; te — you; mohakalilaṁ — delusion-saturated mind; buddhir (buddhiḥ) — discrimination; vyatitariṣyati — departs; tadā — then; gantāsi — you will become; nirvedaṁ — disgusted; śrotavyasya — with what is to be heard; śrutasya — what was heard; ca — and

When from your delusion-saturated mind, your discrimination departs, you will become disgusted with what is to be heard and what was heard. (2.52)

श्रुतिविप्रतिपन्ना ते
यदा स्थास्यति निश्चला ।
समाधावचला बुद्धिस्
तदा योगमवाप्स्यसि ॥ २.५३ ॥

śrutivipratipannā te
yadā sthāsyati niścalā
samādhāvacalā buddhis
tadā yogamavāpsyasi (2.53)

śrutivipratipannā = śruti — scriptural information + vipratipannā — false, misleading; te — you; yadā — when; sthāsyati — will remain; niścalā — unmoving, steady; samādhāvacalābuddhis = samādhau — in deep meditation; acalā — without moving, stable; buddhis (buddhiḥ) — intelligence; tadā — then; yogam — yoga discipline; avāpsyasi — will master

When rejecting misleading scriptural information, your intelligence remains steady without moody variation, being situated in deep meditation, you will master the yoga disciplines. (2.53)

अर्जुन उवाच
स्थितप्रज्ञस्य का भाषा
समाधिस्थस्य केशव ।
स्थितधीः किं प्रभाषेत
किमासीत व्रजेत किम् ॥ २.५४ ॥

arjuna uvāca
sthitaprajñasya kā bhāṣā
samādhisthasya keśava
sthitadhīḥ kiṁ prabhāṣeta
kimāsīta vrajeta kim (2.54)

arjuna — Arjuna; uvāca — said; sthitaprajñasya — of the person who is situated in clear penetrating insight; kā — what; bhāṣā — description; samādhisthasya — one who is anchored in deep meditation; keśava — Keśava, Kṛṣṇa; sthitadhīḥ — one who is steady in objectives; kiṁ — whom; prabhāṣeta — should speak; kim — how; āsīta — should sit; vrajeta — move; kim — how

Arjuna said: In regards to the person who is situated in clear, penetrating insight, would you please describe him? Speak of the person who is anchored in deep meditation, O Keśava Krishna. As for the man who is steady in objectives, how would he speak? How would he sit? How would he act? (2.54)

श्रीभगवानुवाच
प्रजहाति यदा कामान्
सर्वान्पार्थ मनोगतान् ।
आत्मन्येवात्मना तुष्टः
स्थितप्रज्ञस्तदोच्यते ॥ २.५५ ॥

śrībhagavānuvāca
prajahāti yadā kāmān
sarvānpārtha manogatān
ātmanyevātmanā tuṣṭaḥ
sthitaprajñastadocyate (2.55)

śrī bhagavān — the Blessed Lord; uvāca — said; prajahāti — abandons; yadā — when; kāmān — cravings; sarvān — all; pārtha — O son of Pṛthā; manogatān — escapes from mental dominance; ātmanyevātmanā = ātmani — in the spirit + eva — only + ātmanā — by the spirit; tuṣṭaḥ — being self-content; sthitaprajñastadocyate = sthitaprajñaḥ — one whose insight is steady + tadā — then + ucyate — is identified

The Blessed Lord said: When someone abandons all cravings, O son of Pṛthā, and escapes from mental dominance, being self-content, then that person is identified as one with steady insight. (2.55)

दुःखेष्वनुद्विग्नमनाः
सुखेषु विगतस्पृहः ।
वीतरागभयक्रोधः
स्थितधीर्मुनिरुच्यते ॥२.५६ ॥

duḥkheṣvanudvignamanāḥ
sukheṣu vigataspṛhaḥ
vītarāgabhayakrodhaḥ
sthitadhīrmunirucyate (2.56)

duḥkheṣvanudvignamanāḥ = duḥkheṣv (duḥkheṣu) — in miserable conditions + anudvigna — free from worries + manāḥ — mind; sukheṣu — in good conditions; vigataspṛhaḥ — free from excitement; vītarāgabhayakrodhaḥ = vīta — steps aside + rāga — passion + bhaya — fear + krodhaḥ — anger; sthitadhīr = sthitadhīḥ — steady in meditation; munir = muniḥ — wise man; ucyate — is said to be

Furthermore, someone who in miserable conditions remains free from worries, and who in good conditions remains free from excitement, who steps aside from passion, fear and anger, and who is steady in meditation is considered to be a wise man. (2.56)

यः सर्वत्रानभिस्नेहस्
तत्तत्प्राप्य शुभाशुभम् ।
नाभिनन्दति न द्वेष्टि
तस्य प्रज्ञा प्रतिष्ठिता ॥२.५७॥

yaḥ sarvatrānabhisnehas
tattatprāpya śubhāśubham
nābhinandati na dveṣṭi
tasya prajñā pratiṣṭhitā (2.57)

yaḥ- who; sarvatrā — in all circumstances; anabhisnehaḥ — without crippling affections; tattat = tad tad-this or that; prāpya- meeting; śubhāśubham — enjoyable and disturbing factors; nābhinandati = na — not + abhinandati — excited; na — nor; dveṣṭi — distressed; tasya — his; prajñā — reality-piercing consciousness; pratiṣṭhitā - is established

A person who, in all circumstances, is without crippling affections, who, when meeting enjoyable or disturbing factors, does not get excited nor distressed, his reality-piercing consciousness is established. (2.57)

यदा संहरते चायं
कूर्मोऽङ्गानीव सर्वशः।
इन्द्रियाणीन्द्रियार्थेभ्यस्
तस्य प्रज्ञा प्रतिष्ठिता ॥२.५८॥

yadā saṁharate cāyaṁ
kūrmo'ṅgānīva sarvaśaḥ
indriyāṇīndriyārthebhyas
tasya prajñā pratiṣṭhitā (2.58)

yadā — when; saṁharate — pulls; cāyaṁ = ca — and + ayam — this; kūrmo = kūrmaḥ — tortoise; 'ṅgānīva = aṅgānīva = aṅgāni — limbs + iva — like, compared to; sarvaśaḥ — fully; indriyāṇīndriyārthebhyas = indriyani — senses + indriyarthebhyaḥ — attractive things; tasya — his; prajñā — reality-piercing vision; pratiṣṭhitā — is established

When such a person pulls fully out of moods, he or she may be compared to the tortoise with its limbs retracted. The senses are withdrawn from the attractive things in the case of a person whose reality-piercing vision is established. (2.58)

विषया विनिवर्तन्ते
निराहारस्य देहिनः।
रसवर्जं रसोऽप्यस्य
परं दृष्ट्वा निवर्तते॥२.५९॥

viṣayā vinivartante
nirāhārasya dehinaḥ
rasavarjaṁ raso'pyasya
paraṁ dṛṣṭvā nivartate (2.59)

viṣayā = viṣayāḥ — temptations; vinivartante — turn away; nirāhārasya — from(without) indulgence; dehinaḥ — of the embodied soul; rasavarjaṁ = rasa — memory or mental flavor of past indulgences + varjaṁ — except for, besides; raso = rasah — memories (mental flavors); 'pyasya = apyasya = apy (api) — even + asya — of him; paraṁ — higher stage; dṛṣṭvā — having experienced; nivartate — leaves

The temptations themselves turn away from the disciplinary attitude of an ascetic, but the memory of previous indulgences remain with him. When he experiences higher stages, those memories leave him. (2.59)

यततो ह्यपि कौन्तेय
पुरुषस्य विपश्चितः।
इन्द्रियाणि प्रमाथीनि
हरन्ति प्रसभं मनः ॥२.६०॥

yatato hyapi kaunteya
puruṣasya vipaścitaḥ
indriyāṇi pramāthīni
haranti prasabhaṁ manaḥ (2.60)

yatato = yatataḥ — concerning an aspiring seeker; hyapi = hi — indeed + api — also; kaunteya — son of Kuntī; puruṣasya — of the person; vipaścitaḥ — of the discerning educated; indriyāṇi — the senses; pramāthīni — tormenting; haranti — seize, adjust; prasabhaṁ — impulsively, by impulse; manaḥ — mentally

Concerning an aspiring seeker, O son of Kuntī, concerning a discerned educated person, the senses do torment him. By impulses, the senses do adjust his mentality. (2.60)

तानि सर्वाणि संयम्य
युक्त आसीत मत्परः।
वशे हि यस्येन्द्रियाणि
तस्य प्रज्ञा प्रतिष्ठिता ॥२.६१॥

tāni sarvāṇi saṁyamya
yukta āsīta matparaḥ
vaśe hi yasyendriyāṇi
tasya prajñā pratiṣṭhitā (2.61)

tāni — these; sarvāṇi — all (senses); saṁyamya — restraining; yukta — yogically disciplined; āsīta — should sit; matparaḥ — focused on Me, on My interest; vaśe — in control; hi — indeed; yasyendriyāṇi = yasya — of whom + indriyāṇi — of the sensuality; tasya — of him; prajñā — vision; pratiṣṭhitā — anchored

Restraining all these senses, being disciplined in yoga practice, an ascetic should sit, being focused on Me. The vision of a person whose sensuality is controlled, remains anchored in reality. (2.61)

ध्यायतो विषयान्पुंसः
सङ्गस्तेषूपजायते ।
सङ्गात्संजायते कामः
कामात्क्रोधोऽभिजायते ॥२.६२॥

dhyāyato viṣayānpuṁsaḥ
saṅgasteṣūpajāyate
saṅgātsaṁjāyate kāmaḥ
kāmātkrodho'bhijāyate (2.62)

dhyāyato = dhyāyataḥ — considering; viṣayān — sensual objects; puṁsaḥ — a person; saṅgas — attachment; teṣūpajāyate = teṣu — in them + upajāyate — is born, is created; saṅgāt — from attachment; saṁjāyate — is born; kāmaḥ — craving; kāmāt — from craving; krodho = krodhah — anger; 'bhijāyate = abhijāyate — is derived

The act of considering sensual objects, creates in a person, an attachment to them. From attachment comes craving. From this craving anger is derived. (2.62)

क्रोधाद्भवति संमोहः
संमोहात्स्मृतिविभ्रमः ।
स्मृतिभ्रंशाद्बुद्धिनाशो
बुद्धिनाशात्प्रणश्यति ॥२.६३॥

krodhādbhavati saṁmohaḥ
saṁmohātsmṛtivibhramaḥ
smṛtibhraṁśādbuddhināśo
buddhināśātpraṇaśyati (2.63)

krodhād = krodhāt — from anger; bhavati — becomes (comes); saṁmohaḥ — delusion; saṁmohāt — from delusion; smṛti — conscience + vibhramaḥ — vanish; smṛtibhraṁśād = smṛtibhraṁśāt = smṛti — memory, judgement + bhraṁśāt — from fading away; buddhināśo = buddhināśaḥ = buddhi — discerning power + nāśaḥ — lose, affected; buddhināśāt = buddhi — discernment + nāśāt — from loss, from being affected; praṇaśyati — is ruined

From anger, comes delusion. From this delusion, the conscience vanishes. When he loses judgment, his discerning power fades away. Once the discernment is affected, he is ruined. (2.63)

रागद्वेषवियुक्तैस्तु
विषयानिन्द्रियैश्चरन् ।
आत्मवश्यैर्विधेयात्मा
प्रसादमधिगच्छति ॥२.६४॥

rāgadveṣaviyuktaistu
viṣayānindriyaiścaran ।
ātmavaśyairvidheyātmā
prasādamadhigacchati (2.64)

rāgadveṣaviyuktais = rāga — cravings + dveṣa — disliking + viyuktaiḥ — discontinued; tu — if, however; viṣayān — attractive objects; indriyaiścaran = indriyaiḥ — by the senses + caran — interacting; ātmavaśyair = ātmavaśyaiḥ — disciplined person; vidheyātmā — a well-behaved person; prasādam — grace of providence; adhigacchati — gets

If, on the other hand, cravings and dislikings are continued and the attractive objects and senses continue interaction, a disciplined person who is usually well-behaved, gets the grace of providence. (2.64)

प्रसादे सर्वदुःखानां हानिरस्योपजायते । प्रसन्नचेतसो ह्याशु बुद्धिः पर्यवतिष्ठते ॥२.६५॥	prasāde sarvaduḥkhānāṁ hānirasyopajāyate prasannacetaso hyāśu buddhiḥ paryavatiṣṭhate (2.65)

prasāde — the grace of providence producing spiritual peace of mind; sarvaduḥkhānāṁ = sarva — all + duḥkhāṇām — of the emotional distresses; hānir = hāniḥ — cessation, end; asyopajāyate = asya — of him + upajāyate — is produced; prasannacetaso = prasannacetasaḥ = prasanna — peaceful + cetasaḥ— of mind; hyāśu = hy (hi) — indeed + āśu — at once; buddhiḥ — intelligence; paryavatiṣṭhate — becomes stable

By the grace of providence, all the emotional distresses cease for him. Being of a pacified mind, his intelligence at once, becomes stable. (2.65)

नास्ति बुद्धिरयुक्तस्य न चायुक्तस्य भावना । न चाभावयतः शान्तिर् अशान्तस्य कुतः सुखम् ॥२.६६॥	nāsti buddhirayuktasya na cāyuktasya bhāvanā na cābhāvayataḥ śāntir aśāntasya kutaḥ sukham (2.66)

nāsti = na — no + asti — is; buddhir = buddhiḥ — proper discernment; ayuktasya — of the uncontrolled person; na — not; cāyuktasya = ca — and + ayuktasya — of the uncontrolled person; bhāvanā — concentration; na — not; cābhāvayataḥ = ca — and + abhāvayataḥ — a person lacking concentration; śāntir = śāntiḥ — peace; aśāntasya — lacking emotional stability; kutaḥ — how is it to be achieved; sukham — happiness

In comparison, never is there proper discernment in an uncontrolled person. He is not capable of concentration. One who lacks concentration cannot get inner peace. For one who lacks emotional stability, how will happiness be achieved? (2.66)

इन्द्रियाणां हि चरतां यन्मनोऽनुविधीयते । तदस्य हरति प्रज्ञां वायुर्नावमिवाम्भसि ॥२.६७॥	indriyāṇāṁ hi caratāṁ yanmano'nuvidhīyate tadasya harati prajñāṁ vāyurnāvamivāmbhasi (2.67)

indriyāṇām — of the senses; hi — indeed; caratāṁ — wandering; yan = yad — when; mano = manaḥ — the mind; 'nuvidhīyate = anuvidhīyate — is prompted; tadasya = tad — that + asya — of it; harati — it utilizes; prajñāṁ — of the discernment; vāyur = vāyuḥ — the wind; nāvam — a ship; ivāmbhasi = iva — like + ambhasi — in the water

When the mind is prompted by the wandering senses, it utilizes the discernment, just as in water, the wind handles a ship. (2.67)

तस्माद्यस्य महाबाहो निगृहीतानि सर्वशः । इन्द्रियाणीन्द्रियार्थेभ्यस् तस्य प्रज्ञा प्रतिष्ठिता ॥२.६८॥	tasmādyasya mahābāho nigṛhītāni sarvaśaḥ indriyāṇīndriyārthebhyas tasya prajñā pratiṣṭhitā (2.68)

tasmād — therefore; yasya — of the person who; mahābāho — O powerful Arjuna; nigṛhītāni — retracts; sarvaśaḥ — in every interaction; indriyāṇīndriyārthebhyas = indriyāṇi — sensual feelings + indriyārthebhyaḥ — of the attractive objects; tasya — his; prajñā — discernment; pratiṣṭhitā — remains constant

Thus, O Arjuna, concerning the person who, in every interaction retracts the sensual feelings from the attractive objects; his discernment remains constant. (2.68)

या निशा सर्वभूतानां तस्यां जागर्ति संयमी । यस्यां जाग्रति भूतानि सा निशा पश्यतो मुनेः ॥२.६९॥	yā niśā sarvabhūtānāṁ tasyāṁ jāgarti saṁyamī yasyāṁ jāgrati bhūtāni sā niśā paśyato muneḥ (2.69)

yā — which; niśā — void; sarvabhūtānāṁ — all ordinary people; tasyāṁ — in this; jāgarti — is perceptive; saṁyamī — the sense-controlling person; yasyāṁ — in what; jāgrati — is exciting; bhūtāni — the masses of people; sā — that; niśā — is void; paśyato = paśyataḥ — of the perceptive; muneḥ — of the sage

The sense-controlling person is perceptive of that which is void to the ordinary people. What is exciting to the masses of people is void to the perceptive sage. (2.69)

आपूर्यमाणमचलप्रतिष्ठं समुद्रमापः प्रविशन्ति यद्वत् । तद्वत्कामा यं प्रविशन्ति सर्वे स शान्तिमाप्नोति न कामकामी ॥२.७०॥	āpūryamāṇamacalapratiṣṭhaṁ samudramāpaḥ praviśanti yadvat tadvatkāmā yaṁ praviśanti sarve sa śāntimāpnoti na kāmakāmī (2.70)

āpūryamāṇam — becoming filled; acalapratiṣṭhaṁ = acala — not moving about + pratiṣṭham — remaining stationary; samudram — the ocean; āpaḥ — the waters; praviśanti — they enter; yadvat — in which; tadvat — similarly; kāmā = kāmāḥ — cravings; yaṁ — whom; praviśanti — enter, arise; sarve — all; sa — he; śāntim — true satisfaction; āpnoti — gets; na — not; kāmakāmī — one who craves for every desire

Becoming filled, not flowing about, remaining stationary, the ocean absorbs the waters that enter it. Similarly, a person who remains calm when cravings arise gets true satisfaction, but not the person who craves for every desire. (2.70)

विहाय कामान्यः सर्वान्
पुमांश्चरति निःस्पृहः ।
निर्ममो निरहंकारः
स शान्तिमधिगच्छति ॥ २.७१ ॥

vihāya kāmānyaḥ sarvān
pumāṁścarati niḥspṛhaḥ
nirmamo nirahaṁkāraḥ
sa śāntimadhigacchati (2.71)

vihāya — rejects; kāmān — cravings; yaḥ — who; sarvān — all; pumāṁścarati = pumān — person + carati — acts; niḥspṛhaḥ — free of lusty motivation; nirmamo = nirmamaḥ — indifferent to possessions; nirahaṁkāraḥ — free from impulsive assertion; sa — he; śāntim — contentment; adhigacchati — attains

The person who rejects all cravings, whose acts are free of lusty motivation, who is indifferent to possessions, who is free of impulsive assertion, attains contentment. (2.71)

एषा ब्राह्मी स्थितिः पार्थ
नैनां प्राप्य विमुह्यति ।
स्थित्वास्यामन्तकालेऽपि
ब्रह्मनिर्वाणमृच्छति ॥ २.७२ ॥

eṣā brāhmī sthitiḥ pārtha
naināṁ prāpya vimuhyati
sthitvāsyāmantakāle'pi
brahmanirvāṇamṛcchati (2.72)

eṣā - this; brāhmī - divine; sthitiḥ — state; pārtha - son of Pṛthā; naināṁ = na - not + enām - this; prāpya — does have; vimuhyati — is stupified; sthitvā — is fixed; 'syām = asyām — in this; antakāle — at the time of death; 'pi = api — also; brahma — divinity + nirvāṇam — full stoppage of mundane sensuality; ṛcchati — attains

This divine state is required, O son of Pṛthā. If a man does not have this, he is stupefied. At the time of death, the full stoppage of mundane sensuality and the attainment of divinity is attained by one who is fixed in this divine state. (2.72)

CHAPTER 3

Cultural Activity and Renunciation*

अर्जुन उवाच
ज्यायसी चेत्कर्मणस्ते
मता बुद्धिर्जनार्दन ।
तत्किं कर्मणि घोरे मां
नियोजयसि केशव ॥ ३.१ ॥

arjuna uvāca
jyāyasī cetkarmaṇaste
matā buddhirjanārdana
tatkiṁ karmaṇi ghore māṁ
niyojayasi keśava (3.1)

arjuna — Arjuna; uvāca — contested; jyāyasī — is better; cet = ced — if; karmaṇaḥ — than physical action; te — your; matā — idea; buddhirjanārdana = buddhiḥ — mental action + janārdana — motivator of men; tatkiṁ = tat (tad) — them + kiṁ — why; karmaṇi — in action; ghore — in horrible; māṁ — me; niyojayasi — you urge; keśava — handsome-haired one

Arjuna contested: O motivator of men, if it is Your idea that the mental approach is better than the physically-active one, then why do You urge me to commit horrible action, O handsome-haired One? (3.1)

व्यामिश्रेणैव वाक्येन
बुद्धिं मोहयसीव मे ।
तदेकं वद निश्चित्य
येन श्रेयोऽहमाप्नुयाम् ॥ ३.२ ॥

vyāmiśreṇaiva vākyena
buddhiṁ mohayasīva me
tadekaṁ vada niścitya
yena śreyo'hamāpnuyām (3.2)

vyāmiśreṇaiva = vyāmiśreṇa — with this two-way + iva — like this; vākyena — with a proposal; buddhiṁ — intelligence; mohayasīva = mohayasi — you baffle + iva — like this; me — of me; tad — this; ekaṁ — one; vada — tell; niścitya — surely; yena — by which; śreyo = śreyaḥ — the best; 'ham = aham — I; āpnuyām — I should get

You baffle my intelligence with this two-way proposal. Mention one priority, by which I would surely get the best result. (3.2)

श्रीभगवानुवाच
लोकेऽस्मिन्द्विविधा निष्ठा
पुरा प्रोक्ता मयानघ ।
ज्ञानयोगेन सांख्यानां
कर्मयोगेन योगिनाम् ॥ ३.३ ॥

śrībhagavānuvāca
loke'smindvividhā niṣṭhā
purā proktā mayānagha
jñānayogena sāṁkhyānāṁ
karmayogena yoginām (3.3)

**The Mahābhārata contains no chapter headings. This title was assigned by the translator on the basis of verse 4 of this chapter.*

śrī bhagavān — the Blessed Lord; uvāca — said; loke — in this physical world; 'smin = asmin — in this; dvividhā — of the two-fold; niṣṭhā — standard; purā — previously; proktā — was taught; mayā — by me; 'nagha = anagha — O blameless one, good man; jñānayogena — mind regulations by yoga practice; sāṁkhyānāṁ — of the Sāṁkhya philosophical yogis; karmayogena — action regulation by yoga practice; yoginām — of the non-philosophical yogis

The Blessed Lord said: In the physical world, a two-fold standard was previously taught by Me. O Arjuna, my good man. This was mind regulation by the yoga practice of the Sāṁkhya philosophical yogis and the action regulation by the yoga practice of the non- philosophical yogis. (3.3)

न कर्मणामनारम्भान्
नैष्कर्म्यं पुरुषोऽश्नुते ।
न च संन्यसनादेव
सिद्धिं समधिगच्छति ॥ ३.४॥

na karmaṇāmanārambhān
naiṣkarmyaṁ puruṣo'śnute
na ca saṁnyasanādeva
siddhiṁ samadhigacchati (3.4)

na — not; karmaṇām — concerning cultural activity; anārambhān — not being involved; naiṣkarmyaṁ — freedom from cultural activity; puruṣo = puruṣaḥ — a person; 'śnute = aśnute — attains; na — not; ca — and; saṁnyasanādeva = saṁnyasanād (saṁnyasanāt) — from renunciation + eva — alone; siddhiṁ — spiritual perfection; samadhigacchati — achieves

A man does not attain freedom from cultural activity merely by not being involved in social affairs. And not by renunciation alone, does he achieve spiritual perfection. (3.4)

न हि कश्चित्क्षणमपि
जातु तिष्ठत्यकर्मकृत् ।
कार्यते ह्यवशः कर्म
सर्वः प्रकृतिजैर्गुणैः ॥ ३.५॥

na hi kaścitkṣaṇamapi
jātu tiṣṭhatyakarmakṛt
kāryate hyavaśaḥ karma
sarvaḥ prakṛtijairguṇaiḥ (3.5)

na — no; hi — indeed; kaścit — anyone; kṣaṇamapi = kṣaṇam — a moment + api — also; jātu — ever; tiṣṭhatyakarmakṛt = tiṣṭhati — exists + akarmakṛt — not acting; kāryate — caused to act; hyavaśaḥ = hi — indeed + avaśaḥ — against their wishes; karma — vibration; sarvaḥ — everyone; prakṛtijair = prakṛtijaiḥ — produced by material nature; guṇaiḥ — variations of mundane energy

No one, even momentarily, ever exists without vibration. By the variations of mundane energy in material nature, everyone, even against their wishes, is forced to perform. (3.5)

कर्मेन्द्रियाणि संयम्य
य आस्ते मनसा स्मरन् ।
इन्द्रियार्थान्विमूढात्मा
मिथ्याचारः स उच्यते ॥३.६॥

karmendriyāṇi saṁyamya
ya āste manasā smaran
indriyārthānvimūḍhātmā
mithyācāraḥ sa ucyate (3.6)

karmendriyāṇi — bodily limbs; saṁyamya — restraining; ya = yaḥ — who; āste — sits; manasā — by the mind; smaran — remembering; indriyārthān — attractive objects; vimūḍhātmā = vimūḍha — deluded + ātmā — self; mithyācāraḥ — deceiver; sa — he; ucyate — it is declared

A person who while restraining his bodily limbs sits, with the mind remembering attractive objects, is a deceiver. So it is declared. (3.6)

यस्त्विन्द्रियाणि मनसा
नियम्यारभतेऽर्जुन ।
कर्मेन्द्रियैः कर्मयोगम्
असक्तः स विशिष्यते ॥३.७॥

yastvindriyāṇi manasā
niyamyārabhate'rjuna
karmendriyaiḥ karmayogam
asaktaḥ sa viśiṣyate (3.7)

yas (yaḥ)- whosoever; tvindriyāṇi = tv (tu) — however + indriyāṇi — the senses; manasā — by the mind; niyamyārabhate = niyamya — controlling + ārabhate — endeavors; 'rjuna-Arjuna; karmendriyaiḥ — by the limbs; karmayogam — regulating his work by yoga practice; asaktaḥ — without attachment; sa = saḥ — he; viśiṣyate — is superior

However, whosoever endeavors to control the senses by the mind, O Arjuna, and who restricts the limbs through regulating his work by yoga practice, without attachment, is superior. (3.7)

नियतं कुरु कर्म त्वं
कर्म ज्यायो ह्यकर्मणः ।
शरीरयात्रापि च ते
न प्रसिध्येदकर्मणः ॥३.८॥

niyataṁ kuru karma tvaṁ
karma jyāyo hyakarmaṇaḥ
śarīrayātrāpi ca te
na prasidhyedakarmaṇaḥ (3.8)

niyataṁ — moral; kuru — do; karma — cultural duty; tvaṁ — you; karma — performance; jyāyo = jyāyaḥ — better; hy akarmaṇaḥ = hi — indeed + akarmaṇaḥ — than non-action; śarīrayātrāpi = śarīra — body + yātrā — maintenance + api — even; ca — and; te — your; na — not; prasidhyet — could be achieved; akarmaṇaḥ — without activity

Moral action should be done by you. Performance is better than non-performance. Even the maintenance of your body could not be achieved without activity. (3.8)

यज्ञार्थात्कर्मणोऽन्यत्र
लोकोऽयं कर्मबन्धनः ।
तदर्थं कर्म कौन्तेय
मुक्तसङ्गः समाचर ॥३.९॥

yajñārthātkarmaṇo'nyatra
loko'yaṁ karmabandhanaḥ
tadarthaṁ karma kaunteya
muktasaṅgaḥ samācara (3.9)

yajñārthāt = yajña — religious fulfillment and ceremony + ārthāt — for the sake of; karmaṇo (karmaṇaḥ) - from action; 'nyatra = anyatra - besides; loko = lokaḥ — world; 'yaṁ = ayam — this; karmabandhanaḥ — something bound by action; tad — this + arthaṁ — purpose, value; karma — cultural activity; kaunteya — son of Kuntī; muktasaṅgaḥ — freedom from attachment; samācara — act promptly

Besides action for religious fulfillment and ceremony, this world, is action-bound. Act for the sake of religious fulfillment and ceremony, O son of Kuntī. Be free from attachment. Act promptly. (3.9)

सहयज्ञाः प्रजाः सृष्ट्वा
पुरोवाच प्रजापतिः ।
अनेन प्रसविष्यध्वम्
एष वोऽस्त्विष्टकामधुक् ॥३.१०॥

sahayajñāḥ prajāḥ sṛṣṭvā
purovāca prajāpatiḥ
anena prasaviṣyadhvam
eṣa vo'stviṣṭakāmadhuk (3.10)

sahayajñāḥ — along with religious fulfillment and ceremony; prajāḥ — first human beings; sṛṣṭvā — having created; purovāca = pura — long ago + uvāca — said; prajāpatiḥ — procreator Brahma; anena — by this; prasaviṣyadhvam — may you produce; eṣaḥ — this; vo = vaḥ — your; 'stviṣṭakāmadhuk = astviṣṭakāmadhuk = astu — may it be + iṣṭakāmadhuk — for granting desires

Long ago, having created the first human beings, along with religious fulfillment and ceremonies, the Procreator Brahmā said: By this worship procedure, you may be productive. May it cause the fulfillment of your desires. (3.10)

देवान्भावयतानेन
ते देवा भावयन्तु वः ।
परस्परं भावयन्तः
श्रेयः परमवाप्स्यथ ॥३.११॥

devānbhāvayatānena
te devā bhāvayantu vaḥ
parasparaṁ bhāvayantaḥ
śreyaḥ paramavāpsyatha (3.11)

devān — supernatural rulers; bhāvayatānena = bhāvayatā — may you cause to flourish + anena — by this procedure; te — they; devā — the supernatural rulers; bhāvayantu — may they bless you; vaḥ — you; parasparaṁ — each other; bhāvayantaḥ — favorably regarding one another; śreyaḥ — well-being; param — highest; avāpsyatha — you will achieve

By this procedure, you may cause the supernatural rulers to flourish. They, in turn, may bless you. In favorably regarding each other, the highest well-being will be achieved. (3.11)

इष्टान्भोगान्हि वो देवा
दास्यन्ते यज्ञभाविताः ।
तैर्दत्तानप्रदायैभ्यो
यो भुङ्क्ते स्तेन एव सः ॥३.१२॥

iṣṭānbhogānhi vo devā
dāsyante yajñabhāvitāḥ
tairdattānapradāyaibhyo
yo bhuṅkte stena eva saḥ (3.12)

iṣṭān — most desired; bhogān — enjoyable people and things; hi — indeed; vo = vaḥ — to you; devā — supernatural rulers; dāsyante — they will give; yajñabhāvitāḥ — manifested through prescribed austerity and religious ceremony; tair = taiḥ — by those; dattān — given items; apradāyaibhyo = apradāya — not offering + ebhyaḥ — to them; yo = yaḥ — who; bhuṅkte — enjoys; stena — a thief; eva — only; saḥ — he

The supernatural rulers, being manifested through prescribed austerity and religious ceremony, will, indeed, give you the most desired people and things. Whosoever does not offer those given items to them, but who enjoys these, is certainly a thief. (3.12)

यज्ञशिष्टाशिनः सन्तो
मुच्यन्ते सर्वकिल्बिषैः ।
भुञ्जते ते त्वघं पापा
ये पचन्त्यात्मकारणात् ॥३.१३॥

yajñaśiṣṭāśinaḥ santo
mucyante sarvakilbiṣaiḥ
bhuñjate te tvaghaṁ pāpā
ye pacantyātmakāraṇāt (3.13)

yajñaśiṣṭāśinaḥ = yajñaśiṣṭa — sanctified items used after a religious ceremony + āśinaḥ — utilizing; santo = santaḥ — virtuous souls; mucyante — they are released; sarvakilbiṣaiḥ — from all faults; bhuñjate — consume; te — they; tvaghaṁ = tv (tu) — but + aghaṁ — impurity; pāpā — wicked people; ye — who; pacantyātmakāraṇāt = pacanti — prepare + ātma — self + kāraṇāt — for the sake of

(Krishna continued): The virtuous people who utilize the items after they are sanctified by prescribed ceremony, are released from all faults. But the wicked ones who prepare for their own sake, consume their own impurity. (3.13)

अन्नाद्भवन्ति भूतानि
पर्जन्यादन्नसंभवः ।
यज्ञाद्भवति पर्जन्यो
यज्ञः कर्मसमुद्भवः ॥३.१४॥

annādbhavanti bhūtāni
parjanyādannasaṁbhavaḥ
yajñādbhavati parjanyo
yajñaḥ karmasamudbhavaḥ (3.14)

annād=annāt- from nourishment; bhavanti- are produced; bhūtāni - the creatures; parjanyād = parjanyāt — from rain clouds; anna — nourishment; saṁbhavaḥ — originated; yajñād = yajñāt — from prescribed austerity and religious ceremony; bhavati — exists; parjanyo = parjanyaḥ — rain; yajñaḥ — prescribed austerity and religious ceremony; karma — cultural action; samudbhavaḥ — is caused

The creatures are produced from nourishment. From rain clouds, nourishment originated. From prescribed austerity and religious ceremony, rain clouds are produced. And prescribed austerity and religious ceremony are caused by cultural activities. (3.14)

कर्म ब्रह्मोद्भवं विद्धि
ब्रह्माक्षरसमुद्भवम् ।
तस्मात्सर्वगतं ब्रह्म
नित्यं यज्ञे प्रतिष्ठितम् ॥३.१५॥

karma brahmodbhavaṁ viddhi
brahmākṣarasamudbhavam
tasmātsarvagataṁ brahma
nityaṁ yajñe pratiṣṭhitam (3.15)

karma — cultural activity; brahmodbhavaṁ = brahma — the Veda + udbhavaṁ — produced; viddhi — be aware; brahmākṣarasamudbhavam = brahma — Supreme Spirit + akṣara — the unaffected spiritual reality + samudbhavam — produced; tasmāt — hence; sarvagataṁ — all-pervading; brahma — spirit person; nityaṁ — always; yajñe — in prescribed austerity and religious ceremony; pratiṣṭhitam — is situated

Cultural activity is produced from the Personified Veda. The Personified Veda comes from the unaffected Supreme Spirit. Hence the all-pervading Supreme Spirit is always situated in prescribed austerity and religious ceremony. (3.15)

एवं प्रवर्तितं चक्रं
नानुवर्तयतीह यः ।
अघायुरिन्द्रियारामो
मोघं पार्थ स जीवति ॥३.१६॥

evaṁ pravartitaṁ cakraṁ
nānuvartayatīha yaḥ
aghāyurindriyārāmo
moghaṁ pārtha sa jīvati (3.16)

evaṁ — thus; pravartitaṁ — perpetuated; cakraṁ — circular process; nānuvartayatīha = na — not + anuvartayati — cause to be perpetuated + iha — on earth; yaḥ — who; aghāyurindriyārāmo = aghāyuḥ — malicious + indriyārāmaḥ — sensually-happy person; moghaṁ — worthless; pārtha — son of Pṛthā; sa = saḥ — he; jīvati — lives

O son of Pṛthā, a person who does not cause this circular process to be perpetuated here on earth, lives as a malicious, sensually-happy and worthless person. (3.16)

यस्त्वात्मरतिरेव स्याद्
आत्मतृप्तश्च मानवः ।
आत्मन्येव च संतुष्टस्
तस्य कार्यं न विद्यते ॥३.१७॥

yastvātmaratireva syād
ātmatṛptaśca mānavaḥ
ātmanyeva ca saṁtuṣṭas
tasya kāryaṁ na vidyate (3.17)

yastvātmaratireva = yas (yaḥ) — who + tv (tu) — but + ātma — spiritual self + ratir (ratiḥ) — pleased + eva — surely; syāt — should be; ātmatṛptaśca = ātma — self + tṛptaḥ — satisfied + ca — and; mānavaḥ — a human being; ātmanyeva = ātmany (ātmani) — in the self + eva — only; ca — and;

saṁtuṣṭaḥ — content; tasya — of him; kāryaṁ — cultural duty; na — no; vidyate — it is experienced

A person who is spiritually-pleased, self-satisfied and spiritually-content, has no cultural duties. (3.17)

नैव तस्य कृतेनार्थो
नाकृतेनेह कश्चन ।
न चास्य सर्वभूतेषु
कश्चिदर्थव्यपाश्रयः ॥३.१८॥

naiva tasya kṛtenārtho
nākṛteneha kaścana
na cāsya sarvabhūteṣu
kaścidarthavyapāśrayaḥ (3.18)

naiva = na — not + eva — indeed; tasya — regarding him; kṛtenārtho = kṛtena — with action + artho (arthaḥ) — gain; nākṛteneha = na — not + akṛtena — with non-action + iha — in this case; kaścana — anyone; na — not; cāsya = ca — and + asya — of him; sarvabhūteṣu — in all mundane creatures; kaścit — any; arthavyapāśrayaḥ = artha — purpose + vyapāśrayaḥ — depending

The person who does not aspire for gain in an action or in an inaction, is not reliant on any mundane creature. (3.18)

तस्मादसक्तः सततं
कार्यं कर्म समाचर ।
असक्तो ह्याचरन्कर्म
परमाप्नोति पूरुषः ॥३.१९॥

tasmādasaktaḥ satataṁ
kāryaṁ karma samācara
asakto hyācarankarma
paramāpnoti pūruṣaḥ (3.19)

tasmād = tasmāt — therefore; asaktaḥ — unattached; satataṁ — always; kāryaṁ — duty, required tasks; karma — action; samācara — perform; asakto = asaktaḥ — unattached; hyācarankarma = hy (hi) — indeed + ācaran — executing + karma — action; param — the highest stage; āpnoti — gets; pūruṣaḥ — a person

Therefore, being always unattached, perform the action which is your duty. By being detached and executing the required tasks, a person gets the highest stage. (3.19)

कर्मणैव हि संसिद्धिम्
आस्थिता जनकादयः ।
लोकसंग्रहमेवापि
संपश्यन्कर्तुमर्हसि ॥३.२०॥

karmaṇaiva hi saṁsiddhim
āsthitā janakādayaḥ
lokasaṁgrahamevāpi
saṁpaśyankartumarhasi (3.20)

karmaṇaiva = karmaṇa — by cultural activities + eva — alone; hi — indeed; saṁsiddhim — perfection; āsthitā — attained; janakādayaḥ = janaka — Janaka + ādayaḥ — beginning with; loka — world + saṁgraham — maintenance + eva — only + api — only; saṁpaśyan — seeing mentally; kartum — to act; arhasi — you should

Beginning with Janaka, perfection was attained by cultural activities alone. Seeing the necessity for world maintenance, you should act. (3.20)

यद्यदाचरति श्रेष्ठस् तत्तदेवेतरो जनः । स यत्प्रमाणं कुरुते लोकस्तदनुवर्तते ॥३.२१॥	yadyadācarati śreṣṭhas tattadevetaro janaḥ sa yatpramāṇaṁ kurute lokastadanuvartate (3.21)

yadyad — whatever; ācarati — does; śreṣṭhaḥ — the greatest; tattad = tad tad — this and that; evetaro (evetaraḥ) = eva — only + itaraḥ — the others; janaḥ — perform; sa = saḥ — he; yat — what; pramāṇaṁ — trend; kurute — establishes; lokastadanuvartate = lokaḥ — the world + tad — that + anuvartate — pursues

Whatever a great person does, for that only, others aspire. Whatever trend he establishes, the world pursues. (3.21)

न मे पार्थास्ति कर्तव्यं त्रिषु लोकेषु किंचन । नानवाप्तमवाप्तव्यं वर्त एव च कर्मणि ॥३.२२॥	na me pārthāsti kartavyaṁ triṣu lokeṣu kiṁcana nānavāptamavāptavyaṁ varta eva ca karmaṇi (3.22)

na — not; me — of me; pārthāsti = pārtha — O son of Pṛthā + asti — is; kartavyaṁ — should be done; triṣu — in the three divisions; lokeṣu — in the universe; kiṁcana — anything specific; nānavāptamavāptavyaṁ = na — not + anavāptam — not attained + avāptavyam — to be acquired; varta — I function; eva — yet; ca — and; karmaṇi — in cultural activities

For Me, O son of Pṛthā, there is nothing specific that must be done in the three divisions of the universe. And there is nothing that I have not attained nor should acquire, and yet I function in cultural activities. (3.22)

यदि ह्यहं न वर्तेयं जातु कर्मण्यतन्द्रितः । मम वर्त्मानुवर्तन्ते मनुष्याः पार्थ सर्वशः ॥३.२३॥	yadi hyahaṁ na varteyaṁ jātu karmaṇyatandritaḥ mama vartmānuvartante manuṣyāḥ pārtha sarvaśaḥ (3.23)

yadi — if; hyahaṁ = hy (hi) — perchance + ahaṁ — I; na — not; varteyaṁ — should perform; jātu — ever; karmaṇyatandritaḥ = karmaṇy (karmaṇi) — in work + atandritaḥ — attentively; mama — of me, my; vartmānuvartante = vartma — pattern + anuvartante — they follow; manuṣyāḥ — human beings; pārtha — O son of Pṛthā; sarvaśaḥ — in all respects

If perchance, I did not perform attentively, then all human beings, O son of Pṛthā, would follow Me in all respects. (3.23)

उत्सीदेयुरिमे लोका
न कुर्यां कर्म चेदहम् ।
संकरस्य च कर्ता स्याम्
उपहन्यामिमाः प्रजाः ॥३.२४॥

utsīdeyurime lokā
na kuryāṁ karma cedaham
saṁkarasya ca kartā syām
upahanyāmimāḥ prajāḥ (3.24)

utsīdeyur = utsīdeyuh — would perish; ime — these; lokā — worlds; na — not; kuryāṁ — I should engage; karma — cultural activity; cedaham = cet — if + aham — I; saṁkarasya — of the social chaos; ca — and; kartā — producer; syām — I should be; upahanyām — I should destroy; imāḥ — these; prajāḥ — creatures

If I should not engage in cultural activity, these worlds would perish. And I would be a producer of social chaos. I would have destroyed these creatures. (3.24)

सक्ताः कर्मण्यविद्वांसो
यथा कुर्वन्ति भारत ।
कुर्याद्विद्वांस्तथासक्तश्
चिकीर्षुर्लोकसंग्रहम् ॥३.२५॥

saktāḥ karmaṇyavidvāṁso
yathā kurvanti bhārata
kuryādvidvāṁstathāsaktaś
cikīrṣurlokasaṁgraham (3.25)

saktāḥ — attached; karmaṇyavidvāṁso = karmaṇyavidvāṁsaḥ = karmaṇi — in activities + avidvāṁsaḥ — unintelligent; yathā — as; kurvanti — they act; bhārata — O son of the Bharata family; kuryād = kuryāt — he should perform; vidvāṁs — the wise person; tathāsaktaś = tathā — so + asaktaḥ — detached; cikīrṣur = cikīrṣuḥ — intending to do; lokasaṁgraham = loka — society + saṁgraham — maintenance

As the unintelligent people perform with attachment to cultural activity, O son of the Bharata family, so the wise person should act, but in a detached manner, for the maintenance of society. (3.25)

न बुद्धिभेदं जनयेद्
अज्ञानां कर्मसङ्गिनाम् ।
जोषयेत्सर्वकर्माणि
विद्वान्युक्तः समाचरन् ॥३.२६॥

na buddhibhedaṁ janayed
ajñānāṁ karmasaṅginām
joṣayetsarvakarmāṇi
vidvānyuktaḥ samācaran (3.26)

na — not; buddhibhedaṁ = buddhi — intelligence + bhedaṁ — breaking (broken intelligence, indetermination); janayet — should produce; ajñānāṁ — of the simpletons; karmasaṅginām — of those attached to action; joṣayet — should inspire to be satisfied; sarvakarmāṇi — all actions; vidvān — the wise person; yuktaḥ — disciplined; samācaran — performing

One should not produce indetermination in the minds of the simpletons. A wise person should inspire them to be satisfied by action. The wise one should be disciplined in behavior. (3.26)

प्रकृतेः क्रियमाणानि
गुणैः कर्माणि सर्वशः ।
अहंकारविमूढात्मा
कर्ताहमिति मन्यते ॥ ३.२७॥

prakṛteḥ kriyamāṇāni
guṇaiḥ karmāṇi sarvaśaḥ
ahaṁkāravimūḍhātmā
kartāhamiti manyate (3.27)

prakṛteḥ — of the primal mundane energy; kriyamāṇāni — performed; guṇaiḥ — by the variations; karmāṇi — actions; sarvaśaḥ — in all cases; ahaṁkāravimūḍhātmā = ahaṁkāra — falsely-asserted identity + vimūḍha — confused + ātmā — self; kartāham = kartā — performer + aham — I; iti — thus; manyate — he thinks

In all cases, actions are performed by variations of the primal mundane energy. But the identity-confused person thinks: "I am the performer." (3.27)

तत्त्ववित्तु महाबाहो
गुणकर्मविभागयोः।
गुणा गुणेषु वर्तन्त
इति मत्वा न सज्जते ॥ ३.२८॥

tattvavittu mahābāho
guṇakarmavibhāgayoḥ
guṇā guṇeṣu vartanta
iti matvā na sajjate (3.28)

tattvavit — reality-perceiving person; tu — but; mahābāho — O powerful man; guṇakarmavibhāgayoḥ = guṇa — moods of nature + karma — action + vibhāgayoḥ — in two-fold basis; guṇa — the variation of material nature; guṇeṣu — in the variations of material nature; vartanta — they interact; iti — thus; matvā — having thought; na — no; sajjate — is attached

But, O powerful man, having considered that variations of material nature interact with variations of material nature, the reality-perceiving person is not attached to action. (3.28)

प्रकृतेर्गुणसंमूढाः
सज्जन्ते गुणकर्मसु।
तानकृत्स्नविदो मन्दात्
कृत्स्नविन्न विचालयेत् ॥ ३.२९॥

prakṛterguṇasaṁmūḍhāḥ
sajjante guṇakarmasu
tānakṛtsnavido mandāt
kṛtsnavinna vicālayet (3.29)

prakṛter = prakṛteḥ — of subtle material nature; guṇasaṁmūḍhāḥ = guṇa — variations of material nature + saṁmūḍhāḥ — deluded people; sajjante — they are attached; guṇakarmasu — in the mood-motivated activities; tān — them; akṛtsnavido = akṛtsnavidaḥ — partially-knowing; mandāt — foolish people; kṛtsnavin — the person who understands the whole reality; na — not; vicālayet — should unsettle

Those who are deluded by the variations of material nature are attached to mood-motivated activities. The person who understands the reality should not unsettle those foolish people who have partial insight. (3.29)

मयि सर्वाणि कर्माणि
संन्यस्याध्यात्मचेतसा ।
निराशीर्निर्ममो भूत्वा
युध्यस्व विगतज्वरः ॥३.३०॥

mayi sarvāṇi karmāṇi
saṁnyasyādhyātmacetasā
nirāśīrnirmamo bhūtvā
yudhyasva vigatajvaraḥ (3.30)

mayi — to me; sarvāṇi — all; karmāṇi — working power; saṁnyasyādhyātmacetasā = saṁnyasya — entrusting + adhyātmacetasā — by meditation on the Supreme Spirit; nirāśīr — from cravings; nirmamo = nirmamaḥ — indifferent to selfishness; bhūtvā — being; yudhyasva — do fight; vigatajvaraḥ = vigata — departed + jvaraḥ — feverish mood

All your working power should be entrusted to Me. On the Supreme Spirit, you should meditate. Being free from cravings, indifferent to selfishness, do fight. Be a man whose feverish mood has departed. (3.30)

ये मे मतमिदं नित्यम्
अनुतिष्ठन्ति मानवाः ।
श्रद्धावन्तोऽनसूयन्तो
मुच्यन्ते तेऽपि कर्मभिः ॥३.३१॥

ye me matamidaṁ nityam
anutiṣṭhanti mānavāḥ
śraddhāvanto'nasūyanto
mucyante te'pi karmabhiḥ (3.31)

ye — whosoever; me — My; matam — idea; idam — this; nityam — constantly; anutiṣṭhanti — they apply; mānavāḥ — human beings; śraddhāvanto=śraddhāvantaḥ — having faith; 'nasūyanto = anasūyantaḥ — not complaining; mucyante — are freed; te — they; 'pi = api — also; karmabhiḥ — from the consequences of action

Those human beings, who believe My idea, constantly applying it, having faith and not complaining, are freed from the consequences of action. (3.31)

ये त्वेतदभ्यसूयन्तो
नानुतिष्ठन्ति मे मतम् ।
सर्वज्ञानविमूढांस्तान्
विद्धि नष्टानचेतसः ॥३.३२॥

ye tvetadabhyasūyanto
nānutiṣṭhanti me matam
sarvajñānavimūḍhāṁstān
viddhi naṣṭānacetasaḥ (3.32)

ye — who; tvetad = tv (tu) — but + etad — this; abhyasūyanto = abhyasūyantaḥ — discrediting; nānutiṣṭhanti = na — not + anutiṣṭhanti — they practise; me — My; matam — idea; sarvajñānavimūḍhāṁs = sarva — all + jñāna — insight + vimūḍhāṁs — muddled; tān — them; viddhi — know; naṣṭān — jinxed; acetasaḥ — senseless

Know that those who discredit this instruction and do not practice My ideas, being of muddled insight, are jinxed and senseless. (3.32)

सदृशं चेष्टते स्वस्याः
प्रकृतेर्ज्ञानवानपि ।
प्रकृतिं यान्ति भूतानि
निग्रहः किं करिष्यति ॥३.३३॥

sadṛśaṁ ceṣṭate svasyāḥ
prakṛterjñānavānapi
prakṛtiṁ yānti bhūtāni
nigrahaḥ kiṁ kariṣyati (3.33)

sadṛśam — according to; ceṣṭate — one acts; svasyāḥ — from one's own; prakṛter = prakṛteḥ — from material nature; jñānavān — wise man; api — also; prakṛtiṁ — material nature; yānti — they submit; bhūtāni — the creatures; nigrahaḥ — restraint; kiṁ — what; kariṣyati — will do

A human being, even a wise man, acts according to his material nature. The creatures submit to material nature. What will restraint do? (3.33)

इन्द्रियस्येन्द्रियस्यार्थे
रागद्वेषौ व्यवस्थितौ ।
तयोर्न वशमागच्छेत्
तौ ह्यस्य परिपन्थिनौ ॥३.३४॥

indriyasyendriyasyārthe
rāgadveṣau vyavasthitau
tayorna vaśamāgacchet
tau hyasya paripanthinau (3.34)

indriyasyendriyasyārthe = indriyasya — of a sense organ + indriyasya — of a sense organ + arthe — in an attractive object; rāgadveṣau = rāga — the response of liking + dveṣau — the response of disliking; vyavasthitau — deep-seated; tayor = tayoḥ — of these two; na — not; vaśam — power; āgacchet — should be influenced; tau — two; hyasya = hy (hi) — indeed + asya — of him; paripanthinau — two hindrances

The response of liking or disliking that is felt between a sense and an attractive object, is deep-seated. One should not be influenced by the power of these two moods. They are hindrances. (3.34)

श्रेयान्स्वधर्मो विगुणः
परधर्मात्स्वनुष्ठितात् ।
स्वधर्मे निधनं श्रेयः
परधर्मो भयावहः ॥३.३५॥

śreyānsvadharmo viguṇaḥ
paradharmātsvanuṣṭhitāt
svadharme nidhanaṁ śreyaḥ
paradharmo bhayāvahaḥ (3.35)

śreyān — better; svadharmo = svadharmaḥ — one's righteous duty; viguṇaḥ — imperfect; paradharmāt — than the righteous duty of another; svanuṣṭhitāt = sv (su) — good, great + anuṣṭhitāt — than done; svadharme — in one's righteous duty; nidhanaṁ — death; śreyaḥ — it is better; paradharmo = paradharmaḥ — righteous duty of another; bhayāvahaḥ = bhaya — risk + āvahaḥ — bringing on

Better to do one's righteous duty imperfectly, than to do the duty of another with great efficiency. Death is better in the course of one's duty but the task of another is risky. (3.35)

अर्जुन उवाच
अथ केन प्रयुक्तोऽयं
पापं चरति पूरुषः ।
अनिच्छन्नपि वार्ष्णेय
बलादिव नियोजितः ॥३.३६॥

arjuna uvāca
atha kena prayukto'yaṁ
pāpaṁ carati pūruṣaḥ
anicchannapi vārṣṇeya
balādiva niyojitaḥ (3.36)

arjuna — Arjuna; uvāca — said; atha — then; kena — by what?; prayukto = prayuktaḥ — forced; 'yaṁ = ayam — this; pāpaṁ — evil; carati — commits; pūruṣaḥ — a person; anicchannapi = anicchan — unwilling + napi (api) — even; vārṣṇeya — family man of the Vṛṣṇis; balād = balāt — from force; iva — as if; niyojitaḥ — compelled

Arjuna said: Then explain, O family man of the Vṛṣṇis, by what is a person forced to commit an evil unwillingly, just as if he were compelled to do so? (3.36)

श्रीभगवानुवाच
काम एष क्रोध एष
रजोगुणसमुद्भवः।
महाशनो महापाप्मा
विद्ध्येनमिह वैरिणम् ॥३.३७॥

śrībhagavānuvāca
kāma eṣa krodha eṣa
rajoguṇasamudbhavaḥ
mahāśano mahāpāpmā
viddhyenamiha vairiṇam (3.37)

śri bhagavān — the Blessed Lord; uvāca — said; kāma — craving; eṣa — this; krodha — anger; eṣa — this; rajoguṇasamudbhavaḥ = rajo (rajaḥ) — passion + guṇa — emotion + samudbhavaḥ — source; mahāśano (mahāśanaḥ) = mahā — great + aśana — consuming power; mahāpāpmā = mahā — much + pāpmā — damage; viddhyenam = viddhi — recognize + enam — this; iha — in this case; vairiṇam — enemy

The Blessed Lord said: This force is craving. This power is anger. The passionate emotion is the source. It has a great consuming power and does much damage. Recognize it as the enemy in this case. (3.37)

धूमेनाव्रियते वह्निर्
यथादर्शो मलेन च ।
यथोल्बेनावृतो गर्भस्
तथा तेनेदमावृतम् ॥३.३८॥

dhūmenāvriyate vahnir
yathādarśo malena ca
yatholbenāvṛto garbhas
tathā tenedamāvṛtam (3.38)

dhūmenāvriyate = dhūmena — by smoke + āvriyate — is obscured; vahnir = vahniḥ — the sacrificial fire; yathā — similarly; 'darśo = ādarśaḥ — mirror; malena — with dust; ca — and; yatholbenāvṛto = yatholbenāvṛtaḥ = yatho (yatha) — similarly + ulbena — by skin + āvṛtaḥ — is covered; garbhaḥ — embryo; tathā — so; tenedam = tena — by this + idam — this; āvṛtam — is blocked

As the sacrificial fire is obscured by smoke, and similarly as a mirror is shrouded by dust or as an embryo is covered by skin, so a man's insight is blocked by the passionate energy. (3.38)

आवृतं ज्ञानमेतेन
ज्ञानिनो नित्यवैरिणा ।
कामरूपेण कौन्तेय
दुष्पूरेणानलेन च ॥ ३.३९ ॥

āvṛtaṁ jñānametena
jñānino nityavairiṇā
kāmarūpeṇa kaunteya
duṣpūreṇānalena ca (3.39)

āvṛtam — is adjusted; jñānam — discernment; etena — by this; jñānino = jñāninaḥ — educated people; nityavairiṇā = nitya — eternal + vairiṇā — by the enemy; kāmarūpeṇa = kāma — yearning for various things + rūpeṇa — by the sense or form of; kaunteya — son of Kuntī; duṣpūreṇānalena = duspūreṇa — is hard to satisfy + analena — by fire; ca — and

The discernment of educated people is adjusted by their eternal enemy which is the sense of yearning for various things. O son of Kuntī, the lusty power, is as hard to satisfy as it is to keep a fire burning. (3.39)

इन्द्रियाणि मनो बुद्धिर्
अस्याधिष्ठानमुच्यते ।
एतैर्विमोहयत्येष
ज्ञानमावृत्य देहिनम् ॥ ३.४० ॥

indriyāṇi mano buddhir
asyādhiṣṭhānamucyate
etairvimohayatyeṣa
jñānamāvṛtya dehinam (3.40)

indriyāṇi — the senses; mano = manaḥ — the mind; buddhir = buddhiḥ — the intelligence; asyādhiṣṭhānam = asya — if this + adhiṣṭhānam — warehouse; ucyate — it is authoritatively stated; etair = etaiḥ — with these; vimohayatyeṣa = vimohayaty (vimohayati) — confuses + eṣa — this; jñānam — insight; āvṛtya — is shrouded; dehinam — embodied soul

It is authoritatively stated that the senses, the mind and the intelligence are the combined warehouse of the passionate enemy. By these faculties, the lusty power confuses the embodied soul, shrouding his insight. (3.40)

तस्मात्त्वमिन्द्रियाण्यादौ
नियम्य भरतर्षभ ।
पाप्मानं प्रजहिह्येनं
ज्ञानविज्ञाननाशनम् ॥ ३.४१ ॥

tasmāttvamindriyāṇyādau
niyamya bharatarṣabha
pāpmānaṁ prajahihyenaṁ
jñānavijñānanāśanam(3.41)

tasmāt — thus; tvam — you; indriyāṇyādau = indriyāṇi — senses + ādau — initially; niyamya — regulating; bharatarṣabha — powerful man of the Bharata family; pāpmānaṁ — degrading power; prajahi — squelch, destroy; hyenaṁ = hy (hi) — certainly + enaṁ — this; jñānavijñānanāśanam = jñāna — knowledge + vijñāna — discernment + nāśanam — ruining

Thus regulating the senses initially, you should, O powerful man of the Bharata family, squelch this degrading power which ruins knowledge and discernment. (3.41)

इन्द्रियाणि पराण्याहुर्
इन्द्रियेभ्यः परं मनः ।
मनसस्तु परा बुद्धिर्
यो बुद्धेः परतस्तु सः ॥३.४२॥

indriyāṇi parāṇyāhur
indriyebhyaḥ paraṁ manaḥ
manasastu parā buddhir
yo buddheḥ paratastu saḥ (3.42)

indriyāṇi — the senses; parāṇyāhur = parāṇi — are energetic; āhur (āhuḥ) — the ancient psychologists say; indriyebhyaḥ — the senses; paraṁ — more energetic; manaḥ — the mind; manasas — in contrast to the mind; tu — but; parā — more sensitive; buddhir = buddhiḥ — the intelligence; yo = yaḥ — which; buddheḥ — in reference to the intelligence; paratas — most sensitive; tu — but; saḥ — he, the spirit

The ancient psychologists say that the senses are energetic, but in comparison to the senses, the mind is more energetic. In contrast to the mind, the intelligence is even more sensitive. But in reference, the spirit is most elevated. (3.42)

एवं बुद्धेः परं बुद्ध्वा
संस्तभ्यात्मानमात्मना ।
जहि शत्रुं महाबाहो
कामरूपं दुरासदम् ॥३.४३॥

evaṁ buddheḥ paraṁ buddhvā
saṁstabhyātmānamātmanā
jahi śatruṁ mahābāho
kāmarūpaṁ durāsadam (3.43)

evaṁ — thus; buddheḥ — than the intelligence; paraṁ — higher; buddhvā — having understood; saṁstabhyātmānamātmanā = saṁstabhya — keeping together + ātmānam — the personal energies+ ātmanā — by the spirit; jahi — uproot; śatruṁ — enemy; mahābāho — O powerful man; kāmarūpaṁ — form of passionate desire; durāsadam — difficult to grasp

Thus having understood what is higher than intelligence, keeping the personal energies under control of the spirit, uproot, O powerful man, the enemy, the form of passionate desire which is difficult to grasp. (3.43)

CHAPTER 4

Disciplines of Accomplishment*

श्रीभगवानुवाच
इमं विवस्वते योगं
प्रोक्तवानहमव्ययम् ।
विवस्वान्मनवे प्राह
मनुरिक्ष्वाकवेऽब्रवीत् ॥४.१॥

śrībhagavānuvāca
imaṁ vivasvate yogaṁ
proktavānahamavyayam
vivasvānmanave prāha
manurikṣvākave'bravīt (4.1)

śrī bhagavān — the Blessed Lord; uvāca — said; imaṁ — this; vivasvate — to Vivasvat; yogaṁ — yogic skill of controlling personal energies; proktavān — having explained; aham — I; avyayam — perpetual; vivasvān — Vivasvat; manave — to Manu; prāha — explained; manur = manuḥ — Manu; ikṣvākave — to Ikṣvāku; 'bravīt = abravīt — imparted

The Blessed Lord said: I explained to Vivasvat, this perpetual teaching of controlling the personal energies through yoga. Vivasvat explained it to Manu. Manu imparted it to Ikṣvāku. (4.1)

एवं परंपराप्राप्तम्
इमं राजर्षयो विदुः ।
स कालेनेह महता
योगो नष्टः परंतप ॥४.२॥

evaṁ paraṁparāprāptam
imaṁ rājarṣayo viduḥ
sa kāleneha mahatā
yogo naṣṭaḥ paraṁtapa (4.2)

evam — thus; paramparāprāptam = paramparā — a series of teachers + prāptam — received; imaṁ — this; rājarṣayo = rājarṣayaḥ — yogi kings; viduḥ — they knew; sa = saḥ — it; kāleneha = kālena — in time + iha — here on earth; mahatā — long; yogo = yogaḥ — yogic discipline; naṣṭaḥ — was lost; paraṁtapa — O burner of enemy forces

Thus, received through a series of teachers, the yogi kings knew this skill of controlling the personal energies. After a long time, here on earth, this yoga application was lost, O burner of enemy forces. (4.2)

स एवायं मया तेऽद्य
योगः प्रोक्तः पुरातनः ।
भक्तोऽसि मे सखा चेति
रहस्यं ह्येतदुत्तमम् ॥४.३॥

sa evāyaṁ mayā te'dya
yogaḥ proktaḥ purātanaḥ
bhakto'si me sakhā ceti
rahasyaṁ hyetaduttamam (4.3)

The Mahābhārata contains no chapter headings. This title was assigned by the translator on the basis of verse 32 of this.chapter.

sa = saḥ — it; evāyaṁ = eva — indeed + ayam — this; mayā — by me; te — to you; 'dya = adya — today; yogaḥ — yoga technique; proktaḥ — is explained; purātanaḥ — ancient; bhakto = bhaktaḥ — devoted; 'si = asi — you are; me — of me; sakhā — friend; ceti = ca — and + iti — thus; rahasyaṁ — confidential teaching; hyetad = hi — truly + etad — this; uttamam — best

Today, this ancient yoga technique is explained to you by Me, since you are devoted to Me and are My friend. Indeed, this is confidential and is the best teaching. (4.3)

अर्जुन उवाच
अपरं भवतो जन्म
परं जन्म विवस्वतः ।
कथमेतद्विजानीयां
त्वमादौ प्रोक्तवानिति ॥४.४॥

arjuna uvāca
aparaṁ bhavato janma
paraṁ janma vivasvataḥ
kathametadvijānīyāṁ
tvamādau proktavāniti (4.4)

arjuna — Arjuna; uvāca — said; aparaṁ — later; bhavato = bhavataḥ — Your Lordship; janma — birth; paraṁ — earlier; janma — birth; vivasvataḥ — Vivasvat; katham — how; etad — this; vijānīyāṁ — I should understand; tvam — you; ādau — in the beginning, before; proktavān — having explained; iti — thus

Arjuna said: Your Lordship's birth was later. The birth of Vivasvat was earlier. How should I understand that You explained this before? (4.4)

श्रीभगवानुवाच
बहूनि मे व्यतीतानि
जन्मानि तव चार्जुन ।
तान्यहं वेद सर्वाणि
न त्वं वेत्थ परंतप ॥४.५॥

śrībhagavānuvāca
bahūni me vyatītāni
janmāni tava cārjuna
tānyahaṁ veda sarvāṇi
na tvaṁ vettha paraṁtapa (4.5)

śrī bhagavān — the Blessed Lord; uvāca — said; bahūni — many; me — of Me; vyatītāni — transpired; janmāni — births; tava — your; cārjuna = ca — and + arjuna — Arjuna; tānyahaṁ = tāny (tāni) — them + aham — I; veda — I recall; sarvāṇi — all; na — not; tvaṁ — you; vettha — you remember; paraṁtapa — O scorcher of the enemies

The Blessed Lord said: Many of My births transpired, and yours, Arjuna. I recall them all. You do not remember, O scorcher of the enemies. (4.5)

अजोऽपि सन्नव्ययात्मा
भूतानामीश्वरोऽपि सन् ।
प्रकृतिं स्वामधिष्ठाय
संभवाम्यात्ममायया ॥४.६॥

ajo'pi sannavyayātmā
bhūtānāmīśvaro'pi san
prakṛtiṁ svāmadhiṣṭhāya
saṁbhavāmyātmamāyayā (4.6)

ajo = ajaḥ — birthless; 'pi = api — even though; sann = san — being; avyayātmā = avyaya — imperishable + ātmā — person; bhūtānām — of the creatures; īśvaro = īśvaraḥ — Lord; 'pi = api — even; san — being; prakṛtiṁ — material energies; svām — my own; adhiṣṭhāya — controlling; saṁbhavāmyātmamāyayā = sambhavāmy (saṁbhavāmi) — I become visible + ātma — self + māyayā — by supernatural power

Even though I am birthless and My person is imperishable, and even though I am the Lord of the creatures, by controlling My material energies, I become visible by My supernatural power. (4.6)

यदा यदा हि धर्मस्य ग्लानिर्भवति भारत । अभ्युत्थानमधर्मस्य तदात्मानं सृजाम्यहम् ॥४.७॥	yadā yadā hi dharmasya glānirbhavati bhārata abhyutthānamadharmasya tadātmānaṁ sṛjāmyaham (4.7)

yadā yadā — whenever; hi — indeed; dharmasya — of righteousness; glānir = glāniḥ — decrease; bhavati — it is; bhārata — O son of the Bharata family; abhyutthānam — increasing; adharmasya — of unrighteousness, of wickedness; tadā — then; 'tmānaṁ = ātmānaṁ — My self; sṛjāmyaham = sṛjāmy (sṛjāmi) — show + aham — I

Whenever there is a decrease of righteousness, O son of the Bharata family, and when there is an increase of wickedness, then I show Myself. (4.7)

परित्राणाय साधूनां विनाशाय च दुष्कृताम् । धर्मसंस्थापनार्थाय संभवामि युगे युगे ॥४.८॥	paritrāṇāya sādhūnāṁ vināśāya ca duṣkṛtām dharmasaṁsthāpanārthāya saṁbhavāmi yuge yuge (4.8)

paritrāṇāya — to protecting; sādhūnāṁ — of the saintly persons; vināśāya — to destruction; ca — and; duṣkṛtām — of the wicked people; dharmasaṁsthāpanārthāya = dharma — righteousness + saṁsthāpana — the establishing of + arthāya — for the sake of; saṁbhavāmi — I come into visible existence; yuge yuge — from era to era

To protect the saintly people, to destroy the wicked ones, and to establish righteousness, I come into the visible existence from era to era. (4.8)

जन्म कर्म च मे दिव्यम् एवं यो वेत्ति तत्त्वतः । त्यक्त्वा देहं पुनर्जन्म नैति मामेति सोऽर्जुन ॥४.९॥	janma karma ca me divyam evaṁ yo vetti tattvataḥ tyaktvā dehaṁ punarjanma naiti māmeti so'rjuna (4.9)

janma — visitation; karma — deed; ca — and; me — of me; divyam — supernatural; evaṁ — thus; yo = yaḥ — who; vetti — realizes; tattvataḥ — in truth; tyaktvā — abandoning; dehaṁ — body; punarjanma = rebirth; naiti = na — not + eti — goes; mām — to Me; eti — goes; so = saḥ — he; 'rjuna = arjuna — Arjuna

One who knows My supernatural visitation and deeds, who truly realizes this while abandoning his body, does not go for rebirth. He goes to Me, O Arjuna. (4.9)

वीतरागभयक्रोधा
मन्मया मामुपाश्रिताः ।
बहवो ज्ञानतपसा
पूता मद्भावमागताः ॥४.१०॥

vītarāgabhayakrodhā
manmayā māmupāśritāḥ
bahavo jñānatapasā
pūtā madbhāvamāgatāḥ (4.10)

vītarāgabhayakrodhā = vīta — gone + rāga — craving + bhaya — fear + krodhā — anger; manmayā — think of Me; mām — Me; upāśritāḥ — rely on; bahavo = bahavaḥ — many; jñānatapasā — by austerity/education; pūtā — purified; madbhāvam — my level of existence; āgatāḥ — attained

Many, whose cravings, fear and anger are gone, who are totally focused on Me, who are purified by austerity and education, attained My level of existence. (4.10)

ये यथा मां प्रपद्यन्ते
तांस्तथैव भजाम्यहम् ।
मम वर्त्मानुवर्तन्ते
मनुष्याः पार्थ सर्वशः ॥४.११॥

ye yathā māṁ prapadyante
tāṁstathaiva bhajāmyaham
mama vartmānuvartante
manuṣyāḥ pārtha sarvaśaḥ (4.11)

ye — who; yathā — as; māṁ — me; prapadyante — they rely; tāṁs = tan — them; tathaiva = tathā — so + eva — indeed; bhajāmyaham = bhajāmy (bhajāmi) — relate to + aham — I; mama — my; vartmānuvartante = vartma — course of an action + anuvartante — are affected; manuṣyāḥ — human beings; pārtha — son of Pṛthā; sarvaśaḥ — everywhere

As they rely on Me, so I relate to them, O son of Pṛthā. All human beings, everywhere, are affected by My course of action. (4.11)

काङ्क्षन्तः कर्मणां सिद्धिं
यजन्त इह देवताः ।
क्षिप्रं हि मानुषे लोके
सिद्धिर्भवति कर्मजा ॥४.१२॥

kāṅkṣantaḥ karmaṇāṁ siddhiṁ
yajanta iha devatāḥ
kṣipraṁ hi mānuṣe loke
siddhirbhavati karmajā (4.12)

kāṅkṣantaḥ — wanting; karmaṇām — of ritual action; siddhiṁ — success; yajanta — they worship; iha — here on earth; devatāḥ — supernatural authorities; kṣipraṁ — quickly; hi — indeed; mānuṣe — in the humans; loke

— in the world; siddhir = siddhiḥ — fulfillment; bhavati — there is, comes to be; karmajā — produced of ritual action

Wanting their ritual action to succeed, people in the world, worship the supernatural authorities. Quickly in this human world, there is fulfillment which comes from ritual action. (4.12)

चातुर्वर्ण्यं मया सृष्टं
गुणकर्मविभागशः ।
तस्य कर्तारमपि मां
विद्ध्यकर्तारमव्ययम् ॥४.१३॥

cāturvarṇyaṁ mayā sṛṣṭaṁ
guṇakarmavibhāgaśaḥ
tasya kartāramapi māṁ
viddhyakartāramavyayam (4.13)

cāturvarṇyaṁ — the four career categories; mayā — by me; sṛṣṭaṁ — instituted; guṇa - habit; karma - work tendency; vibhāga — distribution; śaḥ — by; tasya — of it; kartāram — creator; api — also; mām — me; viddhyakartāram = viddhy (viddhi) — know + akartāram — one not required to act; avyayam — eternal

According to the distribution of habits and work tendencies, the four career categories were instituted by Me. Know that I am never required to participate. (4.13)

न मां कर्माणि लिम्पन्ति
न मे कर्मफले स्पृहा ।
इति मां योऽभिजानाति
कर्मभिर्न स बध्यते ॥४.१४॥

na māṁ karmāṇi limpanti
na me karmaphale spṛhā
iti māṁ yo'bhijānāti
karmabhirna sa badhyate (4.14)

na — not; māṁ — me; karmāṇi — actions; limpanti — they entrap; na — not; me — of me; karmaphale — in a pay-off; spṛhā — desire; iti — thus; māṁ — me; yo = yaḥ — who; 'bhijānāti = abhijānāti — understands; karmabhir = karmabhih — by actions; na — not; sa = sa — he; badhyate — is entrapped

Actions do not entrap Me. The desire for payoff is not in Me. The person who understands this is not entrapped by action. (4.14)

एवं ज्ञात्वा कृतं कर्म
पूर्वैरपि मुमुक्षुभिः ।
कुरु कर्मैव तस्मात्त्वं
पूर्वैः पूर्वतरं कृतम् ॥४.१५॥

evaṁ jñātvā kṛtaṁ karma
pūrvairapi mumukṣubhiḥ
kuru karmaiva tasmāttvaṁ
pūrvaiḥ pūrvataraṁ kṛtam (4.15)

evaṁ — thus; jñātvā — having understood; kṛtaṁ — done; karma — functional work; pūrvair = pūrvaih — by the ancient rulers like Janaka; api — even; mumukṣubhiḥ — by those who desire liberation; kuru — perform; karmaiva = karma — cultural acts + eva — indeed; tasmāt — therefore; tvaṁ — you; pūrvaiḥ — by the yogi kings like Janaka; pūrvataraṁ — before; kṛtam — performed

Having understood this conclusion, functional work was done, even by the yogi kings who desired liberation. Therefore you should perform cultural acts, just as it was done before. (4.15)

किं कर्म किमकर्मेति	kiṁ karma kimakarmeti
कवयोऽप्यत्र मोहिताः ।	kavayo'pyatra mohitāḥ
तत्ते कर्म प्रवक्ष्यामि	tatte karma pravakṣyāmi
यज्ज्ञात्वा मोक्ष्यसेऽशुभात् ॥४.१६॥	yajjñātvā mokṣyase'śubhāt (4.16)

kiṁ — what; karma — action; kiṁ — what; akarmeti = akarma — no action + iti — thus; kavayaḥ — eloquent philosophers; 'py = api — even; atra — in this matter; mohitāḥ — confused; tat — this; te — to you; karma — action; pravakṣyāmi — I will discuss; yaj = yad — which; jñātvā — knowing; mokṣyase — you will be freed; 'śubhāt = aśubhāt — from undesirable circumstances

What is action? What is not an action? Even eloquent philosophers are confused on this subject. I will discuss the subject of action with you. Knowing this, you will be freed from undesirable circumstances. (4.16)

कर्मणो ह्यपि बोद्धव्यं	karmaṇo hyapi boddhavyaṁ
बोद्धव्यं च विकर्मणः ।	boddhavyaṁ ca vikarmaṇaḥ
अकर्मणश्च बोद्धव्यं	akarmaṇaśca boddhavyaṁ
गहना कर्मणो गतिः ॥४.१७॥	gahanā karmaṇo gatiḥ (4.17)

karmaṇaḥ — of action; hy (hi) — indeed + api — also; boddhavyaṁ — should be known; boddhavyaṁ — should be recognized; ca — and; vikarmaṇaḥ — inappropriate action; akarmaṇaḥ — no action + ca — and; boddhavyaṁ — should be understood; gahanā — difficult to comprehend; karmaṇo = karmaṇaḥ — of action; gatiḥ — the course

Indeed, appropriate action should be known and one should also recognize the inappropriate type. The effect of no action should be understood. The course of action is difficult to comprehend. (4.17)

कर्मण्यकर्म यः पश्येद्	karmaṇyakarma yaḥ paśyed
अकर्मणि च कर्म यः ।	akarmaṇi ca karma yaḥ
स बुद्धिमान्मनुष्येषु	sa buddhimānmanuṣyeṣu
स युक्तः कृत्स्नकर्मकृत् ॥४.१८॥	sa yuktaḥ kṛtsnakarmakṛt (4.18)

karmaṇy (karmaṇi) — in performance + akarma — non-action; yaḥ — who; paśyet — he should see; akarmaṇi — in non-action; ca — and; karma — action; yaḥ — who; sa = saḥ — he; buddhimān — wise person; manuṣyeṣu — of human beings; sa = saḥ — he; yuktaḥ — skilled in yoga; kṛtsnakarmakṛt = kṛtsna — all + karmakṛt — action performance

He who perceived the non-acting factor in a performance and sees an acting factor when there is no action, is the wise person among human beings. He is skilled in yoga and can perform all actions. (4.18)

यस्य सर्वे समारम्भाः
कामसंकल्पवर्जिताः ।
ज्ञानाग्निदग्धकर्माणं
तमाहुः पण्डितं बुधाः ॥४.१९

yasya sarve samārambhāḥ
kāmasaṁkalpavarjitāḥ
jñānāgnidagdhakarmāṇaṁ
tamāhuḥ paṇḍitaṁ budhāḥ (4.19)

yasya — one whom; sarve — all; samārambhāḥ — endeavors; kāmasaṁkalpa varjitāḥ = kāma — desire + saṁkalpa — intention + varjitāḥ — not mixed into; jñānāgni dagdha karmāṇaṁ = jñāna — knowledge + āgni — fiery force + dagdha — burnt, destroyed + karmāṇaṁ — reactionary work; tam — him; āhuḥ — call; paṇḍitaṁ — learned man; budhāḥ — wise man

He for whom desires and intentions are not mixed into his endeavors, who has destroyed reactionary work by the fiery force of his knowledge, he, the wise men call a pandit or learned man. (4.19)

त्यक्त्वा कर्मफलासङ्गं
नित्यतृप्तो निराश्रयः ।
कर्मण्यभिप्रवृत्तोऽपि
नैव किंचित्करोति सः ॥४.२०॥

tyaktvā karmaphalāsaṅgaṁ
nityatṛpto nirāśrayaḥ
karmaṇyabhipravṛtto'pi
naiva kiṁcitkaroti saḥ (4.20)

tyaktvā — given up; karmaphalāsaṅgaṁ = karma — action + phala — pay-off + āsaṅgaṁ — attachment, quest; nityatṛpto (nityatṛptaḥ) = nityaḥ — always + tṛptaḥ — satisfied; nirāśrayaḥ — not dependent; karmaṇy = karmaṇi — in performance; abhipravṛtto = abhipravṛttaḥ — proceeding, functioning; 'pi = api — even; naiva = na — not + eva — indeed; kiṁcit — anything; karoti — does; saḥ — he

Giving up the quest for a payoff from actions, being always satisfied, not depending on anything, he does nothing at all even while performing. (4.20)

निराशीर्यतचित्तात्मा
त्यक्तसर्वपरिग्रहः ।
शारीरं केवलं कर्म
कुर्वन्नाप्नोति किल्बिषम् ॥४.२१॥

nirāśīryatacittātmā
tyaktasarvaparigrahaḥ
śārīraṁ kevalaṁ karma
kurvannāpnoti kilbiṣam (4.21)

nirāśīr — without hoping; yatacittātmā = yata — reserved + citta — thought + ātmā — spirit; tyaktasarvaparigrahaḥ = tyakta — giving up + sarva — all + parigrahaḥ — tendency for grasping; śārīraṁ — body; kevalaṁ — alone; karma — action; kurvan — functioning; nāpnoti = na — not + āpnoti — acquire; kilbiṣam — fault

Without hoping, being reserved in thought and spirit, giving up all tendency for grasping, using the body effectively for action, he does not acquire a fault. (4.21)

यदृच्छालाभसंतुष्टो द्वंद्वातीतो विमत्सरः । समः सिद्धावसिद्धौ च कृत्वापि न निबध्यते ॥४.२२॥	yadṛcchālābhasaṁtuṣṭo dvaṁdvātīto vimatsaraḥ samaḥ siddhāvasiddhau ca kṛtvāpi na nibadhyate (4.22)

yadṛcchā — by chance; lābha — benefit; saṁtuṣṭaḥ — satisfied; dvandvātīto (dvandvātītaḥ) = dvandva — likes and dislikes + atītaḥ — ignoring; vimatsaraḥ — free from envy; samaḥ — even-minded; siddhāv = siddhau — in success; asiddhau — in failure; ca — and; kṛtvā — having performed; 'pi = api — also; na — no; nibadhyate — is implicated

Being satisfied by benefit which comes by chance, ignoring likes and dislikes, being free from envy, even-minded in success and failure, and having performed, a man is still not implicated. (4.22)

गतसङ्गस्य मुक्तस्य ज्ञानावस्थितचेतसः । यज्ञायाचरतः कर्म समग्रं प्रविलीयते ॥४.२३॥	gatasaṅgasya muktasya jñānāvasthitacetasaḥ yajñāyācarataḥ karma samagraṁ pravilīyate (4.23)

gatasaṅgasya = gata — gone + saṅgasya — of attachment; muktasya — of the liberated person; jñānāvasthitacetasaḥ = jñāna — knowledge + avasthita — established + cetasaḥ — of an idea; yajñāyācarataḥ = yajñāya — for austerity and religion + ācarataḥ — doing; karma — action; samagraṁ — completely; pravilīyate — cancels

Concerning a person whose attachment is finished, who is liberated, whose idea is established in knowledge, any of his action which is done solely for austerity and religion, does cancel completely. (4.23)

ब्रह्मार्पणं ब्रह्महविर् ब्रह्माग्नौ ब्रह्मणा हुतम् । ब्रह्मैव तेन गन्तव्यं ब्रह्मकर्मसमाधिना ॥४.२४॥	brahmārpaṇaṁ brahmahavir brahmāgnau brahmaṇā hutam brahmaiva tena gantavyaṁ brahmakarmasamādhinā (4.24)

brahmārpaṇaṁ = brahma — spiritual existence + arpaṇam — ceremonial articles; brahma — spiritual existence; havir = haviḥ — sacrificial ingredients, ghee; brahmāgnau = brahma — spiritual existence + agnau — in fire; brahmaṇā — by the qualified brahmin priest; hutam — offering oblations; brahmaiva = brahma — spiritual existence + eva — indeed; tena — by him; gantavyaṁ — to be attained; brahmakarmasamādhinā = brahma — spiritual existence + karma — activity + samādhinā — by meditative contact

Spiritual existence is the basis of his ceremonial articles. It is the foundation of sacrificial ingredients. The perceptive priest pours the stipulated items into the fiery splendor of spiritual existence. It is the spiritual existence which is attained by a person who keeps contact with the spiritual level while acting. (4.24)

दैवमेवापरे यज्ञं योगिनः पर्युपासते । ब्रह्माग्नावपरे यज्ञं यज्ञेनैवोपजुह्वति ॥४.२५॥	daivamevāpare yajñaṁ yoginaḥ paryupāsate brahmāgnāvapare yajñaṁ yajñenaivopajuhvati (4.25)

daivam — to a supernatural authority; evāpare = eva — indeed + apare — some; yajñaṁ — austerity and religious ceremony; yoginaḥ — yogis; paryupāsate — practise; brahmāgnāv = brahmāgnau — in the fiery brilliance of spiritual existence; apare — others; yajñaṁ — austerity and religious ceremony; yajñenaivopajuhvati = yajñena — by austerity and religious ceremony; eva — indeed + upajuhvati — they offer

Some yogis perform austerity and religious ceremony in relation to a supernatural authority. Others offer austerity and religious ceremony as the sacrifice into the fiery brilliance of spiritual existence. (4.25)

श्रोत्रादीनीन्द्रियाण्यन्ये संयमाग्निषु जुह्वति । शब्दादीन्विषयानन्ये इन्द्रियाग्निषु जुह्वति ॥४.२६॥	śrotrādīnīndriyāṇyanye saṁyamāgniṣu juhvati śabdādīnviṣayānanye indriyāgniṣu juhvati (4.26)

śrotrādīnīndriyāṇy = śrotrādīnīndriyāṇi = śrotra — hearing + ādīni — and related aspects + indriyāṇi — senses; anye — others; saṁyamāgniṣu = saṁyama — restraint + agniṣu — in the fiery power; juhvati — they offer; śabdādīn = śabda — sound + ādīn — and so on; viṣayān — sensual pursuits; anye — others; indriyāgniṣu — in the fiery energy of sensuality; juhvati — they offer

Other yogis offer hearing and other sensual powers into the fiery power of restraint. Some offer sound and other sensual pursuits into the fiery sensual power. (4.26)

सर्वाणीन्द्रियकर्माणि प्राणकर्माणि चापरे । आत्मसंयमयोगाग्नौ जुह्वति ज्ञानदीपिते ॥४.२७॥	sarvāṇīndriyakarmāṇi prāṇakarmāṇi cāpare ātmasaṁyamayogāgnau juhvati jñānadīpite (4.27)

sarvāṇīndriyakarmāṇi = sarvāṇi — all + indriyakarmāṇi — sensual actions; prāṇakarmāṇi = prāṇa — breath function + karmāṇi — activities; cāpare = ca — and + apare — some; ātmasaṁyamayogāgnau = ātmasaṁyama — self-

restraint + yogāgnau — in fiery yoga austerities; juhvati — they offer; jñānadīpite = jñāna — experience + dīpite — illuminated

Some ascetics subject the sensual actions and the breath function to self-restraint by fiery yoga austerities, which are illuminated by experience. (4.27)

द्रव्ययज्ञास्तपोयज्ञा
योगयज्ञास्तथापरे ।
स्वाध्यायज्ञानयज्ञाश्च
यतयः संशितव्रताः ॥४.२८॥

dravyayajñāstapoyajñā
yogayajñāstathāpare
svādhyāyajñānayajñāśca
yatayaḥ saṁśitavratāḥ (4.28)

dravyayajñās = dravya — property + yajñās — austerity and religious ceremony; tapoyajñā = tapo (tapaḥ) — self denial + yajñā — austerity and religious ceremony; yogayajñās = yoga —eight-part yoga process + yajñāḥ — austerity and religious ceremony; tathāpare = tathā — as well as + apare — some others; svādhyāyajñānayajñāśca = svādhyāya — study of the Veda + jñāna — knowledge + yajñāḥ — austerity and religious ceremony + ca — and; yatayaḥ — ascetics; saṁśitavratāḥ = saṁśita — strict + vratāḥ — vows

Persons whose austerity and religious ceremony involve the control of material possession, those whose austerity and religious life involve some self-denial, as well as some others whose penance and religious procedure is the eight-part yoga discipline, and those whose austerity and religious ceremony is the study of the Veda and the acquirement of knowledge, all these are regarded as ascetics with strict vows. (4.28)

अपाने जुह्वति प्राणं
प्राणेऽपानं तथापरे ।
प्राणापानगती रुद्ध्वा
प्राणायामपरायणाः ॥४.२९॥

apāne juhvati prāṇaṁ
prāṇe'pānaṁ tathāpare
prāṇāpānagatī ruddhvā
prāṇāyāmaparāyaṇāḥ (4.29)

apāne — in exhalation; juhvati — they offer; prāṇam — inhalation; prāṇe — in inhalation; 'pānaṁ = apāṇaṁ — in exhalation; tathāpare = tathā — similarly + apare — others; prāṇāpāna gatī = prāṇa — energizing air + apāna — de-energizing air + gatī — channel; ruddhvā — restraining; prāṇāyāmaparāyaṇāḥ = prāṇa — inhaling + āyāma — regulate + parāyaṇāḥ — intent

Some offer inhalation into the exhalation channels; similarly others offer the exhalation into the inhalation channels, thus being determined to restrain the channels of the energizing and de-energizing airs. (4.29)

अपरे नियताहाराः
प्राणान्प्राणेषु जुह्वति ।
सर्वेऽप्येते यज्ञविदो
यज्ञक्षपितकल्मषाः ॥४.३०॥

apare niyatāhārāḥ
prāṇānprāṇeṣu juhvati
sarve'pyete yajñavido
yajñakṣapitakalmaṣāḥ (4.30)

apare — others; niyatāhārāḥ — persons restrained in diet; prāṇān — fresh air; prāṇeṣu — into the previous inhalations; juhvati — impel; sarve — all; 'pyete (apyete) = apy (api) — also + ete — these; yajñavido = yajñavidaḥ — those who know the value of an act of sacrifice; yajñakṣapitakalmaṣāḥ = yajña — austerity and religious ceremony + kṣapita — destroyed, removed + kalmaṣāḥ — impurities

Others who were restrained in diet, impel fresh air into the previously inhaled air. All these ascetics whose impurities were removed by austerity and religious ceremony understand the value of an act of sacrifice. (4.30)

यज्ञशिष्टामृतभुजो
यान्ति ब्रह्म सनातनम्।
नायं लोकोऽस्त्ययज्ञस्य
कुतोऽन्यः कुरुसत्तम ॥४.३१॥

yajñaśiṣṭāmṛtabhujo
yānti brahma sanātanam
nāyaṁ loko'styayajñasya
kuto'nyaḥ kurusattama (4.31)

yajñaśiṣṭāmṛtabhujo = yajñaśiṣṭāmṛtabhujaḥ = yajñaśiṣṭa — the physical result of a sacrifice + amṛta — the psychological enjoyment + bhujaḥ — enjoying; yānti — they go; brahma — to the spiritual region; sanātanam — primeval; nāyaṁ = na — not + ayam — this; loko = lokaḥ — world; 'sty = asty (asti) — is (properly utilized); ayajñasya — of a person who performs no austerity or religious ceremony; kuto = kutaḥ — how can it be?; 'nyaḥ = anyaḥ — other; kurusattama — best of the Kurus

Those who enjoy the physical and psychological results of a sacrifice, go to the primeval spiritual region. This world is not properly utilized by those who do not perform austerity or religious ceremony. How then can the other world be, O best of the Kurus? (4.31)

एवं बहुविधा यज्ञा
वितता ब्रह्मणो मुखे ।
कर्मजान्विद्धि तान्सर्वान्
एवं ज्ञात्वा विमोक्ष्यसे ॥४.३२॥

evaṁ bahuvidhā yajñā
vitatā brahmaṇo mukhe
karmajānviddhi tānsarvān
evaṁ jñātvā vimokṣyase (4.32)

evaṁ — thus; bahuvidhā — many types; yajñā — disciplines of accomplishment; vitatā — expounded; brahmaṇo = brahmaṇaḥ — of spiritual existence; mukhe — in the mouth; karmajān — action-produced; viddhi — know; tān — them; sarvān — all; evaṁ — thus; jñātvā — having realized; vimokṣyase — you will be freed

Many types of disciplines of accomplishment were expounded in the mouth of the spiritual existence. Know them all to be produced from action. Realizing this, O Arjuna, you will be freed. (4.32)

श्रेयान्द्रव्यमयाद्यज्ञाज्	śreyāndravyamayādyajñāj
ज्ञानयज्ञः परंतप ।	jñānayajñaḥ paraṁtapa
सर्वं कर्माखिलं पार्थ	sarvaṁ karmākhilaṁ pārtha
ज्ञाने परिसमाप्यते ॥४.३३॥	jñāne parisamāpyate (4.33)

śreyān — better; dravyamayād = dravyamayāt — than property; yajñāj = yajñāt — than control and ritual regulation; jñānayajñaḥ = jñāna — theoretical knowledge and primitive practical knowledge + yajñaḥ — control and ritual regulation; paraṁtapa — scorcher of the enemy; sarvaṁ — all; karmākhilaṁ = karma — activity + akhilaṁ — without exception; pārtha — son of Pṛthā; jñāne — as conclusion; parisamāpyate — is realized completely

Better than property control and its ritual regulation is knowledge control and its ritual regulation, O scorcher of the enemy. Every activity without exception, O son of Pṛthā, is realized as a conclusion in the final analysis. (4.33)

तद्विद्धि प्रणिपातेन	tadviddhi praṇipātena
परिप्रश्नेन सेवया ।	paripraśnena sevayā
उपदेक्ष्यन्ति ते ज्ञानं	upadekṣyanti te jñānaṁ
ज्ञानिनस्तत्त्वदर्शिनः ॥४.३४॥	jñāninastattvadarśinaḥ (4.34)

tad — this; viddhi — know; praṇipātena — by submitting as a student; paripraśnena — by asking questions; sevayā — by serving as requested; upadekṣyanti — they will teach; te — you; jñānaṁ — knowledge; jñāninaḥ — those who know; tattvadarśinaḥ — perceptive reality-conversant sages

This you ought to know. By submitting yourself as a student, by asking questions and by serving as requested, the perceptive reality-conversant teachers will teach you the knowledge. (4.34)

यज्ज्ञात्वा न पुनर्मोहम्	yajjñātvā na punarmoham
एवं यास्यसि पाण्डव ।	evaṁ yāsyasi pāṇḍava
येन भूतान्यशेषेण	yena bhūtānyaśeṣeṇa
द्रक्ष्यस्यात्मन्यथो मयि ॥४.३५॥	drakṣyasyātmanyatho mayi (4.35)

yaj = yad — which; jñātvā — having known; na — not; punar — again; moham — delusion; evaṁ — thus; yāsyasi — you succumb; pāṇḍava — O son of Pandu; yena — by which; bhūtāny = bhūtāni — living beings; aśeṣeṇa — without exception, all; drakṣyasy = drakṣyasi — you will perceive; ātmany = ātmani — in the self; atho — then; mayi — in me

Having known that experience, you will never again succumb to delusion, O son of Pandu. By that experience, you will perceive all beings in relation to yourself and then in relation to Me. (4.35)

अपि चेदसि पापेभ्यः सर्वेभ्यः पापकृत्तमः । सर्वं ज्ञानप्लवेनैव वृजिनं संतरिष्यसि ॥४.३६॥	api cedasi pāpebhyaḥ sarvebhyaḥ pāpakṛttamaḥ sarvaṁ jñānaplavenaiva vṛjinaṁ saṁtariṣyasi (4.36)

api — even; ced — if; asi — you are; pāpebhyaḥ — of the culprits; sarvebhyaḥ — of all; pāpakṛttamaḥ — most wicked; sarvaṁ — all; jñānaplavenaiva = jñāna — experience + plavena — by conveyance + eva — indeed; vṛjinaṁ — bad tendencies; saṁtariṣyasi — you will overcome

Even if you were the most wicked of the culprits, you will overcome all bad tendencies by the conveyance of this experience. (4.36)

यथैधांसि समिद्धोऽग्निर् भस्मसात्कुरुतेऽर्जुन । ज्ञानाग्निः सर्वकर्माणि भस्मसात्कुरुते तथा ॥४.३७॥	yathaidhāṁsi samiddho'gnir bhasmasātkurute'rjuna jñānāgniḥ sarvakarmāṇi bhasmasātkurute tathā (4.37)

yathaidhāṁsi = yathā — as + idhāṁsi (edhāṁsi) — firewood; samiddho = samiddhaḥ — set on fire; 'gnir = agnir — fire; bhasmasāt kurute — it reduces to ashes; 'rjuna (arjuna)=Arjuna; jñānāgniḥ = jñāna — realize knowledge + agniḥ — fiery potency; sarvakarmāṇi = sarva — all + karmāṇi — actions; bhasmasāt kurute — it reduces to nothing; tathā — so

As when wood is set on fire, it is reduced to ashes, O Arjuna, so the fiery potency of realized knowledge reduces all actions to nothing. (4.37)

न हि ज्ञानेन सदृशं पवित्रमिह विद्यते । तत्स्वयं योगसंसिद्धः कालेनात्मनि विन्दति ॥४.३८॥	na hi jñānena sadṛśaṁ pavitramiha vidyate tatsvayaṁ yogasaṁsiddhaḥ kālenātmani vindati (4.38)

na — nothing; hi — indeed; jñānena — with direct experience; sadṛśaṁ — compared with; pavitram — purifier; iha — in this world; vidyate — is relevant; tat — that realization; svayaṁ — himself; yogasaṁsiddhaḥ = yoga — yoga practice + saṁsiddhaḥ— perfected; kālenātmani = kālena — in time + ātmani — in the self; vindati — he locate

Nothing, indeed, can be compared with direct experience. No other purifier is as relevant in this world. That man who himself is perfected in yoga practice, will in time, locate the realization in himself. (4.38)

श्रद्धावाँल्लभते ज्ञानं
तत्परः संयतेन्द्रियः ।
ज्ञानं लब्ध्वा परां शान्तिम्
अचिरेणाधिगच्छति ॥४.३९॥

śraddhāvāṁllabhate jñānaṁ
tatparaḥ saṁyatendriyaḥ
jñānaṁ labdhvā parāṁ śāntim
acireṇādhigacchati (4.39)

śraddhāvān — one who has faith; labhate — he gets; jñānaṁ — the experience; tatparaḥ = tad — that + paraḥ — being devoted to; saṁyatendriyaḥ = saṁyata — restraining + indriyaḥ — sensual energy; jñānaṁ — experience; labdhvā — having acquired; parāṁ — supreme; śāntim — peace; acireṇādhigacchati = acireṇa — quickly + adhigacchati — goes

One who has faith, gets the experience. Being devoted to restraining the sensual energy, having acquired the experience, he goes quickly to the supreme peace. (4.39)

अज्ञश्चाश्रद्दधानश्च
संशयात्मा विनश्यति ।
नायं लोकोऽस्ति न परो
न सुखं संशयात्मनः ॥४.४०॥

ajñaścāśraddadhānaśca
saṁśayātmā vinaśyati
nāyaṁ loko'sti na paro
na sukhaṁ saṁśayātmanaḥ (4.40)

ajñaścāśraddadhānaśca = ajñaḥ — ignorant person + ca — and + aśraddadhānaḥ — faithless person + ca — and; saṁśayātmā = saṁśaya — doubtful + ātmā — self; vinaśyati — is degraded; nāyaṁ = na — not + ayam — this; loko = lokaḥ — world; 'sti = asti — is; na — not; paro = paraḥ — beyond the physical world; na — not; sukhaṁ — in happiness; saṁśayātmanaḥ = saṁśaya — doubting + ātmanaḥ — for the self

The ignorant person, the faithless one who is doubtful, is degraded. Neither this physical world, nor the dimensions beyond this, nor happiness, is for the person who is doubtful. (4.40)

योगसंन्यस्तकर्माणं
ज्ञानसंछिन्नसंशयम् ।
आत्मवन्तं न कर्माणि
निबध्नन्ति धनंजय ॥४.४१॥

yogasaṁnyastakarmāṇaṁ
jñānasaṁchinnasaṁśayam
ātmavantaṁ na karmāṇi
nibadhnanti dhanaṁjaya (4.41)

yogasaṁnyastakarmāṇaṁ = yoga — yoga technique + saṁnyasta — renounced + karmāṇaṁ — action; jñānasaṁchinnasaṁśayam = jñāna — realized knowledge + saṁchinna — removed + saṁśayam — doubt; ātmavantaṁ — self-composed; na — no; karmāṇi — cultural activities; nibadhnanti — they bind; dhanaṁjaya — O conqueror of wealthy countries

Cultural activities do not implicate a person whose actions are renounced through techniques developed in yoga practice, whose doubt is removed by realized knowledge and who is self-composed, O conqueror of wealthy countries. (4.41)

तस्मादज्ञानसंभूतं
हृत्स्थं ज्ञानासिनात्मनः ।
छित्त्वैनं संशयं योगम्
आतिष्ठोत्तिष्ठ भारत ॥४.४२॥

tasmādajñānasaṁbhūtaṁ
hṛtsthaṁ jñānāsinātmanaḥ
chittvainaṁ saṁśayaṁ yogam
ātiṣṭhottiṣṭha bhārata (4.42)

tasmād = *tasmāt* — *therefore; ajñānasaṁbhūtaṁ* = *ajñāna* — *ignorance* + *saṁbhūtaṁ* — *produced by; hṛtsthaṁ* — *lodged in your being; jñānāsinā* = *jñāna* — *realized knowledge* + *asinā* — *by the cutting effect; 'tmanaḥ* = *ātmanaḥ* — *of yourself; chittvainaṁ* = *chittva* — *having severed entirely* + *enam* — *this; saṁśayam* — *doubt; yogaṁ* — *to yogic technique; ātiṣṭhottiṣṭha* = *ātiṣṭha* — *resort to* + *uttiṣṭha* — *make a stand; bhārata* — *man of the Bharata family*

Therefore having severed entirely, with the cutting instrument of realized knowledge, this doubt that comes from the ignorance, lodged in your being, resort to yogic technique and make a stand, O man of the Bharata family! (4.42)

CHAPTER 5

Disciplined Use of Oppurtunities by a Yogi*

अर्जुन उवाच
संन्यासं कर्मणां कृष्ण
पुनर्योगं च शंससि ।
यच्छ्रेय एतयोरेकं
तन्मे ब्रूहि सुनिश्चितम् ॥५.१॥

arjuna uvāca
saṁnyāsaṁ karmaṇāṁ kṛṣṇa
punaryogaṁ ca śaṁsasi
yacchreya etayorekaṁ
tanme brūhi suniścitam (5.1)

arjuna — Arjuna; uvāca —said; saṁnyāsaṁ — renunciation of involvement; karmaṇām — of social activity; kṛṣṇa — Krishna; punar — again; yogaṁ — the application of yoga austerities to worldly life; ca — and; śaṁsasi — you approved; yacchreya = yad — which + chreya (śreyaḥ) — better; etayor = etayoḥ — of these two; ekaṁ — one; tan — this; me — to me; brūhi — tell; suniścitam — with certainty

Arjuna said: You approved renunciation of social activity and also mentioned the application of yoga to worldly life. Which one of these is better? Tell me this with certainty. (5.1)

श्रीभगवानुवाच
संन्यासः कर्मयोगश्च
निःश्रेयसकरावुभौ ।
तयोस्तु कर्मसंन्यासात्
कर्मयोगो विशिष्यते ॥५.२॥

śrībhagavānuvāca
saṁnyāsaḥ karmayogaśca
niḥśreyasakarāvubhau
tayostu karmasaṁnyāsāt
karmayogo viśiṣyate (5.2)

śrī-bhagavān — the Blessed Lord; uvāca — said; saṁnyāsaḥ — total renunciation of social opportunities; karmayogaśca = karmayogaḥ — disciplined use of social opportunities by a yogi + ca — and; niḥśreyasakarāv = niḥśreyasa — ultimate happiness + karāv (karau) — leading to; ubhau — both; tayos — of the two; tu — but; karmasaṁnyāsāt — than the renunciation of cultural activity; karmayogo = karmayogaḥ — disciplined use of social opportunities by a yogi; viśiṣyate — is better

**The Mahābhārata contains no chapter headings. This title was assigned by the translator on the basis of verse 2 of this chapter.*

The Blessed Lord said: Both methods, the total renunciation of social opportunities and the disciplined use of opportunities by a yogi, lead to ultimate happiness. But of the two aspects, the disciplined use of opportunities in a yogic mood is better than total renunciation of cultural activity. (5.2)

ज्ञेयः स नित्यसंन्यासी
यो न द्वेष्टि न काङ्क्षति ।
निर्द्वंद्वो हि महाबाहो
सुखं बन्धात्प्रमुच्यते ॥५.३॥

jñeyaḥ sa nityasaṁnyāsī
yo na dveṣṭi na kāṅkṣati
nirdvaṁdvo hi mahābāho
sukhaṁ bandhāt pramucyate (5.3)

jñeyaḥ — to be known; sa = saḥ — he; nityasaṁnyāsī = nitya — consistent + saṁnyāsī — a renouncer of social opportunities; yo = yaḥ — who; na — not; dveṣṭi — dislikes; na — not; kāṅkṣati — craves; nirdvandvo = nirdvandvaḥ — indifferent to opposite features; hi — indeed; mahābāho — O strong-armed man; sukhaṁ — easily; bandhāt — from implication; pramucyate — is freed

Indeed, a person who neither dislikes nor craves, who is indifferent to opposite features, should be recognized as a consistent renouncer, O strong-armed man. He is easily freed from implication. (5.3)

सांख्ययोगौ पृथग्बालाः
प्रवदन्ति न पण्डिताः ।
एकमप्यास्थितः सम्यग्
उभयोर्विन्दते फलम् ॥५.४॥

sāṁkhyayogau pṛthagbālāḥ
pravadanti na paṇḍitāḥ
ekamapyāsthitaḥ samyag
ubhayorvindate phalam (5.4)

sāṁkhyayogau = sāṁkhya — Sāṁkhya ideas + yogau — and yoga practices; pṛthagbālāḥ — simple-minded people; pravadanti — they describe; na — not; paṇḍitāḥ — the perceptive speakers; ekam — one; apy = api — even; āsthitaḥ — practiced; samyag — correctly; ubhayor = ubhayoḥ — of either; vindate — one gets; phalam — result

It is the simple-minded people, not the perceptive speakers, who say that Sāṁkhya ideas and yoga practices are separate. Even if one method is practised correctly, the practitioner gets the result of either. (5.4)

यत्सांख्यैः प्राप्यते स्थानं
तद्योगैरपि गम्यते ।
एकं सांख्यं च योगं च
यः पश्यति स पश्यति ॥५.५॥

yatsāṁkhyaiḥ prāpyate sthānaṁ
tadyogairapi gamyate
ekaṁ sāṁkhyaṁ ca yogaṁ ca
yaḥ paśyati sa paśyati (5.5)

yat — whatever; sāṁkhyaiḥ — by the Sāṁkhya experts; prāpyate — is attained; sthānaṁ — the level; tad — that; yogair = yogaiḥ — by the yogis; api — also; gamyate — is reached; ekaṁ — one; sāṁkhyaṁ — samkhya; ca — and; yogaṁ — yoga; ca — and; yaḥ — who; paśyati — perceived; sa = saḥ — he; paśyati — sees

The level obtained by the Sāṁkhya experts is also reached by the yogis. Sāṁkhya and yoga are essentially one. He who perceives that really sees. (5.5)

संन्यासस्तु महाबाहो
दुःखमाप्तुमयोगतः ।
योगयुक्तो मुनिर्ब्रह्म
नचिरेणाधिगच्छति ॥५.६॥

saṁnyāsastu mahābāho
duḥkhamāptumayogataḥ
yogayukto munirbrahma
nacireṇādhigacchati (5.6)

saṁnyāsaḥ — renunciation of opportunity; tu — indeed; mahābāho — O mighty man; duḥkham — difficulty; āptum — to obtain; ayogataḥ — without yoga-proficiency; yogayukto = yogayuktaḥ — yoga-proficient; munir = muniḥ — sage; brahma — spiritual level; nacireṇādhigacchati = nacirena — in no span of time + adhigacchati — reaches.

Renunciation of opportunities is difficult to attain without yoga practice, O mighty man. In the nick of time, a yoga-proficient sage reaches the spiritual plane. (5.6)

योगयुक्तो विशुद्धात्मा
विजितात्मा जितेन्द्रियः ।
सर्वभूतात्मभूतात्मा
कुर्वन्नपि न लिप्यते ॥५.७॥

yogayukto viśuddhātmā
vijitātmā jitendriyaḥ
sarvabhūtātmabhūtātmā
kurvannapi na lipyate (5.7)

yogayukto = yogayuktaḥ — one proficient in yoga; viśuddhātmā — one of purified self; vijitātmā — one who is self-controlled; jitendriyaḥ — one who has conquered his senses; sarvabhūtātmabhūtātmā = sarva — all + bhūta — being + ātma — self + bhūta — being + ātmā — self (sarvabhūtātmabhūtātmā - one who feels related to all beings); kurvan — acting; api — even; na — not; lipyate — is implicated

A person who is proficient in yoga, whose soul is purified, who is self-controlled, who has conquered his senses, whose self feels related to all beings, is not implicated when acting. (5.7)

नैव किंचित्करोमीति
युक्तो मन्येत तत्त्ववित् ।
पश्यञ्शृण्वन्स्पृशञ्जिघ्रन्
अश्नन्गच्छन्स्वपञ्श्वसन् ॥५.८॥

naiva kiṁcitkaromīti
yukto manyeta tattvavit
paśyañśṛṇvanspṛśañjighrann
aśnangacchansvapañśvasan (5.8)

naiva = na — not + eva — indeed; kiṁcit— anything; karomīti = karomi — initiate + iti — thus; yukto = yuktaḥ — proficient in yoga; manyeta — he thinks; tattvavit — knower of reality; paśyan — seeing + śṛṇvan — hearing; spṛśan — touching + jighran — smelling; aśnan — eating; gacchan — walking; svapan — sleeping + śvasan — breathing

"I do not initiate anything." Being proficient in yoga, this is what the knower of reality thinks. While seeing, hearing, touching, smelling, eating, walking, sleeping and breathing, (5.8)

प्रलपन्विसृजन्गृह्णन्
उन्मिषन्निमिषन्नपि ।
इन्द्रियाणीन्द्रियार्थेषु
वर्तन्त इति धारयन् ॥५.९॥

pralapanvisṛjangṛhṇann
unmiṣannimiṣannapi
indriyāṇīndriyārtheṣu
vartanta iti dhārayan (5.9)

pralapan — talking; visṛjan — evacuating; gṛhṇan — holding; unmiṣan — opening the eyelids; nimiṣan — closing the eyelids; api — also; indriyāṇīndriyārtheṣu = indriyāṇi — senses + indriyārtheṣu — in the attractive objects; vartanta — interlock; iti — thus; dhārayan — considers

...while talking, evacuating, holding, opening and closing the eyelids, he considers, "The senses are interlocked with the attractive objects." (5.9)

ब्रह्मण्याधाय कर्माणि
सङ्गं त्यक्त्वा करोति यः ।
लिप्यते न स पापेन
पद्मपत्रमिवाम्भसा ॥५.१०॥

brahmaṇyādhāya karmāṇi
saṅgaṁ tyaktvā karoti yaḥ
lipyate na sa pāpena
padmapatramivāmbhasā (5.10)

brahmaṇy = brahmaṇi — on the spiritual level; ādhāya — putting on, focused on; karmāṇi — actions; saṅgaṁ — attachment; tyaktvā — having discarded; karoti — he acts; yaḥ — who; lipyate — affected; na — not; sa = saḥ — he; pāpena — by necessary violence; padmapatram = padma — lotus + patram — leaf; ivāmbhasā = iva — just as + ambhasā — by water

Being focused on the spiritual level, discarding attachments, his acts are not defiled by necessary violence, just as a lotus leaf is not affected by water. (5.10)

कायेन मनसा बुद्ध्या
केवलैरिन्द्रियैरपि ।
योगिनः कर्म कुर्वन्ति
सङ्गं त्यक्त्वात्मशुद्धये ॥५.११॥

kāyena manasā buddhyā
kevalairindriyairapi
yoginaḥ karma kurvanti
saṅgaṁ tyaktvātmaśuddhaye (5.11)

kāyena — with the body; manasā — with the mind; buddhyā — with the intellect; kevalair = kevalaiḥ — alone; indriyair = indriyaiḥ — by the senses; api — even; yoginaḥ — yogis; karma — cultural activity; kurvanti — they perform; saṅgaṁ — attachment; tyaktvā — having discarded; 'tmaśuddhaye = ātmaśuddhaye = ātma — self + śuddhaye — towards purification

With the body, mind and intelligence, or even with the senses alone, the yogis, having discarded attachment, perform cultural acts for self-purification. (5.11)

युक्तः कर्मफलं त्यक्त्वा
शान्तिमाप्नोति नैष्ठिकीम् ।
अयुक्तः कामकारेण
फले सक्तो निबध्यते ॥५.१२॥

yuktaḥ karmaphalaṁ tyaktvā
śāntimāpnoti naiṣṭhikīm
ayuktaḥ kāmakāreṇa
phale sakto nibadhyate (5.12)

yuktaḥ — proficient in yoga; karmaphalaṁ — reward of cultural activity; tyaktvā — having abandoned; śāntim — peace; āpnoti — obtains; naiṣṭhikīm — steady; ayuktaḥ — a person not proficient in yoga; kāmakāreṇa — by action which is motivated by desire; phale — in result; sakto = saktaḥ — attached; nibadhyate — is bound

The person who is proficient in yoga, and who abandons the rewards of cultural activity, obtains steady peace. The person who is not proficient in yoga, being attached to results, is bound by desire-motivated action. (5.12)

सर्वकर्माणि मनसा
संन्यस्यास्ते सुखं वशी ।
नवद्वारे पुरे देही
नैव कुर्वन्न कारयन् ॥५.१३॥

sarvakarmāṇi manasā
saṁnyasyāste sukhaṁ vaśī
navadvāre pure dehī
naiva kurvanna kārayan (5.13)

sarvakarmāṇi = sarva — all + karmāṇi — actions; manasā — with the mind; saṁnyasyāste = saṁnyasy (saṁnyasi) — renouncing + āste — he sits; sukhaṁ — happily; vaśī — director; navadvāre = nava — nine + dvāre — in the gate; pure — in the city; dehī — the embodied soul; naiva = na — not + eva — indeed; kurvan — acting; na — nor; kārayan — causing activity

Renouncing all action with the mind, the embodied soul resides happily within as the director in the nine-gated city, not acting nor causing activity. (5.13)

न कर्तृत्वं न कर्माणि
लोकस्य सृजति प्रभुः ।
न कर्मफलसंयोगं
स्वभावस्तु प्रवर्तते ॥५.१४॥

na kartṛtvaṁ na karmāṇi
lokasya sṛjati prabhuḥ
na karmaphalasaṁyogaṁ
svabhāvastu pravartate (5.14)

na — not; kartṛtvaṁ — means of action; na — nor; karmāṇi — actions; lokasya — of the creatures; sṛjati — he creates; prabhuḥ — the Lord; na — nor; karmaphalasaṁyogaṁ = karma — action + phala — consequence + saṁyogaṁ — cyclic connection; svabhāvaḥ — inherent nature; tu — but; pravartate — it causes

The Lord does not create the means of action, nor the actions of the creatures, nor the action-consequence cycle. But the inherent nature causes this. (5.14)

नादत्ते कस्यचित्पापं
न चैव सुकृतं विभुः ।
अज्ञानेनावृतं ज्ञानं
तेन मुह्यन्ति जन्तवः ॥५.१५॥

nādatte kasyacitpāpaṁ
na caiva sukṛtaṁ vibhuḥ
ajñānenāvṛtaṁ jñānaṁ
tena muhyanti jantavaḥ (5.15)

nādatte = na — not + ādatte — perceives; kasyacit — of anyone; pāpaṁ — evil consequence; na — not; caiva = ca — and + eva — indeed; sukṛtaṁ — good reaction; vibhuḥ — the Almighty God; ajñānenāvṛtaṁ = ajñānena — by ignorance + avṛtam — shrouded; jñānaṁ — knowledge; tena — through which; muhyanti — they are deluded; jantavaḥ — the people

The Almighty God does not receive from anyone, an evil consequence nor a good reaction. The knowledge of this is shrouded by ignorance through which the people are deluded. (5.15)

ज्ञानेन तु तदज्ञानं
येषां नाशितमात्मनः ।
तेषामादित्यवज्ज्ञानं
प्रकाशयति तत्परम् ॥५.१६॥

jñānena tu tadajñānaṁ
yeṣāṁ nāśitamātmanaḥ
teṣāmādityavajjñānaṁ
prakāśayati tatparam (5.16)

jñānena — by experience; tu — however; tad — this; ajñānaṁ — ignorance; yeṣāṁ — of whom; nāśitam — removed; ātmanaḥ — of the self; teṣām — of them; ādityavaj = ādityavat — like the sun; jñānam — revelation; prakāśayati — causes to appear; tat — that; param — Supreme Truth (explained in two previous verses)

However, for those, in whose souls the ignorance is removed by experience, that revelation of theirs, will cause the Supreme Truth to appear distinctly like the sun. (5.16)

तद्बुद्धयस्तदात्मानस्
तन्निष्ठास्तत्परायणाः ।
गच्छन्त्यपुनरावृत्तिं
ज्ञाननिर्धूतकल्मषाः ॥५.१७॥

tadbuddhayastadātmānas
tanniṣṭhāstatparāyaṇāḥ
gacchantyapunarāvṛttiṁ
jñānanirdhūtakalmaṣāḥ (5.17)

tadbuddhayaḥ — those whose intellects are situated in that supreme truth; tadātmānaḥ — those whose spirits are focused on that supreme truth; tanniṣṭhāḥ — those whose reference is that supreme truth; tatparāyaṇāḥ — those who aspire to that supreme truth as the highest reality; gacchantyapunarāvṛttiṁ = gacchanty (gacchanti) — go + apunar — never again + āvṛttim — rebirth; jñānanirdhūtakalmaṣāḥ = jnana — experience + nirdhūta — removed + kalmaṣāḥ — faults

Those whose intellects are situated in that Supreme Truth, whose souls are focused on it, whose basic reference is that, whose faults are removed by the experience, who aspire to that as the highest reality, never go again to rebirth. (5.17)

विद्याविनयसंपन्ने	vidyāvinayasaṁpanne
ब्राह्मणे गवि हस्तिनि ।	brāhmaṇe gavi hastini
शुनि चैव श्वपाके च	śuni caiva śvapāke ca
पण्डिताः समदर्शिनः ॥५.१८॥	paṇḍitāḥ samadarśinaḥ (5.18)

vidyāvinayasaṁpanne = vidyā — learning + vinaya — trained + saṁpanne — accomplished; brāhmaṇe — in a brahmin; gavi — in a cow; hastini — in an elephant; śuni — in a dog; caiva = ca — and + eva — indeed; śvapāke — in a dog-flesh eater; ca — and; paṇḍitāḥ — scripturally-conversant mystic seers; samadarśinaḥ = sama — common factor + darśinaḥ — observing

In a learned, trained, accomplished brahmin, in a cow, an elephant, a dog, or a dog-flesh eater, the scripturally-conversant mystic seers observe a common factor. (5.18)

इहैव तैर्जितः सर्गो	ihaiva tairjitaḥ sargo
येषां साम्ये स्थितं मनः ।	yeṣāṁ sāmye sthitaṁ manaḥ
निर्दोषं हि समं ब्रह्म	nirdoṣaṁ hi samaṁ brahma
तस्माद्ब्रह्मणि ते स्थिताः ॥५.१९॥	tasmādbrahmaṇi te sthitāḥ (5.19)

ihaiva = iha — here in this world + iva (eva) — indeed; tair = taiḥ — by those; jitaḥ — conquered; sargo = sargaḥ — birth; yeṣāṁ — of whom; sāmye — in impartiality; sthitaṁ — established; manaḥ — mind; nirdoṣaṁ — faultless; hi — indeed; samaṁ — equally disposed; brahma — pure spirit; tasmāt — therefore; brahmaṇi — on the pure spiritual plane; te — they; sthitāḥ — established

Here in this world, birth is conquered by those whose minds are established in impartiality. Indeed, pure spirit is faultless and equally disposed. Therefore they are established on the pure spiritual plane. (5.19)

न प्रहृष्येत्प्रियं प्राप्य	na prahṛṣyetpriyaṁ prāpya
नोद्विजेत्प्राप्य चाप्रियम् ।	nodvijetprāpya cāpriyam
स्थिरबुद्धिरसंमूढो	sthirabuddhirasaṁmūḍho
ब्रह्मविद्ब्रह्मणि स्थितः ॥५.२०॥	brahmavidbrahmaṇi sthitaḥ (5.20)

na — not; prahṛṣyet — should become excited; priyaṁ — dear item or favorable circumstance; prāpya — having attained; nodvijet = na — no + udvijet — should detest; prāpya — having obtained; cāpriyam = ca — and + apriyam — something unpleasant; sthirabuddhir = sthira — stable + buddhiḥ

— intelligent; asaṁmūḍho = asammūḍhaḥ — without confusion; brahmavid — a person who continually experiences the spiritual reality; brahmaṇi — on the spiritual plane; sthitaḥ — situated

Having attained a desired item or favorable circumstance, a person should not become excited. Having attained something unpleasant, he should not detest it. With stable intelligence, without confusion, a person who continually experiences the spiritual reality, remains situated on the spiritual plane. (5.20)

बाह्यस्पर्शेष्वसक्तात्मा
विन्दत्यात्मनि यत्सुखम् ।
स ब्रह्मयोगयुक्तात्मा
सुखमक्षयमश्नुते ॥५.२१॥

bāhyasparśeṣvasaktātmā
vindatyātmani yatsukham
sa brahmayogayuktātmā
sukhamakṣayamaśnute (5.21)

bāhyasparśeṣvasaktātmā = bāhya — external + sparśeṣv (sparśeṣu) — sensation + asakta — not attached + ātmā — soul; vindatyātmani = (vindati) — finds + ātmani — in the spirit; yat — who; sukham — happiness; sa = saḥ — he; brahmayogayuktātmā = brahma — spiritual plane + yoga — yoga process; yukta — linked + ātmā — spirit; sukham — happiness; akṣayam — non-fluctuating; aśnute — makes contact with

The person who is not attached to the external sensations, who finds happiness in the spirit, whose spirit is linked to the spiritual plane through yoga process, makes contact with the non-fluctuating happiness. (5.21)

ये हि संस्पर्शजा भोगा
दुःखयोनय एव ते ।
आद्यन्तवन्तः कौन्तेय
न तेषु रमते बुधः ॥५.२२॥

ye hi saṁsparśajā bhogā
duḥkhayonaya eva te
ādyantavantaḥ kaunteya
na teṣu ramate budhaḥ (5.22)

ye — which; hi — indeed; saṁsparśajā — coming from sensual contact; bhogā — pleasures; duḥkhayonaya = duḥkha — pain + yonayaḥ — sources; eva — indeed; te — they; ādyantavantaḥ = ādy (ādi) — beginnings + anta — ending + vantaḥ — possessed with; kaunteya — O son of Kuntī; na — never; teṣu — in them; ramate — delights; budhaḥ — a wise person

The pleasures that come from sensual contacts are sources of pain. They have a beginning and ending, O son of Kuntī. A wise person never delights in them. (5.22)

शक्नोतीहैव यः सोढुं
प्राक्शरीरविमोक्षणात् ।
कामक्रोधोद्भवं वेगं
स युक्तः स सुखी नरः ॥५.२३॥

śaknotīhaiva yaḥ soḍhuṁ
prākśarīravimokṣaṇāt
kāmakrodhodbhavaṁ vegaṁ
sa yuktaḥ sa sukhī naraḥ (5.23)

śaknotīhaiva = śaknoti — can + iha — here on earth + iva (eva) — indeed; yaḥ — who; soḍhuṁ — to endure; prāk — before; śarīravimokṣaṇāt = śarīra — body + vimokṣaṇāt — from leaving; kāmakrodhodbhavaṁ = kāma — craving + krodha — anger + udbhavaṁ — basis; vegaṁ — impulsion; sa = saḥ — he; yuktaḥ — discipline; sa = saḥ — he; sukhī — happy; naraḥ — human being

The person who, before leaving the body, endures the craving-based, anger-based impulsions, is disciplined. He is a happy human being. (5.23)

योऽन्तःसुखोऽन्तरारामस् तथान्तर्ज्योतिरेव यः । स योगी ब्रह्मनिर्वाणं ब्रह्मभूतोऽधिगच्छति ॥५.२४॥	yo'ntaḥsukho'ntarārāmas tathāntarjyotireva yaḥ sa yogī brahmanirvāṇaṁ brahmabhūto'dhigacchati (5.24)

yo = yaḥ — who; 'ntaḥsukho = antahsukhaḥ — he who is happy within; 'ntarārāmas = antarārāmas — he who is spiritually delighted; tathāntarjyotir (tathāntarjyotiḥ) = tathā — as a result + antarjyotiḥ — he who has brilliant consciousness within; eva — indeed; yaḥ — who; sa = saḥ — he; yogī — yogi; brahmanirvāṇaṁ — stoppage of disturbing sensuality and attainment of constant spirituality; brahmabhūto = brahmabhūtaḥ — absorption on the spiritual plane; 'dhigacchati = adhigacchati — he attains

The person who is happy within, who is spiritually delighted and as a result, experiences the brilliant consciousness, he, that yogi, experiences the stoppage of disturbing sensuality and attains constant spirituality in absorption on the spiritual plane. (5.24)

लभन्ते ब्रह्मनिर्वाणम् ऋषयः क्षीणकल्मषाः । छिन्नद्वैधा यतात्मानः सर्वभूतहिते रताः ॥५.२५॥	labhante brahmanirvāṇam ṛṣayaḥ kṣīṇakalmaṣāḥ chinnadvaidhā yatātmānaḥ sarvabhūtahite ratāḥ (5.25)

labhante — they attain; brahmanirvāṇaṁ — cessation of material existence and a simultaneous absorption in spirituality; ṛṣayaḥ — the seers; kṣīṇakalmaṣāḥ = kṣīṇa — terminates + kalmaṣāḥ — sins, faults; chinnadvaidhā = chinna — removed + dvaidhā — doubts; yatātmānaḥ = yata — restrained + ātmānaḥ — souls; sarvabhūtahite = sarva — all + bhūta — creatures + hite — in welfare; ratāḥ — joy

Those seers whose sins and faults are terminated, whose doubts are removed, whose souls are restrained, who find joy in regarding the welfare of the creatures, attain a cessation of their material existence and a simultaneous absorption in spirituality. (5.25)

कामक्रोधवियुक्तानां
यतीनां यतचेतसाम् ।
अभितो ब्रह्मनिर्वाणं
वर्तते विदितात्मनाम् ॥५.२६॥

kāmakrodhaviyuktānāṁ
yatīnāṁ yatacetasām
abhito brahmanirvāṇaṁ
vartate viditātmanām (5.26)

kāmakrodhaviyuktānāṁ = kāma — desire + krodha — anger + viyuktānāṁ — of the separation from; yatīnāṁ — of the ascetics; yatacetasām — of those whose thinking is restrained; abhito = abhitaḥ — very close; brahmanirvāṇaṁ — cessation of material existence, assumption of enlightened spirituality; vartate — it is; viditātmanām — of those who understand the spiritual self

The cessation of material existence and assumption of enlightened spirituality is soon to be attained by those ascetics whose thinking is restrained and who understand the spiritual self, and are separated from desire and anger. (5.26)

स्पर्शान्कृत्वा बहिर्बाह्यांश्
चक्षुश्चैवान्तरे भ्रुवोः ।
प्राणापानौ समौ कृत्वा
नासाभ्यन्तरचारिणौ ॥५.२७॥

sparśānkṛtvā bahirbāhyāṁś
cakṣuścaivāntare bhruvoḥ
prāṇāpānau samau kṛtvā
nāsābhyantaracāriṇau (5.27)

sparśān — sensual contact; kṛtvā — having done; bahir = bahiḥ — external; bāhyāṁś = bāhyān — excluded; cakṣuścaivāntare = cakṣuḥ — visual focus + ca — and + (eva) — indeed + antare — in between; bhruvoḥ — of the two eyebrows; prāṇāpānau — both inhalation and exhalation; samau — in balance; kṛtvā — having made; nāsābhyantaracāriṇau = nāsa — nose + abhyantara — within + cāriṇau — moving

Excluding the external sensual contacts, and fixing the visual focus between the eyebrows, putting the inhalation and exhalation in balance, moving through the nose. (5.27)

यतेन्द्रियमनोबुद्धिर्
मुनिर्मोक्षपरायणः ।
विगतेच्छाभयक्रोधो
यः सदा मुक्त एव सः ॥५.२८॥

yatendriyamanobuddhir
munirmokṣaparāyaṇaḥ
vigatecchābhayakrodho
yaḥ sadā mukta eva saḥ (5.28)

yatendriyamanobuddhiḥ = yata — controlled + indriya — sensual energy + mano (manah) — mind + buddhiḥ — intelligence; munir = muniḥ — wise person; mokṣaparāyaṇaḥ - one who is dedicated to achieving liberation; vigatecchābhayakrodhaḥ = vigata — gone away + icchā — desire + bhaya — fear + krodho (krodhaḥ) — anger; yaḥ — who; sadā — always; mukta — liberated; eva — indeed; saḥ — he

...the wise man, who is dedicated to achieving liberation, whose sensual energy, mind and intellect are controlled, whose desire, fear and anger are gone, is liberated always. (5.28)

भोक्तारं यज्ञतपसां
सर्वलोकमहेश्वरम् ।
सुहृदं सर्वभूतानां
ज्ञात्वा मां शान्तिमृच्छति ॥५.२९॥

bhoktāraṁ yajñatapasāṁ
sarvalokamaheśvaram
suhṛdaṁ sarvabhūtānāṁ
jñātvā māṁ śāntimṛcchati (5.29)

bhoktāraṁ — enjoyer; yajñatapasāṁ — of the religious ceremonies and austerities; sarvalokamaheśvaram = sarva — all entire + loka — world + maheśvaram — Supreme God; suhṛdaṁ — friend; sarvabhūtānāṁ — of all creatures; jñātvā — recognizing; māṁ — me; śāntim — spiritual peace; ṛcchati — attains

Recognizing Me, as the enjoyer of religious ceremonies and austerities, the Supreme God of the entire world, the friend of the creatures, he attains spiritual peace. (5.29)

CHAPTER 6

Yoga Practice*

श्रीभगवानुवाच
अनाश्रितः कर्मफलं
कार्यं कर्म करोति यः ।
स संन्यासी च योगी च
न निरग्निर्न चाक्रियः ॥६.१॥

śrībhagavānuvāca
anāśritaḥ karmaphalaṁ
kāryaṁ karma karoti yaḥ
sa saṁnyāsī ca yogī ca
na niragnirna cākriyaḥ (6.1)

śrī bhagavān - the Blessed Lord; uvāca — said; anāśritaḥ — not relying on; karmaphalaṁ — result of an action; kāryaṁ — obligation; karma — action; karoti — he fulfills; yaḥ — who; sa = saḥ — he; saṁnyāsī — renouncer; ca — and; yogī — yogi; ca — and; na — not; niragnir = niragniḥ — without a fire ceremony; na — nor; cākriyaḥ = ca — and + akryaḥ — lacking physical activities

The Blessed Lord said: A person who fulfills obligatory action, without depending on the result of the action, is a renouncer, and a yogi, not the one who is without a fire ceremony or who lacks physical activity. (6.1).

यं संन्यासमिति प्राहुर्
योगं तं विद्धि पाण्डव ।
न ह्यसंन्यस्तसंकल्पो
योगी भवति कश्चन ॥६.२॥

yaṁ saṁnyāsamiti prāhur
yogaṁ taṁ viddhi pāṇḍava
na hyasaṁnyastasaṁkalpo
yogī bhavati kaścana (6.2)

yaṁ — that which; saṁnyāsam — renunciation; iti — thus; prāhur = prāhuḥ — the authorities define; yogaṁ — applied yoga; taṁ — it; viddhi — know; pāṇḍava — Arjuna Pandava; na — not; hy = hi — indeed; asaṁnyastasaṁkalpo = (asaṁnyastasaṁkalpaḥ) = asaṁnyasta — without renunciation + saṁkalpaḥ — intention; yogī — yogi; bhavati — becomes; kaścana — anyone

That which the authorities define as renunciation, know it as applied yoga, O Arjuna Pandava. Indeed, no one becomes a yogi without an intention for renunciation. (6.2)

**The Mahābhārata contains no chapter headings. This title was assigned by the translator on the basis of verse 12 of this chapter.*

आरुरुक्षोर्मुनेर्योगं
कर्म कारणमुच्यते ।
योगारूढस्य तस्यैव
शमः कारणमुच्यते ॥६.३॥

āruruksormuneryogaṁ
karma kāraṇamucyate
yogārūḍhasya tasyaiva
śamaḥ kāraṇamucyate (6.3)

āruruksor = āruruksoḥ — of one who strives; muner = muneḥ — of a philosophical man; yogaṁ — yoga expertise; karma — cultural activity; kāraṇam — the means; ucyate — it is remembered; yogārūḍhasya — of one who mastered yoga; tasyaiva = tasya — of him + iva (eva) — indeed; śamaḥ — tranquil method; kāraṇam — the means; ucyate — it is remembered

For a philosophical man who strives for yoga expertise, cultural activity is recommended. For one who has mastered yoga already, the tranquil reserved method is the means. (6.3)

यदा हि नेन्द्रियार्थेषु
न कर्मस्वनुषज्जते ।
सर्वसंकल्पसंन्यासी
योगारूढस्तदोच्यते ॥६.४॥

yadā hi nendriyārtheṣu
na karmasvanuṣajjate
sarvasaṁkalpasaṁnyāsī
yogārūḍhastadocyate (6.4)

yadā — when; hi — indeed; nendriyārtheṣu = na — not + indriyārtheṣu — in attractive objects; na — not; karmasv = karmasu — in performance; anuṣajjate — feels attached; sarvasaṁkalpasaṁnyāsī = sarvasaṁkalpa — all motivations + saṁnyāsī — discarding; yogārūḍhas — proficient in yoga practice; tadocyate = tada — then + ucyate — it is said

Indeed, when having discarded all motivations, a person feels no attachment to attractive objects nor to performance, he is said to be proficient in yoga practice. (6.4)

उद्धरेदात्मनात्मानं
नात्मानमवसादयेत् ।
आत्मैव ह्यात्मनो बन्धुर्
आत्मैव रिपुरात्मनः ॥६.५॥

uddharedātmanātmānaṁ
nātmānamavasādayet
ātmaiva hyātmano bandhur
ātmaiva ripurātmanaḥ (6.5)

uddhared = uddharet — should elevate; ātmanā — by the self; 'tmānaṁ = ātmānam — the self; nātmānam = na — not + ātmānam — the self; avasādayet — should degrade; ātmaiva = ātmā — self + eva — only; hyātmano = hyātmanaḥ = hy (hi) — indeed + ātmanaḥ — of the self; bandhur = bandhuh — friend; ātmaiva = ātmā — self + eva — as well; ripur = ripuḥ — enemy; ātmanaḥ — of the self

One should elevate his being by himself. One should not degrade the self. Indeed, the person should be the friend of himself. Or he could be the enemy as well. (6.5)

बन्धुरात्मात्मनस्तस्य
येनात्मैवात्मना जितः ।
अनात्मनस्तु शत्रुत्वे
वर्तेतात्मैव शत्रुवत् ॥६.६॥

bandhurātmātmanastasya
yenātmaivātmanā jitaḥ
anātmanastu śatrutve
vartetātmaiva śatruvat (6.6)

bandhur = bandhuḥ — friend; ātmā — personal energies; 'tmanas = ātmanas — of the self; tasya — of him; yenātmaivātmanā = yena — by whom + ātmā — self + eva — indeed + ātmanā — by the self; jitaḥ — subdued; anātmanas — of one who is not self-possessed; tu — but; śatrutve — in hostility; vartetātmaiva = varteta — it operates + ātmā - self + eva — indeed; śatruvat — like an enemy

The personal energies are the friend of the person by whom those energies are subdued. But for one whose personality is not self-possessed, the personal energies operate in hostility like an enemy. (6.6)

जितात्मनः प्रशान्तस्य
परमात्मा समाहितः ।
शीतोष्णसुखदुःखेषु
तथा मानावमानयोः ॥६.७॥

jitātmanaḥ praśāntasya
paramātmā samāhitaḥ
śītoṣṇasukhaduḥkheṣu
tathā mānāvamānayoḥ (6.7)

jitātmanaḥ — of the self-controlled person; praśāntasya — of the person who is peaceful; paramātmā — the directive part of the self; samāhitaḥ — composed; śītoṣṇasukhaduḥkheṣu = śīta — cold + uṣṇa — heat + sukha — pleasure + duḥkheṣu — in pain; tathā — also; mānāvamānayoḥ = māna — honor + avamānayoḥ — in dishonor

The directive part of a self-controlled, peaceful person remains composed in the cold, heat, pleasure, pain, and also in honor and dishonor. (6.7)

ज्ञानविज्ञानतृप्तात्मा
कूटस्थो विजितेन्द्रियः ।
युक्त इत्युच्यते योगी
समलोष्टाश्मकाञ्चनः ॥६.८॥

jñānavijñānatṛptātmā
kūṭastho vijitendriyaḥ
yukta ityucyate yogī
samaloṣṭāśmakāñcanaḥ (6.8)

jñānavijñānatṛptātmā = jñāna — knowledge + vijñāna — realized experience + tṛpta — content + ātmā — self; kūṭastho = kūṭasthaḥ — stable; vijitendriyaḥ = vijita - subdued + indriyaḥ — sensual energy; yukta — disciplined in yoga; ityucyate = ity (iti) — thus + ucyate — is called; yogī — yogi; samaloṣṭrāśmakāñcanaḥ = sama — same + loṣṭra — lump of clay + aśma — stone + kāñcanaḥ — gold

The yogi who is satisfied with knowledge and realized experience, who is stable and who has conquered his sensual energy, who regards a lump of clay, a stone or gold in the same way, is said to be disciplined in yoga. (6.8)

सुहृन्मित्रार्युदासीन मध्यस्थद्वेष्यबन्धुषु । साधुष्वपि च पापेषु समबुद्धिर्विशिष्यते ॥६.९॥	suhṛnmitrāryudāsīna madhyasthadveṣya bandhuṣu sādhuṣvapi ca pāpeṣu samabuddhirviśiṣyate (6.9)

suhṛnmitrāryudāsīna = suhṛn (suhṛd) — friend + mitra — acquaintance + ary (ari) — enemy + udāsīna — indifferent; madhyasthadveṣyabandhuṣu = madhyastha — evenly disposed + dvesya — enemy + bandhuṣu — to kinsmen; sādhuṣv = sādhuṣu — in saintly people; api — also; ca — and; pāpeṣu — in sinful people; samabuddhir = samabuddhiḥ — one who exhibits balanced judgement; viśiṣyate — be regarded with distinction

A person who is indifferent to friend, acquaintance, and enemy, who is evenly-disposed to enemies and kinsmen, who exhibits balanced judgment towards saintly people or sinful ones, is to be regarded with distinction. (6.9)

योगी युञ्जीत सततम् आत्मानं रहसि स्थितः । एकाकी यतचित्तात्मा निराशीरपरिग्रहः ॥६.१०॥	yogī yuñjīta satatam ātmānaṁ rahasi sthitaḥ ekākī yatacittātmā nirāśīraparigrahaḥ (6.10)

yogī — yogi; yuñjīta — should concentrate; satatam — constantly; ātmānam — on the self; rahasi — in isolation; sthitaḥ — situated; ekākī — alone; yatacittātmā = yata - controlling + citta - thinking + ātmā — self; nirāśīr — without desire; aparigrahaḥ — without possessions

In isolation, the yogi should constantly concentrate on the self. Being alone, he should be of controlled thinking and subdued self without desire and without possessions. (6.10)

शुचौ देशे प्रतिष्ठाप्य स्थिरमासनमात्मनः । नात्युच्छ्रितं नातिनीचं चैलाजिनकुशोत्तरम् ॥६.११॥	śucau deśe pratiṣṭhāpya sthiramāsanamātmanaḥ nātyucchritaṁ nātinīcaṁ cailājinakuśottaram (6.11)

śucau — in clean; deśe — in place; pratiṣṭhāpya — fixing; sthiram — firm; āsanam — seat; ātmanaḥ — of his self; nātyucchritaṁ = na — not + atyucchritaṁ — too high; nātinīcam = na — not + atinīcam — too low; cailājinakuśottaram = caila - cloth + ajina — antelope skin + kuśa — kusha grass + uttaram — underneath

In a clean place, fixing for himself a firm seat which is not too high, not too low, with a covering layer of cloth, antelope skin and kusha grass underneath, (6.11)

तत्रैकाग्रं मनः कृत्वा यतचित्तेन्द्रियक्रियः । उपविश्यासने युञ्ज्याद् योगमात्मविशुद्धये ॥६.१२॥	tatraikāgraṁ manaḥ kṛtvā yatacittendriyakriyaḥ upaviśyāsane yuñjyād yogamātmaviśuddhaye (6.12)

tatraikāgraṁ = tatra — there + ekāgram — single-focused; manaḥ — mind; kṛtvā — having made; yatacittendriyakriyaḥ = yata - controlled + citta — thought + indriyakriyaḥ — sense energy; upaviśyāsane = upaviśya — seating himself + āsane — in a posture; yuñjād = yuñjāt — should practice; yogamātmaviśuddhaye = yogam — to yoga discipline + ātma — self + viśuddhaye — to purification

...being there, seated in a posture, having the mind focused, the person who controls his thinking and sensual energy, should practise the yoga discipline for self-purification. (6.12)

समं कायशिरोग्रीवं धारयन्नचलं स्थिरः । संप्रेक्ष्य नासिकाग्रं स्वं दिशश्चानवलोकयन् ॥६.१३॥	samaṁ kāyaśirogrīvaṁ dhārayannacalaṁ sthiraḥ saṁprekṣya nāsikāgraṁ svaṁ diśaścānavalokayan (6.13)

samam — balanced; kāyaśirogrīvaṁ = kāya — body + śiro (śiraḥ) — head + grīvam — neck; dhārayan — holding; acalam — without movement; sthiraḥ — steady; saṁprekṣya — gazing at; nāsikāgraṁ = nāsikā — nostril + agram — tip; svam — own; diśaścānavalokayan = diśaḥ — the directions + ca — and + anavalokayan — not looking

Holding the body, head and neck in balance, steady without movement, gaze at the tip of the nose, not looking in any other direction. (6.13)

प्रशान्तात्मा विगतभीर् ब्रह्मचारिव्रते स्थितः । मनः संयम्य मच्चित्तो युक्त आसीत मत्परः ॥६.१४॥	praśāntātmā vigatabhīr brahmacārivrate sthitaḥ manaḥ saṁyamya maccitto yukta āsīta matparaḥ (6.14)

praśāntātmā = praśānta — pacified + ātmā — self; vigatabhīr (vigatabhīḥ) =vigata - gone away + bhīḥ — fear; brahmacārivrate — in the vow of sexual restraint; sthitaḥ — established; manaḥ — mind; saṁyamya — controlling; maccitto = maccittaḥ — though fixed on Me; yukta — disciplined; āsīta — should sit; matparaḥ — devoted to Me

With a pacified self, free from fears, with a vow of sexual restraint firmly practised, with mind controlled and having Me in his thought with his mind concentrated, he should sit, being devoted to Me as the Supreme Objective. (6.14)

युञ्जन्नेवं सदात्मानं
योगी नियतमानसः ।
शान्तिं निर्वाणपरमां
मत्संस्थामधिगच्छति ॥६.१५॥

yuñjannevaṁ sadātmānaṁ
yogī niyatamānasaḥ
śāntiṁ nirvāṇaparamāṁ
matsaṁsthāmadhigacchati (6.15)

yuñjan — disciplining; evaṁ — as described; sadā — continuously; 'tmānaṁ = ātmānam — himself; yogī — yogi; niyatamānasaḥ — one who has a subdued mind; śāntiṁ — spiritual security; nirvāṇaparamāṁ = nirvāṇa - extinction of mundane affinity + paramām — highest living state; matsaṁsthām — existentially positioned with Me; adhigacchati — achieves

Disciplining himself continuously as described, the yogi who has a subdued mind, experiences spiritual security. He achieves the extinction of mundane affinity as he simultaneously attains the highest living state. He achieves an existential position with Me. (6.15)

नात्यश्नतस्तु योगोऽस्ति
न चैकान्तमनश्नतः ।
न चातिस्वप्नशीलस्य
जाग्रतो नैव चार्जुन ॥६.१६॥

nātyaśnatastu yogo'sti
na caikāntamanaśnataḥ
na cātisvapnaśīlasya
jāgrato naiva cārjuna (6.16)

nātyaśnatas = na — not + atyaśnatas — of too much eating; tu — but; yogo = yogaḥ — yoga; 'sti = asti — it is; na — not; caikāntam = ca — and + ekāntam — solely; anaśnataḥ — of not eating at all; na — not; cātisvapnaśīlasya = ca — and + atisvapna - too much sleeping + śīlasya — of habit; jāgrato = jāgrataḥ — of staying awake; naiva = na — nor + eva — indeed; cārjuna = ca — and + arjuna — Arjuna

But Arjuna, yoga practice does not consist of eating too much. And it is not the practice of not eating at all, nor the habit of sleeping too much nor staying awake either. (6.16)

युक्ताहारविहारस्य
युक्तचेष्टस्य कर्मसु ।
युक्तस्वप्नावबोधस्य
योगो भवति दुःखहा ॥६.१७॥

yuktāhāravihārasya
yuktaceṣṭasya karmasu
yuktasvapnāvabodhasya
yogo bhavati duḥkhahā (6.17)

yuktāhāravihārasya = yukta — regulated + āhāra — eating + vihārasya — of leisure; yuktaceṣṭasya = yukta — disciplined + ceṣṭasya — of endeavor; karmasu — in duties; yuktasvapnāvabodhasya = yukta — disciplined +

svapna - sleep + avabodhasya — of waking; yogo = yogah — yoga practice; bhavati — is; duḥkhahā — distress-removing

For a person who is regulated in eating and in leisure, who is disciplined in the endeavor of duties, who is moderate in sleeping and waking, for him, the yoga practice is a distress-remover. (6.17)

यदा विनियतं चित्तम्
आत्मन्येवावतिष्ठते ।
निःस्पृहः सर्वकामेभ्यो
युक्त इत्युच्यते तदा ॥६.१८॥

yadā viniyataṁ cittam
ātmanyevāvatiṣṭhate
niḥspṛhaḥ sarvakāmebhyo
yukta ityucyate tadā (6.18)

yadā — when; viniyataṁ — tightly controlled; cittam — thought; ātmany = ātmani — in the spiritual core self; evāvatiṣṭhate = eva — alone + avatiṣṭhate — is attentive; niḥspṛhaḥ — free from desire; sarvakāmebhyo (sarvakāmebhyaḥ) = sarva — all + kāmebhyaḥ — from cravings; yukta — proficient in yoga; ity = iti — thus; ucyate — is said; tadā — then

When with tightly controlled thought, he is attentive to his spiritual core self alone, being freed from desires and from all cravings, he is said to be proficient in yoga. (6.18)

यथा दीपो निवातस्थो
नेङ्गते सोपमा स्मृता ।
योगिनो यतचित्तस्य
युञ्जतो योगमात्मनः ॥६.१९॥

yathā dīpo nivātastho
neṅgate sopamā smṛtā
yogino yatacittasya
yuñjato yogamātmanaḥ (6.19)

yathā — as; dīpo = dīpaḥ — lamp; nivātastho (nivātasthaḥ) = nivāta — windless + sthaḥ — situated; nengate = na — not + ingate — flickers; sopamā = so (sāḥ) — this + upamā — in comparison; smṛtā — recalled; yogino = yoginaḥ — of the yogi; yatacittasya — of a person whose thinking is restrained; yuñjato = yuñjataḥ — of practising; yogam — yoga; ātmanaḥ — of the self

This comparison is recalled: A lamp in a windless place which does not flicker, and a yogi of controlled thought who performs disciplines in relation to the spiritual self. (6.19)

यत्रोपरमते चित्तं
निरुद्धं योगसेवया ।
यत्र चैवात्मनात्मानं
पश्यन्नात्मनि तुष्यति ॥६.२०॥

yatroparamate cittaṁ
niruddhaṁ yogasevayā
yatra caivātmanātmānaṁ
paśyannātmani tuṣyati (6.20)

yatroparamate = yatra — where + uparamate — it stops; cittaṁ — thinking; niruddhaṁ — restraint; yogasevayā = yoga — yoga discipline + sevayā — by practice; yatra — where; caivātmanā = ca — and + eva — indeed + ātmanā —

by the self; 'tmānaṁ = ātmānam — the self; paśyan — seeing; ātmani — in the self; tuṣyati — is satisfied

At the place where being restrained by yoga practice, thinking stops, and at the place where the yogi perceives the self by the self, he is satisfied in the self. (6.20)

सुखमात्यन्तिकं यत्तद्
बुद्धिग्राह्यमतीन्द्रियम् ।
वेत्ति यत्र न चैवायं
स्थितश्चलति तत्त्वतः ॥६.२१॥

sukhamātyantikaṁ yattad
buddhigrāhyamatīndriyam
vetti yatra na caivāyaṁ
sthitaścalati tattvataḥ (6.21)

sukham — happiness; ātyantikaṁ — continuous; yat = yad — which; tad — this; buddhigrāhyam — grasp by the intellect; atīndriyam — beyond the mundane senses; vetti — he knows; yatra — whereabout; na — not; caivāyam = ca — and + eva — indeed + ayam — this; sthitaścalati = sthitaḥ — established + calati — he shifted; tattvataḥ — the reality

He knows the whereabouts of that continuous happiness, which is grasped by the intellect and which is beyond the mundane senses. And being established, he does not shift from that reality. (6.21)

यं लब्ध्वा चापरं लाभं
मन्यते नाधिकं ततः ।
यस्मिन्स्थितो न दुःखेन
गुरुणापि विचाल्यते ॥६.२२॥

yaṁ labdhvā cāparaṁ lābhaṁ
manyate nādhikaṁ tataḥ
yasminsthito na duḥkhena
guruṇāpi vicālyate (6.22)

yaṁ — which; labdhvā — having attained; cāparaṁ = ca — and + aparaṁ — other; lābhaṁ — attainment; manyate — he thinks; nādhikam = na — not + adhikam — greater; tataḥ — than that; yasmin — which; sthito = sthitaḥ — established; na — not; duḥkhena — by distress; guruṇāpi = guruṇā — by deep + api — also; vicālyate — is drawn away

And having attained that, he thinks there is no greater attainment. Being established in that, he is not drawn away, even by deep distress. (6.22)

तं विद्याद्दुःखसंयोग -
वियोगं योगसंज्ञितम् ।
स निश्चयेन योक्तव्यो
योगोऽनिर्विण्णचेतसा ॥६.२३॥

taṁ vidyādduḥkha-saṁyoga -
viyogaṁ yogasaṁjñitam
sa niścayena yoktavyo
yogo'nirviṇṇacetasā (6.23)

tam — this; vidyād = vidyāt — let it be understood; duḥkhasaṁyoga = duḥkha — emotional distress + saṁyoga — emotional identity with; viyogaṁ — separation; yogasaṁjñitam = yoga — mastery of yoga + saṁjñitam — recognized as; sa = saḥ — this; niścayena — with determination; yoktavyo =

yoktavyaḥ — to be practiced; yogo = yogah — yoga; 'nirviṇṇacetasā (anirviṇṇacetasā) = anirviṇṇa — not depressed + cetasā — with thought

Let it be understood, that this separation from emotional distress is the mastery of yoga. This yoga is to be practised with determination and without depressing thought. (6.23)

संकल्पप्रभवान्कामांस् त्यक्त्वा सर्वानशेषतः । मनसैवेन्द्रियग्रामं विनियम्य समन्ततः ॥६.२४॥	saṁkalpaprabhavānkāmāṁs tyaktvā sarvānaśeṣataḥ manasaivendriyagrāmaṁ viniyamya samantataḥ (6.24)

saṁkalpaprabhavān = saṁkalpa — motive + prabhavān — produced; kāmāṁs — cravings; tyaktvā — having abandoned; sarvān — all; aśeṣataḥ — without exception; manasaivendriyagrāmaṁ = manasā — by mind + eva — indeed + indriyagrāmaṁ — the total sensual energy; viniyamya — controlling; samantataḥ — completely

Abandoning without exception, all desires which are produced from motivation, and completely restraining the total sensual energy by the mind, (6.24)

शनैः शनैरुपरमेद् बुद्ध्या धृतिगृहीतया । आत्मसंस्थं मनः कृत्वा न किंचिदपि चिन्तयेत् ॥६.२५॥	śanaiḥ śanairuparamed buddhyā dhṛtigṛhītayā ātmasaṁsthaṁ manaḥ kṛtvā na kiṁcidapi cintayet (6.25)

śanaiḥ śanair (śanaiḥ) — little by little; uparamed = uparamet — should withdraw from sensual activity; buddhyā — by intelligence; dhṛtigṛhītayā = dhṛti — firmness + gṛhītayā — grasped; ātmasaṁsthaṁ = ātma — spiritual self + saṁsthaṁ — fixed; manah — mind; kṛtvā — having made; na — not; kiṁcit — anything; api — even; cintayet — should think

...little by little, with a firm grasp by the intelligence, he should withdraw from sensual activity. Having made his mind to be fixed on the spiritual self, he should not think of anything. (6.25)

यतो यतो निश्चरति मनश्चञ्चलमस्थिरम् । ततस्ततो नियम्यैतद् आत्मन्येव वशं नयेत् ॥६.२६॥	yato yato niścarati manaścañcalamasthiram tatastato niyamyaitad ātmanyeva vaśaṁ nayet (6.26)

yato yato = yataḥ yataḥ — wherever; niścarati — wanders away; manaścañcalam = manas — mind + cañcalam — drifting; asthiram — unsteady; tatastato = tatastataḥ — from there; niyamyaitad = niyamya —

restrain + etad — it; ātmany (ātmani) — in the self; eva — indeed; vaśam — control; nayet — should direct

To wherever the unsteady, drifty mind wanders, from there he should restrain it. He should direct the mind to control it in the self. (6.26)

प्रशान्तमनसं ह्येनं
योगिनं सुखमुत्तमम् ।
उपैति शान्तरजसं
ब्रह्मभूतमकल्मषम् ॥६.२७॥

praśāntamanasaṁ hyenaṁ
yoginaṁ sukhamuttamam
upaiti śāntarajasaṁ
brahmabhūtamakalmaṣam (6.27)

praśāntamanasaṁ = praśānta — psychologically pacified + manasaṁ — mind; hyenaṁ = hy (hi) — indeed + enam — him; yoginaṁ — yogi; sukham — happiness; uttamam — superior; upaiti — experiences; śāntarajasaṁ = śānta — calmed + rajasam — emotion; brahmabhūtam — spiritual level; akalmaṣam — free from bad tendencies

Indeed, being psychologically pacified, the yogi, whose emotions are calmed, who is on the spiritual plane, who is free from bad tendencies, experiences superior happiness. (6.27)

युञ्जन्नेवं सदात्मानं
योगी विगतकल्मषः ।
सुखेन ब्रह्मसंस्पर्शम्
अत्यन्तं सुखमश्नुते ॥६.२८॥

yuñjannevaṁ sadātmānaṁ
yogī vigatakalmaṣaḥ
sukhena brahmasaṁsparśam
atyantaṁ sukhamaśnute (6.28)

yuñjan — applying yoga disciplines; evaṁ — thus; sadā — constantly; 'tmānaṁ = ātmānam — the self; yogī — yogi; vigatakalmaṣaḥ — free from faults; sukhena — easily; brahmasaṁsparśam — constanting the spiritual plane; atyantaṁ — endless; sukham — happiness; aśnute — attains

Applying the yoga disciplines constantly to the self, the yogi being freed from faults, easily contacting the spiritual plane, attains endless happiness. (6.28)

सर्वभूतस्थमात्मानं
सर्वभूतानि चात्मनि ।
ईक्षते योगयुक्तात्मा
सर्वत्र समदर्शनः ॥६.२९॥

sarvabhūtasthamātmānaṁ
sarvabhūtāni cātmani
īkṣate yogayuktātmā
sarvatra samadarśanaḥ (6.29)

sarvabhūtastham — existing in all mundane creature forms; ātmānaṁ — spirit; sarvabhūtāni — all creatures; cātmani = ca — see + ātmani — in the self; īkṣate — he sees; yogayuktātmā — one who is proficient in yoga; sarvatra — in all cases; samadarśanaḥ — seeing the same

With a spirit existing in every creature, and with every creature based on a spirit, a person who is proficient in yoga, perceives the same existential arrangement in all cases. (6.29)

यो मां पश्यति सर्वत्र सर्वं च मयि पश्यति । तस्याहं न प्रणश्यामि स च मे न प्रणश्यति ॥६.३०॥	yo māṁ paśyati sarvatra sarvaṁ ca mayi paśyati tasyāhaṁ na praṇaśyāmi sa ca me na praṇaśyati (6.30)

yo = yaḥ — who; mām — me; paśyati — sees; sarvatra — in all forms; sarvam — all creatures; ca — and; mayi — in Me; paśyati — sees; tasyāham = tasya — his + aham — I; na — never; praṇaśyāmi — I am out of range; sa = saḥ — he; ca — and; me — my; na — never; praṇaśyati — he is out of view

To him who sees Me in all forms and who sees all creatures in reference to Me, I am never out of range, and he is never out of My view. (6.30)

सर्वभूतस्थितं यो मां भजत्येकत्वमास्थितः । सर्वथा वर्तमानोऽपि स योगी मयि वर्तते ॥६.३१॥	sarvabhūtasthitaṁ yo māṁ bhajatyekatvamāsthitaḥ sarvathā vartamāno'pi sa yogī mayi vartate (6.31)

sarvabhūtasthitam — existentially situated in all creatures; yo = yaḥ — who; māṁ — Me; bhajaty = bhajati — he honors; ekatvam — in harmony; āsthitaḥ — established; sarvathā — in various circumstances; vartamāno = vartamānaḥ — existentially situated; 'pi = api — although; sa = saḥ — he; yogī — yogi; mayi — in Me; vartate — he remains in touch

Although moving in various circumstances, the yogi who is established in that harmony, who honors Me as being existentially situated in all creatures, remains in touch with Me. (6.31)

आत्मौपम्येन सर्वत्र समं पश्यति योऽर्जुन । सुखं वा यदि वा दुःखं स योगी परमो मतः ॥६.३२॥	ātmaupamyena sarvatra samaṁ paśyati yo'rjuna sukhaṁ vā yadi vā duḥkhaṁ sa yogī paramo mataḥ (6.32)

ātmaupamyena = ātma — self + aupamyena — by reference; sarvatra — in all cases; samaṁ — similarity; paśyati — he sees; yo = yaḥ — who; 'rjuna = arjuna — Arjuna; sukhaṁ — pleasurable sensations; vā — or; yadi — regardless; vā — or; duḥkhaṁ — painful sensations; sa = saḥ — he; yogī — yogi; paramo = paramaḥ — highest; mataḥ- considered as

He who, in reference to himself, sees the same facilities in all cases, regardless of pleasure or painful sensations, he, O Arjuna, is considered as the highest yogi. (6.32)

अर्जुन उवाच
योऽयं योगस्त्वया प्रोक्तः
साम्येन मधुसूदन ।
एतस्याहं न पश्यामि
चञ्चलत्वात्स्थितिं स्थिराम् ॥६.३३॥

arjuna uvāca
yo'yaṁ yogastvayā proktaḥ
sāmyena madhusūdana
etasyāhaṁ na paśyāmi
cañcalatvātsthitiṁ sthirām (6.33)

Arjuna — Arjuna; uvāca — said; yo = yah — who; 'yaṁ = ayaṁ — this; yogas — yoga practices; tvayā — by you; proktaḥ — explained; sāmyena — by comparative similarity; madhusūdana — O slayer of Madhu; etasyāhaṁ = etasyā — of this + aham — I; na — not; paśyāmi — see; cañcalatvāt — due to shiftiness; sthitiṁ — position; sthirām — standard

Arjuna said: O slayer of Madhu, due to a shifty vision, I do not see this standard position of a comparatively similar view which is yielded by this yoga practice, declared by You. (6.33)

चञ्चलं हि मनः कृष्ण
प्रमाथि बलवद्दृढम् ।
तस्याहं निग्रहं मन्ये
वायोरिव सुदुष्करम् ॥६.३४॥

cañcalaṁ hi manaḥ kṛṣṇa
pramāthi balavaddṛḍham
tasyāhaṁ nigrahaṁ manye
vāyoriva suduṣkaram (6.34)

cañcalam — unsteady; hi — indeed; manaḥ — the mind; kṛṣṇa — Krishna; pramāthi — troubling; balavat — impulsive; dṛḍham — resistant; tasyāham = tasya — of it + aham — I; nigraham — controlling; manye — I think; vāyor = vāyoḥ — of the wind; iva — compared to; suduṣkaram — very difficult to accomplish

Unsteady indeed is my mind, O Krishna. It is troublesome, impulsive and resistant. I think that controlling it is comparable to controlling the wind. It is very difficult to accomplish. (6.34)

श्रीभगवानुवाच
असंशयं महाबाहो
मनो दुर्निग्रहं चलम्।
अभ्यासेन तु कौन्तेय
वैराग्येण च गृह्यते ॥६.३५॥

śrībhagavānuvāca
asaṁśayaṁ mahābāho
mano durnigrahaṁ calam
abhyāsena tu kaunteya
vairāgyeṇa ca gṛhyate (6.35)

śrībhagavān — the Blessed Lord; uvāca — said; asaṁśayam — undoubtedly; mahābāho — O powerful man; mano = manah — the mind; durnigraham — difficult to control; calam — unsteady; abhyāsena — by practice; tu — however; kaunteya — O son of Kuntī; vairāgyena — by the indifference to response; ca — and; gṛhyate — it is restrained

The Blessed Lord said: Undoubtedly, O powerful man, the mind is difficult to control. It is unsteady. By practice, however, O son of Kuntī, by indifference to its responses, also, it is restrained. (6.35)

असंयतात्मना योगो
दुष्प्राप इति मे मतिः ।
वश्यात्मना तु यतता
शक्योऽवाप्तुमुपायतः ॥ ६.३६ ॥

asaṁyatātmanā yogo
duṣprāpa iti me matiḥ
vaśyātmanā tu yatatā
śakyo'vāptumupāyataḥ (6.36)

asaṁyatātmanā = asaṁyata —indisciplined + ātmanā — by the self; yogo = yogaḥ — yoga; duṣprāpa — difficult to master; iti — thus; me — my; matiḥ — opinion; vaśyātmanā = vaśya — disciplined + ātmanā — by the self; tu — however; yatatā — by endeavor; śakyo = śakyaḥ — possible; 'vāptum = avāptum — to acquire; upāyataḥ —by effective means

For the undisciplined person, yoga is difficult to master. This is My opinion. For the disciplined one, however, by endeavor, it is possible to acquire the skill by an effective means. (6.36)

अर्जुन उवाच
अयतिः श्रद्धयोपेतो
योगाच्चलितमानसः ।
अप्राप्य योगसंसिद्धिं
कां गतिं कृष्ण गच्छति ॥ ६.३७ ॥

arjuna uvāca
ayatiḥ śraddhayopeto
yogāccalitamānasaḥ
aprāpya yogasaṁsiddhiṁ
kāṁ gatiṁ kṛṣṇa gacchati (6.37)

arjuna — Arjuna; uvāca — said; ayatiḥ — indisciplined person; śraddhayopeto = śraddhayopetaḥ = śraddhayā — by faith + upetaḥ — has got; yogāccalitamānasaḥ = yogāc (yogāt) — from yoga practice + calita — deviated + mānasaḥ — mind; aprāpya — not attain; yogasaṁsiddhiṁ — yoga proficiency; kāṁ — what; gatiṁ — course; kṛṣṇa — Krishna; gacchati — he goes

Arjuna said: What about the undisciplined person who has faith? Having deviated from yoga practice, having not attained yoga proficiency, what course does he take, O Krishna? (6.37)

कच्चिन्नोभयविभ्रष्टश्
छिन्नाभ्रमिव नश्यति ।
अप्रतिष्ठो महाबाहो
विमूढो ब्रह्मणः पथि ॥ ६.३८ ॥

kaccinnobhayavibhraṣṭaś
chinnābhramiva naśyati
apratiṣṭho mahābāho
vimūḍho brahmaṇaḥ pathi (6.38)

kaccin = kaccid — is he; nobhayavibhraṣṭaś = na — not + ubhaya — both + vibhraṣṭaḥ — lost out; chinnābhram = chinna — faded + abhram — cloud; iva — like; naśyati — lost; apratiṣṭho = apratiṣṭhaḥ — without foundation; mahābāho — O Almighty Kṛṣṇa; vimūḍho = vimūḍhaḥ — baffled; brahmaṇaḥ — of the spirituality; pathi — on the path

Is he not like a faded cloud, lost from both situations, like being without a foundation? O Almighty Krishna: He is baffled on the path of spirituality. (6.38)

एतन्मे संशयं कृष्ण
छेत्तुमर्हस्यशेषतः।
त्वदन्यः संशयस्यास्य
छेत्ता न ह्युपपद्यते ॥६.३९॥

etanme saṁśayaṁ kṛṣṇa
chettumarhasyaśeṣataḥ
tvadanyaḥ saṁśayasyāsya
chettā na hyupapadyate (6.39)

etan = etad — this; me — of mine; saṁśayam — doubt; kṛṣṇa — Krishna; chettum — remove; arhasy = arhasi — you can; aśeṣataḥ — without reminder, fully; tvadanyaḥ = besides you; saṁśayasyāsya = saṁśayasya — of doubt + asya — of this; chettā — remover of doubt; na — not; hy (hi) — indeed; upapadyate — he exists

You can, O Krishna, remove this doubt of mine fully. Besides You, no other remover of doubt, exists here. (6.39)

श्रीभगवानुवाच
पार्थ नैवेह नामुत्र
विनाशस्तस्य विद्यते ।
न हि कल्याणकृत्कश्चिद्
दुर्गतिं तात गच्छति ॥६.४०॥

śrībhagavānuvāca
pārtha naiveha nāmutra
vināśastasya vidyate
na hi kalyāṇakṛtkaścid
durgatiṁ tāta gacchati (6.40)

śrībhagavān — the Blessed Lord; uvāca — said; pārtha — O son of Pṛthā; naiveha = na — either + eva — indeed + iha — here on earth; namutra = na — nor + amutra — above in the celestial regions; vināśaḥ — loss; tasya — his; vidyate — it is realized; na — not; hy (hi) — indeed; kalyāṇakṛt — performer of pious acts; kaścid — anyone; durgatiṁ — into misfortune; tāta — O ideal one; gacchati — goes down permanently

The Blessed Lord said: O son of Pṛthā, it is realized that neither here on earth nor above in the celestial regions, does the unaccomplished yogi lose his skill. Indeed, O dear Arjuna, no performer of virtuous acts, goes down permanently into misfortune. (6.40)

प्राप्य पुण्यकृताँल्लोकान्
उषित्वा शाश्वतीः समाः ।
शुचीनां श्रीमतां गेहे
योगभ्रष्टोऽभिजायते॥६.४१॥

prāpya puṇyakṛtām̐llokān
uṣitvā śāśvatīḥ samāḥ
śucīnāṁ śrīmatāṁ gehe
yogabhraṣṭo'bhijāyate(6.41)

prāpya — obtaining; puṇyakṛtām — of the performer of virtuous acts; lokān — celestial places; uṣitvā — having lived; śāśvatīḥ — many, many; samāḥ — years; śucīnām — of the purified person; śrīmatām — of the prosperous person; gehe — in the social circumstance; yogabhraṣṭo = yogabhraṣṭaḥ — fallen from yoga; 'bhijāyate = abhijāyate — is born

After obtaining the celestial places where the virtuous souls go, having lived there for many, many years, the fallen yogi is born into the social circumstances of the purified and prosperous people. (6.41)

अथ वा योगिनामेव
कुले भवति धीमताम् ।
एतद्धि दुर्लभतरं
लोके जन्म यदीदृशम् ॥ ६.४२ ॥

atha vā yogināmeva
kule bhavati dhīmatām
etaddhi durlabhataraṁ
loke janma yadīdṛśam (6.42)

atha vā — alternately; yoginām — of the yogi; eva — indeed; kule — in the family situation; bhavati — is born; dhīmatām — of the enlightened people; etad — this; dhi = hi — indeed; durlabhataram — difficult to attain; loke — in this world; janma — birth; yad — which; īdṛśam — such

Alternately, he is born into a family of enlightened people. But such a birth is very difficult to attain in this world. (6.42)

तत्र तं बुद्धिसंयोगं
लभते पौर्वदेहिकम् ।
यतते च ततो भूयः
संसिद्धौ कुरुनन्दन ॥ ६.४३ ॥

tatra taṁ buddhisaṁyogaṁ
labhate paurvadehikam
yatate ca tato bhūyaḥ
saṁsiddhau kurunandana (6.43)

tatra — there; tam — it; buddhisaṁyogam — cumulative intellectual interest; labhate — inspired with; paurvadehikam — from a previous birth; yatate — he strives; ca — and; tato = tataḥ — from that time; bhūyaḥ — again; saṁsiddhau — to perfection; kuru-nandana — O dear son of the Kurus

In that environment, he is inspired with the cumulative intellectual interest from a previous birth. And from that time, he strives again for yoga perfection, O dear son of the Kurus. (6.43)

पूर्वाभ्यासेन तेनैव
ह्रियते ह्यवशोऽपि सः ।
जिज्ञासुरपि योगस्य
शब्दब्रह्मातिवर्तते ॥ ६.४४ ॥

pūrvābhyāsena tenaiva
hriyate hyavaśo'pi saḥ
jijñāsurapi yogasya
śabdabrahmātivartate (6.44)

pūrvābhyāsena = pūrva — previous + abhyāsena — by practice; tenaiva = tena — by it + eva — indeed; hriyate — he is motivated; hy (hi) — indeed; avaśo = avaśaḥ — without conscious desire; 'pi = api — even; saḥ — he; jijñāsuḥ — persistently inquiring; api — even; yogasya — of yoga; śabdabrahmātivartate = śabda — spoken description + brahma — spiritual reality + ativartate — instinctively sees beyond (śabdabrahma — Vedas)

Indeed, by previous practice, he is motivated, even without conscious desire. He who persistently inquires of yoga, instinctively sees beyond the Veda, the spoken description of the spiritual reality. (6.44)

प्रयत्नाद्यतमानस्तु
योगी संशुद्धकिल्बिषः ।
अनेकजन्मसंसिद्धस्
ततोयाति परां गतिम् ॥६.४५॥

prayatnādyatamānastu
yogī saṁśuddhakilbiṣaḥ
anekajanmasaṁsiddhas
tatoyāti parāṁ gatim (6.45)

prayatnāt — from steady effort; yatamānaḥ — consistently controlled; tu — but; yogī — yogi; saṁśuddha — thoroughly cleansed; kilbiṣaḥ — bad tendencies; anekajanmasaṁsiddhas = aneka — not one + janma — birth + saṁsiddhaḥ — perfected; tato = tataḥ — from then onwards; yāti — reaches; parāṁ — supreme; gatim — goal

From a steady effort and a consistently controlled mind, the yogi who is thoroughly cleansed of bad tendencies, who is perfected in many births, reaches the supreme goal. (6.45)

तपस्विभ्योऽधिको योगी
ज्ञानिभ्योऽपि मतोऽधिकः ।
कर्मिभ्यश्चाधिको योगी
तस्माद्योगी भवार्जुन ॥६.४६॥

tapasvibhyo'dhiko yogī
jñānibhyo'pi mato'dhikaḥ
karmibhyaścādhiko yogī
tasmādyogī bhavārjuna (6.46)

tapasvibhyo = tapasvibhyaḥ — to the other types of ascetics; 'dhiko = adhikaḥ — is superior; yogī — yogi; jñānibhyo = jñānibhyaḥ — to the masters of the philosophical theory; 'pi = api — also; mato = mataḥ — is considered to be; 'dhikaḥ = adhikaḥ — is superior; karmibhyaḥ — to the ritual performers; cādhiko (cādhikaḥ) = ca — and + adhikaḥ — is better than; yogī — yogi; tasmād = tasmāt — hence; yogī — yogi; bhavārjuna = bhava — be + arjuna — Arjuna

The yogi is superior to other types of ascetics; he is also considered to be superior to the masters of philosophical theory, and the yogi is better than the ritual performers. Hence, be a yogi, Arjuna. (6.46)

योगिनामपि सर्वेषां
मद्गतेनान्तरात्मना ।
श्रद्धावान्भजते यो मां
स मे युक्ततमो मतः ॥६.४७॥

yogināmapi sarveṣāṁ
madgatenāntarātmanā
śraddhāvānbhajate yo māṁ
sa me yuktatamo mataḥ (6.47)

yoginām — of the yogis; api — also; sarveṣāṁ — of all these; madgatenāntarātmanā = madgatena — attracted to me + antarātmanā — with his soul; śraddhāvān — full of faith; bhajate — worships; yo = yaḥ — who; mām — me; sa = saḥ — he; me — to me; yuktatamo = yuktatamaḥ — most devoted; mataḥ — is regarded

Of all yogis, the one who is attracted to Me with his soul, who worships Me with full faith, is regarded as being most devoted to Me. (6.47)

CHAPTER 7

Krishna: The Ultimate Reality*

श्रीभगवानुवाच
मय्यासक्तमनाः पार्थ
योगं युञ्जन्मदाश्रयः ।
असंशयं समग्रं मां
यथा ज्ञास्यसि तच्छृणु ।७.१॥

śrībhagavānuvāca
mayyāsaktamanāḥ pārtha
yogaṁ yuñjanmadāśrayaḥ
asaṁśayaṁ samagraṁ māṁ
yathā jñāsyasi tacchṛṇu (7.1)

śrībhagavān — the Blessed Lord; uvāca — said; mayy = mayi — in Me; āsaktamanāḥ — attention absorbed in; pārtha — O son of Pṛthā; yogam — yoga; yuñjan — practicing; madasrayah = mad — on me + āśrayah — being dependent; asaṁśayaṁ — without doubt; samagraṁ — fully; māṁ — Me; yathā — as; jñāsyasi — you will know; tac = tad — this; chṛṇ = śṛṇu — hear

The Blessed Lord said: With attention absorbed in Me, O son of Pṛthā, practicing yoga, being dependent on Me, you will know of Me fully without a doubt. Hear of this. (7.1)

ज्ञानं तेऽहं सविज्ञानम्
इदं वक्ष्याम्यशेषतः ।
यज्ज्ञात्वा नेह भूयोऽन्यज्
ज्ञातव्यमवशिष्यते ॥७.२.

jñānaṁ te'haṁ savijñānam
idaṁ vakṣyāmyaśeṣataḥ
yajjñātvā neha bhūyo'nyaj
jñātavyamavaśiṣyate (7.2)

jñānam- information; te — to you; 'ham = aham -I; savijñānam — with experience; idam — this; vakṣyāmy(vakṣyāmi)- I will explain; aśeṣataḥ — without deleting anything; yaj = yad — which; jñātvā — having known; neha = na — not + iha — in this world; bhūyo = bhūyaḥ — further; 'nyaj = anyat — other; jñātavyam — to be discovered; avaśiṣyate — is left

I will explain the information and give the experience to you without deleting anything. Having known that, no other experience would be left to be discovered in this world. (7.2)

मनुष्याणां सहस्त्रेषु
कश्चिद्यतति सिद्धये ।
यततामपि सिद्धानां
कश्चिन्मां वेत्ति तत्त्वतः ॥७.३॥

manuṣyāṇāṁ sahasreṣu
kaścidyatati siddhaye
yatatāmapi siddhānāṁ
kaścinmāṁ vetti tattvataḥ (7.3)

**The Mahābhārata contains no chapter headings. This title was assigned by the translator on the basis of verse 7 of this chapter.*

manuṣyāṇām — of human beings; sahasreṣu — in thousands; kaścid — someone; yatati — strives; siddhaye — to psychological perfection; yatatām — of those who endeavor; api — even; siddhānām — of those who are perfected; kaścin = kaścid — someone; mām — me; vetti — comprehends; tattvataḥ — in truth

Someone, in thousands of human beings, strives for psychological perfection. Of those who endeavor, even of those who are perfected, someone knows Me in truth. (7.3)

भूमिरापोऽनलो वायुः
खं मनो बुद्धिरेव च ।
अहंकार इतीयं मे
भिन्ना प्रकृतिरष्टधा ॥७.४॥

bhūmirāpo'nalo vāyuḥ
khaṁ mano buddhireva ca
ahaṁkāra itīyaṁ me
bhinnā prakṛtiraṣṭadhā (7.4)

bhūmir = bhūmiḥ — solid substance; āpo = āpaḥ — liquid substance; 'nalo = analaḥ — flames; vāyuḥ — gas; kham — space; mano = manaḥ — mindal energy; buddhir = buddhiḥ — intelligence; eva — indeed; ca — and; ahaṁkāra — initiative; itīyam = iti — thus + iyam — this; me — My; bhinnā — apportioned; prakṛtir = prakṛtiḥ — mundane energy; aṣṭadhā — eight-sectioned

Solid substance, liquid substance, flame, gas, space, mindal energy, intelligence, and initiative are My apportioned, eight-sectioned mundane energy. (7.4)

अपरेयमितस्त्वन्यां
प्रकृतिं विद्धि मे पराम् ।
जीवभूतां महाबाहो
ययेदं धार्यते जगत् ॥७.५॥

apareyamitastvanyāṁ
prakṛtiṁ viddhi me parām
jīvabhūtāṁ mahābāho
yayedaṁ dhāryate jagat (7.5)

apareyam = apara — inferior + iyam — this; tv = tu — but; anyām — another; prakṛtiṁ - energy; viddhi — know; me — of Me; parām — higher; jīvabhūtām — the hosts of individual spirits; mahābāho — O strong man; yayedam = yaya — through which + idam — this; dhāryate — is sustained; jagat — universe

That is inferior. But, O strong man, know of My other higher energy which consists of the hosts of individual spirits, through which this universe is sustained. (7.5)

एतद्योनीनि भूतानि
सर्वाणीत्युपधारय ।
अहं कृत्स्नस्य जगतः
प्रभवः प्रलयस्तथा ॥७.६॥

etadyonīni bhūtāni
sarvāṇītyupadhāraya
ahaṁ kṛtsnasya jagataḥ
prabhavaḥ pralayastathā (7.6)

etadyonīni = etad — this + yonīni — multiple origins; bhūtāni — the creatures; sarvāṇīty = sarvāṇi — all + ity (iti) — thus; upadhāraya — understand; aham — I; kṛtsnasya — of the entire; jagataḥ — of the universe; prabhavaḥ — cause of production; pralayaḥ — cause of the destruction; tathā — as well

This higher energy functions as the multiple origins of all creatures. Understand this. I am the cause of production as well as destruction of the entire universe. (7.6)

मत्तः परतरं नान्यत्
किंचिदस्ति धनंजय ।
मयि सर्वमिदं प्रोतं
सूत्रे मणिगणा इव ॥७.७॥

mattaḥ parataraṁ nānyat
kiṁcidasti dhanaṁjaya
mayi sarvamidaṁ protaṁ
sūtre maṇigaṇā iva (7.7)

mattaḥ — than myself; parataram — higher; nānyat = na — not + anyat — other; kiṁcid — anything; asti — is; dhanaṁjaya — O conqueror of rich countries; mayi — on Me; sarvam — all; idam — this; protam — strong; sūtre — on a thread; maṇigaṇā — pearls; iva — like

O conqueror of rich countries, no other reality is higher than Myself. All this existence relies on Me, like pearls strung on a string. (7.7)

रसोऽहमप्सु कौन्तेय
प्रभास्मि शशिसूर्ययोः ।
प्रणवः सर्ववेदेषु
शब्दः खे पौरुषं नृषु ॥७.८॥

raso'hamapsu kaunteya
prabhāsmi śaśisūryayoḥ
praṇavaḥ sarvavedeṣu
śabdaḥ khe pauruṣaṁ nṛṣu(7.8)

raso = rasaḥ — taste; 'ham = aham — I; apsu — in water; kaunteya — O son of Kuntī; prabhāsmi = prabhā — light + asmi — I am; śaśisūryayoḥ — of the sun and moon; praṇavaḥ — of the sacred syllable Om; sarvavedeṣu — in all the Vedas; śabdaḥ — sound; khe — in the atmosphere; pauruṣam — manliness; nṛṣu — in men

I am represented as taste in water, O son of Kuntī . I am signified as light in the moon and sun, as the sacred syllable Om in all the Vedas, as the sound in the atmosphere, as the manliness in men. (7.8)

पुण्यो गन्धः पृथिव्यां च
तेजश्चास्मि विभावसौ ।
जीवनं सर्वभूतेषु
तपश्चास्मि तपस्विषु ॥७.९॥

puṇyo gandhaḥ pṛthivyāṁ ca
tejaścāsmi vibhāvasau
jīvanaṁ sarvabhūteṣu
tapaścāsmi tapasviṣu (7.9)

puṇyo (puṇyaḥ)- wholesome; gandhaḥ odor; pṛthivyām- in the earth; ca - and; tejaḥ — brilliance: cāsmi= ca — and + asmi — I am; vibhavasau — in the sun; jīvanam — life; sarvabhūteṣu — in all creatures; tapaścāsmi = tapaḥ — austerity + ca — and + asmi — I am; tapasviṣu — in the ascetics

I am represented as wholesome odor in the earth. I am sensed by the brilliance in the sun, by the life in all creatures. I am indicated by the austerity of the ascetics. (7.9)

बीजं मां सर्वभूतानां विद्धि पार्थ सनातनम् । बुद्धिर्बुद्धिमतामस्मि तेजस्तेजस्विनामहम् ॥७.१०॥	bījaṁ māṁ sarvabhūtānāṁ viddhi pārtha sanātanam buddhirbuddhimatāmasmi tejastejasvināmaham (7.10)

bījam — primary cause; mām — Me; sarvabhūtānām — of all creatures; viddhi — know; pārtha — O son of Pṛtha; sanātanam — primeval; buddhir = buddhiḥ — intelligence; buddhimatām — of the geniuses; asmi — I am; tejaḥ — splendor; tejasvinām — of the splendrous things; aham — I

Know me as the primeval, primary cause of all creatures, O son of Pṛthā. I can be inferred as the intelligence of the geniuses and glimpsed by the splendor of the splendorous things. (7.10)

बलं बलवतां चाहं कामरागविवर्जितम् । धर्माविरुद्धो भूतेषु कामोऽस्मि भरतर्षभ ॥७.११	balaṁ balavatāṁ cāhaṁ kāmarāgavivarjitam dharmāviruddho bhūteṣu kāmo'smi bharatarṣabha (7.11)

balam — strength; balavatām — of the strong; cāham = ca — and + aham — I; kāmarāgavivarjitam = kāma — selfish desires + rāgavivarjitam — free from passionate urges; dharmāviruddho = dhārmaviruddhaḥ = dharma — Vedic rules of morality + aviruddhaḥ - not opposed to; bhūteṣu — in creatures; kāmo = kāmaḥ — romance; 'smi = asmi — I am; bharatarṣabha — powerful son of the Bharatas

I am indicated as the strength of the strong, which is free from selfish desire and passionate urges. I am supportive of romance which is not opposed to the Vedic rules of morality, O powerful son of the Bharata family. (7.11)

ये चैव सात्त्विका भावा राजसास्तामसाश्च ये । मत्त एवेति तान्विद्धि न त्वहं तेषु ते मयि ॥७.१२॥	ye caiva sāttvikā bhāvā rājasāstāmasāśca ye matta eveti tānviddhi na tvahaṁ teṣu te mayi (7.12)

ye — which; caiva — and indeed; sāttvikā — perceptive clarity; bhāvā — states of being; rājasāḥ — enthusiasm; tāmasāśca = tāmasāḥ — depression + ca — and; ye — which; matta — from Me; eveti = eva — indeed + iti — thus; tān — them; viddhi — know; na — not; tv = tu — but; aham — I; teṣu — in them; te — they; mayi — on Me

Regarding the states of being, which are perceptive clarity, enthusiasm, and depression, know that they are produced by Me. But I am not based in them. They are dependent on Me. (7.12)

त्रिभिर्गुणमयैर्भावैर्
एभिः सर्वमिदं जगत् ।
मोहितं नाभिजानाति
मामेभ्यः परममव्ययम् ॥७.१३॥

tribhirguṇamayairbhāvair
ebhiḥ sarvamidaṁ jagat
mohitaṁ nābhijānāti
māmebhyaḥ paramavyayam (7.13)

tribhir = tribhiḥ — by three; guṇamayair = guṇamayaiḥ — by mundane influence produced; bhāvair = bhāvaiḥ — by states of being; ebhiḥ — by these; sarvam — all; idam — this; jagat — world; mohitam — stupified; nābhijānāti = na — not + abhijānāti — recognizes; mām — Me; ebhyaḥ — than these; param — higher; avyayam — unaffected

All this world is stupefied by the three states of being, which are produced by the mundane influence. The world does not recognize Me, Who is higher than these energies and Who is unaffected. (7.13)

दैवी ह्येषा गुणमयी
मम माया दुरत्यया ।
मामेव ये प्रपद्यन्ते
मायामेतां तरन्ति ते ॥७.१४॥

daivī hyeṣā guṇamayī
mama māyā duratyayā
māmeva ye prapadyante
māyāmetāṁ taranti te (7.14)

daivī — supernatural; hy = hi — indeed; eṣā — this; guṇamayī — quality-controlled; mama — of Me; māyā — magical display; duratyayā — difficult to transcend; mām — Me; eva — indeed; ye — who; prapadyante — they rely on; māyām — bewitching energy; etām — this; taranti — they can see beyond; te — they

Indeed this quality controlled illusion of Mine is supernatural and difficult to transcend. Only those who rely on Me, can see beyond this bewitching energy. (7.14)

न मां दुष्कृतिनो मूढाः
प्रपद्यन्ते नराधमाः ।
माययापहृतज्ञाना
आसुरं भावमाश्रिताः ॥७.१५॥

na māṁ duṣkṛtino mūḍhāḥ
prapadyante narādhamāḥ
māyayāpahṛtajñānā
āsuraṁ bhāvamāśritāḥ (7.15)

na — not; mām — Me; duṣkṛtino = duṣkṛtinaḥ — evil-doers; mūḍhāḥ — confused; prapadyante — they take shelter; narādhamāḥ — lowest of human beings; māyayāpahṛtajñānā = māyayā — by misconception + apahṛta — erased + jñānā — discrimination; āsuram — corrupted; bhāvam — existence; āśritāḥ — attached

The confused evildoers, the lowest of human beings, those whose discrimination is erased by misconceptions, do not take shelter of Me. They are attached to a corrupted existence. (7.15)

चतुर्विधा भजन्ते मां
जनाः सुकृतिनोऽर्जुन ।
आर्तो जिज्ञासुरर्थार्थी
ज्ञानी च भरतर्षभ ॥७.१६॥

caturvidhā bhajante māṁ
janāḥ sukṛtino'rjuna
ārto jijñāsurarthārthī
jñānī ca bharatarṣabha (7.16)

caturvidhā — four kinds; bhajante — worship; mām — Me; janāḥ — people; sukṛtino = sukṛtinaḥ — good people; 'rjuna = arjuna — Arjuna; ārto = ārtaḥ — distressed person; jijñāsur = jijñāsuḥ — inquisitive person; arthārthī — needy person; jñānī — informed person; ca — and; bharatarṣabha — O bullish man of the Bharata family

Four kinds of good people worship Me, O Arjuna: the distressed one, the inquisitive one, the needy one, and the informed one, O bullish man of the Bharata family. (7.16)

तेषां ज्ञानी नित्ययुक्त
एकभक्तिर्विशिष्यते ।
प्रियो हि ज्ञानिनोऽत्यर्थम्
अहं स च मम प्रियः ॥७.१७॥

teṣāṁ jñānī nityayukta
ekabhaktirviśiṣyate
priyo hi jñānino'tyartham
ahaṁ sa ca mama priyaḥ (7.17)

teṣām — of these; jñānī — the informed man; nityayukta — constantly disciplined in yoga; ekabhaktir = ekabhaktiḥ — one who is singularly devoted; viśiṣyate — is distinguished; priyo = priyaḥ — fond; hi — indeed; jñānino = jñāninaḥ — of the informed person; 'tyartham = atyartham — very; aham — I; sa = sah — he; ca — and; mama — of Me; priyaḥ — fond

Of these, the informed man who is constantly disciplined in yoga, being singularly devoted, is distinguished indeed. I am fond of this person and he is fond of Me. (7.17)

उदाराः सर्व एवैते
ज्ञानी त्वात्मैव मे मतम् ।
आस्थितः स हि युक्तात्मा
मामेवानुत्तमां गतिम् ॥७.१८॥

udārāḥ sarva evaite
jñānī tvātmaiva me matam
āsthitaḥ sa hi yuktātmā
māmevānuttamāṁ gatim (7.18)

udārāḥ — exalted; sarva — all; evaite = eva — indeed + ete — these; jñānī — informed person; tv = tu — but; ātmaiva = ātmā — personal self + eva — indeed; me — of Me; matam — is considered; āsthitaḥ — situated with; sa = saḥ — he; hi — truly; yuktātmā — one who is disciplined in yoga practice; mām — Me; evānuttamām = eva — indeed + anuttamām — supreme; gatim — objective

All these are exalted people. But the informed one is considered to be my personal representative. Indeed, he who is disciplined in yoga practice, is situated with Me as the Supreme Objective. (7.18)

बहूनां जन्मनामन्ते
ज्ञानवान्मां प्रपद्यते ।
वासुदेवः सर्वमिति
स महात्मा सुदुर्लभः ॥७.१९॥

bahūnāṁ janmanāmante
jñānavānmāṁ prapadyate
vāsudevaḥ sarvamiti
sa mahātmā sudurlabhaḥ (7.19)

bahūnām — of many; janmanām — of births; ante — at the end; jñānavān — the informed devotee; mām — Me; prapadyate — surrenders to; vāsudevaḥ — son of Vasudeva; sarvam — everything; iti — thus; sa = saḥ — he; mahātmā — great soul; sudurlabhaḥ — hard to locate

At the end of many births, the informed devotee surrenders to Me, thinking that the son of Vasudeva is essential to everything. Such a great soul is hard to locate. (7.19)

कामैस्तैस्तैर्हृतज्ञानाः
प्रपद्यन्तेऽन्यदेवताः ।
तं तं नियममास्थाय
प्रकृत्या नियताः स्वया ॥७.२०॥

kāmaistaistairhṛtajñānāḥ
prapadyante'nyadevatāḥ
taṁ taṁ niyamamāsthāya
prakṛtyā niyatāḥ svayā (7.20)

kāmaiḥ — by desires; taistair = taihtaiḥ — by whose, by these, contrary; hṛtajñānāḥ — persons whose experience is overshadowed; prapadyante — they plead with; 'nyadevatāḥ = anyadevatāḥ = anya — other + devatāḥ — supernatural rulers; taṁtam — this or that; niyamam — religious procedures; āsthāya — following; prakṛtyā — by material nature; niyatāḥ — restricted; svayā — by their own

Persons whose experience was overshadowed by contrary desires, plead with other supernatural rulers, following this or that religious procedure, being restricted by their own material nature. (7.20)

यो यो यां यां तनुं भक्तः
श्रद्धयार्चितुमिच्छति ।
तस्य तस्याचलां श्रद्धां
तामेव विदधाम्यहम् ॥६.२१॥

yo yo yāṁ yāṁ tanuṁ bhaktaḥ
śraddhayārcitumicchati
tasya tasyācalāṁ śraddhāṁ
tāmeva vidadhāmyaham (7.21)

yo yo = yaḥ yaḥ — whoever; yāṁ yām- whatever; tanum — deity form; bhaktaḥ - devotedly worship; śraddhayārcitum = śraddhayā — with belief + arcitum — to worship; icchati - desires; tasya — of him; tasya — of him + acalām - unwavering; śraddhām — confidence; tām — it; eva — indeed; vidadhāmy = vidadhāmi — allow; aham — I

I grant unwavering faith to anyone, who with belief, wants to worship any worshipable deity form. (7.21)

स तया श्रद्धया युक्तस् तस्या राधनमीहते । लभते च ततः कामान् मयैव विहितान्हि तान् ॥७.२२॥	sa tayā śraddhayā yuktas tasyā rādhanamīhate labhate ca tataḥ kāmān mayaiva vihitānhi tān (7.22)

sa = saḥ — he; tayā — with this; śraddhayā — by faith; yuktaḥ — endowed; tasyārādhanam = tasya — of this + ārādhanam — worshipfully petitioning a deity; īhate — thinks of; labhate — gets; ca — and; tataḥ — from that; kāmān — desires; mayaiva = maya — by Me + eva — indeed; vihitān — permitted; hi — truly; tān — them

Being endowed with this confidence, he thinks of worshipfully petitioning the deity and gets from that source, his desires, as those fulfillments are permitted by Me. (7.22)

अन्तवत्तु फलं तेषां तद्भवत्यल्पमेधसाम् । देवान्देवयजो यान्ति मद्भक्ता यान्ति मामपि ॥७.२३॥	antavattu phalaṁ teṣāṁ tadbhavatyalpamedhasām devāndevayajo yānti madbhaktā yānti māmapi (7.23)

antavat — something with an end, short-lived; tu — but; phalam — results; teṣām — of them; tad — this; bhavaty = bhavati — it is; alpamedhasām — of those with little intelligence; devān — supernatural rulers; devayajo = devayajaḥ — those who worship the supernatural rulers; yānti — go; madbhaktā — those who worship Me; yānti — go; mām — to Me; api — surely

But for those with little intelligence, the result is short-lived. The worshippers of the supernatural rulers go to those gods. Those who worship Me, surely go to Me. (7.23)

अव्यक्तं व्यक्तिमापन्नं मन्यन्ते मामबुद्धयः । परं भावमजानन्तो ममाव्ययमनुत्तमम् ॥७.२४॥	avyaktaṁ vyaktimāpannaṁ manyante māmabuddhayaḥ paraṁ bhāvamajānanto mamāvyayamanuttamam (7.24)

avyaktam — that which is beyond the sensual range; vyaktim — that which is grossly perceived; āpannam — within range, limited; manyante — they think; mām — Me; abuddhayaḥ — unintelligent ones; param — higher; bhāvam — being; ajānanto = ajānantaḥ — not realizing; mamāvyayam = mama — of Me + avyayam — imperishable; anuttamam — supermost

Though I am beyond their sensual range, the unintelligent think of Me as being limited to their gross perception. They do not realize My higher existence which is imperishable and supermost. (7.24)

नाहं प्रकाशः सर्वस्य
योगमायासमावृतः ।
मूढोऽयं नाभिजानाति
लोको मामजमव्ययम् ॥७.२५॥

nāhaṁ prakāśaḥ sarvasya
yogamāyāsamāvṛtaḥ
mūḍho'yaṁ nābhijānāti
loko māmajamavyayam (7.25)

nāham = na — not + aham — I; prakāśaḥ — visible; sarvasya — of everyone; yogamāyāsamāvṛtaḥ = yoga — yogically self-controlled + māyā — mystic power + samāvṛtaḥ — shielded; mūḍho = mūḍhaḥ — stupified; 'yam = ayam — this; nābhijānāti = na — not + abhijānāti — recognizes; loko = lokaḥ — population; mām — Me; ajam — not subjected to birth shocks; avyayam — not liable to existential pressures of change

I am not visible to everyone, because I am shielded by My yogicly, self-controlled mystic powers. This stupefied population does not recognize Me as not being subjected to shocks of birth and not being liable to existential pressures of change. (7.25)

वेदाहं समतीतानि
वर्तमानानि चार्जुन ।
भविष्याणि च भूतानि
मां तु वेद न कश्चन ॥७.२६॥

vedāhaṁ samatītāni
vartamānāni cārjuna
bhaviṣyāṇi ca bhūtāni
māṁ tu veda na kaścana (7.26)

vedāham = veda — know + aham — I; samatītāni — the departed souls; vartamānāni — the living creatures; cārjuna = ca — and + arjuna — Arjuna; bhaviṣyāni — those who are to be born; ca — and; bhūtāni — creatures; mām — Me; tu — but; veda — recognizes; na — not; kaścana — anyone

I know the departed souls and the living creatures, O Arjuna, as well as those beings who are to be born. But no one recognizes Me. (7.26)

इच्छाद्वेषसमुत्थेन
द्वंद्वमोहेन भारत ।
सर्वभूतानि संमोहं
सर्गे यान्ति परंतप ॥७.२७॥

icchādveṣasamutthena
dvaṁdvamohena bhārata
sarvabhūtāni saṁmohaṁ
sarge yānti paraṁtapa (7.27)

icchādveṣasamutthena = icchā — liking + dveṣa — disliking + samutthena — through the urge; dvandvamohena = dvandva — two-fold sensuality + mohena — by the delusive influence; bhārata — O man of the Bharata family; sarvabhūtāni — all beings; saṁmoham — delusion; sarge — at the beginning of the creation; yānti — they are influenced by; paraṁtapa — O scorcher of the enemy

O man of the Bharata family, at the beginning of any creation, all beings are influenced by delusion through the urge of liking or disliking and by the delusive influence of the two-fold sensuality. So it is, O scorcher of the enemy. (7.27)

येषां त्वन्तगतं पापं
जनानां पुण्यकर्मणाम् ।
ते द्वंद्वमोहनिर्मुक्ता
भजन्ते मां दृढव्रताः ॥७.२८॥

yeṣāṁ tvantagataṁ pāpaṁ
janānāṁ puṇyakarmaṇām
te dvaṁdvamohanirmuktā
bhajante māṁ dṛḍhavratāḥ (7.28)

yeṣām — of whom; tv = tu — but; antagatam = anta — terminated + gatam — gone; pāpam — sinful propensity; janānām — of people; puṇyakarmaṇām — of persons of righteous actions; te — they; dvandvamohanirmukta = dvandva — two-fold + moha — delusion + nirmuktā — free from; bhajante — worship; mām — Me; dṛḍhavratāḥ — those who maintain firm vows of austerity

But those people whose sinful propensities are terminated, whose actions are righteous, who are free from the two-fold delusion, who are maintaining firm vows of austerity, do worship Me. (7.28)

जरामरणमोक्षाय
मामाश्रित्य यतन्ति ये ।
ते ब्रह्म तद्विदुः कृत्स्नम्
अध्यात्मं कर्म चाखिलम् ॥७.२९॥

jarāmaraṇamokṣāya
māmāśritya yatanti ye
te brahma tadviduḥ kṛtsnam
adhyātmaṁ karma cākhilam (7.29)

jarāmaraṇamokṣāya = jarā — bodily deterioration + maraṇa — bodily death + mokṣāya — to permanent release; mām — Me; āśritya — being dependent; yatanti — strive; ye — who; te — they; brahma — spiritual existence; tad — this; viduḥ — they know; kṛtsnam — complete; adhyātmam — Supreme Self; karma — cultural activity; cākhilam = ca — and + akhilam — entirely

Those who, being dependent on Me, strive for permanent release from bodily deterioration and death, know this spiritual existence completely, as well as the Supreme Spirit and the value of cultural activity. (7.29)

साधिभूताधिदैवं मां
साधियज्ञं च ये विदुः ।
प्रयाणकालेऽपि च मां
ते विदुर्युक्तचेतसः ॥७.३०॥

sādhibhūtādhidaivaṁ māṁ
sādhiyajñaṁ ca ye viduḥ
prayāṇakāle'pi ca māṁ
te viduryuktacetasaḥ (7.30)

sādhibhūtādhidaivam = sa — with + adhibhūta — Lord of mundane beings + adhidaivam — Lord of the supernatural rulers and powers; mām — Me; sādhiyajñam = sa — with + adhiyajñam — Supreme Master of religious discipline; ca — and; ye — who; viduḥ — they know; prayāṇakāle — at the time of final departure from the body; 'pi = api — even; ca — and; mām —

Me; te — they; vidur = viduḥ — know; yuktacetasaḥ — those with concentrated mental focus

Those who know Me as the Lord of mundane beings, Lord of the supernatural rulers and powers, and Supreme Master of religious disciplines, and who know Me even at the time of the final departure from the body, are the ones who know Me with concentrated mental focus. (7.30)

CHAPTER 8

Another Invisible Existence*

अर्जुन उवाच
किं तद्ब्रह्म किमध्यात्मं
किं कर्म पुरुषोत्तम ।
अधिभूतं च किं प्रोक्तम्
अधिदैवं किमुच्यते ॥८.१॥

arjuna uvāca
kiṁ tadbrahma kimadhyātmaṁ
kiṁ karma puruṣottama
adhibhūtaṁ ca kiṁ proktam
adhidaivaṁ kimucyate (8.1)

arjuna — Arjuna; uvāca — said; kim — what; tad — this; brahma — spiritual reality; kim — what; adhyātmam — Supreme Soul; kim — what; karma — cultural activity; puruṣottama — Supermost Personality; adhibhūtam — sum total gross reality; ca — and; kim — what; proktam — authoritatively described as; adhidaivam — Supreme Supernatural Person and Power; kim — what; ucyate — is described

Arjuna said: What is this spiritual reality? What is the Supreme Soul? What is cultural activity, O Supermost Personality? Concerning the sum total gross reality, how is that described authoritatively? And speaking of the Supreme Supernatural Person and Power, what is that described to be? (8.1)

अधियज्ञः कथं कोऽत्र
देहेऽस्मिन्मधुसूदन ।
प्रयाणकाले च कथं
ज्ञेयोऽसि नियतात्मभिः ॥८.२॥

adhiyajñaḥ kathaṁ ko'tra
dehe'sminmadhusūdana
prayāṇakāle ca kathaṁ
jñeyo'si niyatātmabhiḥ (8.2)

adhiyajñaḥ — Supreme Regulator of religious ceremonies and disciplines; katham — how; ko = kaḥ — who; 'tra = atra — here; dehe — in the body; 'smin = asmin — in this; madhusūdana — O slayer of Madhu; prayāṇakāle — at the time of departure from the body; ca — and; katham — how; jñeyo = jñeyaḥ - to be known; 'si = asi — you are; niyatātmabhiḥ = niyata — subdued + ātmabhiḥ — by persons

Who is the Supreme Regulator of religious ceremonies and disciplines? How is He located here in this body, O killer of Madhu? And how, at the time of departure from the body, are You to be known by those persons who are subdued? (8.2)

**The Mahābhārata contains no chapter headings. This title was assigned by the translator on the basis of the verse above*

श्रीभगवानुवाच
अक्षरं ब्रह्म परमं
स्वभावोऽध्यात्ममुच्यते ।
भूतभावोद्भवकरो
विसर्गः कर्मसंज्ञितः ॥८.३॥

śrībhagavānuvāca
akṣaraṁ brahma paramaṁ
svabhāvo'dhyātmamucyate
bhūtabhāvodbhavakaro
visargaḥ karmasaṁjñitaḥ (8.3)

śrībhagavān — the Blessed Lord; uvāca — said; akṣaram — unaffected; brahma — spiritual reality; paramam — supreme; svabhāvo = svabhāvaḥ — personal nature; 'dhyātmam = adhyātmam — supreme soul; ucyate — it is said; bhūtabhāvodbhavakaro = bhūtabhāva — existence of mundane forms + udbhava — production + karo (karaḥ) — causing; visargah — creative power; karmasaṁjñitaḥ = karma — cultural activity + saṁjñitaḥ — is known

The Blessed Lord said: The spiritual reality is unaffected and supreme. The Supreme Soul is described as a personal existence Who causes the production of the mundane world. Cultural action is known as creative power. (8.3)

अधिभूतं क्षरो भावः
पुरुषश्चाधिदैवतम् ।
अधियज्ञोऽहमेवात्र
देहे देहभृतां वर ॥८.४॥

adhibhūtaṁ kṣaro bhāvaḥ
puruṣaścādhidaivatam
adhiyajño'hamevātra
dehe dehabhṛtāṁ vara (8.4)

adhibhūtam — sum total gross reality; kṣaro = kṣaraḥ — ever-changing; bhāvaḥ — nature; puruṣaścādhidaivatam = puruṣa — master of the world + ca — and + adhidaivatam — Lord of the Supernatural rulers and powers; adhiyajño = adhiyajñaḥ — the Supreme Regulator of religious ceremonies and disciplines; 'ham = aham — I; evātra = eva — indeed + atra — here; dehe — in the body; dehabhṛtām vara — O best of the embodied souls

The sum total gross reality is ever-changing nature. The master of the world is the Lord of the supernatural rulers and powers. O best of the embodied souls, I, Who exist here in the body, am the Supreme Regulator of religious ceremonies and disciplines. (8.4)

अन्तकाले च मामेव
स्मरन्मुक्त्वा कलेवरम् ।
यः प्रयाति स मद्भावं
याति नास्त्यत्र संशयः ॥८.५॥

antakāle ca māmeva
smaranmuktvā kalevaram
yaḥ prayāti sa madbhāvaṁ
yāti nāstyatra saṁśayaḥ (8.5)

antakāle — at the end of life; ca — and; mām — Me; eva — in particular; smaran — remembering; muktvā — giving up; kalevaram — body; yaḥ — who; prayāti — departs the body; sa = saḥ — he; madbhāvam — My condition of existence; yāti — is elevated; nāsty (nasti) = na — not + asti — is; atra — here; saṁśayaḥ — doubt

If at the end of one's life, one recalls Me in particular, as one gives up the body, one is elevated to My condition of existence. There is no doubt about this. (8.5)

यं यं वापि स्मरन्भावं त्यजत्यन्ते कलेवरम् । तं तमेवैति कौन्तेय सदा तद्भावभावितः ॥८.६॥	yaṁ yaṁ vāpi smaranbhāvaṁ tyajatyante kalevaram taṁ tamevaiti kaunteya sadā tadbhāvabhāvitaḥ (8.6)

yaṁ yam - whatever; vāpi = va — or + api — also; moreover; smaran — recalling; bhāvam — texture of existence; tyajaty = tyajati — abandons; ante — in the end; kalevaram - the body; taṁtam - that that; evaiti = eva - indeed + eti — is projected; kaunteya - O son of Kuntī; sadā - always; tad — that + bhāva — status of life + bhāvitaḥ — being transformed

Moreover, whatever texture of existence is recalled when a person abandons his body in the end, to that same type of life, he is projected, O son of Kuntī, always being transformed into that status of life. (8.6)

तस्मात्सर्वेषु कालेषु मामनुस्मर युध्य च । मय्यर्पितमनोबुद्धिर् मामेवैष्यस्यसंशयः ॥८.७॥	tasmātsarveṣu kāleṣu māmanusmara yudhya ca mayyarpitamanobuddhir māmevaiṣyasyasaṁśayaḥ (8.7)

tasmāt — therefore; sarveṣu — at all; kāleṣu — at times; mām — Me; anusmara — remember; yudhya — fight; ca — and; mayy = mayi — on Me; arpitamanobuddhir (arpitamanobuddhiḥ) = arpita — anchor + manobuddhiḥ — mind and intelligence; mām — to Me; evaiṣyasy (evaiṣyasi) = eva — indeed + eṣyasi — will be with; asaṁśayaḥ — without doubt

Therefore, at all times, remember Me and fight. Anchor your mind and intelligence on Me. You will be with Me without doubt. (8.7)

अभ्यासयोगयुक्तेन चेतसा नान्यगामिना । परमं पुरुषं दिव्यं याति पार्थानुचिन्तयन् ॥८.८॥	abhyāsayogayuktena cetasā nānyagāminā paramaṁ puruṣaṁ divyaṁ yāti pārthānucintayan (8.8)

abhyāsa — practice;. yoga — yoga; yuktena — by discipline; cetasā — by the mind; nānyagāminā = na — not + anya —other + gāminā — by venturing outward; paramam — supreme; puruṣam — person; divyam — divine; yāti — one goes; pārthānucintayan = pārtha — son of Pṛthā + anucintayan — deeply meditating

With a mind that does not venture outwards, which is disciplined by yoga practice, a person goes to the divine Supreme Person, while deeply meditating, O son of Pṛthā. (8.8)

कविं पुराणमनुशासितारम्
अणोरणीयांसमनुस्मरेद्यः ।
सर्वस्य धातारमचिन्त्यरूपम्
आदित्यवर्णं तमसः परस्तात् ॥८.९॥

kaviṁ purāṇamanuśāsitāram
aṇoraṇīyāṁsamanusmaredyaḥ
sarvasya dhātāram acintyarūpam
ādityavarṇaṁ tamasaḥ parastāt (8.9)

kavim — the person who knows everything; purāṇam — the most ancient; anuśāsitāram — the supreme supervisor; aṇor (aṇoḥ)- than the atom; aṇīyāṁsam — more minute; anusmared (anusmaret)- should meditate on; yaḥ — who; sarvasya — of all; dhātāram — supporter; acintya — unimaginable + rūpam — form; ādityavarṇam = āditya —radiance + varṇam — category; tamasaḥ — grossness; parastāt — distinct form

He who meditates on the Person Who knows everything, the most ancient of people, the Supreme Supervisor, the most minute factor, the one with unimaginable form, with a radiant body, free of grossness, (8.9)

प्रयाणकाले मनसाचलेन
भक्त्या युक्तो योगबलेन चैव ।
भ्रुवोर्मध्ये प्राणमावेश्य सम्यक्
स तं परं पुरुषमुपैति दिव्यम्
॥८.१०॥

prayāṇakāle manasācalena
bhaktyā yukto yogabalena caiva
bhruvormadhye prāṇam āveśya samyak
sa taṁ paraṁ puruṣamupaiti divyam
(8.10)

prayāṇakāle — at the time of death; manasācalena = manasā — by the mind + acalena- by unwavering; bhaktyā — with devotion; yukto = yuktaḥ — connected; yogabalena — with psychological power developed through yoga practice; caiva = ca — and + eva — indeed; bhruvor = bhruvoḥ — of the two eyebrows; madhye — in the middle; prāṇam — energizing breath; āveśya- having caused to enter; samyak — precisely; sa = saḥ — he; tam - this; param — supreme; puruṣam- person; upaiti — he goes; divyam — divine

...and that meditator who even at the time of death, with an unwavering mind, being connected devotedly, with psychological power developed through yoga practice, and having caused the energizing breath to enter between the eyebrows with precision, goes to the Divine Supreme Person. (8.10)

यदक्षरं वेदविदो वदन्ति
विशन्ति यद्यतयो वीतरागाः ।
यदिच्छन्तो ब्रह्मचर्यं चरन्ति
तत्ते पदं संग्रहेण प्रवक्ष्ये ॥८.११॥

yadakṣaraṁ vedavido vadanti
viśanti yadyatayo vītarāgāḥ
yadicchanto brahmacaryaṁ caranti
tatte padaṁ saṁgraheṇa pravakṣye (8.11)

yad — which; akṣaram — imperishable; vedavido = vedavidaḥ — knowers of the Veda; vadanti — they described; viśanti — they enter; yad — which; yatayo = yatayaḥ — ascetics; vītarāgāḥ — free from cravings; yad — which; icchanto = icchantaḥ — desiring; brahmacaryam — life of celibacy; caranti — they follow; tat = tad — this; te — to you; padam — process; saṁgraheṇa — in brief; pravakṣye — I will explain

I will briefly explain the process to you, which the knowers of the Veda describe as imperishable, which the ascetics who are free from cravings enter and who desiring to be transferred there, they follow a life of celibacy. (8.11)

सर्वद्वाराणि संयम्य
मनो हृदि निरुध्य च ।
मूर्ध्न्याधायात्मनः प्राणम्
आस्थितो योगधारणाम् ॥८.१२॥

sarvadvārāṇi saṁyamya
mano hṛdi nirudhya ca
mūrdhnyādhāyātmanaḥ prāṇam
āsthito yogadhāraṇām (8.12)

sarvadvārāṇi = sarva — all + dvārāṇi — entrances; saṁyamya — controlling; mano = manaḥ — mind; hṛdi — in the core of consciousness; nirudhya — confining; ca — and; mūrdhny = mūrdhni — in the brain; ādhāyātmanaḥ = ādhāya — situating + ātmanaḥ — of the soul; prāṇam — energizing breath; āsthito = āsthitaḥ — remain fixed; yogadhāraṇām — yoga concentration

Controlling all openings of the body, and restricting the mind in the core of consciousness, situating the energizing energy of the soul in the brain, remaining fixed in yoga concentration, (8.12)

ओमित्येकाक्षरं ब्रह्म
व्याहरन्मामनुस्मरन् ।
यः प्रयाति त्यजन्देहं
स याति परमां गतिम् ॥८.१३॥

omityekākṣaraṁ brahma
vyāharanmāmanusmaran
yaḥ prayāti tyajandehaṁ
sa yāti paramāṁ gatim (8.13)

om — the uttered sound om; ity = iti — thus saying; ekākṣaram — one syllable; brahma — spiritual reality; vyāharan — chanting; mām — Me; anusmaran — meditating on; yaḥ — who; prayāti — passes on; tyajan — renouncing; deham — body; sa = saḥ — he; yāti — attains; paramām — supreme; gatim — objective

...uttering Om, the one-syllable sound which represents the spiritual reality, meditating on Me, the yogi who passes on, renouncing the body, attains the highest objective. (8.13)

अनन्यचेताः सततं
यो मां स्मरति नित्यशः ।
तस्याहं सुलभः पार्थ
नित्ययुक्तस्य योगिनः ॥८.१४॥

ananyacetāḥ satataṁ
yo māṁ smarati nityaśaḥ
tasyāhaṁ sulabhaḥ pārtha
nityayuktasya yoginaḥ (8.14)

ananyacetāḥ — one whose mind does not go to another focus; satatam — perpetually; yo = yaḥ — who; mām — Me; smarati — he remembers; nityaśaḥ — constantly; tasyāham = tasya — to him + aham — I; sulabhaḥ — easy to reach; pārtha — O son of Pṛthā; nityayuktasya — of one who is constantly disciplined in yoga; yoginaḥ — of the devotee

He whose mind does not go to another focus at any time, who thinks of Me constantly, for that yogi who is constantly disciplined in yoga, I am easy to reach, O son of Pṛthā. (8.14)

मामुपेत्य पुनर्जन्म
दुःखालयमशाश्वतम् ।
नाप्नुवन्ति महात्मानः
संसिद्धिं परमां गताः ॥८.१५॥

māmupetya punarjanma
duḥkhālayamaśāśvatam
nāpnuvanti mahātmānaḥ
saṁsiddhiṁ paramāṁ gatāḥ (8.15)

mām — Me; upetya — approaching; punarjanma — rebirth; duḥkhālayam = duḥkha — misery + ālayam — location; aśāśvatam — shifty; nāpnuvanti = na — not + apnuvanti — subjected to; mahātmānaḥ — great souls; saṁsiddhim — perfect; paramām — supreme; gatāḥ — gone

Approaching me in this way, those great souls who went to supreme perfection are not subjected to rebirth in this shifty, miserable location. (8.15)

आ ब्रह्मभुवनाल्लोकाः
पुनरावर्तिनोऽर्जुन ।
मामुपेत्य तु कौन्तेय
पुनर्जन्म न विद्यते ॥८.१६॥

ā brahmabhuvanāllokāḥ
punarāvartino'rjuna
māmupetya tu kaunteya
punarjanma na vidyate (8.16)

ā — up to; brahmabhuvanāl = brahmabhuvanāt — to Brahmā's world; lokāḥ — populations; punarāvartino = punarāvartinaḥ — subjected to repeated birth and death; 'rjuna = arjuna — Arjuna; mām — Me; upetya — approaching; tu — but; kaunteya — O son of Kuntī; punarjanma — impulsion of rebirth; na — not; vidyate — is experienced

Up to Brahmā's world, the populations are subjected to repeated births and deaths, O Arjuna. But in approaching Me, rebirth is not experienced, O son of Kuntī. (8.16)

सहस्रयुगपर्यन्तम्
अहर्यद्ब्रह्मणो विदुः ।
रात्रिं युगसहस्रान्तां
तेऽहोरात्रविदो जनाः ॥८.१७॥

sahasrayugaparyantam
aharyadbrahmaṇo viduḥ
rātriṁ yugasahasrāntāṁ
te'horātravido janāḥ (8.17)

sahasra — one thousand + yuga — time cycle + paryantam — limit; ahar — day; yad — which; brahmaṇo = brahmaṇaḥ — of Brahmā; viduḥ — they know;

rātrim — night; yugasahasrāntāṁ = yuga — time cycle + sahasra — one thousand + antam — end; te — they; 'horātravido (ahoratravidaḥ) = ahoratra — day and night + vidaḥ — knowers; janāḥ — people

Those who know the day of Brahmā, which has a limit of one thousand time cycles, and the night of Brahmā, which ends in a thousand time cycles, are the people who know day and night. (8.17)

अव्यक्ताद्व्यक्तयः सर्वाः
प्रभवन्त्यहरागमे ।
रात्र्यागमे प्रलीयन्ते
तत्रैवाव्यक्तसंज्ञके ॥८.१८॥

avyaktādvyaktayaḥ sarvāḥ
prabhavantyaharāgame
rātryāgame pralīyante
tatraivāvyaktasaṁjñake (8.18)

avyaktād = avyaktāt — from the invisible world; vyaktayaḥ — the visible world; sarvāḥ — all; prabhavanty = prabhavanti — they are produced; aharāgame — at the beginning of Brahma's day; rātryāgame — at the beginning of Brahma's night; pralīyante — they are reverted back; tatraivāvyaktasaṁjñake = tatra — at the time + eva — indeed + avyakta — invisible world + saṁjñake — is understood as

When the day of Creator Brahmā begins, all this visible world is produced from the invisible world. When his night comes, the manifested energies are reverted back into the invisible world. (8.18)

भूतग्रामः स एवायं
भूत्वा भूत्वा प्रलीयते ।
रात्र्यागमेऽवशः पार्थ
प्रभवत्यहरागमे ॥८.१९॥

bhūtagrāmaḥ sa evāyaṁ
bhūtvā bhūtvā pralīyate
rātryāgame'vaśaḥ pārtha
prabhavatyaharāgame (8.19)

bhūtagrāmaḥ — multitude of beings; sa = saḥ — this; evāyam = eva — indeed + ayam — this; bhūtvā bhūtvā — repeatedly manifesting; pralīyate — is shifted out of visibility; rātryāgame — at the arrival of Brahma's night; 'vaśaḥ = avaśaḥ — happening naturally; pārtha — O son of Pṛthā; prabhavaty = prabhavati — it comes into existence; aharāgame — on the onset of Brahma's day

O son of Pṛthā, this multitude of beings which is repeatedly manifested, is naturally shifted out of visibility at the arrival of each of Brahmā's nights. It again comes into existence at the onset of Brahmā's day. (8.19)

परस्तस्मात्तु भावोऽन्यो
ऽव्यक्तोऽव्यक्तात्सनातनः ।
यः स सर्वेषु भूतेषु
नश्यत्सु न विनश्यति ॥८.२०॥

parastasmāttu bhāvo'nyo
'vyakto'vyaktātsanātanaḥ
yaḥ sa sarveṣu bhūteṣu
naśyatsu na vinaśyati (8.20)

paraḥ — high; tasmāt — than this; tu — but; bhāvo = bhāvaḥ — existence; 'nyo = anyaḥ — another; 'vyakto = avyaktaḥ — invisible; 'vyaktāt = avyaktāt — than the unmanifest state of the dissolvable creation; sanātanaḥ — primeval; yaḥ = which; sa = saḥ — it; sarveṣu — in all; bhūteṣu — in creation; naśyatsu — in the disintegration; na — not; vinaśyati — is disintegrated

But higher than this, there is another invisible existence, which is higher than the primeval unmanifested states of this dissolvable creation. When all these creatures are disintegrated, that is not affected. (8.20)

अव्यक्तोऽक्षर इत्युक्तस्
तमाहुः परमां गतिम् ।
यं प्राप्य न निवर्तन्ते
तद्धाम परमं मम ॥८.२१॥

avyakto'kṣara ityuktas
tamāhuḥ paramāṁ gatim
yaṁ prāpya na nivartante
taddhāma paramaṁ mama (8.21)

avyakto = avyaktaḥ — invisible world; 'kṣara = akṣara — unalterable; ity = iti — thus; uktaḥ — is declared; tam — it; āhuḥ — authorities say; paramām — supreme; gatim — objective; yam — which; prāpya — attaining; na — not; nivartante — return here; tad — that; dhāma — residence; paramam — supreme; mama — My

That invisible world is unalterable, so it is declared. The authorities say that it is the supreme objective. Attaining that, they do not return here. That place is My supreme residence. (8.21)

पुरुषः स परः पार्थ
भक्त्या लभ्यस्त्वनन्यया ।
यस्यान्तःस्थानि भूतानि
येन सर्वमिदं ततम् ॥८.२२॥

puruṣaḥ sa paraḥ pārtha
bhaktyā labhyastvananyayā
yasyāntaḥsthāni bhūtāni
yena sarvamidaṁ tatam (8.22)

puruṣaḥ — person; sa = saḥ — this; paraḥ — supreme; pārtha — O son of Pṛthā; bhaktyā — by a devotional relationship; labhyaḥ — attainable; tv = tu — but; ananyayā — not by any other; yasyāntaḥsthāni = yasya — of which + antaḥsthāni — existing within; bhūtāni — beings; yena — by which; sarvam — all; idam — this; tatam — energized

That Supreme Person, O son of Pṛthā, is attainable through a devotional relationship and not by any other means. Within His influence, all beings exist. By Him, all the universe is energized. (8.22)

यत्र काले त्वनावृत्तिम्
आवृत्तिं चैव योगिनः ।
प्रयाता यान्ति तं कालं
वक्ष्यामि भरतर्षभ ॥८.२३॥

yatra kāle tvanāvṛttim
āvṛttiṁ caiva yoginaḥ
prayātā yānti taṁ kālaṁ
vakṣyāmi bharatarṣabha (8.23)

yatra — where; kāle — in time; tv = tu — but; anāvṛttim — not return; āvṛttim — return; caiva = ca — and + eva — indeed; yoginaḥ — yogis; prayātā — departing; yānti — go; tam — this; kālam — time; vakṣyāmi — I will tell; bharatarṣabha — O bullish man of the Bharata family

O bullish man of the Bharata family, I will tell you of the departure for the yogis who do or do not return. (8.23)

अग्निर्ज्योतिरहः शुक्लः
षण्मासा उत्तरायणम् ।
तत्र प्रयाता गच्छन्ति
ब्रह्म ब्रह्मविदो जनाः ॥८.२४॥

agnirjyotirahaḥ śuklaḥ
ṣaṇmāsā uttarāyaṇam
tatra prayātā gacchanti
brahma brahmavido janāḥ (8.24)

agnir = agniḥ — summer season; jyotir = jyotiḥ — bright atmosphere; ahaḥ — daytime; śuklaḥ — bright moonlight; saṇmāsā — six months; uttarāyaṇam — the time when the sun appears to move north; tatra — at that time; prayātā — departing; gacchanti — they go; brahma — to the spiritual location; brahmavido = brahmavidaḥ — knowers of the spiritual dimension; janāḥ — people

The summer season, the bright atmosphere, the daytime, the bright moonlight, the six months when the sun appears to move north; if at that time, they depart the body, those people who know the spiritual dimension, go to the spiritual location. (8.24)

धूमो रात्रिस्तथा कृष्णः
षण्मासा दक्षिणायनम् ।
तत्र चान्द्रमसं ज्योतिर्
योगी प्राप्य निवर्तते ॥८.२५॥

dhūmo rātristathā kṛṣṇaḥ
ṣaṇmāsā dakṣiṇāyanam
tatra cāndramasaṁ jyotir
yogī prāpya nivartate (8.25)

dhūmo = dhūmaḥ — smoky, misty or hazy season; rātris — night time; tathā — as well as; kṛṣṇaḥ — the dark moon time; saṇmāsā — six months; dakṣiṇāyanam — the time when the sun appears to move south; tatra — at that time; cāndramasam — moon; jyotir = jyotiḥ — light; yogī — yogi; prāpya — attaining; nivartate — is born again

The smoky, misty or hazy season, as well as in the night-time, the dark-moon time, the six months when the sun appears to move south; if the yogi departs at that time, he attains moonlight, after which he is born again. (8.25)

शुक्लकृष्णे गती ह्येते
जगतः शाश्वते मते ।
एकया यात्यनावृत्तिम्
अन्ययावर्तते पुनः ॥८.२६॥

śuklakṛṣṇe gatī hyete
jagataḥ śāśvate mate
ekayā yātyanāvṛttim
anyayāvartate punaḥ (8.26)

śuklakṛṣṇe — light and dark; gatī — two paths; hyete = hy (hi) — indeed + ete — these two; jagataḥ — of the universe; śāśvate — perpetual; mate — is considered; ekayā — by one; yāty = yāti — goes away; anāvṛttim — not return; anyayāvartate = anyayā — by other + āvartate — comes back; punaḥ = punar — again

The light and the dark times are two paths which are considered to be perpetually available for the universe. It is considered so by the authorities. By one, a person goes away not to return; by the other he comes back again. (8.26)

नैते सृती पार्थ जानन्
योगी मुह्यति कश्चन ।
तस्मात्सर्वेषु कालेषु
योगयुक्तो भवार्जुन ॥८.२७॥

naite sṛtī pārtha jānan
yogī muhyati kaścana
tasmātsarveṣu kāleṣu
yogayukto bhavārjuna (8.27)

naite = na — not + ete — these two; sṛtī — two paths; pārtha — O son of Pṛthā; jānan — knowing; yogī — yogi; muhyati — is confused; kaścana — at all; tasmāt — therefore; sarveṣu — in all; kāleṣu — in times; yogayukto = yogayuktaḥ — disciplined in yoga practice; bhavārjuna = bhava — be + arjuna — Arjuna

Knowing these two paths, O son of Pṛthā, the yogi is not confused at all. Therefore at all times, be disciplined in yoga practice, O Arjuna. (8.27)

वेदेषु यज्ञेषु तपःसु चैव
दानेषु यत्पुण्यफलं प्रदिष्टम् ।
अत्येति तत्सर्वमिदं विदित्वा
योगी परं स्थानमुपैति चाद्यम् ॥८.२८॥

vedeṣu yajñeṣu tapaḥsu caiva
dāneṣu yatpuṇyaphalaṁ pradiṣṭam
atyeti tatsarvamidaṁ viditvā
yogī paraṁ sthānamupaiti cādyam
(8.28)

vedeṣu — from study of the Vedas; yajñeṣu — from religious ceremonies and disciplines; tapaḥsu — from austerities; caiva — and indeed; dāneṣu — from scripturally-recommended acts of charity; yat = yad — which; puṇyaphalam — good result; pradiṣṭam — described; atyeti — goes beyond; tat — this; sarvam — all; idam — this; viditvā — having known; yogī — yogi; param — supreme; sthānam — state; upaiti — goes; cadyam = cā — and + adyam — primal

The yogi, having known all this, goes beyond the good results which are derived from study of the Veda, beyond religious ceremonies and disciplines, beyond austerities and beyond offering scripturally-recommended gifts in charity. He goes to the Supreme Primal State. (8.28)

CHAPTER 9

The Devotional Attitude*

श्रीभगवानुवाच
इदं तु ते गुह्यतमं
प्रवक्ष्याम्यनसूयवे ।
ज्ञानं विज्ञानसहितं
यज्ज्ञात्वा मोक्ष्यसेऽशुभात् ॥९.१॥

śrībhagavānuvāca
idaṁ tu te guhyatamaṁ
pravakṣyāmyanasūyave
jñānaṁ vijñānasahitaṁ
yajjñātvā mokṣyase'śubhāt (9.1)

śrībhagavān — the Blessed Lord; uvāca —said; idam — this; tu — but; te — to you; guhyatamam — most secret; pravakṣyāmy = pravakṣyāmi — I will explain; anasūyave — to one who is not cynical; jñānam — knowledge; vijñānasahitaṁ = vijñāna — experienced + sahitam — with; yaj = yad — which; jñātvā — having known; mokṣyase — you will be freed; 'śubhāt = aśubhāt —from impurity

The Blessed Lord said: But I will explain to you who are not cynical, the most secret truths, the knowledge with the experience, which having known, you will be freed from impurities. (9.1)

राजविद्या राजगुह्यं
पवित्रमिदमुत्तमम् ।
प्रत्यक्षावगमं धर्म्यं
सुसुखं कर्तुमव्ययम् ॥९.२॥

rājavidyā rājaguhyaṁ
pavitramidamuttamam
pratyakṣāvagamaṁ dharmyaṁ
susukhaṁ kartumavyayam (9.2)

rājavidyā — ultimate information; rājaguhyam — greatest secret; pavitram — purifier of consciousness; idam — this; uttamam — transcendental; pratyakṣa — by direct experience; avagamam — understood; dharmyam — the principle of religion; su-sukham — very happy; kartum — to execute; avyayam — everlasting

This is the ultimate information, the greatest secret, the purifier of consciousness. It is plain to see, righteous, easy to practise and thoroughly consistent. (9.2)

अश्रद्दधानाः पुरुषा
धर्मस्यास्य परंतप ।
अप्राप्य मां निवर्तन्ते
मृत्युसंसारवर्त्मनि ॥९.३॥

aśraddadhānāḥ puruṣā
dharmasyāsya paraṁtapa
aprāpya māṁ nivartante
mṛtyusaṁsāravartmani (9.3)

**The Mahābhārata contains no chapter headings. This title was assigned by the translator on the basis of verse 26 of this chapter.*

aśraddadhānāḥ — having no faith; puruṣā — people; dharmasyāsya = dharmasya — of the righteous behavior + asya — of this; paraṁtapa — stern subduer of the enemy; aprāpya — not attaining; mām — to Me; nivartante — they are born again; mṛtyusaṁsāravartmani = mṛtyu — death + saṁsāra — cyclic rebirth + vartmani — in the course

People who have no faith in this righteous behavior, who have not attained Me, are born again in the cyclic course of death and rebirth, O stern subduer of the enemy. (9.3)

मया ततमिदं सर्वं
जगदव्यक्तमूर्तिना ।
मत्स्थानि सर्वभूतानि
न चाहं तेष्ववस्थितः ॥९.४॥

mayā tatamidaṁ sarvaṁ
jagadavyaktamūrtinā
matsthāni sarvabhūtāni
na cāhaṁ teṣvavasthitaḥ (9.4)

mayā — by Me; tatam — pervaded; idam — this; sarvam — all; jagad = jagat — world; avyaktamūrtinā = avyakta — invisible + mūrtinā — by form; matsthāni — standing on Me, surviving on Me; sarvabhūtāni — all beings; na — not; cāham = ca — and + aham — I; teṣv = teṣu — in them; avasthitaḥ — standing on, surviving on

This world is pervaded by My invisible form. All beings survive on My energy but I am not surviving on theirs. (9.4)

न च मत्स्थानि भूतानि
पश्य मे योगमैश्वरम् ।
भूतभृन्न च भूतस्थो
ममात्मा भूतभावनः ॥९.५॥

na ca matsthāni bhūtāni
paśya me yogamaiśvaram
bhūtabhṛnna ca bhūtastho
mamātmā bhūtabhāvanaḥ (9.5)

na — not; ca — and; matsthāni — standing on Me, surviving on Me; bhūtāni — beings; paśya — behold; me — My; yogam = yoga — psychological power; aiśvaram — supremacy; bhūtabhṛn = bhūtabhṛt — sustaining beings; na — not; ca — and; bhūtastho = bhūtasthaḥ — existing on the beings; mamātmā = mama — My + ātmā — self; bhūtabhāvanaḥ — causing beings to be

And the created beings are not existing on Me. Behold My psychological supremacy. While sustaining the beings and not existing on them, I Myself cause them to be. (9.5)

यथाकाशस्थितो नित्यं
वायुः सर्वत्रगो महान् ।
तथा सर्वाणि भूतानि
मत्स्थानीत्युपधारय ॥९.६॥

yathākāśasthito nityaṁ
vāyuḥ sarvatrago mahān
tathā sarvāṇi bhūtāni
matsthānītyupadhāraya (9.6)

yathākāśasthito = yathākāśasthitaḥ = yathā — as + ākāśa — space + sthitaḥ — situated; nityam — always; vāyuḥ — wind; sarvatrago = sarvatragaḥ —

everywhere going, pervasive; mahān — powerful; tathā — so; sarvāṇi — all; bhūtāni — beings; matsthānīty (matsthānīti) = matsthānī — exist under Me + iti — thus; upadhāraya — consider thoroughly

As the powerful wind is always situated in space and is pervasive, so all beings exist under My influence. Consider this thoroughly. (9.6)

सर्वभूतानि कौन्तेय
प्रकृतिं यान्ति मामिकाम् ।
कल्पक्षये पुनस्तानि
कल्पादौ विसृजाम्यहम् ॥९.७॥

sarvabhūtāni kaunteya
prakṛtiṁ yānti māmikām
kalpakṣaye punastāni
kalpādau visṛjāmyaham (9.7)

sarvabhūtāni — all beings; kaunteya — son of Kuntī; prakṛtim — material nature; yānti — retrogress into; māmikām — my own; kalpakṣaye — at the end of a day of Brahma; punas = punar — again; tāni — they; kalpādau — at the beginning of a day of Brahma; visṛjāmy = visṛjāmi — I produce; aham — I

O son of Kuntī, all beings retrogress into My own material nature at the end of Brahmā's day. I produce them again at the beginning of Brahmā's next day. (9.7)

प्रकृतिं स्वामवष्टभ्य
विसृजामि पुनः पुनः ।
भूतग्राममिमं कृत्स्नम्
अवशं प्रकृतेर्वशात् ॥९.८॥

prakṛtiṁ svāmavaṣṭabhya
visṛjāmi punaḥ punaḥ
bhūtagrāmamimaṁ kṛtsnam
avaśaṁ prakṛtervaśāt (9.8)

prakṛtim — material nature; svām — own; avaṣṭabhya — supported on, founded on; visṛjāmi — I produce; punaḥ punaḥ — repeated, again and again; bhūtagrāmam — the multitude of beings; imam — this; kṛtsnam — whole; avaśam — powerless; prakṛter = prakṛteḥ — of material nature; vaśāt — in respect to the potency

On the foundation of material nature, I repeatedly produce this whole multitude of beings, which is powerless in respect to the potency of material nature. (9.8)

न च मां तानि कर्माणि
निबध्नन्ति धनंजय ।
उदासीनवदासीनम्
असक्तं तेषु कर्मसु ॥९.९॥

na ca māṁ tāni karmāṇi
nibadhnanti dhanaṁjaya
udāsīnavadāsīnam
asaktaṁ teṣu karmasu (9.9)

na — not; ca — and; mām — Me; tāni — these; karmāṇi — cultural acts; nibadhnanti — they bind; dhanaṁjaya — conqueror of rich countries; udāsīnavat — indifferently; āsīnam —situated; asaktam — unattached; teṣu — in these; karmasu — in cultural actions

And these cultural activities do not bind Me, O conqueror of rich countries. Since I am situated indifferently, I remain unattached to the activities. (9.9)

मयाध्यक्षेण प्रकृतिः
सूयते सचराचरम् ।
हेतुनानेन कौन्तेय
जगद्विपरिवर्तते ॥९.१०॥

mayādhyakṣeṇa prakṛtiḥ
sūyate sacarācaram
hetunānena kaunteya
jagadviparivartate (9.10)

mayā — with Me + adhyakṣeṇa — as supervisor; prakṛtiḥ — material nature; sūyate — produces; sacarācaram — moving and non-moving things; hetunānena = hetunā — by cause of + anena — by this; kaunteya — son of Kuntī; jagad = jagat — world; viparivartate — operates

With Me as the supervisor, material nature produces moving and nonmoving things. By this cause, O son of Kuntī, the universe operates. (9.10)

अवजानन्ति मां मूढा
मानुषीं तनुमाश्रितम् ।
परं भावमजानन्तो
मम भूतमहेश्वरम् ॥९.११॥

avajānanti māṁ mūḍhā
mānuṣīṁ tanumāśritam
paraṁ bhāvamajānanto
mama bhūtamaheśvaram (9.11)

avajānanti — they hold a low opinion; mām — Me; mūḍhā — the foolish people; mānuṣīm — human; tanum — body; āśritam — having assumed; param — higher; bhāvam — being; ajānanto = ajānantaḥ — not knowing; mama — of Me; bhūtamaheśvaram = bhūta — being + maheśvaram — Almighty God

The foolish people, not knowing My higher existence as the Almighty God of the beings, hold a low opinion of Me as having a human body. (9.11)

मोघाशा मोघकर्माणो
मोघज्ञाना विचेतसः ।
राक्षसीमासुरीं चैव
प्रकृतिं मोहिनीं श्रिताः ॥९.१२॥

moghāśā moghakarmāṇo
moghajñānā vicetasaḥ
rākṣasīmāsurīṁ caiva
prakṛtiṁ mohinīṁ śritāḥ (9.12)

moghāśā — people with vain hopes; moghakarmāṇaḥ — people with purposeless actions; moghajñānā — people with incorrect information; vicetasaḥ — without discrimination; rākṣasīm — wicked; āsurīm — devilish; caiva — and indeed; prakṛtim — mode of material nature; mohinīm — deluding feature; śritāḥ — relying on

Persons with vain hopes, purposeless actions, and incorrect information, who lack discrimination, being wicked and devilish, rely on the deluding feature of material nature. (9.12)

महात्मानस्तु मां पार्थ
दैवीं प्रकृतिमाश्रिताः ।
भजन्त्यनन्यमनसो
ज्ञात्वा भूतादिमव्ययम् ॥९.१३॥

mahātmānastu mām̐ pārtha
daivīm̐ prakṛtimāśritāḥ
bhajantyananyamanaso
jñātvā bhūtādimavyayam (9.13)

mahātmānaḥ — great souls; tu — but; mām — Me; pārtha — son of Pṛthā; daivīm — supernatural; prakṛtim — material energy; āśritāḥ — being reliant; bhajanty = bhajanti — they worship; ananyamanaso = ananyamanasaḥ — persons whose minds do not deviate; jñātvā — knowing; bhūtādim — originator of beings; avyayam — constant factor

But great souls, being reliant on the supernatural level of material nature, worship Me, without deviation, knowing Me as the originator of beings, the constant factor. (9.13)

सततं कीर्तयन्तो मां
यतन्तश्च दृढव्रताः ।
नमस्यन्तश्च मां भक्त्या
नित्ययुक्ता उपासते ॥९.१४॥

satatam̐ kīrtayanto mām̐
yatantaśca dṛḍhavratāḥ
namasyantaśca mām̐ bhaktyā
nityayuktā upāsate (9.14)

satatam — always; kīrtayanto = kīrtayantaḥ — glorifying; mām — Me; yatantaśca = yatantaḥ — endeavoring + ca — and; dṛḍhavratāḥ = dṛḍha — firm + vratāḥ — vows; namasyantaśca = namasyantaḥ — paying respects to + ca — and; mām — Me; bhaktyā — with devotion; nityayuktā = nitya — always + yuktā — disciplined; upāsate — worship

Always glorifying Me, endeavoring with firm vows, paying respect to Me with devotion, being always disciplined, they worship Me. (9.14)

ज्ञानयज्ञेन चाप्यन्ये
यजन्तो मामुपासते ।
एकत्वेन पृथक्त्वेन
बहुधा विश्वतोमुखम् ॥९.१५॥

jñānayajñena cāpyanye
yajanto māmupāsate
ekatvena pṛthaktvena
bahudhā viśvatomukham (9.15)

jñānayajñena = jñāna — concept + yajñena — by discipline; cāpy (capi) = ca — and + api — also; anye — others; yajanto = yajantaḥ — performing regulated worship; mām — Me; upāsate — they worship; ekatvena — with the singular basis; pṛthaktvena — as variety; bahudhā — variously shown; viśvatomukham — facing all levels

By the discipline of concepts, others do perform regulated worship of Me as the Singular Basis and as the Variety, facing all levels of reality simultaneously. (9.15)

अहं क्रतुरहं यज्ञः
स्वधाहमहमौषधम् ।
मन्त्रोऽहमहमेवाज्यम्
अहमग्निरहं हुतम् ॥९.१६॥

ahaṁ kraturahaṁ yajñaḥ
svadhāhamahamauṣadham
mantro'hamahamevājyam
ahamagniraham hutam (9.16)

aham — I; kratur — Vedic ritual; aham — I; yajñaḥ — sacrificial ceremony; svadhāham = svadhā — sanctified offering + aham — I; auṣadham — medicinal herb; mantro = mantraḥ — sacred sound; 'ham = aham — I; evājyam = eva — indeed + ājyam — ghee; aham — I; agnir = agniḥ — fire; aham — I; hutam — oblation

I am represented as the Vedic ritual. I may also be seen as the sacrificial ceremony or as the sanctified offering. I may be regarded as the medicinal herb. I may be seen as the ghee, fire or oblation given. (9.16)

पिताहमस्य जगतो
माता धाता पितामहः ।
वेद्यं पवित्रमोंकार
ऋक्साम यजुरेव च ॥९.१७॥

pitāhamasya jagato
mātā dhātā pitāmahaḥ
vedyaṁ pavitramoṁkāra
ṛksāma yajureva ca (9.17)

pitāham = pitā — father + aham — I; asya — of this; jagato = jagataḥ — of the universe; mātā — mother; dhātā — creator; pitāmahaḥ — grandfather; vedyam — subject to be known; pavitram — purifier; oṁkāra — sacred syllable Om; ṛk — Rig Veda; sāma — Sāma Veda; yajur — Yajur Veda; eva — indeed; ca — and

I am the father of this universe, the mother, the creator, the grandfather, the subject of education, the purifier, the sacred syllable Om, the Rig, Sama, and Yajur Vedas. (9.17)

गतिर्भर्ता प्रभुः साक्षी
निवासः शरणं सुहृत् ।
प्रभवः प्रलयः स्थानं
निधानं बीजमव्ययम् ॥९.१८॥

gatirbhartā prabhuḥ sākṣī
nivāsaḥ śaraṇaṁ suhṛt
prabhavaḥ pralayaḥ sthānaṁ
nidhānaṁ bījamavyayam (9.18)

gatir = gatiḥ — objective; bhartā — supporter; prabhuḥ — master; sākṣī — observer; nivāsaḥ — existential residence; śaraṇaṁ — shelter; suhṛt — friend; prabhavaḥ — origin; pralayaḥ — cause of universal disintegration; sthānam — foundation; nidhānam — reservoir of energies; bījam — case; avyayam — non-deteriorating

I am the objective, the supporter, the master, the observer, the existential residence, the shelter, the friend, the origin, the cause of universal integration, the foundation, the reservoir of energies, and the non-deteriorating cause. (9.18)

तपाम्यहमहं वर्षं
निगृह्णाम्युत्सृजामि च ।
अमृतं चैव मृत्युश्च
सदसच्चाहमर्जुन ॥९.१९॥

tapāmyahamahaṁ varṣaṁ
nigṛhṇāmyutsṛjāmi ca
amṛtaṁ caiva mṛtyuśca
sadasaccāhamarjuna (9.19)

tapāmy (tapāmi)- I produce heat; aham — I; aham — I; varṣam — rainfall; nigṛhṇāmy = nigṛhṇāmi — I withhold; utsṛjāmi — I release; ca — and; amṛtam — relatively-long life span of the celestial bodies; caiva — and indeed; mṛtyus- quick death of earthly bodies; ca — and; sad = sat — eternal life; asac = asat — short-term existence; cāham = ca — and + aham — I; arjuna — Arjuna

I produce heat. I withhold and release rainfall. I arrange the relatively-long life span of celestial bodies and the quick death of the earthly ones, as well as the short-term existence and eternal life. (9.19)

त्रैविद्या मां सोमपाः पूतपापा
यज्ञैरिष्ट्वा स्वर्गतिं प्रार्थयन्ते.।
ते पुण्यमासाद्य सुरेन्द्रलोकम्
अश्नन्ति दिव्यान्दिवि देवभोगान् ॥९.२०॥

traividyā māṁ somapāḥ pūtapāpā
yajñairiṣṭvā svargatiṁ prārthayante
te puṇyamāsādya surendralokam
aśnanti divyāndivi devabhogān (9.20)

traividyā — knowers of the three Vedas; mām — Me; somapāḥ — soma drinkers; pūta — reformed; pāpā — bad tendencies; yajñair = yajñaiḥ — with sacrificial procedures; iṣṭvā — worshiping; svargatim — path of heaven; prārthayante — they desire; te — they; puṇyam — merit based; āsādya — attaining; surendra — king of the angelic people; lokam — world; aśnanti — they enjoy; divyān — angelic; divi — in the astral region; devabhogān — celestial delights

The knowers of the three Vedas, the soma drinkers, and those who are reformed of bad tendencies, worship Me with sacrificial procedures. They desire to be transferred to heaven. Attaining the merit-based world of Surendra, the king of the angelic people, they enjoy celestial delights in the astral region. (9.20)

ते तं भुक्त्वा स्वर्गलोकं विशालं
क्षीणे पुण्ये मर्त्यलोकं विशन्ति ।
एवं त्रयीधर्ममनुप्रपन्ना
गतागतं कामकामा लभन्ते ॥९.२१॥

te taṁ bhuktvā svargalokaṁ viśālaṁ
kṣīṇe puṇye martyalokaṁ viśanti
evaṁ trayīdharmam anuprapannā
gatāgataṁ kāmakāmā labhante (9.21)

te — they; tam — it; bhuktvā — having enjoyed; svarga — angelic paradise; lokam — world; viśālam — multi-dimensional; kṣīṇe — in being exhausted; puṇye — in pious merit; martyalokam — world of short life-duration; viśanti — they enter; evam — thus; trayī — three Vedas; dharmam — injunctions for righteous life style; anuprapannā — adhering to; gatāgatam — going away and coming back; kāmakāmā — those who aspire for pleasures and luxuries; labhante — they get the opportunity

Having enjoyed the multi-dimensional, angelic paradise world, exhausting their pious merits, they enter the world of short-life duration. Thus adhering to the tri-part Vedic injunctions for righteous life style, those who aspire for pleasures and luxuries get the opportunity to go to heaven and come back to the earth again. (9.21)

अनन्याश्चिन्तयन्तो मां
ये जनाः पर्युपासते ।
तेषां नित्याभियुक्तानां
योगक्षेमं वहाम्यहम् ॥९.२२॥

ananyāścintayanto māṁ
ye janāḥ paryupāsate
teṣāṁ nityābhiyuktānāṁ
yogakṣemaṁ vahāmyaham (9.22)

ananyāś — to no other person; cintayanto = cintayantaḥ — keeping the mind attuned to; mām — Me; ye — who; janāḥ — people; paryupāsate — they worship; teṣām — concerning them; nityābhiyuktānāṁ = nitya — always + abhiyuktānām — of those who cultivate yoga disciplines; yogakṣemam — welfare; vahāmy = vahāmi — I tend to; aham — I

I tend to the welfare of the persons who worship Me and no other person, who keep their minds attuned to Me, and who always cultivate the yoga disciplines. (9.22)

येऽप्यन्यदेवता भक्ता
यजन्ते श्रद्धयान्विताः ।
तेऽपि मामेव कौन्तेय
यजन्त्यविधिपूर्वकम् ॥९.२३॥

ye'pyanyadevatā bhaktā
yajante śraddhayānvitāḥ
te'pi māmeva kaunteya
yajantyavidhipūrvakam (9.23)

ye — who; 'py = api — even; anyadevatābhaktā = anya — other + devatā — supernatural rulers + bhaktā — worshipping; yajante — they do prescribed ceremonies and disciplines; śraddhayānvitāḥ = śraddhayā — with faith + anvitāḥ — with; te — they; 'pi = api — also; mām — Me; eva — indeed; kaunteya — son of Kuntī; yajanty = yajanti — they do prescribed ceremonies and disciplines; avidhipūrvakam — not by the recommendation

Those who, with religious ceremonies, disciplines and faith, devotedly worship other supernatural rulers, indirectly petition Me, O son of Kuntī, although they do not perform the ceremonies and disciplines by My recommendation. (9.23)

अहं हि सर्वयज्ञानां
भोक्ता च प्रभुरेव च ।
न तु मामभिजानन्ति
तत्त्वेनातश्च्यवन्ति ते ॥९.२४॥

ahaṁ hi sarvayajñānāṁ
bhoktā ca prabhureva ca
na tu māmabhijānanti
tattvenātaścyavanti te (9.24)

aham — I; hi — truly; sarvayajñānām = sarva — all + yajñānām — of religious ceremonies and disciplines; bhoktā — the person who appreciates; ca — and; prabhur = prabhuḥ — master; eva — indeed; ca — and; na — not; tu — but; mām — Me; abhijānanti — they recognize; tattvenātaś = tattvena — by reality + ataḥ — hence; cyavanti — they deviate form the path of virtue; te — they

Indeed I am the Master of all religious ceremonies and disciplines and I am the person Who should appreciate such procedures. But they do not recognize Me; hence they deviate from the path of virtue. (9.24)

यान्ति देवव्रता देवान्
पितॄन्यान्ति पितृव्रताः ।
भूतानि यान्ति भूतेज्या
यान्ति मद्याजिनोऽपि माम् ॥९.२५॥

yānti devavratā devān
pitṝnyānti pitṛvratāḥ
bhūtāni yānti bhūtejyā
yānti madyājino'pi mām (9.25)

yānti — they go; devavratā — those who satisfy the supernatural rulers; devān — supernatural rulers; pitṝn — pious ancestors who exist as departed spirits; yānti — go; pitṛvratāḥ — those who satisfy the pious ancestors; bhūtāni — the ghostly spirits; yānti — go; bhūtejyā — those who satisfy the ghosts; yānti — they go; madyājino = madyājinaḥ — those who satisfy Me; 'pi = api — surely; mām — Me

Those who satisfy the supernatural rulers, go to those authorities. Those who satisfy the pious ancestors, associate with such departed spirits. Those who try to satisfy the ghosts, go to those beings. Those who try to satisfy Me, surely approach Me. (9.25)

पत्रं पुष्पं फलं तोयं
यो मे भक्त्या प्रयच्छति ।
तदहं भक्त्युपहृतम्
अश्नामि प्रयतात्मनः ॥९.२६॥

patraṁ puṣpaṁ phalaṁ toyaṁ
yo me bhaktyā prayacchati
tadahaṁ bhaktyupahṛtam
aśnāmi prayatātmanaḥ (9.26)

patram — leaf; puṣpam — flowers; phalam — fruit; toyam — water; yo = yaḥ — who; me — Me; bhaktyā — with devotion; prayacchati — he offers; tad — that; aham — I; bhaktyupahṛtam = bhakty (bhakti) —devotional + upahṛtam — given; aśnāmi — I accept; prayatātmanaḥ = prayata — disciplined, purified + ātmanaḥ — from the person

I do accept that given devotion from a disciplined, purified person who offers Me a leaf, flower, fruit or water with a devotional attitude. (9.26)

यत्करोषि यदश्नासि
यज्जुहोषि ददासि यत् ।
यत्तपस्यसि कौन्तेय
तत्कुरुष्व मदर्पणम् ॥९.२७॥

yatkaroṣi yadaśnāsi
yajjuhoṣi dadāsi yat
yattapasyasi kaunteya
tatkuruṣva madarpaṇam (9.27)

yat = yad — what; karoṣi — you do; yad — what; aśnāsi — you eat; yaj = yad — what; juhoṣi — you present ceremonially; dadāsi — you gave away; yat = yad — what; yat = yad — what; tapasyasi — you perform as a discipline; kaunteya — son of Kuntī; tat = tad — that; kuruṣva — do; madarpaṇam — offering to Me

Whatever you do, whatever you eat, whatever you present ceremonially, whatever you give away, whatever you perform as a discipline, O son of Kuntī, do that as an offering to Me. (9.27)

शुभाशुभफलैरेवं	śubhāśubhaphalairevaṁ
मोक्ष्यसे कर्मबन्धनैः ।	mokṣyase karmabandhanaiḥ
संन्यासयोगयुक्तात्मा	saṁnyāsayogayuktātmā
विमुक्तो मामुपैष्यसि ॥९.२८॥	vimukto māmupaiṣyasi (9.28)

śubhāśubha- good and bad; phalair (phalaiḥ) -with consequences; evam — thus; mokṣyase — you will be liberated; karmabandhanaiḥ — from the implications of action; saṁnyāsa — renunciation; yoga — yoga; yukta — disciplined; ātmā — self; vimukto = vimuktaḥ — liberated; mām — Me; upaiṣyasi — you will attain

Thus you will be liberated from good and bad consequences and from the implications that come from action. Being liberated by the discipline of yoga as it was applied to renunciation, you will come to Me. (9.28)

समोऽहं सर्वभूतेषु	samo'haṁ sarvabhūteṣu
न मे द्वेष्योऽस्ति न प्रियः ।	na me dveṣyo'sti na priyaḥ
ये भजन्ति तु मां भक्त्या	ye bhajanti tu māṁ bhaktyā
मयि ते तेषु चाप्यहम् ॥९.२९॥	mayi te teṣu cāpyaham (9.29)

samo = samaḥ — equally disposed; 'ham = aham — I; sarvabhūteṣu — to all beings; na — not; me — of Me; dveṣyo = dveṣyaḥ — shunned; 'sti = asti — is; na — not; priyaḥ — especially dear; ye — who; bhajanti — they worship; tu — but; mām — Me; bhaktyā — with devotion; mayi — in Me; te — they; teṣu — in them; cāpy = cāpi — and too; aham — I

I am equally disposed to all beings. No one is shunned by Me nor is anyone especially dear to Me. But those who worship Me with devotion are My favorite and I am special to them too. (9.29)

अपि चेत्सुदुराचारो	api cetsudurācāro
भजते मामनन्यभाक् ।	bhajate māmananyabhāk
साधुरेव स मन्तव्यः	sādhureva sa mantavyaḥ
सम्यग्व्यवसितो हि सः ॥९.३०॥	samyagvyavasito hi saḥ (9.30)

api — also; cet = ced — if; sudurācāro = sudurācāraḥ — wicked person; bhajate — worships; mām — Me; ananyabhāk — without being devoted to another; sādhur = sādhuḥ — saintly; eva — indeed; sa = sah — he; mantavyaḥ — should be considered; samyag = samyac — correctly; vyavasito = vyavasitaḥ — decided; hi — indeed; saḥ — he

If a wicked person worships Me without being devoted to any other authority, he is considered saintly, for he decided correctly. (9.30)

क्षिप्रं भवति धर्मात्मा
शश्वच्छान्तिं निगच्छति ।
कौन्तेय प्रतिजानीहि
न मे भक्तः प्रणश्यति ॥९.३१॥

kṣipraṁ bhavati dharmātmā
śaśvacchāntiṁ nigacchati
kaunteya pratijānīhi
na me bhaktaḥ praṇaśyati (9.31)

kṣipram — quickly; bhavati — he becomes; dharmātmā — a person whose character is virtuous; śaśvacchāntim = śaśvac (śaśvat) — eternal + chāntim (śāntim) — spiritual peace; nigacchati — he experiences; kaunteya — son of Kuntī; pratijānīhi — take note!; na — not; me — of Mine; bhaktaḥ — devotees; praṇaśyati — is ruined permanently

He quickly becomes a person whose character is virtuous. He experiences the eternal spiritual peace. O son of Kuntī, take note of it! No devotee of Mine is ruined permanently. (9.31)

मां हि पार्थ व्यपाश्रित्य
येऽपि स्युः पापयोनयः ।
स्त्रियो वैश्यास्तथा शूद्रास्
तेऽपि यान्ति परां गतिम् ॥९.३२॥

māṁ hi pārtha vyapāśritya
ye'pi syuḥ pāpayonayaḥ
striyo vaiśyāstathā śūdrās
te'pi yānti parāṁ gatim (9.32)

mām — Me; hi — indeed; pārtha — son of Pṛthā; vyapāśritya — by relying on; ye — who; 'pi = api — also; syuḥ — they should be; pāpayonayaḥ — persons from sinful parentage; striyo = striyaḥ — women; vaiśyāḥ — businessmen; tathā — even; śūdrās — laborers; te — they; 'pi = api — also; yānti — they move towards; parām — supreme; gatim — goal

O son of Pṛthā, by relying on Me, even persons from sinful parentage, even women, businessmen, even laborers, do move towards the supreme goal. (9.32)

किं पुनर्ब्राह्मणाः पुण्या
भक्ता राजर्षयस्तथा ।
अनित्यमसुखं लोकम्
इमं प्राप्य भजस्व माम् ॥९.३३॥

kiṁ punarbrāhmaṇāḥ puṇyā
bhaktā rājarṣayastathā
anityamasukhaṁ lokam
imaṁ prāpya bhajasva mām (9.33)

kim — how; punar — more again, more accessible; brāhmaṇāḥ — brahmins; puṇyā — piously-inclined; bhaktā — devoted; rājarṣayaḥ — yogi kings; tathā

— also; anityam — temporary; asukham — miserable; lokam — world; imam — this; prāpya — having acquired; bhajasva — devote yourself; mām — Me

How much more accessible then, is it for the piously-inclined brahmins and yogi kings? Having acquired an opportunity in this temporary, miserable world, you should devote yourself to Me. (9.33)

मन्मना भव मद्भक्तो
मद्याजी मां नमस्कुरु ।
मामेवैष्यसि युक्त्वैवम्
आत्मानं मत्परायणः ॥९.३४॥

manmanā bhava madbhakto
madyājī māṁ namaskuru
māmevaiṣyasi yuktvaivam
ātmānaṁ matparāyaṇaḥ (9.34)

manmanā — one whose mind is fixed on Me; bhava — be; madbhakto = madbhaktaḥ — being devoted to Me; madyājī — performing ceremonial worship of Me; mām — to Me; namaskuru — make obeisance; mām — Me; evaiṣyasi = eva — indeed + esyasi — you will come; yuktvaivam = yuktva — disciplined + evam — thus; ātmānam — self; matparāyaṇaḥ — with Me as the Supreme Objective

With the mind fixed on Me, being devoted to me, performing ceremonial worship to Me, make obeisance to Me. Being thus disciplined, with Me as the Supreme Objective, you will come to Me. (9.34)

CHAPTER 10

A Fraction of Krishna's Splendor*

श्रीभगवानुवाच भूय एव महाबाहो शृणु मे परमं वचः । यत्तेऽहं प्रीयमाणाय वक्ष्यामि हितकाम्यया ॥ १०.१ ॥	śrībhagavānuvāca bhūya eva mahābāho śṛṇu me paramaṁ vacaḥ yatte'haṁ prīyamāṇāya vakṣyāmi hitakāmyayā (10.1)

śrī bhagavān — the Blessed Lord: uvāca — said; bhūya — again; eva — indeed; mahābāho — O powerful man; śṛṇu — hear; me — from Me; paramam — supreme; vacaḥ — information; yat = yad — which; te — to you; 'ham = aham — I; prīyamāṇāya — to one who is beloved; vakṣyāmi — I will explain; hitakāmyayā — desiring your welfare

The Blessed Lord said: Again, O powerful man, hear from Me of the supreme information. Desiring your welfare, I will explain it, O beloved one. (10.1)

न मे विदुः सुरगणाः प्रभवं न महर्षयः . अहमादिर्हि देवानां महर्षीणां च सर्वशः ॥ १०.२ ॥	na me viduḥ suragaṇāḥ prabhavaṁ na maharṣayaḥ ahamādirhi devānāṁ maharṣīṇāṁ ca sarvaśaḥ (10.2)

na — not; me — of Me; viduḥ — they know; suragaṇāḥ — the supernatural rulers; prabhavam — the origin; na — nor; mahārṣayaḥ — great yogi sages; aham — I; ādir = ādiḥ — source; hi — in fact; devānām — of the supernatural rulers; mahārṣīnām — of the great yogi sages; ca — and; sarvaśaḥ — in all respects

The supernatural rulers do not know My origin, nor do the great yogi sages. In all respects, I am the source of the supernatural rulers and the great yogi sages. (10.2)

यो मामजमनादिं च वेत्ति लोकमहेश्वरम् । असंमूढः स मर्त्येषु सर्वपापैः प्रमुच्यते ॥ १०.३ ॥	yo māmajamanādiṁ ca vetti lokamaheśvaram asaṁmūḍhaḥ sa martyeṣu sarvapāpaiḥ pramucyate (10.3)

**The Mahābhārata contains no chapter headings. This title was assigned by the translator on the basis of verse 41 of this chapter.*

yo = yaḥ — who; mām — Me; ajam — birthless; anādim — beginningless; ca — and; vetti — knows; lokamaheśvaram — Almighty God of the world; asaṁmūḍhaḥ — unconfused, perceptive; sa = saḥ — he; martyeṣu — of those who use perishable bodies; sarvapāpaiḥ — from all faults; pramucyate — is freed

Of those who use perishable bodies, the one who regards Me as birthless and beginningless and who knows that I am the Almighty God of the world, is the perceptive person. He is freed from all faults. (10.3)

बुद्धिर्ज्ञानमसंमोहः
क्षमा सत्यं दमः शमः ।
सुखं दुःखं भवोऽभावो
भयं चाभयमेव च ॥१०.४॥

buddhirjñānamasaṁmohaḥ
kṣamā satyaṁ damaḥ śamaḥ
sukhaṁ duḥkhaṁ bhavo'bhāvo
bhayaṁ cābhayameva ca (10.4)

buddhir = buddhiḥ — intelligence; jñānam — knowledge; asaṁmohaḥ — non-confusion, sanity; kṣamā — patience; satyam — truthfulness; damaḥ — self-control; śamaḥ — tranquility; sukham — pleasure; duḥkham — pain; bhavo = bhavaḥ — existence; 'bhāvo = abhāvaḥ — non-existence; bhayam — fear; cābhayam = ca- and + abhayam- fearlessness; eva — indeed; ca — and

Intelligence, knowledge, sanity, patience, truthfulness, self-control, tranquility, pleasure, pain, existence, non-existence, fear, fearlessness... (10.4)

अहिंसा समता तुष्टिस्
तपो दानं यशोऽयशः ।
भवन्ति भावा भूतानां
मत्त एव पृथग्विधाः ॥१०.५॥

ahiṁsā samatā tuṣṭis
tapo dānaṁ yaśo'yaśaḥ
bhavanti bhāvā bhūtānāṁ
matta eva pṛthagvidhāḥ (10..5)

ahiṁsā — non-violence; samatā — impartiality; tuṣṭiḥ — contentment; tapo = tapaḥ — austerity; dānam — charity; yaśo = yaśaḥ — fame; 'yaśaḥ = ayaśaḥ — infamy; bhavanti — are; bhāvā — existential conditions; bhūtānām — of the beings; matta — from Me; eva — alone; pṛthagvidhāḥ — multiple

...non-violence, impartiality, contentment, austerity, charity, fame and infamy, are multiple existential conditions, which are derived from Me alone. (10.5)

महर्षयः सप्त पूर्वे
चत्वारो मनवस्तथा ।
मद्भावा मानसा जाता
येषां लोक इमाः प्रजाः ॥१०.६॥

maharṣayaḥ sapta pūrve
catvāro manavastathā
madbhāvā mānasā jātā
yeṣāṁ loka imāḥ prajāḥ (10.6)

mahārṣayaḥ — great yogi sages; sapta — seven; pūrve — in ancient times, of old; catvāro = catvāraḥ — four celibate boys; manavaḥ — primal sensually-

disciplined pro-creators; tathā — also; madbhāvā — coming from Me; mānasā — mentally; jātā — produced; yeṣāṁ — of whom; loka — universe; imāḥ — these; prajāḥ — creatures

The seven great yogi sages of old, the four celibate boys, and also the primal sexually-disciplined procreators come from Me, being produced mentally. From them, the creatures of this universe evolved. (10.6)

एतां विभूतिं योगं च
मम यो वेत्ति तत्त्वतः ।
सोऽविकम्पेन योगेन
युज्यते नात्र संशयः ॥१०.७॥

etāṁ vibhūtiṁ yogaṁ ca
mama yo vetti tattvataḥ
so'vikampena yogena
yujyate nātra saṁśayaḥ (10.7)

etām — this; vibhūtim — divine glory; yogam — yoga, extensive mystic discipline; ca — and; mama — of My; yo = yaḥ — who; vetti — experience; tattvataḥ — in reality; so = saḥ — he; 'vikampena = avikampena — by consistent; yogena — by yoga practice; yujyate — is harmonized with; nātra = na — not + atra — here; saṁśayaḥ — doubt

Whosoever experiences in reality, this divine glory and extensive mystic discipline of Mine, becomes harmonized with Me by consistent yoga practice. There is no doubt about this. (10.7)

अहं सर्वस्य प्रभवो
मत्तः सर्वं प्रवर्तते ।
इति मत्वा भजन्ते मां
बुधा भावसमन्विताः ॥१०.८॥

ahaṁ sarvasya prabhavo
mattaḥ sarvaṁ pravartate
iti matvā bhajante māṁ
budhā bhāvasamanvitāḥ (10.8)

aham — I; sarvasya — of all; prabhavo = prabhavaḥ — originator; mattaḥ — from Me; sarvam — everything; pravartate — proceeds; iti — thus, in this way; matvā — having thought; bhajante — they worship; mām — Me; budhā — intelligent person; bhāvasamanvitāḥ = bhāva — states of being, meditative ability + samanvitāḥ — endowed with

I am the originator of all. From Me, everything proceeds. Thinking of Me in this way, the intelligent persons, who are endowed with meditative ability, worship Me. (10.8)

मच्चित्ता मद्गतप्राणा
बोधयन्तः परस्परम् ।
कथयन्तश्च मां नित्यं
तुष्यन्ति च रमन्ति च ॥१०.९॥

maccittā madgataprāṇā
bodhayantaḥ parasparam
kathayantaśca māṁ nityaṁ
tuṣyanti ca ramanti ca (10.9)

maccittā — those who think of Me; madgataprāṇā — those who concentrate the life energy onto Me; bodhayantaḥ — enlighten; parasparam — one another; kathayantasca = kathayantaḥ — speaking of + ca — and; mām — of Me;

nityam — constantly; tuṣyanti — they are content; ca — and; ramanti — they are happy; ca — and

Those who think of Me, who concentrate the life energy on Me, who enlighten one another and speak of Me constantly, are content and happy. (10.9)

तेषां सततयुक्तानां भजतां प्रीतिपूर्वकम् । ददामि बुद्धियोगं तं येन मामुपयान्ति ते ॥१०.१०॥	teṣāṁ satatayuktānāṁ bhajatāṁ prītipūrvakam dadāmi buddhiyogaṁ taṁ yena māmupayānti te (10.10)

teṣām — of these; satatayuktānām = satata — constantly + yuktānām — of the disciplined; bhajatām — of the worshippers; prītipūrvakam — with affection; dadāmi — I give; buddhiyogam — technique of insight yoga, application of yoga to the use of intelligence; tam — it; yena — by which; mām — Me; upayānti — they draw near; te — they

Of those who are constantly disciplined, who worship with affection, I give the technique by which they draw near to Me. (10.10)

तेषामेवानुकम्पार्थम् अहमज्ञानजं तमः । नाशयाम्यात्मभावस्थो ज्ञानदीपेन भास्वता ॥१०.११॥	teṣāmevānukampārtham ahamajñānajaṁ tamaḥ nāśayāmyātmabhāvastho jñānadīpena bhāsvatā (10.11)

teṣām — of them; evānukampārtham = eva — indeed + anukampā — assistance + artham — interest; aham — I; ajñānajam — ignorance produced; tamaḥ — stupifying influence of material nature; nāśayāmy = nāśayāmi — I caused to be banished; ātmabhāvastho = ātmabhāvasthaḥ — situated in the self; jñānadīpena = jñāna — knowledge, realized + dīpena — with light, with insight (jñānadīpena — with realized insight); bhāsvatā — clear, shining, clarity of consciousness

In the interest of assisting them, I who am situated within their beings, cause the ignorance produced by the stupefying influence of material nature, to be banished by their clear realized insight. (10.11)

अर्जुन उवाच परं ब्रह्म परं धाम पवित्रं परमं भवान् । पुरुषं शाश्वतं दिव्यम् आदिदेवमजं विभुम् ॥१०.१२॥	arjuna uvāca paraṁ brahma paraṁ dhāma pavitraṁ paramaṁ bhavān puruṣaṁ śāśvataṁ divyam ādidevamajaṁ vibhum (10.12)

arjuna — Arjuna; uvāca — said; param — supreme; brahma — spiritual reality; param — supreme; dhāma — refuge; pavitram — reformer; paramam

— supreme; bhavān — You, O Lord; puruṣam — person; śāśvatam — eternal; divyam — divine; ādidevam — Primal God; ajam — birthless; vibhum — one whose influence spreads everywhere

Arjuna said: Hail to You Who are the Supreme Reality, the Supreme Refuge, the Supreme Reformer, O Lord. You are the eternal divine Person, the Primal God Who is birthless, and Whose influence spreads everywhere. (10.12)

आहुस्त्वामृषयः सर्वे
देवर्षिर्नारदस्तथा ।
असितो देवलो व्यासः
स्वयं चैव ब्रवीषि मे ॥ १०.१३॥

āhustvāmṛṣayaḥ sarve
devarṣirnāradastathā
asito devalo vyāsaḥ
svayaṁ caiva bravīṣi me (10.13)

āhuḥ — they declare; tvām — You; ṛṣayaḥ — yogi sage; sarve — all; devarṣir = devarṣiḥ — supernatural yogi sage; nāradaḥ — Narada; tatha — as well as; asito devalo —Asita Devala; vyāsaḥ — Vyāsa; svayam — your own self; caiva = ca — and + eva — indeed; bravīṣī — You state; me — to Me

All the yogi sages, as well as the supernatural yogi sage Narada, Asita Devala, and Vyasa declare this of You. And You Yourself state this to me. (10.13)

सर्वमेतदृतं मन्ये
यन्मां वदसि केशव ।
न हि ते भगवन्व्यक्तिं
विदुर्देवा न दानवाः ॥ १०.१४॥

sarvametadṛtaṁ manye
yanmāṁ vadasi keśava
na hi te bhagavanvyaktiṁ
vidurdevā na dānavāḥ (10.14)

sarvam — all; etad — this; ṛtam — true; manye — I believe; yan = yad — which; mām — me; vadasi — you say; keśava — O Keshava; na — not; hi — indeed; te — to you; bhagavan — O Blessed Lord; vyaktim — form; vidur = viduḥ — they know; devā — the supernatural rulers; na — nor; dānavāḥ — descendants of Danu, enemies of the supernatural rulers

All that You say to me is true. I believe it, O Keśava. Indeed it is not possible to understand You, O Bhagavan, Blessed Lord. Neither the supernatural rulers nor their enemies, the descendants of Danu, can know Your form. (10.14)

स्वयमेवात्मनात्मानं
वेत्थ त्वं पुरुषोत्तम ।
भूतभावन भूतेश
देवदेव जगत्पते ॥ १०.१५॥

svayamevātmanātmānaṁ
vettha tvaṁ puruṣottama
bhūtabhāvana bhūteśa
devadeva jagatpate (10.15)

svayam — yourself; evātmanā = eva — indeed + ātmanā — by yourself; 'tmānam = ātmānam — yourself; vettha — you know; tvam — you;

puruṣottama — Supreme Person; bhūtabhāvana — one who sustains the existence of all others; bhūteśa — Lord of created beings; devadeva — God of the gods; jagatpate — Lord of the universe

You alone know Yourself, O Supreme Person, O maintainer of the creatures, O Lord of the created beings, O God of gods, O Lord of the universe. (10.15)

वक्तुमर्हस्यशेषेण
दिव्या ह्यात्मविभूतयः ।
याभिर्विभूतिभिर्लोकान्
इमांस्त्वं व्याप्य तिष्ठसि ॥ १०.१६ ॥

vaktumarhasyaśeṣeṇa
divyā hyātmavibhūtayaḥ
yābhirvibhūtibhirlokān
imāṁstvaṁ vyāpya tiṣṭhasi (10.16)

vaktum — to describe; arhasy = arhasi — you can; aśeṣeṇa — without deleting anything, thoroughly; divyā — supernatural; hy = hi — in truth; ātmavibhūtayaḥ — wondrous manifestations of Yourself; yābhir = yābhiḥ — by which; vibhūtibhir = vibhūtibhiḥ — wondrous manifestations; lokān — worlds; imāṁs — these; tvam — you; vyāpya — pervading; tiṣṭhasi — you are situated

Please describe thoroughly, Your supernatural wondrous manifestations by which You pervade these worlds and are situated in them. (10.16)

कथं विद्यामहं योगिंस्
त्वां सदा परिचिन्तयन् ।
केषु केषु च भावेषु
चिन्त्योऽसि भगवन्मया ॥ १०.१७ ॥

kathaṁ vidyāmahaṁ yogiṁs
tvāṁ sadā paricintayan
keṣu keṣu ca bhāveṣu
cintyo'si bhagavanmayā (10.17)

katham — how; vidyām — I will know; aham — I; yogin — O mystic master; tvām — You; sadā — constantly; paricintayan — meditating; keṣukeṣu — in what, in what; ca — and; bhāveṣu — in aspects of existence; cintyo = cintyah — to be considered; 'si = asi — You are; bhagavan — Blessed Lord; mayā — by me

How will I know You, Mystic Master, O Yogi? Is it by constantly meditating? In what aspects of existence are You to be considered by Me, O Blessed Lord? (10.17)

विस्तरेणात्मनो योगं
विभूतिं च जनार्दन ।
भूयः कथय तृप्तिर्हि
शृण्वतो नास्ति मेऽमृतम् ॥ १०.१८ ॥

vistareṇātmano yogaṁ
vibhūtiṁ ca janārdana
bhūyaḥ kathaya tṛptirhi
śṛṇvato nāsti me'mṛtam (10.18)

vistareṇātmano (vistareṇātmanaḥ) = vistareṇa — with detail + ātmanaḥ — of Yourself; yogam — yoga, self-disciplinary methods and the resultant mystic power; vibhūtim — splendrous form; ca — and; janārdana — O motivator of the people; bhūyaḥ — more; kathaya — explain; tṛptir = tṛptiḥ — final satisfaction; hi — indeed; śṛṇvato = śṛṇvataḥ — of hearing; nāsti = na — not + asti — is; me — of me; 'mṛtam = amrtam — sweetness

Explain in more detail about Your self-disciplinary methods and the resultant mystic power and of Your splendorous form, O motivator of the people. There is no final satisfaction for me in hearing Your sweet words. (10.18)

श्रीभगवानुवाच
हन्त ते कथयिष्यामि
दिव्या ह्यात्मविभूतयः ।
प्राधान्यतः कुरुश्रेष्ठ
नास्त्यन्तो विस्तरस्य मे ॥ १०.१९ ॥

śrībhagavānuvāca
hanta te kathayiṣyāmi
divyā hyātmavibhūtayaḥ
prādhānyataḥ kuruśreṣṭha
nāstyanto vistarasya me (10.19)

śrībhagavān — the Blessed Lord; uvāca — said; hanta — listen; te — to you; kathayiṣyāmi — I will talk of; divyā — supernaturally; hy = hi — truly; ātmavibhūtayaḥ — own wondrous forms; prādhānyataḥ — most prominent; kuruśreṣtha — O best of the Kuru clan; nāsty (nasti) = na — not + asti — is; anto = antaḥ — limit; vistarasya — to the influence; me — My

The Blessed Lord said: Listen, I will talk to you of the most prominent of my supernatural manifestations, O best of the Kuru clan, for there is no limit to My influence. (10.19)

अहमात्मा गुडाकेश
सर्वभूताशयस्थितः ।
अहमादिश्च मध्यं च
भूतानामन्त एव च ॥ १०.२० ॥

ahamātmā guḍākeśa
sarvabhūtāśayasthitaḥ
ahamādiśca madhyaṁ ca
bhūtānāmanta eva ca (10.20)

aham — I; ātmā — self; guḍākeśa — sleep-regulator; sarvabhūtāśayasthitaḥ = sarva — all + bhūta — beings + āśaya — mystic resting place + sthitaḥ — situated in; aham — I; ādiśca = ādiḥ — beginning + ca — and; madhyam — middle; ca — and; bhūtānām — of the beings; anta — end; eva — indeed; ca — and

O sleep regulator, I am the person Who is situated in the mystic resting place of all beings. I am responsible for the beginning, middle, and end of all beings. (10.20)

आदित्यानामहं विष्णुर्
ज्योतिषां रविरंशुमान् ।
मरीचिर्मरुतामस्मि
नक्षत्राणामहं शशी ॥ १०.२१ ॥

ādityānāmahaṁ viṣṇur
jyotiṣāṁ raviraṁśumān
marīcirmarutāmasmi
nakṣatrāṇāmahaṁ śaśī (10.21)

ādityānām — of the Adityas; aham — I; viṣṇur = viṣṇuḥ — Vishnu ; jyotiṣām — of lights; ravir = raviḥ — the sun; aṁśumān — radiant; marīcir = marīciḥ — Marici; marutām — of the thunderstormers; asmi — I am; nakṣatrāṇām — of the stars; aham — I; śaśī — the moon

Of the Āditya, I am Vishnu. Of lights, I am represented by the radiant sun. Of the thunderstorms, I am represented by Marīci. Of the stars, I am signified by the moon. (10.21)

वेदानां सामवेदोऽस्मि
देवानामस्मि वासवः ।
इन्द्रियाणां मनश्चास्मि
भूतानामस्मि चेतना ॥१०.२२॥

vedānāṁ sāmavedo'smi
devānāmasmi vāsavaḥ
indriyāṇāṁ manaścāsmi
bhūtānāmasmi cetanā (10.22)

vedānām — of the Vedas; sāmavedo = sāmavedaḥ — Sāma Veda; 'smi = asmi — I am; devānām — of the supernatural rulers; asmi — I am; vāsavaḥ — Vāsava Indra; indriyāṇām — of the senses; manaścāsmi = manas — mind + ca — and + asmi — I am; bhūtānām — of the creature forms; asmi — I am; cetanā — consciousness

Of the Vedas, I am represented by the Sāma Veda. Of the supernatural rulers, I am represented as Vāsava Indra. Of the senses, I am represented as the mind. In creature forms, I am represented as consciousness. (10.22)

रुद्राणां शंकरश्चास्मि
वित्तेशो यक्षरक्षसाम् ।
वसूनां पावकश्चास्मि
मेरुः शिखरिणामहम् ॥१०.२३॥

rudrāṇāṁ śaṁkaraścāsmi
vitteśo yakṣarakṣasām
vasūnāṁ pāvakaścāsmi
meruḥ śikhariṇāmaham (10.23)

rudrāṇām — of the cosmic destroyers; śaṁkaraścāsmi = śaṁkaraḥ — Shankara Shiva + ca — and + asmi — I am; vitteśo = vitteśaḥ - Kubera; yakṣarakṣasām — of the Yakshas and Rakshas; vasūnām — of the Vasus; pāvakaścāsmi = pāvakaḥ — Pavāka + ca — and + asmi — I am; meruḥ — Meru; śikhariṇām — of the mountains; aham — I

Of the cosmic destroyers, I am represented by the Shankara Shiva. Of the Yakshas and Rakshas, I am best represented as Vittesha Kubera. Of the Vasus, I am represented by Pāvaka Agni. Of the mountains, I am represented as Mount Meru. (10.23)

पुरोधसां च मुख्यं मां
विद्धि पार्थ बृहस्पतिम् ।
सेनानीनामहं स्कन्दः
सरसामस्मि सागरः ॥१०.२४॥

purodhasāṁ ca mukhyaṁ māṁ
viddhi pārtha bṛhaspatim
senānīnāmahaṁ skandaḥ
sarasāmasmi sāgaraḥ (10.24)

purodhasām — of the family priest; ca — and; mukhyam — chief; mām — me; viddhi — know; pārtha — son of Pṛthā; bṛhaspatim — Bṛhaspati; senānīnām — of the commanders; aham — I; skandaḥ — Skanda; sarasām — of the seas; asmi — I am; sāgaraḥ — the ocean

O son of Pṛthā, know Me as being represented by Brihaspati, the chief of the family priests. Of military commanders, I am represented by Skanda. Of the seas, I am symbolized by the ocean. (10.24)

महर्षीणां भृगुरहं
गिरामस्म्येकमक्षरम् ।
यज्ञानां जपयज्ञोऽस्मि
स्थावराणां हिमालयः ॥१०.२५॥

maharṣīṇāṁ bhṛguraham
girāmasmyekamakṣaram
yajñānāṁ japayajño'smi
sthāvarāṇāṁ himālayaḥ (10.25)

maharṣīṇām — of the great yogi sages; bhṛgur = bhṛguḥ — Brigu; aham — I; girām — of spoken words; asmy = asmi — I; ekamakṣaram — one-syllable sound; yajñānām — of the religiously-motivated disciplines; japayajño = japayajñaḥ — the discipline of uttering prayers; 'smi = asmi — I am; sthāvarāṇām — of the stationary objects; himālayaḥ — Himalaya

Of the great yogi sages, Bhrigu is one whom I am best represented by. Of the spoken words, I am represented by the one-syllable sound. Of the religiously-motivated disciplines, I am represented best by the discipline of uttering prayers. Of stationary objects, I am best represented by the Himalayas. (10.25)

अश्वत्थः सर्ववृक्षाणां
देवर्षीणां च नारदः ।
गन्धर्वाणां चित्ररथः
सिद्धानां कपिलो मुनिः ॥१०.२६॥

aśvatthaḥ sarvavṛkṣāṇāṁ
devarṣīṇāṁ ca nāradaḥ
gandharvāṇāṁ citrarathaḥ
siddhānāṁ kapilo muniḥ (10.26)

aśvatthaḥ — sacred fig tree; sarvavṛkṣāṇāṁ = sarva — all + vṛksāṇām — of trees; devarṣīṇām — of the celestial supernatural yogi sages; ca — and; nāradaḥ — Narada; gandharvāṇām — of the supernatural singers; citrarathaḥ — Citraratha; siddhānām — of the perfected souls; kapilo = kapilaḥ - Kapila; muniḥ — yogi philosopher

Of all trees, I am best represented by the Ashvattha sacred fig tree. Of the supernatural yogi sages, I am represented by Narada. Of the supernatural singers, it is Chitraratha; of the perfected souls, the yogi philosopher Kapila. (10.26)

उच्चैःश्रवसमश्वानां
विद्धि माममृतोद्भवम् ।
ऐरावतं गजेन्द्राणां
नराणां च नराधिपम् ॥१०.२७॥

uccaiḥśravasamaśvānāṁ
viddhi māmamṛtodbhavam
airāvataṁ gajendrāṇāṁ
narāṇāṁ ca narādhipam (10.27)

uccaihśravasam — the supernatural horse Uccaihśrava; aśvānām — of the horses; viddhi — know; mām — me; amṛtodbhavam = amṛta — a sweet celestial sea + udbhavam — born from; airāvatam — Airāvata; gajendrāṇām — of kingly elephants; narāṇām — of men; ca — and; narādhipam — King of men

Of horses, know Me as represented by the supernatural horse Uccaihśrava, which was born of the sweet celestial sea. Of the kingly elephants, know Me as represented by Airāvata, and know Me as the King of men. (10.27)

आयुधानामहं वज्रं
धेनूनामस्मि कामधुक् ।
प्रजनश्चास्मि कन्दर्पः
सर्पाणामस्मि वासुकिः ॥१०.२८॥

āyudhānāmahaṁ vajraṁ
dhenūnāmasmi kāmadhuk
prajanaścāsmi kandarpaḥ
sarpāṇāmasmi vāsukiḥ (10.28)

āyudhānām — of weapons; aham — I; vajram — supernatural thunderbolt; dhenūnām — of cows; asmi — I am; kāmadhuk — supernatural Kamadhuk cow; prajanaścāsmi = prajanaḥ — begetting + ca — and + asmi — I am; kandarpaḥ — Kandarpa, the god of romance; sarpāṇām — of serpents; asmi — I am; vāsukiḥ — Vāsuki

Of weapons, I am compared to the Vajra supernatural thunderbolt. Of cows, I am represented as the supernatural Kamadhuk. And in the case of begetting, I am represented by Kandarpa, the god of romance. Of serpents, I am represented by Vāsuki. (10.28)

अनन्तश्चास्मि नागानां
वरुणो यादसामहम् ।
पितॄणामर्यमा चास्मि
यमः संयमतामहम् ॥१०.२९॥

anantaścāsmi nāgānāṁ
varuṇo yādasāmaham
pitṝṇāmaryamā cāsmi
yamaḥ saṁyamatāmaham (10.29)

anantaścāsmi = anantaḥ — Ananta + ca — and + asmi — I am; nāgānām — of supernatural snakes; varuṇo = varuṇaḥ — Varuṇa; yādasām — of the aquatics; aham — I; pitṝṇām — of the piously-departed ancestors; aryamā — Aryamā; cāsmi = ca — and + asmi — I am; yamaḥ — Yama; saṁyamatām — of the subduers; aham — I

I am represented by Ananta among the supernatural snakes. I am represented by Varuṇa, among the aquatics. Among the piously-departed spirits, I am represented by Aryamā. Of the subduers, I am represented by Yama. (10.29)

प्रह्लादश्चास्मि दैत्यानां
कालः कलयतामहम् ।
मृगाणां च मृगेन्द्रोऽहं
वैनतेयश्च पक्षिणाम् ॥ १०.३० ॥

prahlādaścāsmi daityānāṁ
kālaḥ kalayatāmaham
mṛgāṇāṁ ca mṛgendro'haṁ
vainateyaśca pakṣiṇām (10.30)

prahlādaścāsmi = prahlādaḥ — Prahlāda + ca — and + asmi — I am; daityānām — of the titan descendants of Diti; kālaḥ — time; kalayatām — of the monitors; aham — I; mṛgāṇām — of the animals; ca — and; mṛgendro = mṛgendraḥ — king of the beasts; 'ham = aham — I; vainateyaśca = vainateyaḥ — son of Vinata + ca — and; pakṣiṇām — of the birds

And I am represented as Prahlāda among the titan descendants of Diti, as time of the monitors, as the king of beasts among the animals, as the son of Vinata among the birds. (10.30)

पवनः पवतामस्मि
रामः शस्त्रभृतामहम्।
झषाणां मकरश्चास्मि
स्रोतसामस्मि जाह्नवी ॥ १०.३१ ॥

pavanaḥ pavatāmasmi
rāmaḥ śastrabhṛtāmaham
jhaṣāṇāṁ makaraścāsmi
srotasāmasmi jāhnavī (10.31)

pavanaḥ — the wind; pavatām — of the cleansers; asmi — I am; rāmaḥ — Rāma; śastrabhṛtām — of the weapon carriers; aham — I; jhaṣāṇām — of sea monsters; makaraścāsmi = makaraḥ — shark + ca — and + asmi — I am; srotasām — of rivers; asmi — I am; jāhnavī — daughter of Jahnu

Among the cleansers, I am best represented by the wind. Of the weapon carriers, I am best represented by Rāma. Of the sea monsters, I am represented by the shark. Of the rivers, I am represented by Jahnu's daughter. (10.31)

सर्गाणामादिरन्तश्च
मध्यं चैवाहमर्जुन ।
अध्यात्मविद्या विद्यानां
वादः प्रवदतामहम् ॥ १०.३२ ॥

sargāṇāmādirantaśca
madhyaṁ caivāhamarjuna
adhyātmavidyā vidyānāṁ
vādaḥ pravadatāmaham (10.32)

sargāṇām — of creations; ādir = ādiḥ — formation; antaśca = antaḥ — ending + ca — and; madhyam — continuation; caivāham = ca — and + eva — indeed + aham — I; arjuna — Arjuna; adhyātmavidyā — knowledge of the Supreme Soul; vidyānām — of sciences; vādaḥ — conclusion; pravadatām — of the logicians; aham — I

Of creations, I am represented by the formation, continuation and ending. O Arjuna, of the sciences, I am knowledge of the Supreme Soul. I am represented by the conclusion of the logicians. (10.32)

अक्षराणामकारोऽस्मि
द्वंद्वः सामासिकस्य च ।
अहमेवाक्षयः कालो
धाताहं विश्वतोमुखः ॥१०.३३॥

akṣarāṇāmakāro'smi
dvaṁdvaḥ sāmāsikasya ca
ahamevākṣayaḥ kālo
dhātāhaṁ viśvatomukhaḥ (10.33)

akṣarāṇām — of letters; akāro = akāraḥ — the letter A; 'smi = asmi — I am; dvandvaḥ — two-word compound; sāmāsikasya — of the word combinations; ca — and; aham — I; evākṣayaḥ = eva — indeed + akṣayaḥ — infinite; kālo = kālaḥ — time; dhātāham = dhātā — Dhātā Brahmā + aham — I; viśvatomukhaḥ — one who faces all directions, four-faced

Of letters, I am represented by the letter A. Of the word combinations, I am represented by the two-word compound. I am comparable to infinite time. I am represented by Dhātā, the four-faced Brahmā. (10.33)

मृत्युः सर्वहरश्चाहम्
उद्भवश्च भविष्यताम् ।
कीर्तिः श्रीर्वाक्च नारीणां
स्मृतिर्मेधा धृतिः क्षमा ॥१०.३४

mṛtyuḥ sarvaharaścāham
udbhavaśca bhaviṣyatām
kīrtiḥ śrīrvākca nārīṇāṁ
smṛtirmedhā dhṛtiḥ kṣamā (10.34)

mṛtyuḥ — death; sarvaharaścāham = sarvaharaḥ — all-devouring + ca — and + aham — I; udbhavaśca = udbhavaḥ — origin + ca — and; bhaviṣyatām — of things which are to be produced; kīrtiḥ — Kīrti, goddess of fame; śrīr = śrīḥ — Shri, goddess of fortune; vāk — Vāk, goddess of speech; ca — and; nārīṇām — of women; smṛtir = smṛtiḥ — Smṛti, goddess of recollection; medhā — Medhā, goddess of counsel; dhṛtiḥ — Dhṛti, goddess of faithfulness; kṣamā — Kṣamā, goddess of patience

I am represented as all-devouring death. I am the foundation of things that are to be produced. And among women, I am represented by Kīrti, the goddess of fame, Śrī, the goddess of fortune, Vāk, the goddess of speech, Smṛti, the goddess of recollection, Medhā, the goddess of counsel, Dhṛti, the goddess of faithfulness and Kṣama, the goddess of patience. (10.34)

बृहत्साम तथा साम्नां
गायत्री छन्दसामहम् ।
मासानां मार्गशीर्षोऽहम्
ऋतूनां कुसुमाकरः ॥१०.३५॥

bṛhatsāma tathā sāmnāṁ
gāyatrī chandasāmaham
māsānāṁ mārgaśīrṣo'ham
ṛtūnāṁ kusumākaraḥ (10.35)

bṛhatsāma — Brihat Sāma Melody; tathā — also; sāmnām — of the Sāma Veda chants; gāyatrī — Gayatri; chandasām — of the poetic hymns; aham — I; māsānām — of months; mārgaśīrṣo = mārgaśīrṣaḥ - November-December lunar month; 'ham = aham — I; ṛtūnām — of seasons; kusumākaraḥ — spring

Of the Sāma Veda chants, the Brihat Sāma melody represents Me. Of the poetic hymns, I am the Gayatri. Of months, I am best represented by the November-December lunar month. Of the seasons, I am best compared to Spring. (10.35)

द्यूतं छलयतामस्मि
तेजस्तेजस्विनामहम् ।
जयोऽस्मि व्यवसायोऽस्मि
सत्त्वं सत्त्ववतामहम् ॥ १०.३६ ॥

dyūtaṁ chalayatāmasmi
tejastejasvināmaham
jayo'smi vyavasāyo'smi
sattvaṁ sattvavatāmaham (10.36)

dyūtam — gambling skill; chalayatām — of the swindlers; asmi — I am; tejaḥ — splendor; tejasvinām — of the splendid things; aham — I; jayo = jayaḥ — victory; 'ham = asmi — I am; vyavasāyo = vyavasāyaḥ — endeavor; 'smi = asmi — I am; sattvam — reality; sattvavatām — of the real things; aham — I

I am represented as the gambling skill of the swindlers. I am compared to the splendor of the splendid things. I am compared to victory and endeavor. I am the reality of the realistic things. (10.36)

वृष्णीनां वासुदेवोऽस्मि
पाण्डवानां धनंजयः ।
मुनीनामप्यहं व्यासः
कवीनामुशना कविः ॥ १०.३७ ॥

vṛṣṇīnāṁ vāsudevo'smi
pāṇḍavānāṁ dhanaṁjayaḥ
munīnāmapyahaṁ vyāsaḥ
kavīnāmuśanā kaviḥ (10.37)

vṛṣṇīnām — of the Vrishnis; vāsudevo = vāsudevaḥ — the son of Vasudeva; 'smi = asmi — I am; pāṇḍavānām — of the Pandavas; dhanaṁjayaḥ — Arjuna; munīnām — of the yogi philosophers; apy = api — also; aham — I; vyāsaḥ — Vyasa; kavīnām — of poets; uśanā — Ushana; kaviḥ — respected poet

Of the Vṛṣṇis, I am the son of Vasudeva. Of the Pāṇḍavas, I am represented by Arjuna. Of the yogi philosophers, I am compared to Vyāsa. Of the poets, I am represented by the respected poet Uśanā. (10.37)

दण्डो दमयतामस्मि
नीतिरस्मि जिगीषताम् ।
मौनं चैवास्मि गुह्यानां
ज्ञानं ज्ञानवतामहम् ॥ १०.३८ ॥

daṇḍo damayatāmasmi
nītirasmi jigīṣatām
maunaṁ caivāsmi guhyānāṁ
jñānaṁ jñānavatāmaham (10.38)

daṇdo = daṇdaḥ — authority to punish; damayatām — of the rulers; asmi — I am; nītir = nītiḥ — morality; asmi — I am; jigīṣatām — of those seeking victory; maunam — silence; caivāsmi = ca — and + eva — indeed + asmi — I am; guhyānām — of secrets; jñānam — knowledge; jñānavatām — of those who know; aham — I

Of rulers, I am the authority to punish. For those seeking victory, I may be compared to the means of morality; of secrets, I am represented by silence. In wise men, I am represented as knowledge. (10.38)

यच्चापि सर्वभूतानां
बीजं तदहमर्जुन ।
न तदस्ति विना यत्स्यान्
मया भूतं चराचरम् ॥ १०.३९ ॥

yaccāpi sarvabhūtānāṁ
bījaṁ tadahamarjuna
na tadasti vinā yatsyān
mayā bhūtaṁ carācaram (10.39)

yac = yad — which; cāpi = ca — and + api — also; sarvabhūtānām — of all created beings; bījam — origin point; tad — that; aham — I; arjuna — Arjuna; na — not; tad — that; asti — is; vinā — without; yat = yad — which; syān = syāt — should be; mayā — through My influence; bhūtam — existing; carācaram — active or stationary

And O Arjuna, I am the origin of all created beings. There is nothing active or stationary which could exist without My influence. (10.39)

नान्तोऽस्ति मम दिव्यानां
विभूतीनां परंतप ।
एष तूद्देशतः प्रोक्तो
विभूतेर्विस्तरो मया ॥ १०.४० ॥

nānto'sti mama divyānāṁ
vibhūtīnāṁ paraṁtapa
eṣa tūddeśataḥ prokto
vibhūtervistaro mayā (10.40)

nānto (nāntaḥ) = na — no + antaḥ — end; 'sti = asti — is; mama — of My; divyānām — of the supernatural; vibhūtīnām — manifestations; paraṁtapa — burner of enemy forces; eṣa — this; tūddeśataḥ = tu — but + uddeśataḥ — for a sample; prokto = proktaḥ — explained; vibhūter = vibhūteḥ — of the opulences; vistaro = vistaraḥ — of the spreading, extensive; mayā — by Me

There is no end to My supernatural manifestations, O burner of the enemy forces. This was explained by Me as a sampling of My extensive opulence. (10.40)

यद्यद्विभूतिमत्सत्त्वं
श्रीमदूर्जितमेव वा ।
तत्तदेवावगच्छ त्वं
मम तेजोंशसंभवम् ॥ १०.४१ ॥

yadyadvibhūtimatsattvaṁ
śrīmadūrjitameva vā
tattadevāvagaccha tvaṁ
mama tejoṁśasaṁbhavam (10.41)

yad yad — what, whatever; vibhūtimat — fantastic; sattvam — real object; śrīmad = śrīmat — prosperous; ūrjitam — powerful; eva — indeed; vā — or; tat tad = tad tat — this, that, any case; evāvagaccha = eva — indeed + avagaccha — realize; tvam — you; mama — of Me; tejo = tejaḥ — splendor; 'ṁśasaṁbhavam (aṁśasaṁbhavam) = aṁśa — fraction + saṁbhavam — origin

You should realize that whatever fantastic existence, whatever prosperous or powerful object there is, in any case, it originates from a fraction of My splendor. (10.41)

अथ वा बहुनैतेन
किं ज्ञातेन तवार्जुन ।
विष्टभ्याहमिदं कृत्स्नम्
एकांशेन स्थितो जगत् ॥ १०.४२ ॥

atha vā bahunaitena
kiṁ jñātena tavārjuna
viṣṭabhyāhamidaṁ kṛtsnam
ekāṁśena sthito jagat (10.42)

athavā — but; bahunaitena = bahunā — with extensive + etena — with this; kim — what is the value?; jñātena — with information; tavārjuna = tava — of you + arjuna — Arjuna; viṣṭabhyāham = viṣṭabhya — supporting + aham — I; idam — this; kṛtsnam — entire; ekāṁśena = eka — one + aṁśena — by a fraction; sthito = sthitaḥ — based, standing; jagat — world

But Arjuna, what is the value of this extensive information? As the foundation, I support this entire universe with a fraction of Myself. (10.42)

CHAPTER 11

The Universal Form*

अर्जुन उवाच
मदनुग्रहाय परमं
गुह्यमध्यात्मसंज्ञितम् ।
यत्त्वयोक्तं वचस्तेन
मोहोऽयं विगतो मम ॥ ११.१ ॥

arjuna uvāca
madanugrahāya paramaṁ
guhyamadhyātmasaṁjñitam
yattvayoktaṁ vacastena
moho'yaṁ vigato mama (11.1)

Arjuna — Arjuna: uvāca — said; madanugrahāya — kindness to me, as a matter of mercy to me; paramaṁ — highest; guhyam — private; adhyātmasaṁjñitam = adhyātma — Supersoul + samjnitam — known as; yad — which; tvayoktaṁ = tvaya — by you + uktam — explained; vacaḥ — lecture; tena — by this; moho = mohaḥ — delusion; 'yam = ayam — this; vigato = vigataḥ — departed; mama — of me (11.1)

Arjuna said: As a matter of mercy to me, the highest, most private information of the Supreme Soul was explained by You in this lecture. Subsequently, the delusion departed from me. (11.1)

भवाप्ययौ हि भूतानां
श्रुतौ विस्तरशो मया ।
त्वत्तः कमलपत्राक्ष
माहात्म्यमपि चाव्ययम् ॥ ११.२ ॥

bhavāpyayau hi bhūtānāṁ
śrutau vistaraśo mayā
tvattaḥ kamalapatrākṣa
māhātmyamapi cāvyayam (11.2)

bhavāpyayau = bhava — origin + apy (api) — also + ayau — ruination; hi — indeed; bhūtānām — of the beings; śrutau — both were heard; vistaraśo = vistaraśaḥ — in detail; mayā — by me; tvattaḥ — from you; kamalapatrākṣa = kamala — lotus + patra — petal + akṣa — eyed; māhātmyam — majestic glory; api — also; cāvyayam = ca — and + avyayam — eternally

The description of the origin and ruination of the beings was heard in detail by me, O Person Whose eyes are shaped like lotus petals. You also described Your eternal majestic glory. (11.2)

एवमेतद्यथात्थ त्वम्
आत्मानं परमेश्वर ।
द्रष्टुमिच्छामि ते रूपम्
ऐश्वरं पुरुषोत्तम ॥ ११.३ ॥

evametadyathāttha tvam
ātmānaṁ parameśvara
draṣṭumicchāmi te rūpam
ĕśvaraṁ puruṣottama (11.3)

**The Mahābhārata contains no chapter headings. This title was assigned by the translator on the basis of verse 16 of this chapter.*

evam — thus; etad — this; yathāttha = yathā — as + attha — you explain; tvam — you; ātmānam — yourself; parameśvara — O Supreme Lord; draṣṭum — to see; icchāmi — I wish; te — your; rūpam — form; aiśvaram — majesty; puruṣottama — O Supreme Person

This is as You explained about Yourself, O Supreme Lord. I wish to see Your Majestic Form, O Supreme Person. (11.3)

मन्यसे यदि तच्छक्यं
मया द्रष्टुमिति प्रभो ।
योगेश्वर ततो मे त्वं
दर्शयात्मानमव्ययम् ॥ ११.४॥

manyase yadi tacchakyaṁ
mayā draṣṭumiti prabho
yogeśvara tato me tvaṁ
darśayātmānamavyayam (11.4)

manyase — you think; yadi — if; tac = tad — that; chakyam = sakyam — possible; mayā — by me; draṣṭum — to see; iti — thus; prabho — O Lord; yogeśvara — Master of yoga technique; tato = tataḥ — then; me — to me; tvam — you; darśayātmānam = darśayā — make it be seen + ātmānam — self; avyayam — eternal

If You think that it is possible for me to see this, O Lord, Master of the yoga technique, then make me see You in that Eternal Form. (11.4)

श्रीभगवानुवाच
पश्य मे पार्थ रूपाणि
शतशोऽथ सहस्रशः ।
नानाविधानि दिव्यानि
नानावर्णाकृतीनि च ॥ ११.५॥

śrībhagavānuvāca
paśya me pārtha rūpāṇi
śataśo'tha sahasraśaḥ
nānāvidhāni divyāni
nānāvarṇākṛtīni ca (11.5)

śrībhagavān — the Blessed Lord; uvāca — said; paśya — see; me — My; pārtha — son of Pṛthā; rūpāṇi — forms; śataśo = śataśaḥ — hundred; 'tha = atha — or; sahasraśaḥ — thousand; nānāvidhāni — variously manifested; divyāni — supernatural; nānāvarṇākṛtīni = nānā — various + varṇa — color + ākṛtīni — shapes + ca — and

The Blessed Lord said: O son of Pṛthā, see My forms in the hundreds or rather in the thousands, variously manifested, supernatural and of the various colors and shapes. (11.5)

पश्यादित्यान्वसून्रुद्रान्
अश्विनौ मरुतस्तथा ।
बहून्यदृष्टपूर्वाणि
पश्याश्चर्याणि भारत ॥ ११.६॥

paśyādityānvasūnrudrān
aśvinau marutastathā
bahūnyadṛṣṭapūrvāṇi
paśyāścaryāṇi bhārata (11.6)

paśyādityān = paśya — look at + ādityān — supernatural rulers; vasūn — Vasus; rudrān — supernatural destroyers; aśvinau — two supernatural doctors; marutaḥ — supernatural stormers; tathā — also; bahūny = bahūni — many; adṛṣṭapūrvāṇi = adṛṣṭa — unseen + pūrvāṇi — before; paśyāścaryāṇi = paśya — view + āścaryāṇi — wonders; bhārata — O relation of the Bharata family

Look at the supernatural rulers, the supernatural destroyers, the two supernatural doctors and the supernatural stormers. View many wonders which were unseen before, O relation of the Bharata family. (11.6)

इहैकस्थं जगत्कृत्स्नं
पश्याद्य सचराचरम् ।
मम देहे गुडाकेश
यच्चान्यद्द्रष्टुमिच्छसि ॥११.७॥

ihaikasthaṁ jagatkṛtsnaṁ
paśyādya sacarācaram
mama dehe guḍākeśa
yaccānyaddraṣṭumicchasi (11.7)

ihaikastham = iha — here + ekastham — situated in one reality; jagat — universe; kṛtsnam — entire; paśyādya = pasya — see + adya — now; sacarācaram — with active and inactive; mama — of Me; dehe — in the body; guḍākeśa — O conqueror of sleep; yac = yad — what; cānyad = cānyat = ca — and + anyat — other; draṣṭum — to see; icchasi — you desire

Here, O conqueror of sleep, you see the entire universe with all active and inactive manifestations, situated as one reality, in My body. And observe any other manifestations which you desire to see. (11.7)

न तु मां शक्यसे द्रष्टुम्
अनेनैव स्वचक्षुषा ।
दिव्यं ददामि ते चक्षुः
पश्य मे योगमैश्वरम् ॥११.८॥ ॥

na tu māṁ śakyase draṣṭum
anenaiva svacakṣuṣā
divyaṁ dadāmi te cakṣuḥ
paśya me yogamaiśvaram (11.8)

na — not; tu — but; mām — Me; śakyase — you can; draṣṭum — to see; anenaiva = anena — by this + iva (eva) — indeed; svacakṣuṣā — with your vision; divyam — supernatural; dadāmi — I give; te — to you; cakṣuḥ — sight; paśya — look at; me — Me; yogam — mystic power; aiśvaram — majesty

But you cannot see with your vision. I give you supernatural sight to look at My mystic majesty. (11.8)

संजय उवाच
एवमुक्त्वा ततो राजन्
महायोगेश्वरो हरिः ।
दर्शयामास पार्थाय
परमं रूपमैश्वरम् ॥११.९॥

saṁjaya uvāca
evamuktvā tato rājan
mahāyogeśvaro hariḥ
darśayāmāsa pārthāya
paramam rūpamaiśvaram (11.9)

saṁjaya — Sanjaya; uvāca — said; evam — thus; uktvā — having said; tato = tataḥ — then; rājan — O King; mahāyogeśvaro = mahāyogeśvaraḥ — the great master of yoga; hariḥ — Hari, the God Vishnu; darśayāmāsa — reveals; pārthāya — to the son of Pritha; paramam — supreme; rūpam — form; aiśvaram — supernatural glory

Sanjaya said: O King, having said that, the great Master of yoga, Hari, the God Vishnu, revealed to the son of Pṛthā, the Supreme Form, the supernatural glory. (11.9)

अनेकवक्त्रनयनम्
अनेकाद्भुतदर्शनम् ।
अनेकदिव्याभरणं
दिव्यानेकोद्यतायुधम् ॥ ११.१० ॥

anekavaktranayanam
anekādbhutadarśanam
anekadivyābharaṇaṁ
divyānekodyatāyudham (11.10)

anekavaktranayanam = aneka — countless + vaktra — mouth + nayanam — eye; anekādbhutadarśanam = aneka — countless + adbhuta — wonders + darśanam — vision; anekadivyābharaṇaṁ = aneka — countless + divya — supernatural + ābharaṇam — ornament; divyānekodyatāyudham = divya — supernatural + aneka — countless + udyata — uplifted + āyudham — weapon

Countless mouths, eyes, wondrous visions, countless supernatural ornaments, supernatural uplifted weapons, (11.10)

दिव्यमाल्याम्बरधरं
दिव्यगन्धानुलेपनम् ।
सर्वाश्चर्यमयं देवम्
अनन्तं विश्वतोमुखम् ॥ ११.११ ॥

divyamālyāmbaradharaṁ
divyagandhānulepanam
sarvāścaryamayaṁ devam
anantaṁ viśvatomukham (11.11)

divyamālyāmbaradharam = divya — supernatural + mālya — garland + ambara — garment + dharam — wearing; divyagandhānulepanam = divya — supernatural + gandha — perfume + anulepanam — ointment; sarvāścaryamayam = sarvaścarya — all wonder + mayam — made of; devam — God; anantam — infinite; viśvatomukham — facing all directions

...wearing supernatural garlands and garments, with supernatural perfumes and ointments, appearing all wonderful, the God appeared infinite as He faced all directions. (11.11)

दिवि सूर्यसहस्रस्य
भवेद्युगपदुत्थिता ।
यदि भाः सदृशी सा स्याद्
भासस्तस्य महात्मनः ॥ ११.१२ ॥

divi sūryasahasrasya
bhavedyugapadutthitā
yadi bhāḥ sadṛśī sā syād
bhāsastasya mahātmanaḥ(11.12)

divi — in the sky; sūryasahasrasya = sūrya — sun + sahasrasya — of one thousand; bhaved = bhavet — should be; yugapad — at once; utthitā — risen;

yadi — if; bhāḥ — brilliance; sadṛśi — such; sā — it; syād — it might be; bhāsaḥ — of brightness; tasya — of it; mahātmanaḥ — of the great personality

Imagine in the sky, a thousand suns, being at once risen together. If such a brilliance were to be, it might be compared to that Great Personality. (11.12)

तत्रैकस्थं जगत्कृत्स्नं
प्रविभक्तमनेकधा ।
अपश्यद्देवदेवस्य
शरीरे पाण्डवस्तदा ॥११.१३॥

tatraikasthaṁ jagatkṛtsnaṁ
pravibhaktamanekadhā
apaśyaddevadevasya
śarīre pāṇḍavas tadā (11.13)

tatraikastham = tatra — there + ekastham — one position; jagat — universe; kṛtsnam — entire; pravibhaktam — divided; anekadhā — in many ways; apaśyad = apaśyat — he saw; devadevasya — of the God of gods; śarīre — in the body; pāṇḍavas — Arjuna Pandava; tadā — then

There the entire universe existed as one reality divided in many ways. Arjuna Pandava then saw the God of gods in that body. (11.13)

ततः स विस्मयाविष्टो
हृष्टरोमा धनंजयः ।
प्रणम्य शिरसा देवं
कृताञ्जलिरभाषत ॥११.१४॥

tataḥ sa vismayāviṣṭo
hṛṣṭaromā dhanaṁjayaḥ
praṇamya śirasā devaṁ
kṛtāñjalirabhāṣata (11.14)

tataḥ — then; sa = saḥ — he; vismayāviṣṭo = vismayāviṣṭaḥ — one who is amazed; hṛṣṭaromā — one whose hair is bristled; dhanamjayaḥ — Arjuna, conqueror of rich countries; praṇamya — bowing; śirasā — with the head; devam — God; kṛtāñjalir = kṛtāñjaliḥ — making reverence with palms pressed for prayers; abhāsata — he spoke

Then he, who was amazed, whose hair bristled, Arjuna, the conqueror of rich countries, bowing his head to the God, with palm pressed for prayers, spoke. (11.14)

अर्जुन उवाच
पश्यामि देवांस्तव देव देहे
सर्वांस्तथा भूतविशेषसंघान् ।
ब्रह्माणमीशं कमलासनस्थम्
ऋषींश्च सर्वानुरगांश्च दिव्यान् ॥११.१५॥

arjuna uvāca
paśyāmi devāṁstava deva dehe
sarvāṁstathā bhūtaviśeṣasaṁghān
brahmāṇamīśaṁ kamalāsanastham
ṛṣīṁśca sarvānuragāṁśca divyān (11.15)

arjuna — Arjuna; uvāca — said; paśyāmi — I see; devāṁs — spiritual rulers; tava — your; deva — O God; dehe — in the body; sarvāṁs — all; tathā — as well as; bhūtaviśeṣasaṁghān = bhūta — being + viśeṣa — variety + saṁghān — assembled; brahmāṇam — Lord Brahmā; īśam — Lord; kamalāsanasthaṁ = kamala — lotus + āsana — seat + stham — situated; ṛṣīṁśca = ṛṣīn — yogi sages + ca — and; sarvān — all; uragāṁśca = uragān — serpents + ca — and; divyān — supernatural

Arjuna said: I see the supernatural rulers in Your body, O God, as well as all varieties of beings assembled there, Lord Brahmā, who is lotus-seated, all the yogi sages and the supernatural serpents. (11.15)

अनेकबाहूदरवक्त्रनेत्रं
पश्यामि त्वां सर्वतोऽनन्तरूपम् ।
नान्तं न मध्यं न पुनस्तवादिं
पश्यामि विश्वेश्वर विश्वरूप ॥ ११.१६ ॥

anekabāhūdaravaktranetraṁ
paśyāmi tvām sarvato'nantarūpam
nāntaṁ na madhyaṁ na punastavādiṁ
paśyāmi viśveśvara viśvarūpa (11.16)

anekabāhūdaravaktranetram = aneka — countless + bāhu — arm + udara — belly + vaktra — face + netram — eye; paśyāmi — I see; tvām — you; sarvato = sarvataḥ — all directions; 'nantarūpam = anantarūpam = ananta — infinite + rūpam — form; nāntam = na — not + antam — end; na — not; madhyam — middle; na — no; punas = punar — again even; tavādim = tava — of you + ādim — beginning; paśyāmi — I observe; viśveśvara — O Lord of all; viśvarūpa — form of everything

There are countless arms, bellies, faces, and eyes. I see You in all directions, O person of infinite form. There is no end, no middle, nor even a beginning of You. I observe You, O Lord of all, O Form of everything. (11.16)

किरीटिनं गदिनं चक्रिणं च
तेजोराशिं सर्वतो दीप्तिमन्तम् ।
पश्यामि त्वां दुर्निरीक्ष्यं समन्ताद्
दीप्तानलार्कद्युतिमप्रमेयम् ॥ ११.१७॥

kirīṭinaṁ gadinaṁ cakriṇaṁ ca
tejorāśiṁ sarvato dīptimantam
paśyāmi tvāṁ durnirīkṣyaṁ samantād
dīptānalārkadyutim aprameyam (11.17)

kirīṭinam — crowned; gadinam — armed with a club; cakriṇam — bearing a discs; ca — and; tejorāśim = tejo — splendor + rāśim — a mass; sarvato = sarvataḥ — on all sides; dīptimantam — shining wondrously; paśyāmi — I see; tvām — you; durnirīkṣyam — difficult to behold; samantād = samantāt — in entirety; dīptānalārkadyutim = dīpta — blazing + anala — fire + arka — sun + dyutim — effulgence; aprameyam — immeasurable

This Form is crowned, armed with a club, bearing a discus, a mass of splendor on all sides, shining wondrously with immeasurable radiance of the sun and blazing fire. I see You in entirety, You Who are difficult to behold. (11.17)

त्वमक्षरं परमं वेदितव्यं
त्वमस्य विश्वस्य परं निधानम् ।
त्वमव्ययः शाश्वतधर्मगोप्ता
सनातनस्त्वं पुरुषो मतो मे ॥ ११.१८॥

tvamakṣaraṁ paramaṁ veditavyaṁ
tvamasya viśvasya paraṁ nidhānam
tvamavyayaḥ śāśvatadharmagoptā
sanātanastvaṁ puruṣo mato me (11.18)

tvam — you; akṣaram — imperishable; paramam — supreme; veditavyam — to be revealed; tvam — you; asya — of it; viśvasya — of all; param — ultimate; nidhānam — shelter; tvam — you; avyayaḥ — imperishable; śāśvatadharmagoptā = śāśvata — eternal + dharma — law + goptā — guardian; sanātanaḥ — most ancient; tvam — you; puruṣo = puruṣaḥ — person; mato = mataḥ — thought; me — of me

You are the indestructible Supreme Reality, to be realized. You are the ultimate shelter of all. You are the imperishable, eternal guardian of law. It seems to me that You are the most ancient person. (11.18)

अनादिमध्यान्तमनन्तवीर्यम्
अनन्तबाहुं शशिसूर्यनेत्रम्
पश्यामि त्वां दीप्तहुताशवक्त्रं
स्वतेजसा विश्वमिदं तपन्तम् ॥११.१९॥

Anādimadhyāntam anantavīryam
anantabāhuṁ śaśisūryanetram
paśyāmi tvāṁ dīptahutāśavaktraṁ
svatejasā viśvamidaṁ tapantam (11.19)

anādimadhyāntam = an — without + ādi — beginning + madhya — middle + antam — end; anantavīryam = ananta — unlimited + vīryam — manly power; anantabāhuṁ = ananta — unlimited + bāhum — arm; śaśisūryanetram = śaśi — moon + sūrya — sun + netram — eye; paśyāmi — I see; tvām — you; dīptahutāśavaktraṁ = dīpta — blazing + hutāśa — oblation-eating + vaktram — mouth; svatejasā — with Your splendor; viśvam — universe; idam — this; tapantam — heating

You who are without beginning, middle, or ending, Who has infinite manly power, Who has unlimited arms, Who has the sun and moon as Your eyes, I see You, with the blazing oblation-eating mouth, heating this universe with Your Own splendor. (11.19)

द्यावापृथिव्योरिदमन्तरं हि
व्याप्तं त्वयैकेन दिशश्च सर्वाः ।
दृष्ट्वाद्भुतं रूपम् उग्रं तवेदं
लोकत्रयं प्रव्यथितं महात्मन् ॥११.२०॥

dyāvāpṛthivyoridam antaraṁ hi
vyāptaṁ tvayaikena diśaścasarvāḥ
dṛṣṭvādbhutaṁ rūpam ugraṁ tavedaṁ
lokatrayaṁ pravyathitaṁ mahātman (11.20)

dyāvāpṛthivyor = dyāvāpṛthivyoḥ — of heaven and earth; idam — this; antaram — space between; hi — indeed; vyāptam - pervaded; tvayaikena = tvaya — by you + ekena - alone; diśaḥ — directions; ca — and; sarvāḥ — all; dṛṣtvā — having seen + adbhutam — marvelous; rūpam — form; ugram — terrible; tavedam = tava — your + idam — this; lokatrayam = loka — world + trayam — three; pravyathitam — trembling; mahātman — O great personality

In all directions, the space between heaven and earth is pervaded by You alone. Seeing Your marvelous Form, of a terrible feature, the three worlds tremble, O great Personality. (11.20)

अमी हि त्वा सुरसंघा विशन्ति
केचिद्भीताः प्राञ्जलयो गृणन्ति ।
स्वस्तीत्युक्त्वा महर्षिसिद्धसंघाः
स्तुवन्ति त्वां स्तुतिभिः पुष्कलाभिः
॥ ११.२१ ॥

amī hi tvā surasaṁghā viśanti
kecidbhītāḥ prāñjalayo gṛṇanti
svastītyuktvā maharṣisiddhasaṁghāḥ
stuvanti tvāṁ stutibhiḥ puṣkalābhiḥ
(11.21)

amī — those; hi — truly; tvām — you; surasaṁghā = sura — supernatural ruler + saṁghā — groups; viśanti — they enter; kecid — some; bhītāḥ — terrified; prāñjalayo = prāñjalayaḥ — bowing with palms pressed together; gṛṇanti — they offer praise; svastīty = svastīti = sv (su) — suitable + asti — there be + iti — thus; uktvā — saying; maharṣisiddhasaṁghāḥ = mahārṣi — great yogi sages + siddha — perfected yogis + saṁghāḥ — groups; stuvanti — they praise; tvām — you; stutibhiḥ — with glorification; puṣkalābhiḥ — with lavish

Those groups of supernatural rulers enter You. Some being terrified, bowing with palms pressed together, offer praise. "May everything be suitable," they say. The groups of great yogi sages and perfected yogis praise You with lavish glorification. (11.21)

रुद्रादित्या वसवो ये च साध्या
विश्वेऽश्विनौ मरुतश्चोष्मपाश्च ।
गन्धर्वयक्षासुरसिद्धसंघा
वीक्षन्ते त्वां विस्मिताश्चैव सर्वे ॥ ११.२२॥

rudrādityā vasavo ye ca sādhyā
viśve'śvinau marutaścoṣmapāśca
gandharvayakṣā surasiddhasaṁghā
vīkṣante tvām vismitāś caiva
sarve(11.22)

rudrādityā = rudra — supernatural destroyers + ādityāḥ — supernatural rulers; vasavo = vasavaḥ — Vasus, assistants to supernatural rulers; ye — who; ca — and; sādhyā — Sādhya, guardian angels; viśve — Vishvadevas supernatural priests; 'śvinau = aśvinau — two primal supernatural doctors; marutaścoṣmapāś = marutaḥ — supernatural stormers + ca — and + uṣmapāḥ — spirits who take vapor bodies; ca — and; gandharvayakṣāsurasiddhasaṁghā = gandharva — celestial musicians + yakṣa — spirits guarding natural resources + asura — supernatural rebels + siddha — perfected souls + saṁghā — groups; vīkṣante — they behold; tvām — you; vismitāścaiva = vismitāḥ — amazed + ca — and + iva (eva) — indeed; sarve — all

The supernatural destroyers, the supernatural rulers, the assistants to those rulers, these and the Sādhya guardian angels, the Vishvadeva supernatural priests, the two primal supernatural doctors, the supernatural stormers, the spirits who take vapor bodies, the groups of celestial musicians, the spirits guarding natural resources, the supernatural rebels and the perfected souls, behold You. And they are all amazed. (11.22)

रूपं महत्ते बहुवक्त्रनेत्रं
महाबाहो बहुबाहूरुपादम् ।
बहूदरं बहुदंष्ट्राकरालं
दृष्ट्वा लोकाः प्रव्यथितास्तथाहम्॥ ११.२३॥

rūpaṁ mahatte bahuvaktranetraṁ
mahābāho bahubāhūrupādam
bahūdaraṁ bahudaṁṣṭrākarālaṁ
dṛṣṭvā lokāḥ pravyathitās tathāham
(11.23)

rūpam — form; mahat — great; te — your; bahuvaktranetram = bahu — many + vaktra — mouth + netram — eye; mahābāho — O mighty-armed Person; bahubāhūrupādam = bahu — many + bāhu — arm + ūru — thigh + pādam — foot; bahūdaram = bahu — many + udaram — belly; bahudaṁṣṭrākarālam = bahu — many + daṁṣṭrā — teeth + karālam — terrible; dṛṣṭvā — having seen; lokāḥ — the world; pravyathitāḥ — trembling; tathā — as well as; 'ham = aham — I

O mighty-armed Person, having seen Your great Form with many mouths, and many arms, thighs, and feet, many bellies and many terrible teeth, the worlds tremble as well as I. (11.23)

नभःस्पृशं दीप्तमनेकवर्णं
व्यात्ताननं दीप्तविशालनेत्रम् ।
दृष्ट्वा हि त्वां प्रव्यथितान्तरात्मा
धृतिं न विन्दामि शमं च विष्णो ॥११.२४॥

nabhaḥspṛśaṁ dīptamanekavarṇaṁ
vyāttānanaṁ dīptaviśālanetram
dṛṣṭvā hi tvāṁ pravyathitāntarātmā
dhṛtiṁ na vindāmi śamaṁ ca viṣṇo
(11.24)

nabhaḥspṛśaṁ = nabhaḥ — sky + spṛśaṁ — touching, extending; dīptam — glowing; aneka — many; varṇam — colors; vyātta — open; ānanam — mouths; dīpta — glowing; viśāla — very great; netram — eyes; dṛṣṭvā — seeing; hi — certainly; tvām — You; pravyathita — perturbed; antaḥ — within; ātmā — soul; dhṛtim — steadiness; na — not; vindāmi — I have; śamam — mental tranquillity; ca — also; viṣṇo — O Lord Viṣṇu.

Having seen You, sky extending, blazing, multi-colored, with gaping mouths and blazing vast eyes, there is a shivering in my soul. I find no courage, nor stability, O God Vishnu. (11.24)

दंष्ट्राकरालानि च ते मुखानि
दृष्ट्वैव कालानलसंनिभानि ।
दिशो न जाने न लभे च शर्म
प्रसीद देवेश जगन्निवास ॥११.२५॥

daṁṣṭrākarālāni ca te mukhāni
dṛṣṭvaiva kālānalasaṁnibhāni
diśo na jāne na labhe ca śarma
prasīda deveśa jagannivāsa (11.25)

daṁṣṭrā — teeth; karālāni — terrible; ca — also; te — Your; mukhāni — faces; dṛṣṭvā — seeing; eva — thus; kāla-anala — the fire of death; sannibhāni — as if; diśaḥ — the directions; na — not; jāne — I know; na — not; labhe — I obtain; ca — and; śarma — grace; prasīda — be pleased; deva-īśa — O Lord of all lords; jagat-nivāsa — O refuge of the worlds

And seeing Your Form with many mouths, having terrible teeth, glowing like the fire of universal destruction, I cannot determine the cardinal points. I do not find any peace of mind. Have mercy, O Lord of the gods, Abode of the universe. (11.25)

अमी च त्वां धृतराष्ट्रस्य पुत्राः
सर्वे सहैवावनिपालसंघैः ।
भीष्मो द्रोणः सूतपुत्रस्तथासौ
सहास्मदीयैरपि योधमुख्यैः ॥११.२६॥

amī ca tvāṁ dhṛtarāṣṭrasya putrāḥ
sarve sahaivāvanipāla saṁghaiḥ
bhīṣmo droṇaḥ sūtaputrastathāsau
sahāsmadīyairapi yodhamukhyaiḥ
(11.26)

amī — those; ca — and; tvāṁ — you; dhṛtarāṣṭrasya — of Dhṛtarāṣṭra; putrāḥ — sons; sarve — all; sahaivāvanipālasaṁghaiḥ = saha — with + eva — indeed+avanipāla — rulers of the earth + saṁghaiḥ — with groups; bhīṣmo = bhīṣmaḥ — Bhishma; droṇaḥ — Droṇa; sūtaputraḥ — Karna, son of the charioteer; tathāsau=tathā — as well as + asau — that; sahāsmadīyair= saha — along with +asmadīyaiḥ — with ours; api — also; yodhamukhyaiḥ — with chief warriors

And those, all the sons of Dhṛtarāṣṭra, along with the groups of rulers, Bhishma, Droṇa, as well as that son of the charioteer, along with our men and also our chief warriors, are in contrast to You. (11.26)

वक्त्राणि ते त्वरमाणा विशन्ति
दंष्ट्राकरालानि भयानकानि ।
केचिद्विलग्ना दशनान्तरेषु
संदृश्यन्ते चूर्णितैरुत्तमाङ्गैः ॥११.२७॥

vaktrāṇi te tvaramāṇā viśanti
daṁṣṭrākarālāni bhayānakāni
kecidvilagnā daśanāntareṣu
saṁdṛśyante cūrṇitair uttamāṅgaiḥ
(11.27)

vaktrāṇi — mouths; te — your; tvaramāṇā — speedily; viśanti — they enter; daṁṣṭrākarālāni = daṁṣṭrā — teeth + karālāni — dreadful; bhayānakāni — fearful; kecid (kecit) — some: vilagnā — clinging: daśanāntareṣu = daśana — tooth + antareṣu — in between; saṁdṛśyante — they are seen'; cūrṇitaiḥ — with crushed; uttamāṅgaiḥ — with heads

They speedily enter Your fearful mouths, which have dreadful teeth. Some cling between the teeth. They are seen with crushed heads. (11.27)

यथा नदीनां बहवोऽम्बुवेगाः
समुद्रमेवाभिमुखा द्रवन्ति ।
तथा तवामी नरलोकवीरा
विशन्ति वक्त्राण्यभिविज्वलन्ति ॥११.२८॥

yathā nadīnāṁ bahavo'mbuvegāḥ
samudramevābhimukhā dravanti
tathā tavāmī naralokavīrā
viśanti vaktrāṇyabhivijvalanti
(11.28)

yathā — as; nadīnāṁ — of the rivers; bahavo — bahavaḥ — many; 'mbuvegāḥ — ambuvegāḥ — water currents; samudram — sea; evābhimukhā — eva —

indeed + abhimukhā — facing towards; dravanti — they flow; tathā —so; tavāmī — tava — of you + ami — those; naralokavīrā = nara — man + loka — world + vīrā —heroes; viśanti — they enter; vaktràni — mouths; abhivijvalanti — they are flaming

As the water currents of many rivers flow to the sea, so the earthly heroes enter Your mouths, which are flaming. (11.28)

यथा प्रदीप्तं ज्वलनं पतंगा
विशन्ति नाशाय समृद्धवेगाः ।
तथैव नाशाय विशन्ति लोकास्
तवापि वक्त्राणि समृद्धवेगाः ॥ ११.२९॥

yathā pradīptaṁ jvalanaṁ pataṁgā
viśanti nāśāya samṛddhavegāḥ
tathaiva nāśāya viśanti lokās
tavāpi vaktrāṇi samṛddhavegāḥ (11.29)

yathā — as; pradīptaṁ — blazing; jvalanaṁ —fire; pataṁgā — moths; viśanti — enter; nāśāya — to destruction; samṛddhavegāḥ — with great speed; tathaiva -tathā —so + iva (eva) — indeed; nāśāya — to ruination; viśanti — enter; lokāh — worlds; tavāpi = lava — you + api — also; vaktrāṇi — mouths; samṛddhavegāḥ — with great speed

As moths speedily enter a blazing fire to destruction, so to ruination, the worlds enter Your mouths with great speed. (11.29)

लेलिह्यसे ग्रसमानः समन्ताल्
लोकान्समग्रान्वदनैर्ज्वलद्भिः ।
तेजोभिरापूर्य जगत्समग्रं
भासस्तवोग्राः प्रतपन्ति विष्णो ॥ ११.३०॥

lelihyase grasamānaḥ samantāl
lokānsamagrānvadanai jvaladbhiḥ
tejobhirāpūrya jagatsamagraṁ
bhāsastavogrāḥ pratapanti viṣṇo
(11.30)

lelihyase — you lick; grasamānaḥ — swallow; samantāt — from all sides; lokān — the worlds; samagrān —all: vadanaiḥ — with mouths; jvaladbhiḥ — with flaming; tejobhiḥ — with splendor; āpūrya — filling;jagat — universe; samagraṁ — all; bhāsaḥ — rays; tavogrāḥ - tava —your + ugrāh — horrible; pratapanti — burns; viṣṇo — O Lord Vishnu

You lick, swallowing from all sides, all the worlds with Your flaming mouths, filling the universes with splendor, Your horrible blazing rays burn it, O Lord Vishnu . (11.30)

आख्याहि मे को भवानुग्ररूपो
नमोऽस्तु ते देववर प्रसीद ।
विज्ञातुमिच्छामि भवन्तमाद्यं
न हि प्रजानामि तव प्रवृत्तिम् ॥ ११.३१॥

ākhyāhi me ko bhavānugrarūpo
namo'stu te devavara prasīda
vijñātumicchāmi bhavantamādyaṁ
na hi prajānāmi tava pravṛttim (11.31)

ākhyāhi — explain; me — to me; ko = kaḥ — who; bhavān — respected person; ugrarūpo — ugrarūpaḥ — of terrible form; namo = namaḥ — homage; 'stu — astu — may it be; te — to you; devavara — best of the gods; prasīda — have mercy; vijnātum — to understand; icchāmi — I want; bhavantam — Your lordship; ādyaṁ — primal person: na — not: hi — indeed; prajānāmi — I know; tava — your; pravṛttim — intention

Explain to me who You are, O respected Person of terrible form. I gave my homage to You, O best of gods. Have mercy! I want to understand You, O Primal Person. I do not know Your intentions. (11.31)

श्रीभगवानुवाच
कालोऽस्मि लोकक्षयकृत्प्रवृद्धो
लोकान्समाहर्तुमिह प्रवृत्तः ।
ऋतेऽपि त्वा न भविष्यन्ति सर्वे
येऽवस्थिताः प्रत्यनीकेषु योधाः ॥ ११.३२ ॥

śrībhagavānuvāca
kālo'smi lokakṣayakṛt pravṛddho
lokānsamāhartumiha pravṛttaḥ
ṛte'pi tvāṁ na bhaviṣyanti sarve
ye'vasthitāḥ pratyanīkeṣu yodhāḥ
(11.32)

śrī bhagavān — the Blessed Lord; uvāca — said; kālo — kālah — time-limit; 'smi = asmi — I am; lokaksayakrt — loka — world + ksaya — destruction + kit — causing; pravṛddho — pravṛddhaḥ — mighty; lokān — worlds; samāhartum — to annihilate; iha — here; pravṛttaḥ — appeared; ṛte — without; 'pi = api — also; tvāṁ —you na — not, cease; bhaviṣyanti — they will live; sarve — all; ye — who ; 'vasthitāḥ = avasthitāḥ — armored; pratyanikeṣu — on both armies; yodhāḥ — warriors

The Blessed Lord said: I am the time limit, the mighty world-destroying Cause, appearing here to annihilate the worlds. Even without you, all the armored warriors, in both armies will cease to live. (11.32)

तस्मात्त्वमुत्तिष्ठ यशो लभस्व
जित्वा शत्रून्भुङ्क्ष्व राज्यं समृद्धम् ।
मयैवैते निहताः पूर्वमेव
निमित्तमात्रं भव सव्यसाचिन् ॥
११.३३ ॥

tasmāttvamuttiṣṭha yaśo labhasva
jitvā śatrūnbhuṅkṣva rājyaṁ samṛddham
mayaivaite nihatāḥ pūrvameva
nimittamātraṁ bhava savyasācin (11.33)

tasmāt — therefore; tvam — you; uttiṣṭha — stand; yaśo — yaśaḥ — glory; labhasva — get; jitvā — having conquered; śatrūn — enemies; bhuṅkṣva — enjoy; rājyaṁ — country; samṛddham — prosperous; mayaivaite — mayā — by me + eva — indeed + ete — these; nihatāḥ — supernaturally-destroyed; pūrvam — already; eva — indeed; nimittamātraṁ = nimitta — agent + mātraṁ — only; bhava — be; savyasācin — O ambidextrous archer

Therefore you should stand up! Get the glory! Having conquered the enemies, enjoy a prosperous country. These fellows are supernaturally disposed by Me already. Be only the agent, O ambidextrous archer. (11.33)

द्रोणं च भीष्मं च जयद्रथं च
कर्णं तथान्यानपि योधवीरान् ।
मया हतांस्त्वं जहि मा व्यथिष्ठा
युध्यस्व जेतासि रणे सपत्नान् ॥ ११.३४॥

droṇaṁ ca bhīṣmaṁ ca jayadrathaṁ ca
karṇaṁ tathānyānapi yodhavīrān
mayā hatāṁstvaṁ jahi mā vyathiṣṭhā
yudhyasva jetāsi raṇe sapatnān (11.34)

droṇaḥ — Droṇa; ca — and; bhīṣmaṁ — Bhishma; ca — and; jayadrathaṁ — Jayadratha; ca —.and; karṇaṁ — Karṇa; tathānyān = tathā — as well as; anyān — others; api — also: yodhavīrān — battle heroes; mayā — by me; hatāṁ — supernaturally hurt; tvaṁ — you; jahi — physically kill; mā — not; vyathiṣṭhā — hesitate; yudhyasva — fight; jetāsi — you will conquer; raṇe — in battle; sapatnān — enemies

Droṇa, Bhishma, Jayadratha, and Karṇa, as well as other battle heroes, were supernaturally hurt by Me. You may physically kill them. Do not hesitate. Fight! You will conquer the enemies in battle. (11.34)

संजय उवाच
एतच्छ्रुत्वा वचनं केशवस्य
कृताञ्जलिर्वेपमानः किरीटी ।
नमस्कृत्वा भूय एवाह कृष्णं
सगद्गदं भीतभीतः प्रणम्य ॥ ११.३५॥

saṁjaya uvāca
etacchrutvā vacanaṁ keśavasya
kṛtāñjalirvepamānaḥ kirīṭī
namaskṛtvā bhūya evāha kṛṣṇaṁ
sagadgadaṁ bhītabhītaḥ praṇamya (11.35)

saṁjaya — Sanjaya; uvāca — said; etat — this; śrutvā — having heard; vacanaṁ — speech; keśavasya — of the handsome-haired Krsna; kṛtāñjalil— offering respects with joined palms; vepamānah — trembling; kirīṭī — Arjuna, the crowned one; namaskṛtvā = namaḥ — obeisances + krtvā — having made; bhūya — again; evāha = eva — indeed + aha — said; kṛṣṇaṁ — Kṛṣṇaṁ; sagadgadaṁ — stutteringly; bhītabhītaḥ — very frightened; praṇamya — prostrations

Sanjaya said: Having heard the speech of the handsome-haired Krishna, Arjuna, the crowned one, who was trembling, offered respect with joined palms. Bowing again, he stutteringly, with much fright and prostrations, spoke to Krishna. (11.35)

अर्जुन उवाच
स्थाने हृषीकेश तव प्रकीर्त्या
जगत्प्रहृष्यत्यनुरज्यते च ।
रक्षांसि भीतानि दिशो द्रवन्ति
सर्वे नमस्यन्ति च सिद्धसंघाः ॥ ११.३६॥

arjuna uvāca
sthāne hṛṣīkeśa tava prakīrtyā
jagatprahṛṣyatyanurajyate ca
rakṣāṁsi bhītāni diśo dravanti
sarve namasyanti ca siddhasaṁghāḥ
(11.36)

Arjuna — Arjuna; uvāca — said; sthāne — in position; hṛṣīkeśa — masterful controller of the senses; tava — your; prakīrtyā — by fame; jagat — universe; prahṛṣyati — rejoices; anurajyate — is delighted; ca — and; prahṛṣyati —

demons; bhītāni — terrified; diśo = diśaḥ — directions; dravanti — they flee; sarve — all; namasyanti — they will reverentially bow; ca — and; siddhasaṁghāḥ — groups of perfected souls

Arjuna said: Everything is in position, O Hṛṣīkeśa, masterful controller of the senses. The universe rejoices and is delighted by Your fame. The demons being terrified, flee in all directions. All the groups of perfected souls will reverentially bow to You. (11.36)

कस्माच्च ते न नमेरन्महात्मन्
गरीयसे ब्रह्मणोऽप्यादिकर्त्रे ।
अनन्त देवेश जगन्निवास
त्वमक्षरं सदसत्तत्परं यत् ॥ ११.३७॥

kasmācca te na nameranmahātman
garīyase brahmaṇo'pyādikartre
ananta deveśa jagannivāsa
tvamakṣaraṁ sadasattat paraṁ yat (11.37)

kasmāt — why; ca — and; te — to you; na — not; nameran — they should bow; mahātmān — O great soul; garīyase — greater; brahmaṇaḥ — than Brahma; 'pi = api — also; ādikartre — ādi — original + kartre — to the creator; ananta — infinite: deveśa — lord of the gods; jagan (jagat) — universe + nivāsa — resort; tvam — you; akṣaraṁ — imperishable basis of energies; sat — sum total permanent life; asat — sum total temporary existence; tatparaṁ — that which is beyond; yat = yad — whatever

And why should they not bow to You, O great soul, original creator, Who is also greater than Brahmā, Who is the infinite Lord of the gods, the resort of the world? You are the imperishable basis of energies, the sum total permanent life, the sum total temporary existence, and whatever is beyond all that. (11.37)

त्वमादिदेवः पुरुषः पुराणस्
त्वमस्य विश्वस्य परं निधानम् ।
वेत्तासि वेद्यं च परं च धाम
त्वया ततं विश्वमनन्तरूप ॥ ११.३८॥

tvamādidevaḥ puruṣaḥ purāṇas
tvamasya viśvasya paraṁ nidhānam
vettāsi vedyaṁ ca paraṁ ca dhāma
tvayā tataṁ viśvamanantarūpa (11.38)

tvam — you; ādidevaḥ— first God; puruṣaḥ — spirit; purāṇaḥ — most ancient; tvam — you; asya — of it; viśvasya — of the universe; paraṁ — supreme; nidhānam — refuge; vettāsi = vettā — knower + asi — you are; vedyaṁ — that which is to be known; ca — and; paraṁ — ultimate; ca — and; dhāma — sanctuary; tvayā — by you; tataṁ — pervaded; viśvam — universe; anantarūpa — Person of Infinite Form

You are the First God, the most ancient spirit. You are the knower, You are the supreme refuge of all the worlds. You are that which is to be known. You are the ultimate sanctuary. By You, the universe is pervaded, O Person of Infinite Form. (11.38)

वायुर्यमोऽग्निर्वरुणः शशाङ्कः
प्रजापतिस्त्वं प्रपितामहश्च ।
नमो नमस्तेऽस्तु सहस्रकृत्वः
पुनश्च भूयोऽपि नमो नमस्ते ॥ ११.३९॥

vāyuryamo'gnirvaruṇaḥ śaśāṅkaḥ
prajāpatistvaṁ prapitāmahaśca
namo namaste'stu sahasrakṛtvaḥ
punaśca bhūyo'pi namo namaste (11.39)

vāyuḥ — Vāyu wind regulator; yamo — yamaḥ — Yama, Death Supervisor; 'gniḥ = agniḥ = Agni, fire controller; varuṇaḥ — Varuṇa, Master of the waters; śaśāṅkaḥ — Śaśāṅka — moon lord; prajāpatiḥ — procreator Brahmā; tvaṁ — you; prapitāmahaḥ — father of Brahmā; ca — and; namo — namaḥ — obeisances: namaḥ — obeisances repeated; te — to you; 'stu = astu — let it be; sahasrakṛtvaḥ — a thousand times made; punasca — punaḥ (punar) — again + ca — and; bhūyo — bhuyaḥ — again; 'pi — api — also; namo — namaḥ — obeisances repeated; te — to you

You are represented by Vāyu, the wind regulator; Yama, the death supervisor; Agni, the fire controller; Varuṇa, the master of the waters; Śāśaṅka, the moon Lord; Procreator Brahmā; and you are the father of Brahmā. Obeisances unto You a thousand times repeatedly. Again and again, honor to You! (11.39)

नमः पुरस्तादथ पृष्ठतस्ते
नमोऽस्तु ते सर्वत एव सर्व ।
अनन्तवीर्यामितविक्रमस्त्वं
सर्वं समाप्नोषि ततोऽसि सर्वः ॥ ११.४०॥

namaḥ purastādatha pṛṣṭhataste
namo'stu te sarvata eva sarva
anantavīryāmita vikramastvaṁ
sarvaṁ samāpnoṣi tato'si sarvaḥ
(11.40)

namaḥ — reverence; purstāt — from in front; atha — and then; pṛṣṭhataḥ — from behind; te — to you; namo — namaḥ — obeisances; 'stu = astu — let there be; te — to you; sarvata — on all sides; eva — also; sarva — sum total reality; anantavīryāmitavikramaḥ = ananta — infinite + vīrya — power + amita — immeasurable + vikramaḥ — might; tvaṁ — you; sarvaṁ — everything; samāpnoṣi — you penetrate; tato = tataḥ — thus, in that sense; 'si — asi — you are; sarvaḥ — everything

Reverence to You from the front, from behind. Let there be obeisances to You on all sides, O sum total Reality. You are infinite power, immeasurable might. You penetrate everything. In that sense, You are Everything. (11.40)

सखेति मत्वा प्रसभं यदुक्तं
हे कृष्ण हे यादव हे सखेति.।
अजानता महिमानं तवेदं
मया प्रमादात्प्रणयेन वापि ॥ ११.४१॥

sakheti matvā prasabhaṁ yaduktaṁ
he kṛṣṇa he yādava he sakheti
ajānatā mahimānaṁ tavedaṁ
mayā pramādāt praṇayena vāpi (11.41)

sakheti = sakhā — friend + iti — such as; matvā — considering; prasabhaṁ — impulsively; yat — whatever; uktaṁ — was said; he — hey; kṛṣṇa — Kṛṣṇa ; he — hey; yādava — family man of the Yadus; he — hey; sakheti — sakhā — buddy + iti — thus; ajānatā — through ignorance; mahimānaṁ — majestic supernatural glory; tavedaṁ = tava — your + idam — this; mayā — by me; pramādāt — from familiarity; pranayena- with affection; vāpi = va — or + api — even

Whatever was said impulsively, considering You as a friend, such as, "Hey, Krishna! Hey, family man of the Yadus! Hey, buddy!" was done by me through ignorance of Your majestic supernatural glory or even by affectionate familiarity. (11.41)

यच्चावहासार्थमसत्कृतोऽसि
विहारशय्यासनभोजनेषु ।
एकोऽथ वाप्यच्युत तत्समक्षं
तत्क्षामये त्वामहमप्रमेयम् ॥ ११.४२ ॥

yaccāvahāsārthamasatkṛto'si
vihāraśayyāsanabhojaneṣu
eko'tha vāpyacyut tatsamakṣaṁ
tatkṣāmaye tvām ahamaprameyam
(11.42)

Yat — that; cāvahāsārtham = ca — and + avahāsa — joking + artham — intention; asatkṛto — asatkṛtaḥ — disrespectfully; 'si = asi — you are; vihāraśayyāsanabhojaneṣu = vihāra — play + śayyā — couch + āsana — sitting + bhojaneṣu — in dining; eko = ekaḥ — alone, privately; 'thavāpi = athavāpi = athava — nor + api — also; acyuta — O infallible Kṛṣṇa ; tatsamakṣaṁ — before the public; tat = tad—that; kṣāmaye — I ask forgiveness; tvām — of you; aham — I; aprameyam — one who is boundless

And with intent to joke, You were disrespectfully treated, while playing, while on a couch, while sitting, while dining privately or even in public, O infallible Krishna. For that I ask forgiveness of You Who are boundless. (11.42)

पितासि लोकस्य चराचरस्य
त्वमस्य पूज्यश्च गुरुर्गरीयान् ।
न त्वत्समोऽस्त्यभ्यधिकः कुतोऽन्यो
लोकत्रयेऽप्यप्रतिमप्रभाव ॥ ११.४३ ॥

pitāsi lokasya carācarasya
tvamasya pūjyaśca gururgarīyān
na tvatsamo'styabhyadhikaḥ kuto'nyo
lokatraye'pyapratim aprabhāva (11.43)

pitāsi = pitā — father + asi—you are; lokasya — of the world; carācarasya — of the moving and non-moving; tvam — you; asya — of this; pūjyaśca = pūjyaḥ — worshipable + ca — and; guruḥ — spiritual master; garīyān — gravest; na — not; tvatsamo = tvatsamaḥ= tyat (tvam) —you + samaḥ — similar, like; 'sti = asti — there is; abhyadhikaḥ — greater; kuto = kulaḥ— how; 'nyo = anyaḥ — other; lokatraye — in the three partitions of the universe; 'pi = api — also; apratimaprabhāva — person of incomparable splendor

You are the father of the world, of the moving and non-moving objects. You are the worshipable and gravest spiritual master. There is none like You in the three partitions of the universe. How could anyone be greater, O person of incomparable splendor? (11.43)

तस्मात्प्रणम्य प्रणिधाय कायं
प्रसादये त्वामहमीशमीड्यम् ।
पितेव पुत्रस्य सखेव सख्युः
प्रियः प्रियायार्हसि देव सोढुम् ॥ ११.४४॥

tasmātpraṇamya praṇidhāya kāyaṁ
prasādaye tvāmahamīśamīḍyam
piteva putrasya sakheva sakhyuḥ
priyaḥ priyāyārhasi deva soḍhum
(11.44)

tasmāt — therefore; praṇamya — bowing with reverence; praṇidhāya — lying down; kāyaṁ — body; prasadaye — I ask mercy; tvām — you; aham — of you; īśam — Lord; īḍyam — to be praised; piteva = pitā— father + eva — as; putrasya — of a son; sakheva = sakhā — friend + eva — as; sakhyuḥ — of a chum; priyaḥ — beloved; priyāyārhasi = priyāya — to a lover + arhasi — you should; deva — O God; soḍhum— to be merciful

Therefore, bowing with reverence, lying my body down, I ask for mercy of You, O Lord Who is to be praised. As a father to a son, as a friend to his chum, as a beloved to a lover, You should be merciful, O God. (11.44)

अदृष्टपूर्वं हृषितोऽस्मि दृष्ट्वा
भयेन च प्रव्यथितं मनो मे ।
तदेव मे दर्शय देव रूपं
प्रसीद देवेश जगन्निवास ॥ ११.४५॥

adṛṣṭapūrvaṁ hṛṣito'smi dṛṣṭvā
bhayena ca pravyathitaṁ mano me
tadeva me darśaya deva rūpaṁ
prasīda deveśa jagannivāsa (11.45)

adṛṣṭapūrvaṁ = adṛṣṭa—never seen + pūrvaṁ — previously; hṛṣiṭo = hṛṣitaḥ — delighted; 'smi = asmi — I am; dṛṣṭvā — having seen; bhayena — with fear; ca — and, but; pravyathitaṁ — trembling; mano = manaḥ— mind; me — my; tat — that; eva — indeed: me — to me; darśaya — to see; deva — O God; rūpaṁ — God-form; prasīda — have mercy; deveśa — Lord of gods; jagannivāsa — shelter of the world

Seeing what was never seen before, I am delighted but my mind trembles with fear. Now, O God, cause me to see the God-form. Have mercy, O Lord of the gods, shelter of the world. (11.45)

किरीटिनं गदिनं चक्रहस्तम्
इच्छामि त्वां द्रष्टुमहं तथैव ।
तेनैव रूपेण चतुर्भुजेन
सहस्रबाहो भव विश्वमूर्ते ॥ ११.४६॥

kirīṭinaṁ gadinaṁ cakrahastam
icchāmi tvāṁ draṣṭumah tathaiva
tenaiva rūpeṇa caturbhujena
sahasrabāho bhava viśvamūrte (11.46)

kirīṭinaṁ — form which wears a crown, gadinaṁ — form which is armed with a disc; cakrahastaṁ — for with a club in hand; icchāmi — I wish; tvāṁ — you; draṣṭum — to see; aham — I; tathaiva - tathii — as requested + eva — indeed; tenaiva — tena -with this + eva — indeed; rūpeṇa — with the form;

caturbhujena — with four arms; sahasrabāho — O thousand-armed person; bhava — become; viśvamūrte — person of universal dimensions

I wish to see You wearing a crown, armed with a club, and with a disc in hand, as requested. Please become that four-armed form, O thousand-armed Person, O Person of universal dimensions. (11.46)

श्रीभगवानुवाच
मया प्रसन्नेन तवार्जुनेदं
रूपं परं दर्शितमात्मयोगात् ।
तेजोमयं विश्वमनन्तमाद्यं
यन्मे त्वदन्येन न दृष्टपूर्वम् ॥ ११.४७॥

śrībhagavānuvāca
mayā prasannena tavārjunedaṁ
rūpaṁ paraṁ darśitam ātmayogāt
tejomayaṁ viśvamanantam ādyaṁ
yanme tvadanyena na dṛṣṭapūrvam
(11.47)

śrī bhagavān — the Blessed Lord; uvāca — said; mayā — by me; prasannena — by grace; tavārjunedaṁ = tava — to you + arjuna — Arjuna+ idam — this; rūpaṁ — form; param — supreme; darśitaṁ — manifested; ātmayogāt — from my yoga power: tejomayaṁ — made of supernatural energy; viśvam — universal; anantam — infinite; ādyaṁ — primal; yat — which; me — my; tvadanyena = tvad — besides you + anyena — by any other; na — not; dṛṣṭapūrvam = dṛṣṭa — seen + pūrvam — before

The Blessed Lord said: By My grace to you Arjuna, this Supreme Form was manifested from My yoga power. This Form of Mine which is made of supernatural energy, being universal, infinite and primal, was never seen by another other person besides you. (11.47)

न वेदयज्ञाध्ययनैर्न दानैर्
न च क्रियाभिर्न तपोभिरुग्रैः ।
एवंरूपः शक्य अहं नृलोके
द्रष्टुं त्वदन्येन कुरुप्रवीर ॥ ११.४८॥

na vedayajñādhyayanairna dānair
na ca kriyābhirna tapobhirugraiḥ
evaṁrūpaḥ śakya ahaṁ nṛloke
draṣṭuṁ tvadanyena kurupravīra (11.48)

Na — not; vedayajñādhyayanaiḥ = veda — Veda + yajñā — by sacrificial ceremonies + adyayanaiḥ — by education; na — nor; danaiḥ — by charity as recommended in the Vedic literature; na — not; ca — and; kriyābhiḥ — by special ritual acts; na — not; tapobhiḥ — by austerities; ugraiḥ — by strenuous; evam — as such; rūpaḥ — form; śakya = śakye — can; ahaṁ — I; nṛloke — in the world of human beings; drastuṁ — to see; tvadanyena = tvad — except you + anyena — by another; kurupravīra — great hero of the Kurus

Not by Vedic sacrificial ceremonies, nor by Vedic education, not by offering charity as recommended in the Vedic literatures and not by special ritual acts, nor by strenuous austerities, can I be seen in such a form in this world of human beings except through the method used by you, O great hero of the Kurus. (11.48)

मा ते व्यथा मा च विमूढभावो
दृष्ट्वा रूपं घोरमीदृङ्ममेदम् ।
व्यपेतभीः प्रीतमनाः पुनस्त्वं
तदेव मे रूपमिदं प्रपश्य ॥ ११.४९ ॥

mā te vyathā mā ca vimūḍhabhāvo
dṛṣṭvā rūpaṁ ghoramīdṛṅmamedam
vyapetabhīḥ prītamanāḥ punastvaṁ
tadeva me rūpamidaṁ prapaśya (11.49)

Mā — not; te — of you; vyathā — should tremble; mā — not; ca — and; vimūḍhabhāvo = vimūḍhabhāvaḥ — confused state; dṛṣṭvā — having seen; rūpam — form; ghoram — ghastly; īdṛn = īdṛḥ — such; mamedam = mama — of my + idam — this; vyapetabhīḥ = vyapeta — freed from + bhīḥ — fear; prītamanāḥ — cheerful in mind; punaḥ — again; tvam — you; tat — you; eva — indeed; me — of me; rūpam — form; idam — this; prapaśya — look at

You should not tremble nor be confused after seeing this, My ghastly form. Be free from fear and be cheerful of mind. Again look at this form of Mine. (11.49)

संजय उवाच
इत्यर्जुनं वासुदेवस्तथोक्त्वा
स्वकं रूपं दर्शयामास भूयः ।
आश्वासयामास च भीतमेनं
भूत्वा पुनः सौम्यवपुर्महात्मा ॥ ११.५० ॥

saṁjaya uvāca
ityarjunaṁ vāsudevas tathoktvā
svakaṁ rūpaṁ darśayāmāsa bhūyaḥ
āśvāsayāmāsa ca bhītamenaṁ
bhūtvā punaḥ saumyavapur
mahātmā (11.50)

Saṁjaya — Sanjaya; uvāca — said; iti — thus; arjunam = Arjuna; vāsudevaḥ — Kṛṣṇa , the son of Vasudeva; tathoktvā = tathā — thus + uktvā — having said; svakaṁ — his own; rūpaṁ — divine form; darśayāmāsa — he revealed; bhūyaḥ — again; āsvāsayāmāsa — he caused to be calm; ca — and; bhītam — frightened person; enam — this; bhūtvā — having assumed; punaḥ = punar — again; saumyavapuḥ = saumya — pleasing + vapuḥ — attractive appearance; mahātmā — great person

Sanjaya said: Krishna, the son of Vasudeva, having said this to Arjuna, revealed His own Divine Form. And once again that great person assumed the pleasing, attractive form and caused the frightened Arjuna to be calm. (11.50)

अर्जुन उवाच
दृष्ट्वेदं मानुषं रूपं
तव सौम्यं जनार्दन ।
इदानीमस्मि संवृत्तः
सचेताः प्रकृतिं गतः ॥ ११.५१ ॥

arjuna uvāca
dṛṣṭvedaṁ mānuṣaṁ rūpaṁ
tava saumyaṁ janārdana
idānīmasmi saṁvṛttaḥ
sacetāḥ prakṛtiṁ gataḥ (11.51)

arjuna — Arjuna; uvāca — said; dṛṣṭvedaṁ = dṛṣṭvā — having seen + idam — this; mānuṣaṁ — human: rūpaṁ — form; tava — of you; saumyam — gentle; janārdana — O motivator of human beings; idānīm — now; asmi — I am; saṁvṛttaḥ — satisfied; sacetāḥ — with mind; prakṛtiṁ — to human nature, to normal condition; gataḥ — gone back, returned

Arjuna said: Seeing this gentle, human-like Form of Yours, O Janardana, motivator of human beings, I am satisfied with my mind returned to the normal condition. (11.51)

श्रीभगवानुवाच
सुदुर्दर्शमिदं रूपं
दृष्टवानसि यन्मम ।
देवा अप्यस्य रूपस्य
नित्यं दर्शनकाङ्क्षिणः ॥११.५२॥

śrībhagavānuvāca
sudurdarśamidaṁ rūpaṁ
dṛṣṭavānasi yanmama
devā apyasya rūpasya
nityaṁ darśanakāṅkṣiṇaḥ (11.52)

śrī bhagavān — The Blessed Lord; uvāca — said; sudurdarsam — difficult to perceive; idam — this; rūpaṁ — form; dṛṣṭvān — having seen; asi — you are; yat — which; mamā — of mine; deva — supernatural rulers; api — also; asya — of this; rūpasya — of the form; nityam — always; darśanakāṅkṣiṇaḥ = darśana — sight + kāṅkṣiṇaḥ — wishing

The Blessed Lord said: This Form of Mine which you saw, is difficult to perceive. Even the supernatural rulers always wish for the sight of this Form. (11.52)

नाहं वेदैर्न तपसा
न दानेन न चेज्यया ।
शक्य एवंविधो द्रष्टुं
दृष्टवानसि मां यथा ॥११.५३॥

nāhaṁ vedairna tapasā
na dānena na cejyayā
śakya evaṁvidho draṣṭuṁ
dṛṣṭavānasi māṁ yathā (11.53)

nāhaṁ = na — neither + aham — I; vedaiḥ — by Vedic study; na — nor; tapasā — by austerity; na — nor; dānena — by charily; na — not; cejyayā = ca — and + ijyayā — by sacrificial ceremony; śakya = śakye — I can; evaṁvidho = evaṁvidhaḥ — in that way; draṣṭuṁ — to see; dṛṣṭavān — having seen; asi — you are; mām — me; yathā — as

Neither by Vedic study, nor by austerity, nor by charity, and not by sacrificial ceremony, can I be seen in the way you saw Me. (11.53)

भक्त्या त्वनन्यया शक्य
अहमेवंविधोऽर्जुन ।
ज्ञातुं द्रष्टुं च तत्त्वेन
प्रवेष्टुं च परंतप ॥११.५४॥

bhaktyā tvananyayā śakya
ahamevaṁvidho'rjuna
jñātuṁ draṣṭuṁ ca tattvena
praveṣṭuṁ ca paraṁtapa (11.54)

Bhaktyā — by devotion; tu — only; ananyayā — not in another way, undistracted; śakya = śakye — I can; aham — 1; evaṁvidho = evaṁvidhaḥ — in that way; 'rjuna = arjuna — Arjuna; jñātuṁ — to be known; draṣṭuṁ —to see; ca — and; tattvena — by reality; praveṣṭuṁ — to communicate with; ca — and; paraṁtapa — scorcher of the enemies

By undistracted devotion only, O Arjuna, can I be known, seen in reality, and communicated with, O scorcher of enemies. (11.54)

मत्कर्मकृन्मत्परमो
मद्भक्तः सङ्गवर्जितः ।
निर्वैरः सर्वभूतेषु
यः स मामेति पाण्डव ॥ ११.५५॥

matkarmakṛnmatparamo
madbhaktaḥ saṅgavarjitaḥ
nirvairaḥ sarvabhūteṣu
yaḥ sa mām eti pāṇḍava (11.55)

matkarmakṛt — doing my word; matparamo - matparamaḥ — depending on me; madbhaktaḥ — being devoted to me; saṅgavarjitaḥ = sariga — attachment + varjitaḥ — abandoned; nirvairaḥ — free from hostility; sarvabhūteṣu — to all beings; yah — who; sa = saḥ — he; mām — to me; eti — comes; pāṇḍava — son of Pandu

Whosoever does My work, depending on Me, being devoted to Me, abandoning attachment, being freed from hostility towards all beings, comes to Me, O son of Pṛthā. (11.55)

CHAPTER 12

The Most Disciplined Yogi*

अर्जुन उवाच
एवं सततयुक्ता ये
भक्तास्त्वां पर्युपासते ।
ये चाप्यक्षरमव्यक्तं
तेषां के योगवित्तमाः ॥१२.१॥

arjuna uvāca
evaṁ satatayuktā ye
bhaktāstvāṁ paryupāsate
ye cāpyakṣaramavyaktaṁ
teṣāṁ ke yogavittamāḥ (12.1)

arjuna — Arjuna; uvāca — said; evaṁ — thus; satatayuktā = satata— constantly + yuktā — disciplined in yoga; ye — who; bhaktāh — devoted; tvam —you; paryupāsate — they cherish; ye — who; cāpi = ca — and + api — also; akṣaram — imperishable; avyaktaṁ — invisible existence; teṣāṁ — of them; ke — which; yogavittamāḥ — those who have the highest knowledge of yoga

Arjuna said: Of those who are constantly disciplined in yoga, being also devoted to You, and those who cherish the imperishable invisible existence, which of these two have the highest knowledge of the yoga techniques? (12.1)

श्रीभगवानुवाच
मय्यावेश्य मनो ये मां
नित्ययुक्ता उपासते ।
श्रद्धया परयोपेतास्
ते.मे युक्ततमा मताः ॥१२.२॥

śrībhagavānuvāca
mayyāveśya mano ye māṁ
nityayuktā upāsate
śraddhayā parayopetās
te me yuktatamā matāḥ (12.2)

Śrībhagavān — the Blessed Lord;uvāca — said; mayyāveśya = mayi-on me + āveśya — focusing on: mano = manaḥ — mind; ye — who; māṁ — me; nityayuktā — those who are always disciplined in yoga; upāsate — they worship; śraddhayā — with faith; parayopetās = parayā — with the highest degree; + upetāḥ — endowed; te they; me — to me; yuktatamā — most disciplined; matāḥ — considered

The Blessed Lord said: Those whose minds are focused on Me, who are always disciplined in yoga, who are always involved in worship of Me, who are endowed with the highest degree of faith, they are considered to be the most disciplined. (12.2)

**The Mahābhārata contains no chapter headings. This title was assigned by the translator on the basis of verse 2 of this chapter.*

ये त्वक्षरमनिर्देश्यम्
अव्यक्तं पर्युपासते ।
सर्वत्रगमचिन्त्यं च
कूटस्थमचलं ध्रुवम् ॥१२.३॥

ye tvakṣaramanirdeśyam
avyaktaṁ paryupāsate
sarvatragamacintyaṁ ca
kūṭasthamacalaṁ dhruvam (12.3)

ye — who; tu — but; akṣaram — imperishable; anirdeśyam — undefinable; avyaktaṁ— invisible; paryupāsate — they cherish; sarvatragam — all-pervading; acintyam — inconceivable; ca — and; kūṭastham — unchanging; acalaṁ —- immovable; dhruvam — constant

But those who cherish the imperishable, undefinable, invisible, all-pervading, inconceivable, unchanging, immovable, constant reality, (12.3)

संनियम्येन्द्रियग्रामं
सर्वत्र समबुद्धयः ।
ते प्राप्नुवन्ति मामेव
सर्वभूतहिते रताः ॥१२.४॥

saṁniyamyendriyagrāmaṁ
sarvatra samabuddhayaḥ
te prāpnuvanti māmeva
sarvabhūtahite ratāḥ (12.4)

saṁniyamyendriyagrāmaṁ = saṁniyamya — controlling + indriyagrāmaṁ — all sensual energies; sarvatra — in all respects; samabuddhayaḥ — even-minded; te — them; prāpnuvanti — they attain; mām — me; eva — also; sarvabhūtahite = sarvabhūta — all creatures + hite — in the welfare; ratāḥ — rejoicing

...by controlling all sensual energies, being even-minded in all respects, rejoicing in the welfare of all creatures, they also attain Me. (12.4)

क्लेशोऽधिकतरस्तेषाम्
अव्यक्तासक्तचेतसाम् ।
अव्यक्ता हि गतिर्दुःखं
देहवद्भिरवाप्यते ॥१२.५॥

kleśo'dhikatarasteṣām
avyaktāsaktacetasām
avyaktā hi gatirduḥkhaṁ
dehavadbhiravāpyate (12.5)

kleśo — kleśaḥ — exertion; 'dhikataraḥ = adhikataraḥ — greater; tesam — of them; avyaktāsaktacetasām — avyakta — invisible existence + āsakta — attached + cetasām — of minds; avyaktā — invisible reality; hi — truly; gatiḥ — goal; duḥkhaṁ — difficult; dehavadbhiḥ — by the human beings; avāpyate — is attained

The mental exertion of those whose minds are attached to the invisible existence is greater. The goal of reaching that invisible reality is attained with difficulty by the human beings. (12.5)

ये तु सर्वाणि कर्माणि
मयि संन्यस्य मत्पराः ।
अनन्येनैव योगेन
मां ध्यायन्त उपासते ॥ १२.६ ॥

ye tu sarvāṇi karmāṇi
mayi saṁnyasya matparāḥ
ananyenaiva yogena
māṁ dhyāyanta upāsate (12.6)

ye — who; tu — but; sarvāṇi — all; karmāṇi — actions; mayi — in me; saṁnyasya — deferring: matparāḥ — regarding me as the most important factor; ananyenaiva = ananyena — without another, undistracted + eva — indeed; yogena — with yoga discipline; māṁ — me; dhyayānta — meditating on; upāsate — they worship

But those who defer all actions to Me, regarding Me as the most important factor, who meditate on Me with undistracted yoga discipline, do worship Me. (12.6)

तेषामहं समुद्धर्ता
मृत्युसंसारसागरात् ।
भवामि नचिरात्पार्थ
मय्यावेशितचेतसाम् ॥ १२.७ ॥

teṣāmahaṁ samuddhartā
mṛtyusaṁsārasāgarāt
bhavāmi nacirātpārtha
mayyāveśitacetasām (12.7)

teṣām — of those; aham — I; samuddhartā — delivered; mṛtyusaṁsārasāgarāt = mṛtyu — death + saṁsāra — reincarnations + sāgarāt — from the vast existence; bhavāmi — I am; nacirāt — soon; pārtha — son of Pṛthā; mayyāveśitacetasām = mayi — in me + āveśita — intently, invested in + cetasām — of thoughts

I am the deliverer of those devotees, rescuing them from the vast existence of death and reincarnation. O son of Pṛthā, I soon deliver those devotees whose thoughts are intently invested in Me. (12.7)

मय्येव मन आधत्स्व
मयि बुद्धिं निवेशय ।
निवसिष्यसि मय्येव
अत ऊर्ध्वं न संशयः ॥ १२.८ ॥

mayyeva mana ādhatsva
mayi buddhiṁ niveśaya
nivasiṣyasi mayyeva
ata ūrdhvaṁ na saṁśayaḥ (12.8)

mayyeva = mayi — on me + eva — alone; mana — mind; ādhatsva — place; mayi — on me; buddhiṁ — intellect; niveśaya — cause to be absorbed; nivasiṣyasi — you will be focused: mayyeva = mayi — in me + eva — indeed; ata ūrdhvaṁ — from now onwards; na — not; saṁśayaḥ — doubt

Placing your mind on Me alone, causing your intellect to be absorbed in Me alone, you will be focused on Me from now onward. There is no doubt about this. (12.8)

अथ चित्तं समाधातुं
न शक्नोषि मयि स्थिरम् ।
अभ्यासयोगेन ततो
मामिच्छाप्तुं धनंजय ॥१२.९॥

atha cittaṁ samādhātuṁ
na śaknoṣi mayi sthiram
abhyāsayogena tato
māmicchāptuṁ dhanaṁjaya (12.9)

atha — if however; cittam — thought; samādhātum — to anchor; na — not; śaknoṣi — you can; mayi — on me; sthiram — steadily; abhyāsayogena = abhyāsa — practice + yogena — by yoga; tato = tataḥ — then; mām — me; icchāptum = iccha — with + āptuṁ — to attain; dhanaṁjaya — conqueror of wealthy countries

If, however, you cannot steadily anchor your thoughts on Me, then by yoga practice, try to attain Me, O conqueror of wealthy countries. (12.9)

अभ्यासेऽप्यसमर्थोऽसि
मत्कर्मपरमो भव ।
मदर्थमपि कर्माणि
कुर्वन्सिद्धिमवाप्स्यसि ॥१२.१०॥

abhyāse'pyasamartho'si
matkarmaparamo bhava
madarthamapi karmāṇi
kurvansiddhimavāpsyasi (12.10)

abhyāse — in practice; 'pi = api — perchance; asamartho = asamarthaḥ — incapable; 'si = asi — you are; matkarmaparamo = matkarmaparamaḥ = matkarma — my work + paramaḥ — be absorbed; bhava — be; madartham — for my sake; api — even; karmāṇi — activities; kurvan — doing; siddhim — perfection; avāpsyasi — you will attain

But if perchance, you are incapable of such practice, then by being absorbed in My work, or even by doing activities for My sake, you will attain perfection. (12.10)

अथैतदप्यशक्तोऽसि
कर्तुं मद्योगमाश्रितः ।
सर्वकर्मफलत्यागं
ततः कुरु यतात्मवान् ॥१२.११॥

athaitadapyaśakto'si
kartuṁ madyogamāśritaḥ
sarvakarmaphalatyāgaṁ
tataḥ kuru yatātmavān (12.11)

athaitat = atha — if + etat — this; api — even: aśakto = aśaktaḥ — unable; 'si = asi — you are; kartum — to do; madyogam — my yoga; aśritaḥ — resorting to; sarvakarmaphalatyāgaṁ = sarvakarmaphala — all results of action + tyāgam — abandoning; tataḥ — then; kuru — act; yatātmavān — with restraint

If you are unable to even do this, then resorting to My yoga process, abandoning all results of action, act with self restraint. (12.11)

श्रेयो हि ज्ञानमभ्यासाज्
ज्ञानाद्ध्यानं विशिष्यते ।
ध्यानात्कर्मफलत्यागस्
त्यागाच्छान्तिरनन्तरम् ॥१२.१२॥

śreyo hi jñānamabhyāsāj
jñānāddhyānaṁ viśiṣyate
dhyānātkarmaphalatyāgas
tyāgācchāntiranantaram (12.12)

śreyo = śreyaḥ — better; hi — indeed; jñānam — derived knowledge, experience; abhyāsāt — from the practice; jñānāt — than derived knowledge; dhyānaṁ — meditation; viśiṣyate — is superior; dhyānāt — than meditation; karmaphalatyāgaḥ = karmaphala — results of action + tyāgaḥ — renunciation; tyāgāt — from renunciation; śāntiḥ — spiritual peace; anantaram — instantly

Indeed, derived knowledge is better than practice. Meditation is superior to derived knowledge. Renunciation of results is better than meditation. From such renunciation, spiritual peace is instantly gained. (12.12)

अद्वेष्टा सर्वभूतानां
मैत्रः करुण एव च ।
निर्ममो निरहंकारः
समदुःखसुखः क्षमी ॥१२.१३॥

adveṣṭā sarvabhūtānāṁ
maitraḥ karuṇa eva ca
nirmamo nirahaṁkāraḥ
samaduḥkhasukhaḥ kṣamī (12.13)

adveṣṭā — one who does not dislike; sarvabhūtānāṁ — all creatures; maitraḥ — friendly; karuṇa — compassionate; eva — indeed; ca — and; nirmamo = nirmamaḥ — free from attachment to possessions; nirahaṁkāraḥ — free from the propensity of, "I am the creator of my actions"; samaduḥkhasukhaḥ = sama — equally disposed + duḥkha — pain + sukhaḥ — pleasure; kṣamī — be patient

One who does not dislike any of the creatures, who is friendly and compassionate, free from attachment to possessions, free from the propensity of "I am the creator of my actions," being equally disposed towards pain and pleasure, being patient, (12.13)

संतुष्टः सततं योगी
यतात्मा दृढनिश्चयः ।
मय्यर्पितमनोबुद्धिर्
यो मद्भक्तः स मे प्रियः ॥१२.१४॥

saṁtuṣṭaḥ satataṁ yogī
yatātmā dṛḍhaniścayaḥ
mayyarpitamanobuddhir
yo madbhaktaḥ sa me priyaḥ (12.14)

saṁtuṣṭaḥ — contented; satataṁ — always; yogī — yogi; yatātmā — one with a controlled self; draḍhaniścayaḥ — determined; mayi — on me; arpitamanobuddhiḥ - arpita — focused + mano = manas — mind + buddhiḥ — intellect; yo = yaḥ — who; madbhaktaḥ — devoted to me; sa = saḥ — he; me — of me; priyaḥ — dear

...the yogi who is always content, who has a controlled self, who is determined, whose mind and intellect are focused on Me, who is devoted to Me, is dear to Me. (12.14)

यस्मान्नोद्विजते लोको लोकान्नोद्विजते च यः । हर्षामर्षभयोद्वेगैर् मुक्तो यः स च मे प्रियः ॥१२.१५॥	yasmānnodvijate loko lokānnodvijate ca yaḥ harṣāmarṣabhayodvegair mukto yaḥ sa ca me priyaḥ (12.15)

yasmāt — from whom; nodvijate = na — not + udvijate — is repulsed; loko = lokaḥ — world; lokat — from the world; nodvijate = na— not + udvijate— is repulsed; ca — and; yaḥ— who; harṣāmarṣabhayodvegaiḥ = harṣa — excitement + amarṣa — impatience + bhaya —fear + udvegaiḥ — with distress; mukto = muktaḥ — freed; yaḥ — who; sa = saḥ — he; ca — and; me — of me; priyaḥ — dear

He from whom the world is not repulsed, and who is not repulsed from the world, who is free from excitement, impatience, fear and distress, is dear to Me. (12.15)

अनपेक्षः शुचिर्दक्ष उदासीनो गतव्यथः । सर्वारम्भपरित्यागी यो मद्भक्तः स मे प्रियः ॥१२.१६॥	anapekṣaḥ śucirdakṣa udāsīno gatavyathaḥ sarvārambhaparityāgī yo madbhaktaḥ sa me priyaḥ (12.16)

anapekṣaḥ — impartial; śuciḥ — hygienic; dakṣa — competent; udāsīno = udasīnāḥ — indifferent; gatavyathaḥ — one whose anxieties are gone; sarvārambhaparityāgī = sarva — all + ārambha — undertaking + parityāgi — abandoning; yo = yaḥ — who; madbhaktaḥ — devoted to me; sa = saḥ — he; me — of me; priyaḥ — dear

He who is impartial, hygienic, competent, indifferent, whose anxieties are gone, who abandoned all personal undertakings, and who is devoted to Me, is dear to Me. (12.16)

यो न हृष्यति न द्वेष्टि न शोचति न काङ्क्षति । शुभाशुभपरित्यागी भक्तिमान्यः स मे प्रियः ॥१२.१७॥	yo na hṛṣyati na dveṣṭi na śocati na kāṅkṣati śubhāśubhaparityāgī bhaktimānyaḥ sa me priyaḥ (12.17)

yo = yaḥ — who; na — not; hṛṣyāti — rejoice; na — not; dveṣṭi — hates; na — not;śocati — laments; na — not; kāṅkṣati — craves; śubhāśubhaparityāgī = subhasubha — agreeable and disagreeable + parityāgī — leaving aside; bhaktimān — full of devotion; yaḥ — who; sa = saḥ— he; me — of me; priyaḥ — dear

One who does not rejoice, nor hate, nor lament, nor crave, who left aside what is agreeable and disagreeable, who is full of devotion, is dear to Me. (12.17)

समः शत्रौ च मित्रे च
तथा मानावमानयोः ।
शीतोष्णसुखदुःखेषु
समः सङ्गविवर्जितः ॥१२.१८॥

samaḥ śatrau ca mitre ca
tathā mānāvamānayoḥ
śītoṣṇasukhaduḥkheṣu
samaḥ saṅgavivarjitaḥ (12.18)

samaḥ — equally disposed; śatrau — and to an enemy; ca — and; mitre — to friend; ca — and; tathā — similar; mānāpamānayoḥ — in honor and dishonor; śītoṣṇasukhaduḥkheṣu = *śīta — cold + uṣṇa — heat + sukha — happiness + duḥkheṣu — in distress; samaḥ — same; saṅgavivarjitaḥ = saṅga — attachment + vivarjitaḥ — freedom from*

Being equally disposed to an enemy and a friend, with a similar attitude in honor and dishonor, in cold and heat, happiness and distress, being free from attachment, (12.18)

तुल्यनिन्दास्तुतिर्मौनी
संतुष्टो येन केनचित् ।
अनिकेतः स्थिरमतिर्
भक्तिमान्मे प्रियो नरः ॥१२.१९॥

tulyanindāstutirmaunī
saṁtuṣṭo yena kenacit
aniketaḥ sthiramatir
bhaktimānme priyo naraḥ (12.19)

tulyanindāstutiḥ = tulya — relates to + nindā — condemnation + stutiḥ — glorification; maunī — silent; saṁtuṣṭo = saṁtuṣṭaḥ — content; yena — with what; kenacit = kenacid — with anything; aniketaḥ — without a house; sthiramatiḥ = sthira — steady + matiḥ — mind; bhaktimān — full of devotion; me — of me; priyo = priyaḥ — dear; naraḥ — person

...one who relates equally to condemnation and glorification, who is silent, content with anything, who is unattached to home, who has a steady mind, and who is full of devotion, that person is dear to Me.(12.19)

ये तु धर्म्यामृतमिदं
यथोक्तं पर्युपासते ।
श्रद्दधाना मत्परमा
भक्तास्तेऽतीव मे प्रियाः ॥१२.२०॥

ye tu dharmyāmṛtamidaṁ
yathoktaṁ paryupāsate
śraddadhānā matparamā
bhaktāste'tīva me priyāḥ (12.20)

ye — who; tu — but; dharmyāmṛtam = dharmya — codes of behavior + amṛtam — life-giving; idam — this; yathoktaṁ = yathā — as + uktaṁ — declared; paryupāsate — they honor; śraddhānā — having confidence; matparamā — absorbed in me as top priority; bhaktāḥ — be devoted; te — they; 'tīva = atīva — very very: me — to me; priyaḥ — dear

Those who honor these life-giving codes of behavior, who have confidence, being intent on Me as top-priority, being devoted, are very dear. (12.20)

CHAPTER 13

Material Nature

The Person

The Living Space*

अर्जुन उवाच
प्रकृतिं पुरुषं चैव
क्षेत्रं क्षेत्रज्ञमेव च ।
एतद्वेदितुमिच्छामि
ज्ञानं ज्ञेयं च केशव ॥ १३.१ ॥

arjuna uvāca
prakṛtiṁ puruṣaṁ caiva
kṣetraṁ kṣetrajñameva ca
etadveditumicchāmi
jñānaṁ jñeyaṁ ca keśava (13.1)

arjuna — Arjuna; uvāca — said; prakṛtiṁ — material nature; puruṣaṁ — person; caiva — and indeed; kṣetraṁ — the living space; kṣetrajñam — the experiencer of the living space; eva — indeed; ca — and; etad — this; veditum — to know; icchāmi — I wish; jñānaṁ— conclusion; jñeyaṁ— what is to be experienced; ca — and; keśava — pretty-haired one

Arjuna said: What is material nature? What is the person? What is the living space? Who is the experiencer of the living space? I wish to know this. What is a conclusion? And what is experienced, O Keshava, pretty-haired One? (13.1)

श्रीभगवानुवाच
इदं शरीरं कौन्तेय
क्षेत्रमित्यभिधीयते ।
एतद्यो वेत्ति तं प्राहुः
क्षेत्रज्ञ इति तद्विदः. ॥ १३.२ ॥

śrībhagavānuvāca
idaṁ śarīraṁ kaunteya
kṣetramityabhidhīyate
etadyo vetti taṁ prāhuḥ
kṣetrajña iti tadvidaḥ(13.2)

śrī bhagavān — The Blessed Lord; uvāca — said; idaṁ— this; śarīraṁ— earthly body; kaunteya — O son of Kuntī ; kṣetraṁ — the living space; iti — thus; abhidhīyate — it is called; etat — this; yo = yaḥ— who; vetti — knows; taṁ—him; prāhuḥ — they declare; kṣetrajña — experiencer of the living space; iti—thus; tadvidaḥ — of those knowledgeable of that

**The Mahābhārata contains no chapter headings. This title was assigned by the translator on the basis of verse 1. of this chapter.*

The Blessed Lord said: This, the earthly body, O son of Kuntī, is called the living space. Those who are knowledgeable of this, declare the person who understands this to be the experiencer of the living space. (13.2)

क्षेत्रज्ञं चापि मां विद्धि
सर्वक्षेत्रेषु भारत ।
क्षेत्रक्षेत्रज्ञयोर्ज्ञानं
यत्तज्ज्ञानं मतं मम ॥ १३.३

kṣetrajñaṁ cāpi māṁ viddhi
sarvakṣetreṣu bhārata
kṣetrakṣetrajñayorjñānaṁ
yattajjñānaṁ mataṁ mama (13.3)

kṣetrajñam — the experiencer of the living space; cāpi = ca—and + api—also; māṁ -me, viddhi—know; sarvakṣetreṣu — I all living spaces; bhārata —O man of the Bhārata family; kṣetrakṣetrajñayoḥ — of the living space and the experiencer of it; jñānaṁ — information; yat — which; tat — that; jñānaṁ — knowledge; mataṁ -considered; mama — by me

Know also, that I am the experiencer of all living spaces, O man of the Bharata family. Information of the living space and the experiencer of it, is considered by Me to be knowledge. (13.3)

तत्क्षेत्रं यच्च यादृक् च
यद्विकारि यतश्च यत् ।
स च यो यत्प्रभावश्च
तत्समासेन मे श्रृणु ॥ १३.४॥

tatkṣetraṁ yacca yādṛk ca
yadvikāri yataśca yat
sa ca yo yatprabhāvaśca
tatsamāsena me śṛṇu (13.4)

tat - tad — this; kṣetraṁ — living space; yat — what; ca — and; yadṛk — what kind?; ca — and; yadvikāri = yad —what + vikāri— changes; yataśca - yataḥ— what causes?; ca — and; yat — what; sa = saḥ— he; ca — and; yo - yaḥ— who; yatprabhāvaḥ- yat (yad) — what + prabhāvaḥ— potential + ca — and; tat = tad — that; samāsena — with brevity, in brief; me — of me; śṛṇu — hear

As for this living space, as for what is, as for what kind of environment it is, as for the changes it endures, as to what causes it to change, as for he who is involved, as for his potential, hear from Me of that in brief. (13.4)

ऋषिभिर्बहुधा गीतं
छन्दोभिर्विविधैः पृथक् ।
ब्रह्मसूत्रपदैश्चैव
हेतुमद्भिर्विनिश्चितैः ॥ १३.५॥

ṛṣibhirbahudhā gītaṁ
chandobhirvividhaiḥ pṛthak
brahmasūtrapadaiścaiva
hetumadbhirviniścitaiḥ (13.5)

ṛṣibhiḥ — by the yogī sages; bahudhā — many times; gītaṁ — recited; chandobhiḥ — with Vedic hymns; vividhaiḥ— with various; pṛthak — distinctly; brahmasūtrapadaiścaiva = brahmasūtrapadaiḥ — with Brahma-sūtra verses + ca — and, eva — indeed; hetumadbhiḥ — with sound logic; viniścataiḥ — with definite, conclusive

This was distinctly recited many times with the various Vedic hymns and with the Brahma Sūtras, conclusively with sound logic, by the great yogi sages. (13.5)

महाभूतान्यहंकारो
बुद्धिरव्यक्तमेव च ।
इन्द्रियाणि दशैकं च
पञ्च चेन्द्रियगोचराः ॥ १३.६ ॥

mahābhūtānyahaṁkāro
buddhiravyaktameva ca
indriyāṇi daśaikaṁ ca
pañca cendriyagocarāḥ (13.6)

mahābhūtāni — major elements; ahaṁkāro = ahaṁkāraḥ- ahaṁ — I, person + kāraḥ — doing, initiative to act; buddhiḥ — intellect; avyaktam — unmanifesled energy; eva — indeed; ca — and; indriyāṇi — senses; daśaikaṁ= dasa — ten + ekam — one; ca — and; pañca — five; cendriyagocarāḥ = ca — and + indriyagocarāḥ — attractive objects

The major categories of the elements, the personal initiative, the intellect, the unmanifested energy, the ten and one senses, the five attractive objects, (13.6)

इच्छा द्वेषः सुखं दुःखं
संघातश्चेतना धृतिः ।
एतत्क्षेत्रं समासेन
सविकारमुदाहृतम् ॥ १३.७ ॥

icchā dveṣaḥ sukhaṁ duḥkhaṁ
saṁghātaścetanā dhṛtiḥ
etatkṣetraṁ samāsena
savikāramudāhṛtam (13.7)

Icchā — desire; dveṣaḥ — hatred; sukhaṁ — pleasure; duḥkhaṁ — pain: saṁghātaścetanā = saṁghātaḥ — the whole body + cetana — consciousness; dhṛtiḥ — conviction: etat = etad — this; kṣetraṁ — living space; samāsena — with brevity, briefly; savikāram — with changes; udāhṛtam — described

...desire, hatred, pleasure, pain, the whole body, consciousness and conviction; this is described with brevity, as the living space with its changes. (13.7)

अमानित्वमदम्भित्वम्
अहिंसा क्षान्तिरार्जवम् ।
आचार्योपासनं शौचं
स्थैर्यमात्मविनिग्रहः ॥ १३.८ ॥

amānitvamadambhitvam
ahiṁsā kṣāntirārjavam
ācāryopāsanaṁ śaucaṁ
sthairyamātmavinigrahaḥ (13.8)

amānitvaṁ — a lack of pride; adambhitvam — freedom from deceit; ahiṁsā — non-violence; kṣāntiḥ — patience; ārjavam — straightforwardness; ācāryopāsanaṁ — sitting near a teacher, attendance to a teacher; śaucaṁ — purity; sthairyam — stability; ātmavinigrahaḥ = ātma — self + vinigrahaḥ — restraint

Lack of pride, freedom from deceit, non-violence, patience, straightforwardness, attendance to a teacher, purity, stability and self-restraint, (13.8)

इन्द्रियार्थेषु वैराग्यम्
अनहंकार एव च ।
जन्ममृत्युजराव्याधि-
दुःखदोषानुदर्शनम् ॥ १३.९ ॥

indriyārtheṣu vairāgyam
anahaṁkāra eva ca
janmamṛtyujarāvyādhi-
duḥkhadoṣānudarśanam (13.9)

indriyārtheṣu — towards the attractive objects; vairāgyam — indifference; anahaṁkāra = an — absence of + ahaṁkāra — motivated initiative; eva — indeed; ca — and; janmamṛtyujarāvyādhi =janma — birth + mṛtyu —death + jarā — old age + vyādhi — disease; duḥkhadoṣānudarśanam = duḥkha — suffering + doṣa — danger + anudarśanam — perception

..indifference towards the attractive objects, absence of motivated initiative, the perception of the danger of birth, death, old age, disease, and suffering, (13.9)

असक्तिरनभिष्वङ्गः
पुत्रदारगृहादिषु ।
नित्यं च समचित्तत्वम्
इष्टानिष्टोपपत्तिषु ॥ १३.१० ॥

asaktiranabhiṣvaṅgaḥ
putradāragṛhādiṣu
nityaṁ ca samacittatvam
iṣṭāniṣṭopapattiṣu (13.10)

asaktiḥ — non-attachment, social detachment: anabhiṣvaṅgaḥ — absence of emotional affection: putradāragṛhādiṣu = putra — child + dāra — wife + gṛha —home + ādiṣu — beginning with, whatever is related to; nityaṁ — always; ca — and: samacittatvam — even-mindedness; iṣṭāniṣṭopapattiṣu = iṣṭa — undesired + aniṣṭa — not wanted + upapattiṣu — in matters

...social and emotional detachment towards child, wife, a home and whatever is related to social life, being always even-minded towards what is desired and what is not wanted, (13.10)

मयि चानन्ययोगेन
भक्तिरव्यभिचारिणी ।
विविक्तदेशसेवित्वम्
अरतिर्जनसंसदि ॥ १३.११ ॥

mayi cānanyayogena
bhaktiravyabhicāriṇī
viviktadeśasevitvam
aratirjanasaṁsadi (13.11)

mayi — in me; cānanyayogena = ca — and + ananya — no other + yogena — with yoga practice; bhaktiḥ — devotion: avyabhicārinī — not wandering away, unwavering; viviktadeśasevitvam = vivikta — secluded + deśa— place + sevitvam — resorting; aratiḥ — having a dislike; janasaṁsadi — in crowds of human beings

...unswerving devotion to Me, with no other discipline but yoga practice, resorting to a secluded place, having a dislike for crowds of human beings, (13.11)

अध्यात्मज्ञाननित्यत्वं
तत्त्वज्ञानार्थदर्शनम् ।
एतज्ज्ञानमिति प्रोक्तम्
अज्ञानं यदतोऽन्यथा ॥ १३.१२ ॥

adhyātmajñānanityatvaṁ
tattvajñānārthadarśanam
etajjñānamiti proktam
ajñānaṁ yadato'nyathā (13.12)

adhyātmajñananityatvam = adhyātma — Supreme Spirit + jñana — information + nityatvam — constantly; tattvajñānārtha darśanam = tattva — reality + jñāna — science + artha — value+ darśanam —perceiving; etat— this; jñānam — knowledge; iti — thus; proktam — declared as; ajñānaṁ — ignorance; yat — whatever; ato = ataḥ — to this; 'nyathā = anyathā — otherwise , contrary

...constantly considering information about the Supreme Spirit, perceiving the value of the science of reality; this is declared as knowledge. Whatever is contrary to this, is ignorance. (13.12)

ज्ञेयं यत्तत्प्रवक्ष्यामि
यज्ज्ञात्वामृतमश्नुते ।
अनादिमत्परं ब्रह्म
न सत्तन्नासदुच्यते ॥ १३.१३ ॥

jñeyaṁ yattatpravakṣyāmi
yajjñātvāmṛtamaśnute
anādimatparaṁ brahma
na sattannāsaducyate (13.13)

jṇeyaṁ — to be known, the desired subject; yat — which; tat — that; pravakṣyāmi — I will explain; yat — which; jñātvā — knowing; 'mṛtam = amṛtam — eternal life; aśnute — he gets in touch with; anādimat — beginningless; paraṁ — supreme; brahma — reality; na - not; sat — substantial; tat — this; nāsat = na — not + asat — non-substantial; ucyate — is said

I will explain that which is to be experienced, knowing which one gets in touch with eternal life. The beginningless Supreme Reality is said to be neither substantial nor insubstantial. (13.13)

सर्वतःपाणिपादं तत्
सर्वतोक्षिशिरोमुखम् ।
सर्वतःश्रुतिमल्लोके
सर्वमावृत्य तिष्ठति ॥ १३.१४ ॥

sarvataḥpāṇipādaṁ tat
sarvatokṣiśiromukham
sarvataḥśrutimalloke
sarvamāvṛtya tiṣṭhati (13.14)

sarvataḥ — everywhere; pāṇi — hand; pādaṁ — foot; tat = tad — this; sarvato = sarvataḥ — everywhere; 'kṣiśiromukham= akṣiśiromukham= akṣi— eye + śiraḥ — head + mukham — face; sarvasaḥśrutimat - sarvasaḥ — everywhere + śrutimat — having hearing ability; loke — in the world; sarvam — all; āvṛtya — ranging over; tiṣṭhati — stands

Everywhere is Its hands and feet, everywhere Its eyes, head and face, everywhere is Its hearing ability in this world; It stands, ranging over all. (13.14)

सर्वेन्द्रियगुणाभासं
सर्वेन्द्रियविवर्जितम् ।
असक्तं सर्वभृच्चैव
निर्गुणं गुणभोक्तृ च ॥१३.१५॥

sarvendriyaguṇābhāsaṁ
sarvendriyavivarjitam
asaktaṁ sarvabhṛccaiva
nirguṇaṁ guṇabhoktṛ ca (13.15)

sarvendriyaguṇābhāsaṁ = sarva —all + indriyaḥ — sensual + guṇa — mood + ābhāsaṁ — appearance; sarvendriyavivarjitam = sarva — all + indriya — sensuousness + vivarjitam — freedom from; asaktaṁ — unattached; sarvabhṛt — maintaining everything; caiva = ca — and + eva — indeed; nirguṇaṁ — free from the influence of material nature; guṇabhoktṛ — experiencer of the modes of material nature; ca — and

It has the appearance of having all sensual moods, and It is freed from sensuousness. Though unattached, It maintains everything. Though free from the influence of material nature, It is the experiencer of that influence nevertheless. (13.15)

बहिरन्तश्च भूतानाम्
अचरं चरमेव च ।
सूक्ष्मत्वात्तदविज्ञेयं
दूरस्थं चान्तिके च तत् ॥१३.१६॥

bahirantaśca bhūtānām
acaraṁ carameva ca
sūkṣmatvāttadavijñeyaṁ
dūrasthaṁ cāntike ca tat (13.16)

bahiḥ — outside; antaḥ — inside; ca — and; bhūtānām — of the beings; acaraṁ — non-moving; caram — moving; eva — indeed; ca — and; sūkṣmatvāt — from subtlety; tat — this; avijñeyaṁ — not to be comprehended; dūrasthaṁ — situated far off; cāntike = ca — and + antike — in the location; ca — and; tat = tad — this

It is outside and inside the moving and non-moving beings. Because of Its subtlety, this beginningless Supreme Reality is not comprehended. This Reality is situated far away and it is in the location as well. (13.16)

अविभक्तं च भूतेषु
विभक्तमिव च स्थितम् ।
भूतभर्तृ च तज्ज्ञेयं
ग्रसिष्णु प्रभविष्णु च ॥१३.१७॥

avibhaktaṁ ca bhūteṣu
vibhaktamiva ca sthitam
bhūtabhartṛ ca tajjñeyaṁ
grasiṣṇu prabhaviṣṇu ca (13.17)

avibhaktam — undivided: ca — and; bhūteṣu — among the beings: vibhaktam — divided; iva — as if; ca — and; sthitam — remaining; bhūtabhartṛ = bhūta — being + bhartṛ — sustainer; ca — and; tat — this; jñeyaṁ — to be known; grasiṣṇu — absorber; prabhaviṣṇu — producer; ca — and

It is undivided among the beings, but It appears as if It is divided in each. It is the sustainer of the beings and this should be known. It is the absorber and producer. (13.17)

ज्योतिषामपि तज्ज्योतिस्
तमसः परमुच्यते ।
ज्ञानं ज्ञेयं ज्ञानगम्यं
हृदि सर्वस्य विष्ठितम् ॥ १३.१८ ॥

jyotiṣāmapi tajjyotis
tamasaḥ paramucyate
jñānaṁ jñeyaṁ jñānagamyaṁ
hṛdi sarvasya viṣṭhitam (13.18)

jyotiṣām — of luminaries; api — also; tat = tad — this; jyotiḥ — light; tamasaḥ — of gross or subtle darkness; param-beyond; ucyate — declared to be; jñānaṁ — information; jñeyaṁ — education; jñānagamyaṁ = jñāna — education + gamyam — goal; hṛdi — in the psychological core; sarvasya — of all; viṣṭhitam — situated

This is declared as the light of the luminaries, but It is beyond gross or subtle darkness. It is the information, the education and the goal of education. It is situated in the psychological core of all beings. (13.18)

इति क्षेत्रं तथा ज्ञानं
ज्ञेयं चोक्तं समासतः ।
मद्भक्त एतद्विज्ञाय
मद्भावायोपपद्यते ॥ १३.१९ ॥

iti kṣetraṁ tathā jñānaṁ
jñeyaṁ coktaṁ samāsataḥ
madbhakta etadvijñāya
madbhāvāyopapadyate (13.19)

iti — thus; kṣetraṁ— the living space, the psychological environment; tathā — as well as; jñanaṁ — standard knowledge; jñeyaṁ — what is to be known; coktaṁ- ca -and + uktaṁ — described: samāsataḥ — in brief; madbhakta — my devotee; etad — this: vijñāya — experiencing; madbhāvāyopapadyate = madbhāvāya — to my state of being + upapadyate — draws near

Thus the psychological environment as well as the standard knowledge and what is to be known, was described in brief. Experiencing this, My devotee draws near to My state of being. (13.19)

प्रकृतिं पुरुषं चैव
विद्ध्यनादी उभावपि ।
विकारांश्च गुणांश्चैव
विद्धि प्रकृतिसंभवान्॥ १३.२० ॥

prakṛtiṁ puruṣaṁ caiva
viddhyanādī ubhāvapi
vikārāṁśca guṇāṁścaiva
viddhi prakṛtisaṁbhavān (13.20)

prakṛtiṁ — material nature; puruṣaṁ — spiritual personality; caiva = ca — and + eva — indeed; viddhi — know; anādī — beginningless; ubhau — both; api — also; vikārān — changes of the living space (see 13.4); ca — and; guṇāṁ — moods; caiva = ca— and + eva — indeed; viddhi — know; prakṛtisaṁbhavān = prakṛti — material nature + saṁbhavān — produced

Know that both material nature and the spiritual personality are beginningless, and know that the changes of the living space and the moods of material nature are produced from material nature. (13.20)

कार्यकारणकर्तृत्वे
हेतुः प्रकृतिरुच्यते ।
पुरुषः सुखदुःखानां
भोक्तृत्वे हेतुरुच्यते ॥ १३.२१ ॥

kāryakāraṇakartṛtve
hetuḥ prakṛtirucyate
puruṣaḥ sukhaduḥkhānāṁ
bhoktṛtve heturucyate (13.21)

kāryakaraṇakartṛtve = kārya — created work + karaṇa — sensual potency as a cause + kartṛtve — agency; hetuḥ — cause; prakṛtiḥ — material nature; ucyate — is said; puruṣaḥ — the spiritual personality; sukhaduḥkhānāṁ — of pleasure and pain; bhoktṛtve — in terms of experiencing; hetuḥ — cause; ucyate — is said

Material nature is said to be the cause in terms of created work, sensual potency and agency. The spiritual personality is said to be the cause in terms of experiencing pleasure and pain. (13.21)

पुरुषः प्रकृतिस्थो हि
भुङ्क्ते प्रकृतिजान्गुणान् ।
कारणं गुणसङ्गोऽस्य
सदसद्योनिजन्मसु ॥ १३.२२ ॥

puruṣaḥ prakṛtistho hi
bhuṅkte prakṛtijānguṇān
kāraṇaṁ guṇasaṅgo'sya
sadasadyonijanmasu (13.22)

puruṣaḥ — spirit; prakṛtistho - prakṛtisthaḥ — situated in material nature; hi — indeed: bhuṅkte — experiencing; prakṛtijān — produced on material nature; guṇān — the modes of material nature; kāraṇaṁ — the source; guṇasaṅgo = guṇasaṅgaḥ — attachment to the influence of material nature; 'sya = asya —of it: sadasadyonijanmasu = sad (sat) — reality + asad (asat) — unrealistic + yoni — birth situations + janmasu — birth

The spirit, being situated in material nature, experiences the modes which were produced by that nature. Attachment to the modes is the cause of the spirit's emergence from realistic and unrealistic situations. (13.22)

उपद्रष्टानुमन्ता च
भर्ता भोक्ता महेश्वरः ।
परमात्मेति चाप्युक्तो
देहेऽस्मिन्पुरुषः परः ॥ १३.२३ ॥

upadraṣṭānumantā ca
bhartā bhoktā maheśvaraḥ
paramātmeti cāpyukto
dehe'sminpuruṣaḥ paraḥ (13.23)

upadraṣṭānumantā = upadraṣṭā —observer + anumantā — permitter; ca — and; bhartā — supporter; bhoktā — experiencer; maheśvaraḥ — Supreme Lord; paramātmeti = paramātmā — Supreme Soul + iti — thus; cāpi — and also; ukto = uktaḥ — is called; dehe — in the body; 'smin = asmin — in this; puruṣaḥ — spirit; paraḥ — highest

The observer, the permitter, the supporter, the experiencer, the Supreme Lord and the Supreme Soul as He is called, He is the highest spirit in the body. (13.23)

य एवं वेत्ति पुरुषं
प्रकृतिं च गुणैः सह ।
सर्वथा वर्तमानोऽपि
न स भूयोऽभिजायते ॥ १३.२४॥

ya evaṁ vetti puruṣaṁ
prakṛtiṁ ca guṇaiḥ saha
sarvathā vartamāno'pi
na sa bhūyo'bhijāyate (13.24)

ya = yaḥ — who; evaṁ — thus; vetti — knows; puruṣaṁ — spiritual person; prakṛtiṁ — material nature; ca — and; guṇaiḥ — with the variations of material nature; saha — with; sarvathā — in whatever way; vartamāno = vartamānaḥ — existing presently, present condition; 'pi = api — also; na — not; sa = saḥ — he; bhūyo = bhūyaḥ — again; 'bhijāyate = abhijāyate — is horn

He who knows the spiritual person and material nature, along with the variations of material nature, is not born again, regardless of his present condition. (13.24)

ध्यानेनात्मनि पश्यन्ति
केचिदात्मानमात्मना ।
अन्ये सांख्येन योगेन
कर्मयोगेन चापरे ॥ १३.२५॥

dhyānenātmani paśyanti
kecidātmānamātmanā
anye sāṁkhyena yogena
karmayogena cāpare (13.25)

dhyānenātmani = dhyānena — through meditative perception + ātmani — in the spirit; paśyānti — they perceive; kecit — some; ātmānam — by the spirit; ātmanā — -the spirit; anye — others; sāṁkhyena — by sāṁkhyena philosophical conclusions; yogena — by yoga practice; karmayogena — by yogic disciplined action; cāpare = ca —and + apare — others

Some perceive the spirit by the spirit through meditative perception of the spirit. Others do so with Sāṁkhya philosophical conclusions and others by yogic disciplined action. (13.25)

अन्ये त्वेवमजानन्तः
श्रुत्वान्येभ्य उपासते ।
तेऽपि चातितरन्त्येव
मृत्युं श्रुतिपरायणाः ॥ १३.२६॥

anye tvevamajānantaḥ
śrutvānyebhya upāsate
te'pi cātitarantyeva
mṛtyuṁ śrutiparāyaṇāḥ (13.26)

anye — others; tu — but; evam — thus; ajānantaḥ — not knowing; śrutvānyebhya = śrutvā — hearing + anyebhya — from others; upāsate — they worship; te — they; 'pi = api — also; catitaranti = ca — and + atitaranti — transcend; eva — indeed; mṛtyuṁ — death: śrutiparāyaṇāḥ = śruti — hearing + parāyaṇāḥ — putting confidence in as the highest

But some, though they are ignorant, hear from others. They worship and by their confidence in what is heard, they also transcend death. (13.26)

यावत्संजायते किंचित् सत्त्वं स्थावरजङ्गमम् । क्षेत्रक्षेत्रज्ञसंयोगात् तद्विद्धि भरतर्षभ ॥ १३.२७	yāvatsaṁjāyate kiṁcit sattvaṁ sthāvarajaṅgamam kṣetrakṣetrajñasaṁyogāt tadviddhi bharatarṣabha(13.27)

yāvat — as for; saṁjāyate — is born; kiṁcit = kiṁcid — anything, whatever; sattvaṁ — existence; sthāvarajaṅgamam= sthāvara — stationary + jaṅgamam — moving; kṣetrakṣetrajñasaṁyogāt = kṣetra — living space + kṣetrajña — experiencer + saṁyogāt from the synthesis; tat — that; viddhi — know; bharataṛsabha — strong man of the Bharatas

As for anything that is produced in this existence, be it a stationary or moving object, know, O strong man of the Bharatas, that it is produced from a synthesis of the experiencer and the living space. (13.27)

समं सर्वेषु भूतेषु तिष्ठन्तं परमेश्वरम् । विनश्यत्स्वविनश्यन्तं यः पश्यति स पश्यति ॥ १३.२८॥	samaṁ sarveṣu bhūteṣu tiṣṭhantaṁ parameśvaram vinaśyatsvavinaśyantaṁ yaḥ paśyati sa paśyati (13.28)

Samam — similar; sarveṣu — in all; bhūteṣu — in beings; tiṣṭhantaṁ — situated; parmeśvaram — Supreme Lord; vinaśyatsu — in disintegrations; avinaśyantaṁ — not perishing; yaḥ — who; paśyati—perceive; sa = saḥ — he', paśyati — really sees

The Supreme Lord is similarly situated in all beings without perishing when they disintegrate. He who perceives that, really sees. (13.28)

समं पश्यन्हि सर्वत्र समवस्थितमीश्वरम् । न हिनस्त्यात्मनात्मानं ततो याति परां गतिम् ॥ १३.२९॥	samaṁ paśyanhi sarvatra samavasthitamīśvaram na hinastyātmanātmānaṁ tato yāti parāṁ gatim (13.29)

samaṁ — same; paśyan — seeing; hi — indeed; sarvatra — everywhere; samavasthitam — same established; īśvaram — Lord; na — not; hinasti — degrade; ātmānātmānaṁ = ātmanā — by the soul + ātmānaṁ — the soul; tato = tataḥ — subsequently; yāti — goes; parām — supreme; gatim — destination

Seeing the same Lord being situated everywhere, he does not degrade the soul by his own soul. Subsequently, he goes to the supreme destination. (13.29)

प्रकृत्यैव च कर्माणि क्रियमाणानि सर्वशः । यः पश्यति तथात्मानम् अकर्तारं स पश्यति ॥ १३.३०	prakṛtyaiva ca karmāṇi kriyamāṇāni sarvaśaḥ yaḥ paśyati tathātmānam akartāraṁ sa paśyati (13.30)

prakṛtyaiva = prakṛtya — by material nature + eva — indeed: ca — and; karmāṇi — actions; kriyamāṇāni — performed; sarvaśaḥ — in all cases, yaḥ — who; paśyati — he sees; tathātmānam = tathā— as regarding + ātmānam — self; akartāraṁ — non-doer; sa = saḥ— he: paśyati — truly sees

He who sees, that in all cases, the actions are performed by material nature, and who regards himself as a non-doer, truly sees. (13.30)

यदा भूतपृथग्भावम्
एकस्थमनुपश्यति ।
तत एव च विस्तारं
ब्रह्म संपद्यते तदा ॥ १३.३१ ॥

yadā bhūtapṛthagbhāvam
ekasthamanupaśyati
tata eva ca vistāraṁ
brahma saṁpadyate tadā (13.31)

yadā — when; bhūtapṛthagbhāvam = bhūta — being + pṛthak — various + bhāvam — existential state: ekastham — based in one foundation; anupaśyati — be sees; tata — from that conclusion; eva — only; ca — and; vistāraṁ — extending, emanating; brahma — spiritual plane; saṁpadyate — he reaches: tadā — then

When a person sees that all the various states of being are based on a single foundation, and only from that everything emanates, then he reaches the spiritual plane. (13.31)

अनादित्वान्निर्गुणत्वात्
परमात्मायमव्ययः ।
शरीरस्थोऽपि कौन्तेय
न करोति न लिप्यते ॥ १३.३२ ॥

anāditvānnirguṇatvāt
paramātmāyamavyayaḥ
śarīrastho'pi kaunteya
na karoti na lipyate (13.32)

anāditvāt = due to being without a beginning; nirguṇatvāt — due to being devoid of the influence of material nature; paramātmāyam = paramātmā — Supreme Soul + ayam — this; avyayaḥ — imperishable; śarīrastho = śarīrasthaḥ — situated in the material body; 'pi = api — even though; kaunteya — O son of Kuntī ; na — not; karoti — he does; na — not; lipyate — become contaminated

Since this imperishable Supreme Lord is beginningless and devoid of the influence of material nature, even though He is situated in the material body, O son of Kuntī, He does not act or become contaminated. (13.32)

यथा सर्वगतं सौक्ष्म्याद्
आकाशं नोपलिप्यते ।
सर्वत्रावस्थितो देहे
तथात्मा नोपलिप्यते ॥ १३.३३ ॥

yathā sarvagataṁ saukṣmyād
ākāśaṁ nopalipyate
sarvatrāvasthito dehe
tathātmā nopalipyate (13.33)

yathā — as; sarvagataṁ — all-pervading; saukṣmyāt — as by subtlety; ākāśaṁ — sky. nopalipyate = na — not + upalipyate — is polluted; sarvatrāvasthito = sarvatra — all over +avasthitaḥ — situated; dehe — in the body; tathātmā = tathā — so + ātmā — soul; nopalipyate = na — not + upalipyate — affected

As by subtlety, the all-pervading space is not polluted, so the soul, though situated all over the body, is not affected actually. (13.33)

यथा प्रकाशयत्येकः
कृत्स्नं लोकमिमं रविः ।
क्षेत्रं क्षेत्री तथा कृत्स्नं
प्रकाशयति भारत ॥ १३.३४॥

yathā prakāśayatyekaḥ
kṛtsnaṁ lokamimaṁ raviḥ
kṣetraṁ kṣetrī tathā kṛtsnaṁ
prakāśayati bhārata (13.34)

yathā — as; prakāśayati — illuminates; ekaḥ — one, alone; kṛtsnaṁ — whole; lokam — world; imaṁ — this; raviḥ — sun; kṣetraṁ — living space; kṣetrī — the user of the living space; tathā — so; kṛtsnaṁ — entire; prakāśayati — gives feeling; bhārata — O man of the Bhārata family

As the sun alone illuminates the whole world, O man of the Bharata family, so the user of the living space gives feeling to the entire psyche. (13.34)

क्षेत्रक्षेत्रज्ञयोरेवम्
अन्तरं ज्ञानचक्षुषा ।
भूतप्रकृतिमोक्षं च
ये विदुर्यान्ति ते परम् ॥ १३.३५॥

kṣetrakṣetrajñayorevam
antaraṁ jñānacakṣuṣā
bhūtaprakṛtimokṣaṁ ca
ye viduryānti te param (13.35)

kṣetrakṣetrajñayoḥ — of the experiencer and the living space; evam — thus; antaraṁ - difference; jñānacakṣuṣā - jñāna — perceptive knowledge + cakṣuṣā — intuitive vision; bhūtaprakṛtimokṣaṁ = bhūta — being + prakṛti—material nature + mokṣaṁ — liberation; ca — and; ye — who: viduḥ — they know; yānti — they go; te — they; param — supreme

Those who by intuitive perception know the difference between the living space and the experiencer, as well as the liberation of the living being from material nature, go to the Supreme. (13.35)

CHAPTER 14

The Extensive Mundane Reality*

श्रीभगवानुवाच
परं भूयः प्रवक्ष्यामि
ज्ञानानां ज्ञानमुत्तमम् ।
यज्ज्ञात्वा मुनयः सर्वे
परां सिद्धिमितो गताः ॥ १४.१ ॥

śrībhagavānuvāca
paraṁ bhūyaḥ pravakṣyāmi
jñānānāṁ jñānamuttamam
yajjñātvā munayaḥ sarve
parāṁ siddhimito gatāḥ (14.1)

śrī bhagavān — the Blessed Lord; uvāca — said; paraṁ — highest; bhūyaḥ — further; pravakṣyāmi — I will explain; jñānānāṁ — of the knowledges; jñānam — information; uttamam — the very best; yat — which; jñātvā— having experienced; munayaḥ — yogī philosophers; sarve — all; parāṁ — supreme; siddhim — perfection; ito = itaḥ — from here; gatāḥ — done

The Blessed Lord said: I will explain more, giving the highest information of all knowledges, the very best. Having experienced that, all the yogi philosophers went away from here to the Supreme Perfection. (14.1)

इदं ज्ञानमुपाश्रित्य
मम साधर्म्यमागताः ।
सर्गेऽपि नोपजायन्ते
प्रलये न व्यथन्ति च ॥ १४.२ ॥

idaṁ jñānamupāśritya
mama sādharmyamāgatāḥ
sarge'pi nopajāyante
pralaye na vyathanti ca (14.2)

idaṁ — this; jñānam — experience; upāśritya — resorting to; mama — my; sādharmyam — a nature that is similar; āgatāḥ — transformed into; sarge — at the time of the universal creation; 'pi = api — even; nopajāyante = na — not + upajāyante — they are born; pralaye — at the time of universal dissolution; na — not; vyathanti — disturbed; ca — and

Resorting to this experience, being transformed into a nature that is similar to My own, they are not born even at the time of the universal creation, nor are they disturbed at the time of dissolution. (14.2)

मम योनिर्महद्ब्रह्म
तस्मिन्गर्भं दधाम्यहम् ।
संभवः सर्वभूतानां
ततो भवति भारत ॥ १४.३ ॥

mama yonirmahadbrahma
tasmingarbhaṁ dadhāmyaham
saṁbhavaḥ sarvabhūtānāṁ
tato bhavati bhārata (14.3)

**The Mahābhārata contains no chapter headings. This title was assigned by the translator on the basis of verse 3 of this chapter.*

mama — my; yoniḥ — womb; mahat — extensive; brahma —reality; tasmin — into it; garbhaṁ — essence; dadhāmi — I impregnate; aham — I; saṁbhavaḥ — origin; sarvabhūtānāṁ — of all beings: tato = tataḥ — from that; bhavati — comes into being; bhārata — O man of the Bharata family

The extensive mundane reality is My womb. I impregnate the essence into it. The origin of all beings comes from that reality, O man of the Bharata family. (14.3)

सर्वयोनिषु कौन्तेय
मूर्तयः संभवन्ति याः ।
तासां ब्रह्म महद्योनिर्
अहं बीजप्रदः पिता ॥१४.४॥

sarvayoniṣu kaunteya
mūrtayaḥ saṁbhavanti yāḥ
tāsāṁ brahma mahadyonir
ahaṁ bījapradaḥ pitā (14.4)

sarvayoniṣu — in all wombs; kaunteya — O son of Kuntī ; mūrtayaḥ- forms; saṁbhavanti — they are produced; yāḥ— which; tāsāṁ — of them; brahmā — mundane reality; mahat — great; yoniḥ — giving; aham — I; bījapradaḥ — seed-giving; pitā — father

Forms are produced in all types of wombs, O son of Kuntī, I am the seed-giving father. The extensive mundane reality is the great womb. (14.4)

सत्त्वं रजस्तम इति
गुणाः प्रकृतिसंभवाः ।
निबध्नन्ति महाबाहो
देहे देहिनमव्ययम् ॥१४.५॥

sattvaṁ rajastama iti
guṇāḥ prakṛtisaṁbhavāḥ
nibadhnanti mahābāho
dehe dehinamavyayam (14.5)

sattvaṁ — clarity; rajaḥ — impulsion; tama — retardation; iti — thus; guṇāḥ — influences; prakṛtisaṁbhavāḥ = prakṛti— material nature + saṁbhavāḥ — produced of; nibadhnanti — they captivate; mahābāho — O great-armed hero; dehe — in the body; dehinaṁ — embodied soul; avyayam — imperishable

Clarity, impulsion and retardation are the influences produced of material nature. They captivate the imperishable embodied soul in the body, O strong-armed hero. (14.5)

तत्र सत्त्वं निर्मलत्वात्
प्रकाशकमनामयम् ।
सुखसङ्गेन बध्नाति
ज्ञानसङ्गेन चानघ ॥१४.६॥

tatra sattvaṁ nirmalatvāt
prakāśakamanāmayam
sukhasaṅgena badhnāti
jñānasaṅgena cānagha (14.6)

tatra — regarding these; sattvaṁ — clarifying influence; nirmalatvāt — relatively free from perceptive impurities; prakāśakam — illuminating; anāmayam — free from disease; sukhasaṅgena = sukha — happiness + saṅgena — by attachment; badhnāti — it binds; jñānasaṅgena = jñāna— knowledge of expertise + saṅgena — by attachment; cānagha = ca — and + anagha — sinless one

Regarding these influences, the clarifying one is relatively free from perceptive impurities. It is illuminating and free from disease, but by granting an attachment to happiness and to expertise, it captivates a person, O sinless one. (14.6)

रजो रागात्मकंविद्धि तृष्णासङ्गसमुद्भवम् । तन्निबध्नाति कौन्तेय कर्मसङ्गेन देहिनम् ॥ १४.७॥	rajo rāgātmakaṁviddhi tṛṣṇāsaṅgasamudbhavam tannibadhnāti kaunteya karmasaṅgena dehinam (14.7)

rajo - rajaḥ — impulsive influence; rāgātmakaṁ — characterized by passion; viddhi — know; tṛṣṇāsaṅgasamudbhavam= tṛṣṇā— desire + saṅga — earnest + samudbhavam — produced from; tat — this; nibadhnāti — it captivates; kaunteya — O son of Kuntī ; karmasaṅgena — by attachment to activity; dehināṁ — the embodied soul

Know that the impulsive influence is characterized by passion. It is produced from earnest desire and attachment. O son of Kuntī , this mode captivates the embodied soul by an attachment to activity. (14.7)

तमस्त्वज्ञानजं विद्धि मोहनं सर्वदेहिनाम् । प्रमादालस्यनिद्राभिस् तन्निबध्नाति भारत ॥ १४.८॥	tamastvajñānajaṁ viddhi mohanaṁ sarvadehinām pramādālasyanidrābhis tannibadhnāti bhārata (14.8)

tamaḥ — depressing mode; tu — but; ajñānajaṁ — produced of insensibility; viddhi — know; mohanam — confusion; sarvadehināṁ — of all embodied beings; pramādālasyanidrābhiḥ = pramāda — inattentiveness + ālasya — laziness + nidrābhiḥ - sleep; tat — this; nibadhnāti — captivates; bhārata — O man of the Bharata family

But know that the depressing mode is produced of insensibility which is the confusion of all embodied beings. This captivates by inattentiveness, laziness and sleep, O man of the Bharata family. (14.8)

सत्त्वं सुखे सञ्जयति रजः कर्मणि भारत । ज्ञानमावृत्य तु तमः प्रमादे सञ्जयत्युत ॥ १४.९॥	sattvaṁ sukhe sañjayati rajaḥ karmaṇi bhārata jñānamāvṛtya tu tamaḥ pramāde sañjayatyuta (14.9)

sattvaṁ — clarifying influence; sukhe — in happiness; sañjayati — causes attachment; rajaḥ — impulsive influence; karmaṇi — to action; bhārata — O Bharata family man; jñānam — experience; āvṛtya — obscuring; tu — but;

tamaḥ — depressing mode; pramāde — to negligence; sañjayati — causes attachment; uta — even

The clarifying influence causes attachment to happiness. The impulsive one causes a need for action, O Bharata family man. But the depressing mode obscures experience and causes attachment to negligence. (14.9)

रजस्तमश्चाभिभूय सत्त्वं भवति भारत । रजः सत्त्वं तमश्चैव तमः सत्त्वं रजस्तथा ॥१४.१०॥	rajastamaścābhibhūya sattvaṁ bhavati bhārata rajaḥ sattvaṁ tamaścaiva tamaḥ sattvaṁ rajastathā (14.10)

rajaḥ — impulsiveness; tamaścābhibhūya = tamaḥ — depression + ca — and + abhibhūya — predominating over; sattvaṁ — clarity; bhavati — emerges; bhārata — O Bharata family man; rajaḥ — impulsiveness; sattvaṁ — clarity; tamaścaiva = tamaḥ — depression + caiva — and indeed; tamaḥ — depression; sattvaṁ — clarity; rajaḥ — impulsion; tathā — similarly

When predominating over impulsiveness and depression, clarity emerges, O Bharata family man. Depression rises, predominating over impulsiveness and clarity. Similarly, impulsion takes control over depression and clarity. (14.10)

सर्वद्वारेषु देहेऽस्मिन् प्रकाश उपजायते । ज्ञानं यदा तदा विद्याद् विवृद्धं सत्त्वमित्युत ॥१४.११॥	sarvadvāreṣu dehe'smin prakāśa upajāyate jñānaṁ yadā tadā vidyād vivṛddhaṁ sattvamityuta (14.11)

sarvadvāreṣu — in all openings; dehe — in the body; 'smin = asmin — in this; prakāśa — clear perception: upajāyate — is felt; jñānaṁ — true knowledge; yadā — when; tadā — tlien; vidyāt — it should be concluded; vivṛddhaṁ — dominant; sattvam — clarifying mode; iti — thus; uta — indeed

When clear perception, true knowledge, is felt in all openings of the body, then it should be concluded that the clarifying mode is predominant. (14.11)

लोभः प्रवृत्तिरारम्भः कर्मणामशमः स्पृहा । रजस्येतानि जायन्ते विवृद्धे भरतर्षभ ॥१४.१२॥	lobhaḥ pravṛttirārambhaḥ karmaṇāmaśamaḥ spṛhā rajasyetāni jāyante vivṛddhe bharatarṣabha (14.12)

lobhaḥ = greed; pravṛttiḥ — over-exertion; ārambhaḥ — rash undertaking; karmaṇām — of action; aśamaḥ — restlessness; spṛhā — craving; rājasī — in impulsiveness; etāni — those; jāyante — are produced; vivṛddhe — in the dominance; bharatarṣabha — strong man of the Bharatas

Greed, overexertion, rash undertakings, restlessness and craving, these are produced when impulsiveness is predominant, O strong man of the Bharatas. (14.12)

अप्रकाशोऽप्रवृत्तिश्च
प्रमादो मोह एव च ।
तमस्येतानि जायन्ते
विवृद्धे कुरुनन्दन ॥१४.१३॥

aprakāśo'pravṛttiśca
pramādo moha eva ca
tamasyetāni jāyante
vivṛddhe kurunandana (14.13)

aprakāśo = aprakāśaḥ — tack of claiity; 'pravṛttiśca = apravṛttiśca = apravṛttiḥ — lack of energy + ca — and; pramādo = pramādaḥ — inattentiveness; mohā — confusion; eva — indeed; ca — and; tamasī — in depression; etāni — these; jāyante — they emerge; vivṛddhe — in the dominance; kurunandana — O dear son of the Kurus

Lack of clarity, lack of energy, inattentiveness and confusion emerge when depression is predominant, O dear son of the Kurus. (14.13)

यदा सत्त्वे प्रवृद्धे तु
प्रलयं याति देहभृत् ।
तदोत्तमविदां लोकान्
अमलान्प्रतिपद्यते ॥१४.१४॥

yadā sattve pravṛddhe tu
pralayaṁ yāti dehabhṛt
tadottamavidāṁ lokān
amalānpratipadyate (14.14)

yadā — when; sattve — in clarity; pravṛddhe — under the dominance of; tu — but; pralayaṁ — death experience; yāti — he goes; dehabhṛt — the embodied soul; tadottamavidāṁ = tadā — then + uttamavidāṁ — of those who know the supreme; lokān — worlds; amalan — pure; pratipadyate — he is transferred

When the embodied soul goes through the death experience while under the dominance of the clarifying mode, he is transferred to the pure world of those who know the Supreme. (14.14)

रजसि प्रलयं गत्वा
कर्मसङ्गिषु जायते ।
तथा प्रलीनस्तमसि
मूढयोनिषु जायते ॥१४.१५॥

rajasi pralayaṁ gatvā
karmasaṅgiṣu jāyate
tathā pralīnastamasi
mūḍhayoniṣu jāyate (14.15)

rajasi — in the impulsive mode; pralayam — death experience; gatvā — having gone: karmasaṅgiṣu = karmā — work + saṅgiṣu — among people who are prone; jāyate — is born; tathā — likewise; pralīnaḥ — dying; tamasi — in the depressive mode; mūḍhayoniṣu = mūḍha — ignorant; yoniṣu — in the wombs or species; jāyate — is born

Having gone through the death experience in the impulsive mode, the soul is born among the work-prone people; likewise when dying in the depressive mode, the soul takes birth from the wombs of the ignorant species. (14.15)

कर्मणः सुकृतस्याहुः
सात्त्विकं निर्मलं फलम् ।
रजसस्तु फलं दुःखम्
अज्ञानं तमसः फलम् ॥ १४.१६ ॥

karmaṇaḥ sukṛtasyāhuḥ
sāttvikaṁ nirmalaṁ phalam
rajasastu phalaṁ duḥkham
ajñānaṁ tamasaḥ phalam (14.16)

karmaṇaḥ — of action; sukṛtasyāhuḥ = sukṛtasya — of well-performed + āhuḥ — the authorities say; sāttvikaṁ — of the clarifying mode; nirmalaṁ — free of defects; phalam — result: rajasaḥ — of impulsion; tu — but; phalaṁ — result; duḥkham — distress; ajñānaṁ — ignorance; tamasaḥ — of the depressing mode; phalam — consequences

The authorities say that the result of a well-performed action is in the clarifying mode and is free of defects. But the result of an impulsive act is distress, while the consequence of a depressive act is ignorance. (14.16)

सत्त्वात्संजायते ज्ञानं
रजसो लोभ एव च ।
प्रमादमोहौ तमसो
भवतोऽज्ञानमेव च ॥ १४.१७ ॥

sattvātsaṁjāyate jñānaṁ
rajaso lobha eva ca
pramādamohau tamaso
bhavato'jñānameva ca (14.17)

sattvāt — from clarity; saṁjāyate — is produced;jñānaṁ — factual knowledge; rajaso = rajasaḥ — from impulsion; lobha — greed; eva — indeed; ca — and; pramādamohau — inattentiveness and confusion; tamaso = tamasaḥ — from depression; bhavato = bhavataḥ — they come; 'jñānam = ajñānam — ignorance: eva — indeed: ca — and

Factual knowledge is produced from clarity. Greed comes from impulsion. Inattentiveness, confusion, and ignorance come from depression. (14.17)

ऊर्ध्वं गच्छन्ति सत्त्वस्था
मध्ये तिष्ठन्ति राजसाः ।
जघन्यगुणवृत्तस्था
अधो गच्छन्ति तामसाः ॥ १४.१८ ॥

ūrdhvaṁ gacchanti sattvasthā
madhye tiṣṭhanti rājasāḥ
jaghanyaguṇavṛttasthā
adho gacchanti tāmasāḥ (14.18)

ūrdhvaṁ — upward; gacchanti — they go; sattvasthā — situated in clarity; madhye in the middle; tiṣṭhanti — they are situated; rājasāḥ — those who are impulsive; jaghanyaguṇavṛttisthā = jaghanya — lowest + guṇavṛttasthā — situated in the influence of the material energy; adho = adhaḥ — downward; gacchanti — they go; tāmasāḥ those who are retarded

Those who are anchored in clarity, go upward. Those who are impulsive are situated in the middle. Those who are habituated to the lowest influence of the material energy, the retarded people, go downward. (14.18)

नान्यं गुणेभ्यः कर्तारं
यदा द्रष्टानुपश्यति ।
गुणेभ्यश्च परं वेत्ति
मद्भावं सोऽधिगच्छति ॥ १४.१९ ॥

nānyaṁ guṇebhyaḥ kartāraṁ
yadā draṣṭānupaśyati
guṇebhyaśca paraṁ vetti
madbhāvaṁ so'dhigacchati (14.19)

nānyaṁ = na — not + anyam — other; guṇebhyaḥ — than the influences of material nature; kartāraṁ — the performer; yadā — when; draṣṭānupaśyati = draṣṭā — observer + anupaśyati — he perceives; guṇebhyaḥ— than the influences of material nature + ca — and; paraṁ — higher; vetti — he knows; madbhāvaṁ — my level of existence; so = saḥ — he; 'dhigacchati = adhigacchati — he reaches

When the observer perceives no performer besides the influences of material nature and knows what is higher than those influences, he reaches My level of existence. (14.19)

गुणानेतानतीत्य त्रीन्
देही देहसमुद्भवान् ।
जन्ममृत्युजरादुःखैर्
विमुक्तोऽमृतमश्नुते ॥ १४.२० ॥

guṇānetānatītya trīn
dehī dehasamudbhavān
janmamṛtyujarāduḥkhair
vimukto'mṛtamaśnute (14.20)

guṇān — the influences of material nature; etān — these; atītya — transcends; trīn three; dehī — embodied soul; dehasamudbhavān - dcha — body + samudbhavān — formulated in; janmamṛtyujarāduḥkhaiḥ = janma — birth + mṛtyu — death +jarā old age + duḥkhaiḥ — with distress; vimuktaḥ — released; 'mṛtam = amṛtam — immortality; aśnute — he attains

When the embodied soul transcends these three influences of material nature which are formulated in the body, he is released from birth, death, old age, and distress, and attains immortality. (14.20)

अर्जुन उवाच
कैर्लिङ्गैस्त्रीन्गुणानेतान्
अतीतो भवति प्रभो ।
किमाचारः कथं चैतांस्
त्रीन्गुणानतिवर्तते ॥ १४.२१ ॥

arjuna uvāca
kairliṅgaistrīnguṇānetān
atīto bhavati prabho
kimācāraḥ kathaṁ caitāṁs
trīnguṇānativartate (14.21)

arjuna — Arjuna; uvāca — said; kaiḥ — by what; liṅgaiḥ — by features; trīn — three; guṇān — influences; etān — these; atīto = atītaḥ — transcending; bhavati — he is; prabho — respectful Lord; kimācāraḥ = kim — what + ācāraḥ — conduct; kathaṁ how; caitān = ca — and + etān — these; trîn — three; guṇān — influences; ativartate - he transcends

Arjuna said: In regards to a person who transcended the three influences of material nature, by what features is he recognized, O respectful Lord? What is his conduct? And how does he transcend the three influences? (14.21)

श्रीभगवानुवाच
प्रकाशं च प्रवृत्तिं च
मोहमेव च पाण्डव ।
न द्वेष्टि संप्रवृत्तानि
न निवृत्तानि काङ्क्षति ॥१४.२२॥

śrībhagavānuvāca
prakāśaṁ ca pravṛttiṁ ca
mohameva ca pāṇḍava
na dveṣṭi saṁpravṛttāni
na nivṛttāni kāṅkṣati (14.22)

śrī bhagavān — the Blessed Lord; uvāca — said; prakāśaṁ — enlightenment; ca — and; pravṛttiṁ — enthusiasm; ca — and; moham — depression; eva — indeed; ca — and; pāṇḍava — O son of Pandu; na — not; dveṣṭi — scorns; saṁpravṛttāni — presence; na — nor; nivṛttāni — absence; kāṅkṣati — yearns for

The Blessed Lord said: O son of Pandu, he does not scorn nor does he yearn for the presence or absence of enlightenment, enthusiasm or depression. (14.22)

दासीनवदासीनो
गुणैर्यो न विचाल्यते ।
गुणा वर्तन्त इत्येव
योऽवतिष्ठति नेङ्गते ॥१४.२३॥

udāsīnavadāsīno
guṇairyo na vicālyate
guṇā vartanta ityeva
yo'vatiṣṭhati neṅgate (14.23)

udāsinavat — detached; āsīnaḥ — sitting, existing; guṇaiḥ — by the influences of material nature; yaḥ — who; na — not; vicālyate — he is affected; guṇā — the mundane influences; vartanta. — they operate; iti — thus (thinking that); eva — indeed: yo = yaḥ — who; 'vatiṣṭhati - avatiṣṭhati — he is spiritually situated; neṅgate = na — not + iṅgate — he becomes excited

Being situated in the body, but being detached, not being affected by the influences of material nature, considering that the modes are operating naturally, he who is spiritually-situated, who does not become excited, (14.23)

समदुःखसुखः स्वस्थः
समलोष्टाश्मकाञ्चनः ।
तुल्यप्रियाप्रियो धीरस्
तुल्यनिन्दात्मसंस्तुतिः ॥१४.२४॥

samaduḥkhasukhaḥ svasthaḥ
samaloṣṭāśmakāñcanaḥ
tulyapriyāpriyo dhīras
tulyanindātmasaṁstutiḥ (14.24)

samaduḥkhasukhaḥ = samā — equally regarded + duḥkha — pain + sukhaḥ — pleasure; svasthaḥ — self-situated; samaloṣṭāśmakāñcanaḥ = samā — regarded in the same way + loṣṭa — lump of clay + aśmā — stone + kāñcanaḥ — gold; tulyapriyāpriyo = tulyapriyāpriyaḥ = tulya — treated equally + priya — loved ones + apriyaḥ — despised person; dhīraḥ — one who is steady of mind; tulyanindātmasaṁstutiḥ = tulya — regarded equally + nindā — condemnation + ātmā — self + saṁstutiḥ — congratulation

...to whom pain and pleasure are equally regarded, who is self-situated, to whom a lump of clay, a stone or gold, are regarded in the same way, by whom a loved one and a despised person are treated equally, who is steady of mind, to whom condemnation and congratulations are regarded equally, (14.24)

मानावमानयोस्तुल्यस्
तुल्यो मित्रारिपक्षयोः ।
सर्वारम्भपरित्यागी
गुणातीतः स उच्यते ॥१४.२५॥

mānāvamānayostulyas
tulyo mitrāripakṣayoḥ
sarvārambhaparityāgī
guṇātītaḥ sa ucyate (14.25)

mānāvamānayoḥ — in honor and dishonor; tulyaḥ — equally-disposed; tulyo = tulyaḥ — impartial; mitrāripakṣayoḥ — to friend or foe; sarvārambhaparityāgī = sarvā — all + ārambha — undertaking + parityāgī — renouncing; guṇatītaḥ = guṇa — mundane influence + atītaḥ — transcending; sā = saḥ— he; ucyate — is said to be

...who is equally disposed to honor and dishonor, who is impartial to friend or foe, who has renounced all undertakings, is said to have transcended the mundane influences. (14.25)

मां च योऽव्यभिचारेण
भक्तियोगेन सेवते ।
स गुणान्समतीत्यैतान्
ब्रह्मभूयाय कल्पते ॥१४.२६॥

māṁ ca yo'vyabhicāreṇa
bhaktiyogena sevate
sa guṇānsamatītyaitān
brahmabhūyāya kalpate (14.26)

māṁ — me; ca — and; yo = yaḥ — who; 'vyabhicāreṇa = avyabhicāreṇa — with unwavering; bhaktiyogena — by yogically-disciplincd affection; sevate — serves; sā = saḥ— he; guṇān — the mundane influences; samatītyaitān = samatītya — transcending + etān— these; brahmabhūyāya — absorbing in spiritual existence: kalpate — is suited

And a person who serves Me with unwavering, yogicly-disciplined affection and who transcends these mundane influences, is suited for absorption in spiritual existence. (14.26)

ब्रह्मणो हि प्रतिष्ठाहम्
अमृतस्याव्ययस्य च ।
शाश्वतस्य च धर्मस्य
सुखस्यैकान्तिकस्य च ॥१४.२७॥

brahmaṇo hi pratiṣṭhāham
amṛtasyāvyayasya ca
śāśvatasya ca dharmasya
sukhasyaikāntikasya ca (14.27)

brahmaṇo = *brahmaṇaḥ* — *of spiritual existence; hi* — *indeed; pratiṣṭhāham* = *pratiṣṭhā* — *basis* + *aham* — *I; amṛtasyāvyayasya* = *amṛtasya* — *of the immortal* + *avyayasya* — *of the imperishable; ca* — *and; śāśvatasya* — *of the perpetual; ca* — *and; dharmasya* — *of the rules for social conduct; sukhasyaikāntikasya* = *sukhasya*— *of happiness* + *ekāntikasya* — *of the absolute; ca* — *and*

...for I am the basis of the immortal, imperishable spiritual existence and of the perpetual rules of social conduct and of absolute happiness. (14.27)

CHAPTER 15

Two Types of Spirits*

श्रीभगवानुवाच
ऊर्ध्वमूलमधःशाखम्
अश्वत्थं प्राहुरव्ययम् ।
छन्दांसि यस्य पर्णानि
यस्तं वेद स वेदवित् ॥ १५.१ ॥

śrībhagavānuvāca
ūrdhvamūlamadhaḥśākham
aśvatthaṁ prāhuravyayam
chandāṁsi yasya parṇāni
yastaṁ veda sa vedavit (15.1)

śrī bhagavān — The Blessed Lord; uvāca — said; ūrdhvamūtam = urdhva — upward + mūlam — root; adhaḥśākham = adhaḥ — below + śākham — branch; aśvatthaṁ — ashvattha tree; prāhuḥ — the yogī sages say; avyayam — imperishable; chandāṁsi -Vedic hymns; yasya — or what which; parṇāni — leaves; yaḥ — who; taṁ — this; veda — knows; sa = saḥ— he; vedavit — knower of the Vedas

The Blessed Lord said: The yogi sages say that there is an imperishable Ashvattha tree which has a root going upwards and a trunk downwards, the leaves of which are the Vedic hymns. He who knows this is a knower of the Vedas. (15.1)

अधश्चोर्ध्वं प्रसृतास्तस्य शाखा
गुणप्रवृद्धा विषयप्रवालाः ।
अधश्च मूलान्यनुसंततानि
कर्मानुबन्धीनि मनुष्यलोके ॥ १५.२ ॥

adhaścordhvaṁ prasṛtāstasya śākhā
guṇapravṛddhā viṣayapravālāḥ
adhaśca mūlānyanusaṁtatāni
karmānubandhīni manuṣyaloke (15.2)

Adhaścordhvaṁ = adhaḥ — downward + ca — and + urdhvam — upward; prasṛtāḥ — widely spreading; tasya — of it; śākhā — branches; guṇa — mundane influence; pravrddhā — nourished; viṣayapravālāḥ = viṣaya — attractive objects + pravālāḥ — sprouts; adhaśca = adhaḥ — below + ca — and; mūlāni — roots;— stretched out; karmānubandhīni = karmā — action + anubandhīni — promoting; manuṣyaloke = manuṣya — of human being + loke — in the world

Branches spread from it, upwards and downwards. It is nourished by the mundane influences and the attractive objects are its sprouts. The roots are spread below, promoting action in the world of human beings. (15.2)

**The Mahābhārata contains no chapter headings .This title was assigned by the translator on the basis of verse 15 of this chapter.*

न रूपमस्येह तथोपलभ्यते
नान्तो न चादिर्न च संप्रतिष्ठा ।
अश्वत्थमेनं सुविरूढमूलम्
असङ्गशस्त्रेण दृढेन छित्त्वा ॥ १५.३

na rūpamasyeha tathopalabhyate
nānto na cādirna ca saṁpratiṣṭhā
aśvatthamenaṁ suvirūḍhamūlam
asaṅgaśastreṇa dṛḍhena chittvā(15.3)

na — not; rūpam — form; asyeha - asya — of it + iha — in this dimension; tathopalabhyate = tathā — thus + upalabhyate — it is perceived; nānto = nāntah = na — not + antaḥ — end; na — nor; cādiḥ = ca — and + ādiḥ — end; na — nor; ca — and; saṁpratiṣṭhā — foundation; aśvatthaṁ — ashvattha tree; enam — this; suvirūḍhamūtam = suvirūḍha — well-developed + mūlam — root; asaṅgaśastreṇa = asaṅga — non-attachment + śastreṇa — with the axe; dṛḍhena — with the strong; chittvā — cutting down

Its form is not perceived in this dimension, nor its end, nor beginning nor foundation. With the strong ax of non-attachment, cut down this Ashvattha tree with its well-developed roots. (15.3)

ततः पदं तत्परिमार्गितव्यं
यस्मिन्गता न निवर्तन्ति भूयः ।
तमेव चाद्यं पुरुषं प्रपद्ये
यतः प्रवृत्तिः प्रसृता पुराणी. ॥ १५.४॥

tataḥ padaṁ tatparimārgitavyaṁ
yasmingatā na nivartanti bhūyaḥ
tameva cādyaṁ puruṣaṁ prapadye
yataḥ pravṛttiḥ prasṛtā purāṇī(15.4)

tataḥ — then; padaṁ— please; tat— that; parimārgitavyaṁ — to be sought; yasmin — to which; gatā — some; na — not; nivartanti — they return; bhūyaḥ — again; tam — that; eva — indeed; cādyaṁ = ca — and + ādyaṁ — primal; puruṣaṁ — person; prapadye — I take shelter; yataḥ — from whom; pravṛttiḥ — creation; prasṛtā — emerged; purāṇī — in primeval limes

Then that place is to be sought, to which having gone, the spirits do not return to this world again. One should think: I take shelter with that Primal Person, from Whom the creation emerged in primeval times. (15.4)

निर्मानमोहा जितसङ्गदोषा
अध्यात्मनित्या विनिवृत्तकामाः ।
द्वंद्वैर्विमुक्ताः सुखदुःखसंज्ञैर्
गच्छन्त्यमूढाः पदमव्ययं तत् ॥ १५.५

nirmānamohā jitasaṅgadoṣā
adhyātmanityā vinivṛttakāmāḥ
dvaṁdvairvimuktāḥ sukhaduḥkha-
saṁjñair
gacchantyamūḍhāḥ padamavyayaṁ
tat (15.5)

nirmāna — devoid of pride ; mohā — confusion; jita — conquered ; saṅga — attachment ; doṣā — faults; adhyātmanityā = adhyātma — Supreme Spirit + nityā — constantly; vinivṛtta — ceased; kāmāḥ — cravings; dvandvaiḥ — by dualities; vimuktāḥ — freed; sukhaduḥkha — pleasure-pain ; saṁjñaiḥ — known as; gacchanti — they go; amūḍhāḥ — the undeluded souls; padam — place; avyayam — imperishable; tat = tad — that

Those who are devoid of pride and confusion, who have conquered the faults of attachment, who constantly stay with the Supreme Spirit, whose cravings have ceased, who are freed from the dualities known as pleasure and pain, these undeluded souls go to that imperishable place. (15.5)

न तद्भासयते सूर्यो न शशाङ्को न पावकः । यद्गत्वा न निवर्तन्ते तद्धाम परमं मम ॥ १५.६ ॥	na tadbhāsayate sūryo na śaśāṅko na pāvakaḥ yadgatvā na nivartante taddhāma paramaṁ mama (15.6)

na — not; tat — that; bhāsayate — illuminates; sūryo = sūryaḥ — the sun; na — nor; sasaḥko = śaśāṅkaḥ — moon; na — nor; pāvakaḥ — fire; yat — which; gatvā — having gone; na — never; nivartante — they return; tat — that; dhāmā — residence; paramaṁ — supreme; mama — my

The sun does not illuminate that place, nor the moon, nor the fire. Having gone to that location, they never return. That is My supreme residence. (15.6)

ममैवांशो जीवलोके जीवभूतः सनातनः । मनःषष्ठानीन्द्रियाणि प्रकृतिस्थानि कर्षति ॥ १५.७ ॥	mamaivāṁśo jīvaloke jīvabhūtaḥ sanātanaḥ manaḥṣaṣṭhānīndriyāṇi prakṛtisthāni karṣati (15.7)

mamaivāṁśaḥ = mama — my + eva — indeed + aṁśaḥ — partner; jīvaloke = jīva — individualized conditioned being + loke — in the world; jīvabhūtaḥ individual soul; sanātanaḥ — eternal; manaḥ — mind; ṣaṣṭhānindriyāṇi = saṣṭhāni — sixth + indriyāṇi — sense, detection device; prakṛtisthāni — mundane; karṣati — draws

My partner is in this world of individualized conditioned beings. He is an eternal individual soul but he draws to himself the mundane senses of which the mind is the sixth detection device. (15.7)

शरीरं यदवाप्नोति यच्चाप्युत्क्रामतीश्वरः । गृहीत्वैतानि संयाति वायुर्गन्धानिवाशयात् ॥ १५.८ ॥	śarīraṁ yadavāpnoti yaccāpyutkrāmatīśvaraḥ gṛhītvaitāni saṁyāti vāyurgandhānivāśayāt (15.8)

śarīraṁ — by body; yad — which; avāpnoti — he acquires; yat — which; cāpi — and also; utkrāmatīśvaraḥ = utkrāmati — departs from + īśvaraḥ — master; gṛhītvaitāni = gṛhītvā — taking + etāni — these; saṁyāti — he goes; vāyuḥ — wind; gandhān — perfumes; ivāśayāt = ivā — just as + āśayāt — from source

Regardless of whichever body that master acquires, or whichever one he departs from, he goes taking these senses along, just as the wind goes with the perfumes from their source. (15.8)

श्रोत्रं चक्षुः स्पर्शनं च
रसनं घ्राणमेव च ।
अधिष्ठाय मनश्चायं
विषयानुपसेवते ॥१५.९॥

śrotraṁ cakṣuḥ sparśanaṁ ca
rasanaṁ ghrāṇameva ca
adhiṣṭhāya manaścāyaṁ
viṣayānupasevate (15.9)

śrotraṁ — hearing; cakṣuḥ — vision; sparśanaṁ — sense of touch; ca — and; rasanaṁ — taste; ghrāṇaṁ — smell; eva — indeed; ca — and; adhiṣṭhāya — governing ; manaścāyaṁ = manaḥ — mind;-- ca — and + ayaṁ — this; viṣayān — attractive objects; upasevate — becomes addicted

While governing the sense of hearing, the vision, the sense of touch, the sense of taste, the sense of smell and the mind, My partner becomes addicted to the attractive objects. (15.9)

उत्क्रामन्तं स्थितं वापि
भुञ्जानं वा गुणान्वितम् ।
विमूढा नानुपश्यन्ति
पश्यन्ति ज्ञानचक्षुषः ॥१५.१०॥

utkrāmantaṁ sthitaṁ vāpi
bhuñjānaṁ vā guṇānvitam
vimūḍhā nānupaśyanti
paśyanti jñānacakṣuṣaḥ (15.10)

utkrāmantaṁ — departing; sthitaṁ — remaining; vāpi = vā — or + api — also; bhuñjānaṁ — exploiting; vā — or; guṇānvitam — under the influence of material nature; vimūḍhā — idiots; nānupaśyanti = na — not + aupaśyanti — they perceived; paśyanti — they perceive; jñānacakṣuṣaḥ — vision of reality

The idiots do not perceive how the spirit departs or remains or exploits under the influence of material nature. But those who have the vision of reality do perceive this. (15.10)

यतन्तो योगिनश्चैनं
पश्यन्त्यात्मन्यवस्थितम् ।
यतन्तोऽप्यकृतात्मानो
नैनं पश्यन्त्यचेतसः ॥१५.११॥

yatanto yoginaścainaṁ
paśyantyātmanyavasthitam
yatanto'pyakṛtātmāno
nainaṁ paśyantyacetasaḥ (15.11)

yatanto = yatantaḥ — endeavoring; yoginaścainaṁ = yoginaḥ — yogis + ca — and + enam — this (spirit); paśyānti — they sec; ātmani — in the self; avasthitam — situated; yatanto = yatantaḥ — exertion; 'pi = api — even; akṛtātmāno — akṛtātmānaḥ = akṛta — not in order, imperfect + ātmānaḥ — self; nainaṁ= na — not + enam — this (spirit); paśyanti — they see; acetasaḥ — thoughtless ones

The endeavoring yogis see the spirit as being situated in itself; but even with exertion, the imperfected souls, the thoughtless ones, do not perceive it. (15.11)

यदादित्यगतं तेजो जगद्भासयतेऽखिलम् । यच्चन्द्रमसि यच्चाग्नौ तत्तेजो विद्धि मामकम् ॥१५.१२॥	yadādityagataṁ tejo jagadbhāsayate'khilam yaccandramasi yaccāgnau tattejo viddhi māmakam (15.12)

yat — which; ādityagatam — sun-yielding; tejo = tejaḥ — splendor; jagat — universe; bhāsayate — illuminates; 'khitam = akhitam — completely; yat — which; candramasi — in the mood; yat — which; cāgnau = ca — and + āgnau — in fire; tat — that; tejo = tejaḥ — splendor; viddhi — knows; māmakam — mine

That sun-yielding splendor which illuminates the universe completely, which is in the moon and which is in fire; know that splendor to be Mine. (15.12)

गामाविश्य च भूतानि धारयाम्यहमोजसा । पुष्णामि चौषधीः सर्वाः सोमो भूत्वा रसात्मकः ॥१५.१३॥	gāmāviśya ca bhūtāni dhārayāmyahamojasā puṣṇāmi cauṣadhīḥ sarvāḥ somo bhūtvā rasātmakaḥ (15.13)

gām — the earth; āviśya — penetrating; ca — and; bhūtāni — beings; dhārayāmi — I support; aham — I; ojasā — with potency; puṣṇāmi — I cause to thrive; cauṣadhīḥ = ca — and + auṣadhīḥ — plants; sarvāḥ — all; somo = somaḥ — moon; bhūtvā — having influenced; rasātmakaḥ — sap-producing

And penetrating the earth, I support all beings with potency. And having influenced the sap-producing moon, I cause all plants to thrive. (15.13)

अहं वैश्वानरो भूत्वा प्राणिनां देहमाश्रितः । प्राणापानसमायुक्तः पचाम्यन्नं चतुर्विधम् ॥१५.१४॥	ahaṁ vaiśvānaro bhūtvā prāṇināṁ dehamāśritaḥ prāṇāpānasamāyuktaḥ pacāmyannaṁ caturvidham (15.14)

Aham — I; vaiśvānaro = vaiśvānaraḥ — Vaiśvānara, a supernatural being, digestive heat; bhūtvā — becoming; prāṇinām — of the breathing beings; deham — body; āśritaḥ — entering; prāṇāpānasamāyuktaḥ= prāṇāpāna— inhaled and exhaled breath + samāyuktaḥ — combining; pacāmi — digest; annam —food; caturvidham —four kinds

Becoming the Vaiśvānara digestive heat, I, entering the body of all breathing beings and combining with the inhaled and exhaled breath, digest the four kinds of foodstuffs. (15.14)

सर्वस्य चाहं हृदि संनिविष्टो
मत्तः स्मृतिर्ज्ञानमपोहनं च ।
वेदैश्च सर्वैरहमेव वेद्यो
वेदान्तकृद्वेदविदेव चाहम् ॥ १५.१५॥

sarvasya cāhaṁ hṛdi saṁniviṣṭo
mattaḥ smṛtirjñānam apohanaṁ ca
vedaiśca sarvairahameva vedyo
vedāntakṛdvedavideva cāham(15.15)

sarvasya — of all; cāhaṁ = ca — and + aham — I; hṛdi — in the central, psyche; saṁniviṣṭo - saṁniviṣṭaḥ — entered; mattaḥ — from me; smṛtiḥ — memoiy; jñānam — knowledge; apohanaṁ — reasoning; ca — and; vedaiśca = vedaiḥ — by the Vedas + ca — and; sarvaiḥ — by all; aham — I; eva — indeed; vedyo = vedyaḥ— to be known; vedāntakṛt = vedānta — Vedānta + kṛt — maker, author; vedavit — knower of the Vcdas; eva — indeed; cāham = ca — and + aham — I

And I entered the central psyche of all beings. From Me comes memory, knowledge and reasoning. By all the Vedas, I am to be known. I am the author of Vedānta and the knower of the Vedas. (15.15)

द्वाविमौ पुरुषौ लोके
क्षरश्चाक्षर एव च ।
क्षरः सर्वाणि भूतानि
कूटस्थोऽक्षर उच्यते ॥ १५.१६॥

dvāvimau puruṣau loke
kṣaraścākṣara eva ca
kṣaraḥ sarvāṇi bhūtāni
kūṭastho'kṣara ucyate (15.16)

dvau — two; imau — these two; puruṣau — two spirits; loke — in the world; kṣaraścākṣara = kṣaraḥ — affected + ca — and + akṣara — unaffected; eva — indeed; ca — and; kṣaraḥ — affected; sarvāṇi — all; bhūtāni — mundane creatures; kūṭastho = kūṭasthaḥ — stable soul ; 'kṣara = akṣara — unaffected; ucyate — is said to be

These two types of spirits are in this world, namely the affected ones and the unaffected ones. All mundane creatures are affected. The stable soul is said to be unaffected. (15.16)

उत्तमः पुरुषस्त्वन्यः
परमात्मेत्युदाहृतः ।
यो लोकत्रयमाविश्य
बिभर्त्यव्यय ईश्वरः ॥ १५.१७॥

uttamaḥ puruṣastvanyaḥ
paramātmetyudāhṛtaḥ
yo lokatrayamāviśya
bibhartyavyaya īśvaraḥ (15.17)

uttamaḥ — higher: puruṣaḥ — spirit; tu — but; anyaḥ — another; paramātmeti = paramātmā — Supreme Spirit + iti — tims; udāhṛtaḥ — is called; yo = yaḥ — who; lokatrayam — three worlds; āviśya — entering; bibharti — supports; avyaya — eternal; īśvaraḥ — Lord

But the highest spirit is in another category. He is called the Supreme Spirit, Who having entered the three worlds as the eternal Lord, supports it. (15.17)

यस्मात्क्षरमतीतोऽहम्
अक्षरादपि चोत्तमः ।
अतोऽस्मि लोके वेदे च
प्रथितः पुरुषोत्तमः ॥ १५.१८॥

yasmātkṣaramatīto'ham
akṣarādapi cottamaḥ
ato'smi loke vede ca
prathitaḥ puruṣottamaḥ (15.18)

yasmāt — since; kṣaram — effected; atīto = atītaḥ — beyond; 'ham = aham — I; akṣarāt — than the unaffected spirits; api — even; cottamaḥ = ca — and + uttamaḥ — higher; ato = ataḥ — hence; 'smi = asmi — I am; loke — in the world; vede — in the Veda; ca — and; prathitaḥ — known as; puruṣottamaḥ — Supreme Person

Since I am beyond the affected spirits and I am even higher than the unaffected ones, I am known in the world and in the Vedas as the Supreme Person. (15.18)

यो मामेवमसंमूढो
जानाति पुरुषोत्तमम् ।
स सर्वविद्भजति मां
सर्वभावेन भारत ॥ १५.१९॥

yo māmevamasaṁmūḍho
jānāti puruṣottamam
sa sarvavidbhajati māṁ
sarvabhāvena bhārata (15.19)

yo = yaḥ — who; mām — me; evam — in this way; asaṁmūḍho = asaṁmūḍhaḥ — undeluded; jānāti — knows; puruṣottamam — Supreme Person; sa — he; sarvavit — all-knowing, knowledgeable; bhajati — worships; mām — me; sarvabhāvena — with all being; bhārata — O man of the Bharata family

In this way, he who is undeluded, who knows Me as the Supreme Person, he being knowledgeable, worships Me with all his being, O man of the Bharata family. (15.19)

इति गुह्यतमं शास्त्रम्
इदमुक्तं मयानघ ।
एतद्बुद्ध्वा बुद्धिमान्स्यात्
कृतकृत्यश्च भारत ॥ १५.२०॥

iti guhyatamaṁ śāstram
idamuktaṁ mayānagha
etadbuddhvā buddhimānsyāt
kṛtakṛtyaśca bhārata (15.20)

iti — thus; guhyatamaṁ — most secret; śāstram — teaching; idam — this; uktaṁ— is declared; mayā — by me; 'nagha= anagha — O blameless man; etat — this; buddhvā — having realized; buddhimān —wise; syāt — he should become; kṛtakṛtyaśca = kṛtakṛtyaḥ — with duties accomplished + ca — and; bhārata — O descendant of Bharata

Thus the most secret teaching is declared by Me, O blameless man. Having realized this, O descendant of the Bharatas, one becomes a wise person, whose duties are accomplished. (15.20)

CHAPTER 16

Two Types of Created Beings*

श्रीभगवानुवाच
अभयं सत्त्वसंशुद्धिर्
ज्ञानयोगव्यवस्थितिः ।
दानं दमश्च यज्ञश्च
स्वाध्यायस्तप आर्जवम् ॥ १६.१ ॥

śrībhagavānuvāca
abhayaṁ sattvasaṁśuddhir
jñānayogavyavasthitiḥ
dānaṁ damaśca yajñaśca
svādhyāyastapa ārjavam (16.1)

Śrī bhagavān — The Blessed Lord; uvāca — said; abhayaṁ — fearlessness; sattvasaṁśuddhiḥ = sattva — existence, being + saṁśuddhiḥ — purity; jñānayogavyavasthitiḥ = jñāna — mental concept + yoga — application of yoga + vyavasthitiḥ — consistence; dānaṁ — charily; damaśca — damaḥ — self-restraint + ca — and; yajñaśca- yajñaḥ — worship ceremony + ca — and; svādhyāyaḥ — recitation of scripture; tapa — austerity; ārjayam — straight-forwardness

The Blessed Lord said: Fearlessness, purity of being, consistency in application of yoga to mental concepts, charity, self-restraint, worship ceremony, recitation of scripture, austerity and straight-forwardness, (16.1)

अहिंसा सत्यमक्रोधस्
त्यागः शान्तिरपैशुनम् ।
दया भूतेष्वलोलुप्त्वं
मार्दवं ह्रीरचापलम् ॥ १६.२ ॥

ahiṁsā satyamakrodhas
tyāgaḥ śāntirapaiśunam
dayā bhūteṣvaloluptvaṁ
mārdavaṁ hrīracāpalam (16.2)

ahiṁsā — non-violence; satyam — recognition of reality; akrodhaḥ — absence oí anger: tyāgaḥ — abandonment of consequences; śāntiḥ — spiritual security; apaiśunam — absence of destructive criticism; dayā — compassion: bhūteṣu — in beings; aloluptvam — freedom from craving: mārdavaṁ — gentleness; hrīḥ — modesty; acāpalam —absence of fickleness

...non-violence, recognition of reality, absence of anger, abandonment of consequences, spiritual security, absence of destructive criticism, compassion for the beings, freedom from craving, gentleness, modesty, absence of fickleness, (16.2)

**The Mahābhārata contains no chapter headings. This title was assigned by the translator on the basis of verse 6 of this chapter.*

तेजः क्षमा धृतिः शौचम्
अद्रोहो नातिमानिता ।
भवन्ति संपदं दैवीम्
अभिजातस्य भारत ॥१६.३॥

tejaḥ kṣamā dhṛtiḥ śaucam
adroho nātimānitā
bhavanti saṁpadaṁ daivīm
abhijātasya bhārata (16.3)

tejaḥ — vigor; kṣamā — forbearance; dhṛtiḥ — strong-mindedness; śaucam — purity; adroho = adrohaḥ — freedom from hatred; nātimānitā = na — not + ātimānitā — conceit; bhavanti — they are; saṁpadaṁ — nature; daivīm — godly; abhijātasya — of those born; bhārata — O desendant of Bharata

...vigor, forbearance, strong-mindedness, purity, freedom from hatred, and the freedom from conceit; these are the talents of those born with the godly nature, O descendant of Bharata. (16.3)

दम्भो दर्पोऽतिमानश्च
क्रोधः पारुष्यमेव च ।
अज्ञानं चाभिजातस्य
पार्थ संपदमासुरीम् ॥१६.४॥

dambho darpo'timānaśca
krodhaḥ pāruṣyameva ca
ajñānaṁ cābhijātasya
pārtha saṁpadamāsurīm (16.4)

dambho = dambhaḥ — deceit; darpo — darpaḥ — arrogance; 'bhimānaśca = abhimānaśca = abhimānaḥ — conceit + ca — and: krodhaḥ — anger; pāruṣyam — abusive language; eva — indeed; ca — and; ajñānaṁ — lack of knowledge; cābhijātasya = ca — and + abhijātasya — of those born; pārtha — son of Pṛthā; saṁpadam — tendency; āsurīm — those with a wicked nature

Deceit, arrogance, conceit, anger, abusive language, and lack of knowledge are the tendencies of those born with a wicked nature, O son of Pṛthā. (16.4)

दैवी संपद्विमोक्षाय
निबन्धायासुरी मता ।
मा शुचः संपदं दैवीम्
अभिजातोऽसि पाण्डव ॥१६.५॥

daivī saṁpadvimokṣāya
nibandhāyāsurī matā
mā śucaḥ saṁpadaṁ daivīm
abhijāto'si pāṇḍava (16.5)

daivī — godly: saṁpad — talent; vimokṣāya — to liberation; nibandhāyāsurī = nibandhāyā — to bondage + āsurī — wicked tendency; matā — considered to be; mā — not; śucaḥ — worry, saṁpadaṁ — nature; daivīm — godly; abhijāto = abhijātaḥ — born; 'si = asi — you are; pāṇḍava — son of Pandu

The godly talent is conducive to liberation. It is considered that the wicked tendencies facilitate bondage. Do not worry. You are endowed with the godly nature, O son of Pandu. (16.5)

द्वौ भूतसर्गौ लोकेऽस्मिन्
दैव आसुर एव च ।
दैवो विस्तरशः प्रोक्त
आसुरं पार्थ मे श‍ृणु ॥१६.६॥

dvau bhūtasargau loke'smin
daiva āsura eva ca
daivo vistaraśaḥ prokta
āsuraṁ pārtha me śṛṇu (16.6)

dvau — two; bhūtasargau = bhūta — being + sargau — two created types; loke — in the world; 'smin = asmin — in this; daiva — godly; āsura — wicked; eva — indeed; ca — and; daivo = daivah — godly type; viṣṭaraśaḥ — in detail; prokta — explained; āsuraṁ — wicked: pārtha — son of Pṛthā; me — from me; śṛṇu — hear

There are two types of created beings in this world, the godly type and the wicked. The godly type was explained in detail. Hear from me of the wicked, O son of Pṛthā. (16.6)

प्रवृत्तिं च निवृत्तिं च
जना न विदुरासुराः ।
न शौचं नापि चाचारो
न सत्यं तेषु विद्यते ॥१६.७॥

pravṛttiṁ ca nivṛttiṁ ca
janā na vidurāsurāḥ
na śaucaṁ nāpi cācāro
na satyaṁ teṣu vidyate (16.7)

pravṛttiṁ — what to do; ca — and; nivṛttiṁ — what not to do; ca — and; janā — people; na — not; viduḥ — they know; āsurāḥ — wicked; na — neither; śaucaṁ — cleanliness; nāpi = na — nor + api — also; cācāro = cācāraḥ = ca — and + ācāraḥ — good conduct; na — nor; satyam — realism; teṣu — in them; vidyate — is found

The wicked people do not know what to do and what not to do. Neither cleanliness or even good conduct, nor realism is found in them. (16.7)

असत्यमप्रतिष्ठं ते
जगदाहुरनीश्वरम् ।
अपरस्परसंभूतं
किमन्यत्कामहैतुकम् ॥१६.८॥

asatyamapratiṣṭhaṁ te
jagadāhuranīśvaram
aparasparasaṁbhūtaṁ
kimanyatkāmahaitukam (16.8)

asatyam — unreal; apratiṣṭhaṁ — without a foundation; te — they; jagat — the world; āhuḥ — they say; anīśvaram — without a Supreme Lord; aparasparasaṁbhūtaṁ = aparaspara — without a series of causes + saṁbhūtaṁ — produced; kim — what?; anyat — other cause; kāmahaitukam = kāma — sensual urge + haitukam — caused

They say that the universe is unreal, without a foundation, without a Supreme Lord, without a series of causes. They explain, saying, "Sexual urge is the cause. What other basis could there be?" (16.8)

एतां दृष्टिमवष्टभ्य
नष्टात्मानोऽल्पबुद्धयः ।
प्रभवन्त्युग्रकर्माणः
क्षयाय जगतोऽहिताः ॥ १६.९ ॥

etāṁ dṛṣṭimavaṣṭabhya
naṣṭātmāno'lpabuddhayaḥ
prabhavantyugrakarmāṇaḥ
kṣayāya jagato'hitāḥ (16.9)

etāṁ — this; dṛṣṭim — view; avaṣṭabhya — holding; naṣṭātmāno — naṣṭātmānaḥ = naṣṭa — lost + ātmānaḥ — to their spiritual selves; 'lpabuddhayaḥ = alpabuddhayaḥ = alpa — negligible + buddhayaḥ — intelligence; prabhavanti — they become; ugrakarmāṇaḥ = ugra — cruel + karmāṇaḥ — acts; kṣayāya — to destruction; jagato = jagataḥ — of the world; 'hitāḥ = ahitāḥ — enemies

Holding this view, men who lost track of their spirituality, who have negligible intelligence, who commit cruel acts, become enemies for the destruction of the world. (16.9)

काममाश्रित्य दुष्पूरं
दम्भमानमदान्विताः ।
मोहाद्गृहीत्वासद्ग्राहान्
प्रवर्तन्तेऽशुचिव्रताः ॥ १६.१०

kāmamāśritya duṣpūraṁ
dambhamānamadānvitāḥ
mohādgṛhītvāsadgrāhān
pravartante'śucivratāḥ (16.10)

kāmam — lusty urge; āśritya — relying; duṣpūraṁ — non-fulfilling; dambhamānamadānvitāḥ = dambba — hypocrisy + māna — pride + mada — intoxicated + anvitāḥ — possessed by; mohāt — from delusion; gṛhītvā — having accepted; 'sadgrāhān = asadgrāhān = asad (asat) — unrealistic + grāhān — views; pravartante — they proceed; 'śucivratāḥ = aśucivratāh = aśuci — impure + vratāḥ — objectives

Being reliant on the non-fulfilling lusty urge, possessed of hypocrisy, pride, and intoxication, having accepted unrealistic views, through delusion, they proceed with impure objectives. (16.10)

चिन्तामपरिमेयां च
प्रलयान्तामुपाश्रिताः ।
कामोपभोगपरमा
एतावदिति निश्चिताः ॥ १६.११ ॥

cintāmaparimeyāṁ ca
pralayāntāmupāśritāḥ
kāmopabhogaparamā
etāvaditi niścitāḥ (16.11)

Citām — worry; aparimeyāṁ — endless; ca — and; pralayāntām — ending at death; upāśritāḥ — clinging; kāmopabhogaparamā = kāma — lust + upabhoga — enjoyment + paramā — highest aim; etāvat — so much; iti — thus; niścitāḥ — convinced

And clinging to endless worries which end at the time of death, with lusty enjoyment as the highest aim, being convinced that this is all there is, (16.11)

आशापाशशतैर्बद्धाः
कामक्रोधपरायणाः ।
ईहन्ते कामभोगार्थम्
अन्यायेनार्थसंचयान् ॥ १६.१२॥

āśāpāśaśatairbaddhāḥ
kāmakrodhaparāyaṇāḥ
īhante kāmabhogārtham
anyāyenārthasaṁcayān (16.12)

āśāpāśaśataiḥ = āśāpāśa — frustrating expectations + śataiḥ — by a hundred; baddhāḥ — bound; kāmakrodhaparāyaṇāḥ = kāma — craving + krodha — anger + parāyaṇāḥ — cherishing; īhante — they strive to acquire; kāmabhogārtham = kāma — craving + bhoga — pleasure + artham — fulfillment; anyāyenārthasañcayān = anyāyena — with any other + artha — money + sañcayān — huge sums

...bound by hundreds of frustrating expectations, cherishing craving and anger, using any means, they strive to acquire huge sums of money for the fulfillment of craving and pleasure. (16.12)

इदमद्य मया लब्धम्
इदं प्राप्स्ये मनोरथम् ।
इदमस्तीदमपि मे
भविष्यति पुनर्धनम् ॥ १६.१३

idamadya mayā labdham
idaṁ prāpsye manoratham
idamastīdamapi me
bhaviṣyati punardhanam (16.13)

idam — this; adya — today; mayā — by me; labdham — obtained; idaṁ — this; prāpsye — I will fulfill; manoratham — fantasy; idam — this; astīdam = asti — it is + idam — this; api — also; me — mine; bhaviṣyati — willl be; punaḥ — again, also; dhanam — wealth

Thinking: "This was obtained by me today, I will fulfill this fantasy. This is it. This wealth will also be mine. (16.13)

असौ मया हतः शत्रुर्
हनिष्ये चापरानपि ।
ईश्वरोऽहमहं भोगी
सिद्धोऽहं बलवान्सुखी ॥ १६.१४॥

asau mayā hataḥ śatrur
haniṣye cāparānapi
īśvaro'hamahaṁ bhogī
siddho'haṁ balavānsukhī (16.14)

asau — that; mayā — by me; hataḥ — was killed; śatruḥ — enemy; haniṣye — I will kill; cāparān = ca — and + aparān — others; api — as well as; īśvaro = īśvaraḥ — controller; 'ham = aham — I; aham — I; bhogī — enjoyer; siddho = siddhaḥ — successful; aham = aham — I; balavān — powerful; sukhī — happy

"That enemy was killed by me, I will kill others as well. I am the controller. I am the enjoyer. I am successful, powerful and happy. (16.14)

आढ्योऽभिजनवानस्मि
कोऽन्योऽस्ति सदृशो मया ।
यक्ष्ये दास्यामि मोदिष्य
इत्यज्ञानविमोहिताः ॥ १६.१५॥

āḍhyo'bhijanavānasmi
ko'nyo'sti sadṛśo mayā
yakṣye dāsyāmi modiṣya
ityajñānavimohitāḥ (16.15)

āḍhyo = ādhyaḥ — rich; 'bhijanavān = abhijanavān — upper class; asmi — I am; ko = kaḥ — who; 'nyo = anyaḥ — other; 'sti = asti — there is; sadraśo = sadraśaḥ — like; mayā — me; yakṣye — I will perform religious ceremony; dāsyāmi — I will give in, donate; — I will make merry; iti — thus is said; ajñānavimohitāḥ = ajñāna -ignorance + vimohitāḥ — those who are deluded

"I am rich and upper class. Who is there besides me? I will perform religious ceremony. I will donate. I will make merry." This is what is said by those who are deluded by ignorance. (16.15)

अनेकचित्तविभ्रान्ता
मोहजालसमावृताः ।
प्रसक्ताः कामभोगेषु
पतन्ति नरकेऽशुचौ ॥१६.१६॥

anekacittavibhrāntā
mohajālasamāvṛtāḥ
prasaktāḥ kāmabhogeṣu
patanti narake'śucau (16.16)

anekacittavibhrāntā = aneka — many + citta — idea + vibhrāntā — carried away; mohajālasamāvṛtāh = moha — delusion + jāla — entanglement + samāvṛtāḥ — occupied by; prasaktāḥ —being attached; kāmabhogeṣu = kāma — craving + bhogeṣu — in enjoyments; patanti — they fall; narake — in hellish condition; 'śucau = aśucau — unclean

Being carried away by many ideas, being occupied by entangling delusions, being attached by cravings and enjoyments, they fall into an unclean, hellish condition. (16.16)

आत्मसंभाविताः स्तब्धा
धनमानमदान्विताः ।
यजन्ते नामयज्ञैस्ते
दम्भेनाविधिपूर्वकम् ॥१६.१७॥

ātmasaṁbhāvitāḥ stabdhā
dhanamānamadānvitāḥ
yajante nāmayajñaiste
dambhenāvidhipūrvakam (16.17)

ātmasaṁbhāvitāḥ — self-conceited; stabdhā — stubborn; dhanamānamadānvitāḥ = dhanamāna — arrogance of having money + mada — pride +anvitāḥ — possessed with; yajante — they worship in ceremony; nāmayajñaiḥ — with religious ceremony in name only; te — they; dambhenāvidhipūrvakam - dambhena — with hyprocrisy + avidhipurvakam — with reference to Vedic injunction

Self-conceited, stubborn, possessed of pride and the arrogance of having money, with hypocrisy and without reference to Vedic injunctions, they worship in ceremonies that are religious in name only. (16.17)

अहंकारं बलं दर्पं
कामं क्रोधं च संश्रिताः ।
मामात्मपरदेहेषु
प्रद्विषन्तोऽभ्यसूयकाः ॥१६.१८॥

ahaṁkāraṁ balaṁ darpaṁ
kāmaṁ krodhaṁ ca saṁśritāḥ
māmātmaparadeheṣu
pradviṣanto'bhyasūyakāḥ (16.18)

ahaṁkāraṁ — misplaced self-identity; balam — brute force; darpaṁ — arrogance; kāmaṁ — craving; krodhaṁ — anger; ca — and; saṁśritāḥ — clinging to; mām — me; ātmaparadeheṣu = ātma — self + para — other + deheṣu — in bodies; pradviṣanto = pradviṣantaḥ — disliking; 'bhyasūyakāḥ = abhyasūyakāḥ — those who are envious

Clinging to a misplaced self-identity, brute force, arrogance, craving and anger, those who are envious dislike Me, in their own bodies and in those of others. (16.18)

तानहं द्विषतः क्रूरान्
संसारेषु नराधमान् ।
क्षिपाम्यजस्रमशुभान्
आसुरीष्वेव योनिषु ॥१६.१९

tānahaṁ dviṣataḥ krūrān
saṁsāreṣu narādhamān
kṣipāmyajasramaśubhān
āsurīṣveva yoniṣu (16.19)

tān — them; aham — I; dviṣataḥ — those who are despising; krūrān — those who are cruel; saṁsāreṣu — in the cycles of rebirth; narādhamān — lowest of humans; kṣipāmi — I hurl; ajasram — constantly; aśubhān — the vicious; āsurīṣu — into the wicked people; eva — indeed; yoniṣu — in the wombs

I constantly hurl the despising cruel, vicious, lowest of humans into the cycles of rebirth in the wombs of wicked people. (16.19)

आसुरीं योनिमापन्ना
मूढा जन्मनि जन्मनि ।
मामप्राप्यैव कौन्तेय
ततो यान्त्यधमां गतिम् ॥१६.२०॥

āsurīṁ yonimāpannā
mūḍhā janmani janmani
māmaprāpyaiva kaunteya
tato yāntyadhamāṁ gatim (16.20)

āsurīṁ — the wicked people; yonim — womb; āpannā — entering; mūḍhā — the blockheads; janmani janmani — in birth, in birth again; mām — me; aprāpyaivā = aprāpya — associating + eva — indeed; kaunteya — O son of Kuntī ; tato = tataḥ — thence; yānti — they traverse; adhamāṁ — lowest; gatim — route of transmigrations

Thus, O son of Kuntī, entering the wombs of the wicked people, the blockheads, after not associating with Me in birth after birth, traverse the lowest route of transmigration. (16.20)

त्रिविधं नरकस्येदं
द्वारं नाशनमात्मनः ।
कामः क्रोधस्तथा लोभस्
तस्मादेतत्त्रयं त्यजेत् ॥१६.२१॥

trividhaṁ narakasyedaṁ
dvāraṁ nāśanamātmanaḥ
kāmaḥ krodhastathā lobhas
tasmādetattrayaṁ tyajet (16.21)

trividhaṁ — threefold; narakasyedaṁ = narakasya — of hell + idam — this; dvāraṁ — avenues; nāśanam — destructive of, degrading towards; ātmanaḥ — of the self; kāmaḥ — craving; krodhaḥ — anger; tathā— as well; lobhaḥ —

greed; tasmāt — therefore; etat — this; trayam — three-fold; tyajet — should abandon

Craving, anger and greed are the three avenues of hell which degrade the soul. Therefore one should abandon this threefold influence. (16.21)

एतैर्विमुक्तः कौन्तेय तमोद्वारैस्त्रिभिर्नरः । आचरत्यात्मनः श्रेयस् ततो याति परां गतिम् ॥१६.२२॥	etairvimuktaḥ kaunteya tamodvāraistribhirnaraḥ ācaratyātmanaḥ śreyas tato yāti paraṁ gatim (16.22)

etair (etaiḥ) — by these; vimuktaḥ — released; kaunteya — son of Kuntī ; tamodvārais = tamo (tamaḥ) — depression + dvāraiḥ — by avanues; tribhir (tribhiḥ) — by three; naraḥ — a person; ācaratyātmanaḥ = ācarati — he serves + ātmanaḥ — of the self; śreyaḥ — best interest; tato (tataḥ) — then; yāti — goes; paraṁ — supreme; gatim — destination

Being released from these three avenues of depression, O son of Kuntī, a person serves his best interest and then goes to the highest destination. (16.22)

यः शास्त्रविधिमुत्सृज्य वर्तते कामकारतः । न स सिद्धिमवाप्नोति न सुखं न परां गतिम् ॥१६.२३॥	yaḥ śāstravidhimutsṛjya vartate kāmakārataḥ na sa siddhimavāpnoti na sukhaṁ na paraṁ gatim (16.23)

yaḥ — who; śāstravidhim — scriptural injunction; utsṛjya — discarding; vartate — he follows; kāmakārataḥ — impulsion, inclination; na — not; sa = saḥ — he; siddhim — perfection; avāpnoti — attains; na — nor; sukhaṁ — happiness; na — nor; paraṁ — highest; gatim — destination

Whosoever discards the scriptural injunctions, and follows the impulsive inclinations, does not get perfection or happiness or the supreme destination. (16.23)

तस्माच्छास्त्रं प्रमाणं ते कार्याकार्यव्यवस्थितौ । ज्ञात्वा शास्त्रविधानोक्तं कर्म कर्तुमिहार्हसि ॥१६.२४॥	tasmācchāstraṁ pramāṇaṁ te kāryākāryavyavasthitau jñātvā śāstravidhānoktaṁ karma kartumihārhasi (16.24)

tasmāt — therefore; śāstram — scripture; pramāṇaṁ — recommendation; te — your; karyākāryavyavasthitau = kārya — duty + akārya — non-duty + vyavasthitau — setting; jñātvā —knowing; śāstravidhānoktaṁ = śāstravidhāna — scriptural rules + uktaṁ — prescribed; karma — action; kartum — to perform; ihārhasi = ihā — here in this world + arhasi — you can

Therefore, setting your standard of duty and non-duty by scriptural recommendation, knowing the scriptural rules prescribed, you should perform actions in this world. (16.24)

CHAPTER 17

Three Types of Confidences*

अर्जुन उवाच
ये शास्त्रविधिमुत्सृज्य
यजन्ते श्रद्धयान्विताः ।
तेषां निष्ठा तु का कृष्ण
सत्त्वमाहो रजस्तमः ॥ १७.१ ॥

arjuna uvāca
ye śāstravidhimutsṛjya
yajante śraddhayānvitāḥ
teṣāṁ niṣṭhā tu kā kṛṣṇa
sattvamāho rajastamaḥ (17.1)

arjuna — Arjuna; uvāca — said; ye — who; śastravidhim — scriptural injunction; utsṛjya — disregarding; yajante — they perform religiously—motivated ceremony and austerity; śraddhayānvitāḥ — with full confidence; teṣāṁ — of them; niṣṭhā — position; tu — but; kā — what; kṛṣṇa — O Krishna; sattvaṁ — clarity; āho — is it?; rajaḥ — impulsion; tamaḥ—depression

Arjuna said: Concerning those who disregard scriptural injunction, but who with full confidence perform religiously-motivated ceremonies and austerities, what indeed, is their position, O Krishna? Is it clarity, impulsion or depression? (17.1)

श्रीभगवानुवाच
त्रिविधा भवति श्रद्धा
देहिनां सा स्वभावजा ।
सात्त्विकी राजसी चैव
तामसी चेति तां शृणु ॥ १७.२ ॥

śrībhagavānuvāca
trividhā bhavati śraddhā
dehināṁ sā svabhāvajā
sāttvikī rājasī caiva
tāmasī ceti tāṁ śṛṇu (17.2)

śrī bhagavān — The Blessed Lord; uvāca — said; trividhā — three types; bhavati — there is; śraddhā — confidence; dehināṁ — of the embodied souls; sā — anyone; svabhāvajā — produced from innate tendency; sāttvikī — clarifying; rājasī — motivating; caiva — and indeed; tāmasī — depression; ceti = ca — and + iti — thus; tāṁ — this; śṛṇu — hear

The Blessed Lord said: According to innate tendency, there are three types of confidences of the embodied souls. These are clarifying, motivating and depressing. Hear about this. (17.2)

**The Mahābhārata contains no chapter headings. This title was assigned by the translator on the basis of verse 2 of this chapter.*

सत्त्वानुरूपा सर्वस्य
श्रद्धा भवति भारत ।
श्रद्धामयोऽयं पुरुषो
यो यच्छ्रद्धः स एव सः ॥१७.३॥

sattvānurūpā sarvasya
śraddhā bhavati bhārata
śraddhāmayo'yaṁ puruṣo
yo yacchraddhaḥ sa eva saḥ (17.3)

sattvānurūpā = sattva — essential nature + anurūpā — according to; sarvasya — of every person; śraddhā — confidence; bhavati — becomes manifest; bhārata — O man of the Bharata family; śraddhāmayaḥ — made of faith, trend of confidence; 'yaṁ = ayaṁ — this; puruṣo = puruṣaḥ — human being; yo = yaḥ — who; yacchraddhah = yac (yad) — which + chraddhah (śraddhaḥ) — faith; sa = saḥ — he; eva — only: saḥ — he

Confidence becomes manifest according to the essential nature of the person, O man of the Bharata family. A human being follows his trend of confidence. Whatever type of faith he has, that he expresses only. (17.3)

यजन्ते सात्त्विका देवान्
यक्षरक्षांसि राजसाः ।
प्रेतान्भूतगणांश्चान्ये
यजन्ते तामसा जनाः ॥१७.४॥

yajante sāttvikā devān
yakṣarakṣāṁsi rājasāḥ
pretānbhūtagaṇāṁścānye
yajante tāmasā janāḥ (17.4)

yajante — they worship; sāttvikā — clear-minded people; devān — supernatural riders; yakṣarakṣāṁsi = yakṣa — passionate sorcerers + rakṣāṁsi — to cannibalistic powerful humans; rājasāḥ — impulsive people; pretān — the departed spirits; bhūtagaṇāṁścānye — bhūtagaṇān — hordes of ghosts + ca — and + anye — others; yajante — they petition; tāmasā = retarded; janāḥ — people

The clear-minded people worship the supernatural rulers. The impulsive ones worship the passionate sorcerors and the cannibalistic humans. The others, the retarded people, petition the departed spirits and the hordes of ghosts. (17.4)

अशास्त्रविहितं घोरं
तप्यन्ते ये तपो जनाः ।
दम्भाहंकारसंयुक्ताः
कामरागबलान्विताः ॥१७.५॥

aśāstravihitaṁ ghoraṁ
tapyante ye tapo janāḥ
dambhāhaṁkāra-saṁyuktāḥ
kāmarāgabalānvitāḥ (17.5)

aśāstravihitaṁ = aśāstra — not of scripture + vihitaṁ — recommended; ghoraṁ — terrible; tapyante — tbey endure; ye — who; tapo — tapaḥ — austerity; janāḥ — people; dambhāhaṁkārasaṁyuktāḥ — dambha — deceit + ahaṁkāra — misplaced identity + saṁyuktāḥ — enthused with; kāmarāgabalānvitāḥ = kāma — craving + rāga — rage + bala — brute force + anvitāḥ — possessed with

People who endure terrible austerities which are not recommended in the scripture, people who are enthused with deceit and misplaced identity, who are possessed with craving, rage and brute force, (17.5)

कर्शयन्तः शरीरस्थं
भूतग्राममचेतसः ।
मां चैवान्तःशरीरस्थं
तान्विद्ध्यासुरनिश्चयान् ॥ १७.६ ॥

karśayantaḥ śarīrasthaṁ
bhūtagrāmamacetasaḥ
māṁ caivāntaḥśarīrasthaṁ
tānviddhyāsuraniścayān (17.6)

karśayantaḥ — torturing, troubling; śarīrasthaṁ — within the body; bhūtagrāmam — collection of elements; acetasaḥ — senseless; māṁ — me; caivantaḥ = ca — and + eva — indeed + antaḥ — within; śarīrasthaṁ — within the body; tān — them; viddhi — know; — āsura — wicked + niścayān — intentions

...those who torture the collection of the elements which comprise the body, who also trouble Me within the body, know that they have wicked intentions. (17.6)

आहारस्त्वपि सर्वस्य
त्रिविधो भवति प्रियः ।
यज्ञस्तपस्तथा दानं
तेषां भेदमिमं शृणु ॥ १७.७॥

āhārastvapi sarvasya
trividho bhavati priyaḥ
yajñastapastathā dānaṁ
teṣāṁ bhedamimaṁ śṛṇu (17.7)

āhāraḥ — food; tu — but; api — as well; sarvasya — of all; trividho = trividhaḥ — three kinds; bhavati — is; priyaḥ — likes; yajñaḥ — religious ceremony; tapaḥ — austerity; tathā — as; dānaṁ — charity; teṣāṁ — of them; bhedam — difference; imaṁ — this; śṛṇu — hear

But food as well, which is liked by all, is of three kinds as are religious ceremony, austerity and charity. Hear of the difference between them. (17.7)

आयुःसत्त्वबलारोग्य-
सुखप्रीतिविवर्धनाः ।
रस्याः स्निग्धाः स्थिरा हृद्या
आहाराः सात्त्विकप्रियाः ॥ १७.८॥

āyuḥsattvabalārogya-
sukhaprītivivardhanāḥ
rasyāḥ snigdhāḥ sthirā hṛdyā
āhārāḥ sāttvikapriyāḥ (17.8)

āyuḥsattvabalārogya = āyuḥ — duration of life + sattva — spiritual well-being + bala — strength + ārogya — health; sukhaprītivivardhanāḥ = sukha — happiness + prīti — satisfaction + vivardhanāḥ — increasing; rasyāḥ — juicy; snigdhāḥ — milky; sthirā — sustaining; hṛdyā — palatable; āhārāḥ — foods; sātvikapriyāḥ — dear to the clear-minded people

Foods which increase the duration of the life, the spiritual well-being, strength, health, happiness and satisfaction, which are juicy, milky, sustaining and palatable, are eatables which are dear to the clear-minded people. (17.8)

कट्वम्ललवणात्युष्ण-
तीक्ष्णरूक्षविदाहिनः ।
आहारा राजसस्येष्टा
दुःखशोकामयप्रदाः ॥ १७.९ ॥

kaṭvamlalavaṇātyuṣṇa-
tīkṣṇarūkṣavidāhinaḥ
āhārā rājasasyeṣṭā
duḥkhaśokāmayapradāḥ (17.9)

kaṭvamlalavaṇātyuṣṇa = kaṭv (kaṭu) — pungent + amla — sour + lavaṇa — salt; atyuṣṇa — peppery; tīkṣnarūkṣavidāhinaḥ — tīkṣṇa — acidic + rūkṣa — dry + vidāhinaḥ — overheated; āhārā — foods; rājasasyeṣṭā — rajasasya — of the passionate people + iṣṭā — desired; duḥkhaśokāmayapradāḥ = duḥkha — pain + śoka — misery + āmaya — sickness + pradāḥ — causing

Foods which are pungent, sour, salty, peppery, acidic, dry and overheated, are desired by the passionate people. These foods cause pain, misery and sickness. (17.9)

यातयामं गतरसं
पूति पर्युषितं च यत् ।
उच्छिष्टमपि चामेध्यं
भोजनं तामसप्रियम् ॥ १७.१० ॥

yātayāmaṁ gatarasaṁ
pūti paryuṣitaṁ ca yat
ucchiṣṭamapi cāmedhyaṁ
bhojanaṁ tāmasapriyam (17.10)

yātayāmaṁ — stale; gatarasaṁ — tasteless; pūti — rotten; paryuṣitaṁ — left over; ca — and; yat = yad — which; ucchiṣṭam — rejected; api — also; cāmedhyam = ca — and + amedhyaṁ — unfit for religious ceremony; bhojanaṁ — food; tāmasapriyam — cherished by the depressed people

Food which is stale, tasteless, and rotten, which was left over, as well as that which is rejected or unfit for religious ceremony, is cherished by the depressed people. (17.10)

अफलाकाङ्क्षिभिर्यज्ञो
विधिदृष्टो य इज्यते ।
यष्टव्यमेवेति मनः
समाधाय स सात्त्विकः ॥ १७.११ ॥

aphalākāṅkṣibhiryajño
vidhidṛṣṭo ya ijyate
yaṣṭavyameveti manaḥ
samādhāya sa sāttvikaḥ (17.11)

aphalākāṅkṣibhiḥ = aphalā — no benefits + kāṅkṣibhiḥ — desiring; yajño = yajñaḥ — a religious discipline or ceremony; vidhidṛṣṭo — vidhidṛṣṭaḥ = vidhi — scripture + dṛṣṭaḥ — observing; ya — who; ijyate — is offered; yaṣṭavyam — to be sacrificed; eveti = eva — indeed + iti — thus; manaḥ — mind; samādhāya — concentrating; sa — it; sāttvikaḥ — realistic

A religious discipline or ceremony in observance of the scripture, by those who do not desire a benefit and who, while concentrating, think, "This is to be sacrificed," is a ceremony of the realistic type. (17.11)

अभिसंधाय तु फलं
दम्भार्थमपि चैव यत् ।
इज्यते भरतश्रेष्ठ
तं यज्ञं विद्धि राजसम् ॥ १७.१२

abhisaṁdhāya tu phalaṁ
dambhārthamapi caiva yat
ijyate bharataśreṣṭha
taṁ yajñaṁ viddhi rājasam (17.12)

abhisandhāya — kept in mind; tu — but; phalam — benefit; dambhārtham — for the sake of outsmarting the deity; api — also; caiva — and indeed; yat = yad — which; ijyate — is offered; bharataśreṣṭha — best of the Bhāratas; tam — this; yajñaṁ — disciplined worship; viddhi — know; rājasam — impulsive

But when a benefit is kept in mind and when the motive is to outsmart the deity, know, O best of the Bharatas, that the disciplinary worship offered is based on impulsion. (17.12)

विधिहीनमसृष्टान्नं
मन्त्रहीनमदक्षिणम् ।
श्रद्धाविरहितं यज्ञं
तामसं परिचक्षते ॥ १७.१३ ॥

vidhihīnamasṛṣṭānnaṁ
mantrahīnamadakṣiṇam
śraddhāvirahitaṁ yajñaṁ
tāmasaṁ paricakṣate (17.13)

vidhihīnam — scripture neglected; asṛṣṭānnaṁ = asṛṣṭa — not offered + annam — food; mantrahīnam — Vedic hymn not recited; adakṣiṇam — no fee for the priest; śraddhāvirahitaṁ — confidence lacking; yajñaṁ — disciplinary worship; tāmasaṁ — depressive; paricakṣate — they regard

When scripture is neglected, food is not offered, Vedic hymns not recited, a fee not given to the priest, and confidence is lacking, regard that disciplinary worship as depressive. (17.13)

देवद्विजगुरुप्राज्ञ-
पूजनं शौचमार्जवम् ।
ब्रह्मचर्यमहिंसा च
शारीरं तप उच्यते ॥ १७.१४ ॥

devadvijagurprājña-
pūjanaṁ śaucamārjavam
brahmacaryamahiṁsā ca
śārīraṁ tapa ucyate (17.14)

devadvijagurprājña = deva — supernatural ruler + dvija = those who are qualified by sacred thread ceremony + guru — spiritual teacher + prājña — wise man; pūjanaṁ — reverential respect; śaucam — purity; ārjavam — straightforwardness; brahmacaryam — celibacy; ahiṁsa — non—violence; ca — and; śārīraṁ — body; tapa — austerity; ucyate — is said to be

Reverential respect of the supernatural rulers, of those who are qualified by the sacred thread ceremony, of the spiritual teacher, and of the wise man, purity, straightforwardness, celibacy and non-violence, are said to be austerity of the body. (17.14)

अनुद्वेगकरं वाक्यं
सत्यं प्रियहितं च यत् ।
स्वाध्यायाभ्यसनं चैव
वाङ्मयं तप उच्यते ॥ १७.१५ ॥

anudvegakaraṁ vākyaṁ
satyaṁ priyahitaṁ ca yat
svādhyāyābhyasanaṁ caiva
vāṅmayaṁ tapa ucyate (17.15)

anudvegakaraṁ — not causing distress; vākyaṁ — speech; satyam — truthful; priyaḥitam — agreeable and beneficial; ca — and; yat = yad — which; svādhyāyābhyasanaṁ = svādhyāya — recitation of scripture + abhyasanaṁ — practice, regularity; caiva — and indeed; vāṅmayaṁ — speech-made; tapa — discipline; ucyate — is called

Speech which does not cause distress, and is truthful, agreeable and beneficial, as well as regular recitation of the scriptures is the discipline of speech. (17.15)

मनःप्रसादः सौम्यत्वं
मौनमात्मविनिग्रहः ।
भावसंशुद्धिरित्येतत्
तपो मानसमुच्यते ॥ १७.१६ ॥

manaḥprasādaḥ saumyatvaṁ
maunamātmavinigrahaḥ
bhāvasaṁśuddhirityetat
tapo mānasamucyate (17.16)

manaḥprasādaḥ = manah — mind + prasādaḥ — peace; saumayatvaṁ — gentleness; maunam — silence; ātmavinigrahaḥ — self—restraint; bhāvasaṁśuddhiḥ = bhāva — being + saṁśuddhiḥ — purity; iti — thus, etat = etad — this; tapo = tapaḥ — discipline; mānasam — of the mind; ucyate — is called

Peace of mind, gentleness, silence, self restraint, and purity of being, this is called discipline of mind. (17.16)

श्रद्धया परया तप्तं
तपस्तत्त्रिविधं नरैः ।
अफलाकाङ्क्षिभिर्युक्तैः
सात्त्विकं परिचक्षते ॥ १७.१७ ॥

śraddhayā parayā taptaṁ
tapastattrividhaṁ naraiḥ
aphalākāṅkṣibhiryuktaiḥ
sāttvikaṁ paricakṣate (17.17)

śraddhayā — with faith; parayā — with the highest; taptam — performed; tapaḥ — austerity; tat = tad — this; trividham — three-fold; naraih — by people; aphalākāṅkṣibhiḥ — by those who do not aspire for a benefit; yuktaiḥ — by those disciplined in yoga; sāttvikaṁ — realilstic; paricakṣate — they consider

When this threefold austerity is performed with the highest faith by yogicly-disciplined people who do not aspire for a benefit, the authorities consider it to be realistic. (17.17)

सत्कारमानपूजार्थं
तपो दम्भेन चैव यत् ।
क्रियते तदिह प्रोक्तं
राजसं चलमध्रुवम् ॥ १७.१८ ॥

satkāramānapūjārthaṁ
tapo dambhena caiva yat
kriyate tadiha proktaṁ
rājasaṁ calamadhruvam (17.18)

satkāramānapūjārthaṁ = satkāra — reputation +māna — respect + pūjā — reverence + arthaṁ — for the sake of; tapo — tapaḥ — austerity; dambhena — with trickery; caiva — and indeed; yat = yad — which; kriyate — performed; tat — this; iha — in this world; proktaṁ — is declared; rājasaṁ — impulsive; calam — shifty; adhruvam — temporary

Austerity which, in this world is performed with trickery for the sake of reputation, respect and reverence, is declared to be impulsive, shifty and temporary. (17.18)

मूढग्राहेणात्मनो यत्
पीडया क्रियते तपः ।
परस्योत्सादनार्थं वा
तत्तामसमुदाहृतम् ॥ १७.१९ ॥

mūḍhagrāheṇātmano yat
pīḍayā kriyate tapaḥ
parasyotsādanārthaṁ vā
tattāmasamudāhṛtam (17.19)

mūḍhagrāheṇātmano = mūḍha — foolish + grāheṇa= by miṣṭaken ideas + ātmano (ātmanaḥ) — of the self; yat — yad — which; pīḍayā — with torture; kriyate — is performed; tapaḥ — austerity; parasyotsādanārthaṁ = parasya — of someone else + utsādana — harming + artham — purpose; vā — or; tat — that; tāmasam — depressive; udāhṛtam — said to be

Austerity performed with foolish, mistaken ideas, and with torture or for the purpose of harming someone else, is said to be depressive. (17.19)

दातव्यमिति यद्दानं
दीयतेऽनुपकारिणे ।
देशे काले च पात्रे च
तद्दानं सात्त्विकं स्मृतम् ॥ १७.२० ॥

dātavyamiti yaddānaṁ
dīyate'nupakāriṇe
deśe kāle ca pātre ca
taddānaṁ sāttvikaṁ smṛtam (17.20)

dātavyam — to be given; iti — thus; yat — which; dānaṁ — gift; dīyate — is given: 'nupakāriṇe = anupakāriṇe — to one who has not done a prior favor; deśe — in proper place; kāle — at the proper time: ca — and; pātre — to as worthy person; ca — and; tat — that; dānaṁ — gift; sāttvikaṁ — virtuous; smṛtam — remembered as

A gift given to one who has not done a prior favor, in the proper place and time and to a worthy person, is remembered as being virtuous. (17.20)

यत्तु प्रत्युपकारार्थं
फलमुद्दिश्य वा पुनः ।
दीयते च परिक्लिष्टं
तद्दानं राजसं स्मृतम् ॥ १७.२१ ॥

yattu pratyupakārārthaṁ
phalamuddiśya vā punaḥ
dīyate ca parikliṣṭaṁ
taddānaṁ rājasaṁ smṛtam (17.21)

yat — which; tu — but; pratyupakārārthaṁ — for a compensation; phalam — a result; uddiśya— pointing to, hoping; vā — or; punaḥ — alternately; dīyate — is given; ca — and; parikliṣṭaṁ — grudgingly: tat — that; dānaṁ — gift; rājasaṁ — impulsive; smṛtam — mentally noted

But the gift which is given grudgingly for a compensation or alternately hoping for a reward, is mentally noted as being impulsive. (17.21)

अदेशकाले यद्दानम्
अपात्रेभ्यश्च दीयते ।
असत्कृतमवज्ञातं
तत्तामसमुदाहृतम् ॥ १७.२२ ॥

adeśakāle yaddānam
apātrebhyaśca dīyate
asatkṛtamavajñātaṁ
tattāmasamudāhṛtam (17.22)

adeśakāle — at the wrong place and time; yat — wbich; dānam — gift; apātrebhyaśca = apātrebhyaḥ — to a worthy person + ca — and; dīyate — is given; asatkṛtam — without paying respect; avajñātaṁ — without due consideration; tat = tad — that; tāmasam — depressive mode; udāhrtam — is said to be

That gift which is given in the wrong place and time, to an unworthy person, without paying respect, without due consideration, is said to be of the depressive mode. (17.22)

ओं तत्सदिति निर्देशो
ब्रह्मणस्त्रिविधः स्मृतः ।
ब्राह्मणास्तेन वेदाश्च
यज्ञाश्च विहिताः पुरा ॥ १७.२३ ॥

oṁ tatsaditi nirdeśo
brahmaṇastrividhaḥ smṛtaḥ
brāhmaṇāstena vedāśca
yajñāśca vihitāḥ purā (17.23)

oṁ — Om; tat = Tat; sat = Sat; iti — pronouncement; nirdeśo = nirdeśaḥ — designation; brahmaṇaḥ — of spiritual reality; trividhaḥ — three-fold; smrtah — is known; brahmaṇaḥ — by the brahmins; tena — by this; vedāsca = vedāh — of the Vedas + ca — and; yajnāśca = yajnāḥ — religious disciplines and ceremony + ca — and; vihitāḥ — prescribed; purā — anciently

The pronouncement Om Tat Sat is known as the threefold designation of spiritual reality. By this expression, the brahmins, the Vedas, and the prescribed religious disciplines and ceremonies were ordained in ancient times. (17.23)

तस्मादोमित्युदाहृत्य
यज्ञदानतपःक्रियाः ।
प्रवर्तन्ते विधानोक्ताः
सततं ब्रह्मवादिनाम् ॥ १७.२४ ॥

tasmādomityudāhṛtya
yajñadānatapaḥkriyāḥ
pravartante vidhānoktāḥ
satataṁ brahmavādinām (17.24)

tasmāt — hence: om — the sound Om; iti — thus; udāhṛtya — uttering; yajñadānatapaḥkriyāḥ — yajña — sacrifice + dāna — charity + tapaḥ — austerity + kriyaḥ — acts; pravartante — they begin; vidhānoktāḥ = vidhāna — prescription + uktāḥ — said; satatam — always; brahmavādinām — of the spiritual masters

Hence as prescribed in the Vedic scriptures, acts of sacrifice, charity, and austerity always begin by the spiritual masters while uttering the sound Om. (17.24)

तदित्यनभिसंधाय
फलं यज्ञतपःक्रियाः ।
दानक्रियाश्च विविधाः
क्रियन्ते मोक्षकाङ्क्षिभिः ॥ १७.२५ ॥

tadityanabhisaṁdhāya
phalaṁ yajñatapaḥkriyāḥ
dānakriyāśca vividhāḥ
kriyante mokṣakāṅkṣibhiḥ (17.25)

tat — Tat; iti — saying; anabhisaṁdhāya — without an interest; phalam — benefit; yajñatapaḥkriyāḥ = yajña — sacrifice + tapaḥ — austerity + kriyaḥ — actions; dānakriyāśca = dānakriyāḥ— acts of charity + ca — and; vividhāḥ — various types; kriyante — are performed; mokṣakāṅkṣibhiḥ — by those who desire liberation

While saying Tat without an interest in a benefit, acts of sacrifice, austerity and various types of charity are performed by those who are desirous of liberation. (17.25)

सद्भावे साधुभावे च
सदित्येतत्प्रयुज्यते ।
प्रशस्ते कर्मणि तथा
सच्छब्दः पार्थ युज्यते ॥ १७.२६ ॥

sadbhāve sādhubhāve ca
sadityetatprayujyate
praśaste karmaṇi tathā
sacchabdaḥ pārtha yujyate (17.26)

sadbhāve — sad (sat) — reality + bhāve — in meaning; sādhubhāve = sādhu — excellence + bhāve — in meaning; ca — and; sat — reality, that which is productive of reality; iti — thus; etat = etad — this; prayujyate — is used; praśaste — is praiseworthy; karmāṇi — in action; tathā — also; sacchabdaḥ — sat + śabdaḥ — word; pārtha — son of Pṛthā; yujyate — is used

The word Sat is used to mean reality and excellence and also for a praiseworthy act, O son of Pṛthā. (17.26)

यज्ञे तपसि दाने च
स्थितिः सदिति चोच्यते ।
कर्म चैव तदर्थीयं
सदित्येवाभिधीयते ॥ १७.२७॥

yajñe tapasi dāne ca
sthitiḥ saditi cocyate
karma caiva tadarthīyaṁ
sadityevābhidhīyate (17.27)

yajñe — in sacrifice; tapasi — in austerity; dāne — in charity; ca — and; sthitiḥ — steady application; sat — realism; iti — thus; cocyate = ca — and + ucyate — is designated; karma — action; caiva — and indeed; tadarthīyaṁ — for the purpose of that; sat — realistic; iti — thus; evābhidhīyate = eva — indeed + abhidhīyate — is designated

Steady application in sacrifice, austerity and charity, is also called Sat. An action which is supportive of this purpose is also designated as Sat. (17.27)

अश्रद्धया हुतं दत्तं
तपस्तप्तं कृतं च यत् ।
असदित्युच्यते पार्थ
न च तत्प्रेत्य नो इह ॥ १७.२८॥

aśraddhayā hutaṁ dattaṁ
tapastaptaṁ kṛtaṁ ca yat
asadityucyate pārtha
na ca tatpretya no iha (17.28)

aśraddhayā — with a lack of faith; hutaṁ — oblation; dattaṁ — offered; tapaḥ — austerity; taptaṁ — performed; kṛtaṁ — done; ca — and; yat — which; asat — unrealistic; iti — thus; ucyate — is called; pārtha— son of Prthà; na —no; ca — and; tat — that; pretya — hereafter; no = naḥ — to us; iha — here

An oblation offered with a lack of faith and austerity performed in the same way is called asat, unrealistic, O son of Pṛtha. And that has no value to us here or in the hereafter. (17.28)

CHAPTER 18

The Most Secret of All Information*

अर्जुन उवाच
संन्यासस्य महाबाहो
तत्त्वमिच्छामि वेदितुम् ।
त्यागस्य च हृषीकेश
पृथक्केशिनिषूदन ॥ १८.१ ॥

arjuna uvāca
saṁnyāsasya mahābāho
tattvamicchāmi veditum
tyāgasya ca hṛṣīkeśa
pṛthakkeśiniṣūdana (18.1)

arjuna — Arjuna ; uvāca — said; saṁnyāsasya — of the rejection of opportunity;mahābāho — O strong-armed hero; tattvam — fact; icchāmi — I want; veditum — to know; tyāgasya — of the rejection of consequences; ca — and; hṛṣīkesa — O Hṛṣīkeśa ; pṛthak — distinguish; keśiniṣūdāna — slayer of Keshi

Arjuna said: Regarding the rejection of opportunity, O strong-armed hero, I want to know the fact. And regarding the rejection of consequences, O Hṛṣīkeśa, distinguish these, O slayer of Keshi. (18.1)

श्रीभगवानुवाच
काम्यानां कर्मणां न्यासं
संन्यासं कवयो विदुः ।
सर्वकर्मफलत्यागं
प्राहुस्त्यागं विचक्षणाः ॥ १८.२ ॥

śrībhagavānuvāca
kāmyānāṁ karmaṇāṁ nyāsaṁ
saṁnyāsaṁ kavayo viduḥ
sarvakarmaphalatyāgaṁ
prāhustyāgaṁ vicakṣaṇāḥ (18.2)

śrī bhagavān — The Blessed Lord; uvāca — said; śrī kāmyānāṁ — prompted by craving; karmaṇāṁ — of actions; nyāsaṁ— renunciation; saṁnyāsaṁ — rejection of opportunity; kavayo — kavayaḥ — authoritative speakers; viduḥ — know; sarvakarmaphalatyāgaṁ= sarva — all + karma — action + phala — benefit + tyāgaṁ — abandonment; prāhuḥ — they declare; tyāgaṁ — rejection of consequences; vicakṣaṇāḥ — the clear-sighted person

The Blessed Lord said: The authoritative speakers know the rejection of opportunity as renunciation of actions which are prompted by craving. The clear-sighted seers declare the abandonment of the results of benefit-motivated action as the rejection of consequences. (18.2)

**The Mahābhārata contains no chapter headings. This title was assigned by the translator on the basis of verse 64 of this chapter.*

त्याज्यं दोषवदित्येके
कर्म प्राहुर्मनीषिणः ।
यज्ञदानतपःकर्म
न त्याज्यमिति चापरे ॥१८.३॥

tyājyaṁ doṣavadityeke
karma prāhurmanīṣiṇaḥ
yajñadānatapaḥkarma
na tyājyamiti cāpare (18.3)

tyājyaṁ — to be abandoned; doṣāvat — full of fault; iti — thus; eke — some; karma — action; prāhur= prāhuḥ — they declare; manīṣaṇaḥ — philosophers; yajñadānatapaḥkarma = yajña — sacrifice + dāna — charity + tapaḥ — austerity + karma — action; na — not; tyājyam — be abandoned; iti — thus; cāpare = ca — and + apare — others

Some philosophers declare that action is to be abandoned, since it is full of faults. Some others say that acts of sacrifice, charity and austerity are not to be abandoned. (18.3)

निश्चयं शृणु मे तत्र
त्यागे भरतसत्तम ।
त्यागो हि पुरुषव्याघ्र
त्रिविधः संप्रकीर्तितः ॥१८.४॥

niścayaṁ śṛṇu me tatra
tyāge bharatasattama
tyāgo hi puruṣavyāghra
trividhaḥ saṁprakīrtitaḥ (18.4)

niścayaṁ — view; śṛṇu — hear; me — my; tatra — here, on this matter; tyāge — in the abandonment of consequences; bharatasattama — best of the Bharatas; — tyāgo (tyāgaḥ) — abandonment of consequences; hi — indeed; puruṣavyāghra — tiger among men; trividhaḥ — three-fold; saṁprakīrtitaḥ — designated

Hear my view on this matter of abandonment of the consequences of action, O best of the Bharatas. The abandonment of consequences, O tiger among men, is designated as being threefold. (18.4)

यज्ञदानतपःकर्म
न त्याज्यं कार्यमेव तत् ।
यज्ञो दानं तपश्चैव
पावनानि मनीषिणाम् ॥१८.५॥

yajñadānatapaḥkarma
na tyājyaṁ kāryameva tat
yajño dānaṁ tapaścaiva
pāvanāni manīṣiṇām (18.5)

yajñadānatapaḥkrama = yajña — sacrifice + dāna — charity + tapaḥ — austerity + karma — action; na — not; tyājyaṁ — to be abandoned; kāryam — to be performed; eva — indeed; tat — tad — this; yajño — yajñaḥ — sacrifice; dānaṁ — charily; tapaścaiva = tapaḥ — austerity + caiva — and indeed; pāvanāni — purificatory acts; manīṣiṇāṁ — for the wise men

Acts of sacrifice, charity, and austerity are not to be abandoned but should be performed. Sacrifice, charity and austerity are purificatory acts even for the wise men. (18.5)

एतान्यपि तु कर्माणि
सङ्गं त्यक्त्वा फलानि च ।
कर्तव्यानीति मे पार्थ
निश्चितं मतमुत्तमम् ॥ १८.६ ॥

etānyapi tu karmāṇi
saṅgaṁ tyaktvā phalāni ca
kartavyānīti me pārtha
niścitaṁ matamuttamam (18.6)

etāni — these; api — also; tu — but; karmāṇi — actions; saṅgaṁ — attachment; tyaktvā — giving up; phalāni — results; ca — and; kartvyānīti = kartvyāni — to be done + iti — thus; me — my; pārtha — O son of Pṛthā; niścitaṁ — definitely; matam — opinion; uttamam — highest

But these actions are to be performed by giving up attachment to results, O son of Pṛthā. This is definitely My highest opinion. (18.6)

नियतस्य तु संन्यासः
कर्मणो नोपपद्यते ।
मोहात्तस्य परित्यागस्
तामसः परिकीर्तितः ॥ १८.७ ॥

niyatasya tu saṁnyāsaḥ
karmaṇo nopapadyate
mohāttasya parityāgas
tāmasaḥ parikīrtitaḥ (18.7)

niyatasya — of obligation; tu — but; saṁnyāsaḥ — renunciation; karmaṇo (karmaṇaḥ) — of action; nopapadyate = na — not + upapadyate — it is proper; mohāt — from delusion; tasya — of it; parityāgaḥ — rejection; tāmasaḥ — influence of depression; parikīrtitaḥ — is said to be

But renunciation of obligatory actions is not proper. The rejection of it on the basis of delusion, is said to occur by the influence of depression. (18.7)

दुःखमित्येव यत्कर्म
कायक्लेशभयात्त्यजेत् ।
स कृत्वा राजसं त्यागं
नैव त्यागफलं लभेत् ॥ १८.८ ॥

duḥkhamityeva yatkarma
kāyakleśabhayāttyajet
sa kṛtvā rājasaṁ tyāgaṁ
naiva tyāgaphalaṁ labhet (18.8)

duḥkham — difficult: ityeva = iti — thus + eva — indeed; yat = yad — which; karma — action; kāyakleśabhayāt = kāya — body + kleśa — suffering + bhayāt — from fear; tyajet — should abandon; sa — saḥ — he; kṛtvā — having performed: rājasaṁ — impulsive influence; tyāgaṁ — renunciation; naiva — na — not + eva — indeed; tyāgaphalam — result of renunciation; labhet — should obtain

He who abandons action because of difficulty or because of a fear of bodily suffering, performs impulsive renunciation. He would not obtain the desired result of that renunciation. (18.8)

कार्यमित्येव यत्कर्म
नियतं क्रियतेऽर्जुन ।
सङ्गं त्यक्त्वा फलं चैव
स त्यागः सात्त्विको मतः ॥१८.९॥

kāryamityeva yatkarma
niyataṁ kriyate'rjuna
saṅgaṁ tyaktvā phalaṁ caiva
sa tyāgaḥ sāttviko mataḥ
(18.9)

káryam — to be done; ityeva — iti — thus + eva — indeed; yat — which; karma — action; niyataṁ — disciplinary manner; kriyate — is performed; 'rjuna= arjuna — Arjuna: saṅgaṁ — attachment; tyaktvā — abandoning; phalaṁ — result; caiva — and indeed; sa = saḥ — it; tyāgaḥ — renunciation; sāttviko = sāttvikaḥ — of the clarifying mode; mataḥ — is considered

O Arjuna, when an action is done in a disciplinary manner, because it is to be performed, and with renunciation of the attachment to the results, it is considered to be in the clarifying mode. (18.9)

न द्वेष्ट्यकुशलं कर्म
कुशले नानुषज्जते ।
त्यागी सत्त्वसमाविष्टो
मेधावी छिन्नसंशयः ॥१८.१०॥

na dveṣṭyakuśalaṁ karma
kuśale nānuṣajjate
tyāgī sattvasamāviṣṭo
medhāvī chinnasaṁśayaḥ (18.10)

na — not; dveṣṭi — hates; akuśalaṁ — disagreeable; karma — action; kuśale — is agreeable; nānuṣajjate = na — not + anuśajjate — is attached; tyāgī — renouncer; sattvasamāviṣṭo = sattva — clarity + samāviṣṭo (samāviṣṭah) — filled with; medhāvi — wise man; chinnasaṁśayaḥ = chinna — removed+ saṁśayaḥ — doubt

The renouncer who is filled with clarity, the wise man whose doubts are removed, does not hate disagreeable action, nor is he attached to agreeable performance. (18.10)

न हि देहभृता शक्यं
त्यक्तुं कर्माण्यशेषतः ।
यस्तु कर्मफलत्यागी
स त्यागीत्यभिधीयते ॥१८.११॥

na hi dehabhṛtā śakyaṁ
tyaktuṁ karmāṇyaśeṣataḥ
yastu karmaphalatyāgī
sa tyāgītyabhidhīyate (18.11)

na — not; hi — indeed; dehabhṛtā — by the body-supported; śakyaṁ — possible; tyaktuṁ — to abandon; karmāṇi — actions; aśeṣataḥ — completely; yaḥ — who; tu — but; karmaphalatyāgī — karma — action + phala — result + tyāgī — remover; sa = saḥ — he; tyāgīti = tyāgī — renunciate + iti — thus; abhidhīyate — is called

Indeed it is not possible for the body-supported beings to abandon actions completely. But whosoever is the renouncer of the results of actions is called a renunciate. (18.11)

अनिष्टमिष्टं मिश्रं च
त्रिविधं कर्मणः फलम् ।
भवत्यत्यागिनां प्रेत्य
न तु संन्यासिनां क्वचित् ॥ १८.१२ ॥

anistamistaṁ miśraṁ ca
trividhaṁ karmaṇaḥ phalam
bhavatyatyāgināṁ pretya
na tu saṁnyāsināṁ kvacit (18.12)

anistam — undesired; istaṁ — desired: miśraṁ — mixed; ca — and; trividham — three types; karmaṇaḥ — of action; phalam — result; bhavati — it is; atyāgināṁ — of those who do not renounce results; pretya — departing; na — not; tu — but: saṁnyāsināṁ — of the renouncers; kvacit — any at all

Undesired, desired and mixed are the three types of results of actions that occur for the departing souls who do not renounce results. But for the renouncers of opportunity, there is no result at all. (18.12)

पञ्चैतानि महाबाहो
कारणानि निबोध मे ।
सांख्ये कृतान्ते प्रोक्तानि
सिद्धये सर्वकर्मणाम् ॥ १८.१३ ॥

pañcaitāni mahābāho
kāraṇāni nibodha me
sāṁkhye kṛtānte proktāni
siddhaye sarvakarmaṇām (18.13)

pañcaitāni — pañca — five + tāni — these; mahābāho — O mighty-armed man; kāraṇāni — factors; nibodha — learn; me — from me; sāṁkhye — in Sāṁkhya philosophy; krtānte — in conclusion, in doctrīne; proktāni — declared; siddhaye — in accomplishment; sarvakarmaṇām — of all actions

Learn from Me, O mighty-armed man, of the five factors declared in the Sāṁkhya doctrine for the accomplishment of all actions. (18.13)

अधिष्ठानं तथा कर्ता
करणं च पृथग्विधम् ।
विविधाश्च पृथक्चेष्टा
दैवं चैवात्र पञ्चमम् ॥ १८.१४ ॥

adhiṣṭhānaṁ tathā kartā
karaṇaṁ ca pṛthagvidham
vividhāśca pṛthakceṣṭā
daivaṁ caivātra pañcama (18.14)

adhiṣṭhānaṁ — location; tathā — as well as; kartā — the agent; karaṇaṁ — the instrument; ca — and; prthagvidham — various kinds; vividhāśca = vividhāḥ — various + ca — and; pṛthakceṣṭa — movements; daivam — destiny; caivātra — ca — and + eva — indeed + atra — here in this case; pañcamam — the fifth

The location, the agent, the various instruments, the various movements, and destiny, the fifth factor. (18.14)

शरीरवाङ्मनोभिर्यत्
कर्म प्रारभते नरः ।
न्याय्यं वा विपरीतं वा
पञ्चैते तस्य हेतवः ॥ १८.१५ ॥

śarīravāṅmanobhiryat
karma prārabhate naraḥ
nyāyyaṁ vā viparītaṁ vā
pañcaite tasya hetavaḥ (18.15)

śarīravāṅmanobhiḥ = śarīra — body + vān(vās) — speech + manobhiḥ — with mind; yat = yad — whatever; karma — project; prārabhate — he undertakes; naraḥ — a human being; nyāyyaṁ — moral; vā — or; viparītam — immoral; vā — or; pañcaite — pañca — five + ete — these; tasya — of it; hetayaḥ — factors

As for whatever project a human being undertakes with body, speech and mind, regardless of it being moral or immoral, these are its five factors. (18.15)

तत्रैवं सति कर्तारम् आत्मानं केवलं तु यः । पश्यत्यकृतबुद्धित्वान् न स पश्यति दुर्मतिः ॥१८.१६॥	tatraivaṁ sati kartāram ātmānaṁ kevalaṁ tu yaḥ paśyatyakṛtabuddhitvān na sa paśyati durmatiḥ (18.16)

tatraivaṁ = tatra — here, in this case + evam — thus; sati — in reality, correctly; kartāram — agent; ātmānaṁ — self; kevalam — only; tu — but; yaḥ— who; paśyati — he regards; akṛtabuddhitvāt = akṛta — undone, defective + buddhitvāt — due to intellect; na — not; sa = saḥ — he; paśyati — he perceives; durmatiḥ — idiot

In that case, whosoever regards himself as the only agent, does not perceive correctly. This is due to the defective intellect of the idiot. (18.16)

यस्य नाहंकृतो भावो बुद्धिर्यस्य न लिप्यते । हत्वापि स इमाँल्लोकान् न हन्ति न निबध्यते ॥१८.१७॥	yasya nāhaṁkṛto bhāvo buddhiryasya na lipyate hatvāpi sa imām̐llokān na hanti na nibadhyate (18.17)

yasya — regarding who; nāhaṁkṛto = na — not + ahaṁkṛto (ahaṁkṛtaḥ) — falsely assertive; bhāvo = bhāvaḥ — attitude: buddhiḥ— intellect; yasya — of whom; na — not; lipyate — is clouded; hatvāpi = hatvā — having slain + api — even; sa = saḥ — he; imān — these; lokān — people; na — not; hanti — he slays; na — not; nibadhyate — is implicated

Regarding the person whose attitude is not falsely assertive, whose intellect is not clouded, even after slaying these people, he would not have slain or have been implicated. (18.17)

ज्ञानं ज्ञेयं परिज्ञाता त्रिविधा कर्मचोदना । करणं कर्म कर्तेति त्रिविधः कर्मसंग्रहः ॥१८.१८॥	jñānaṁ jñeyaṁ parijñātā trividhā karmacodanā karaṇaṁ karma karteti trividhaḥ karmasaṁgrahaḥ (18.18)

jñānaṁ — experience; jñeyaṁ — the item of research; parijñātā— the experience; trividhā — three aspects; karmacodanā= karma — action + codanā — impetus for; karaṇaṁ — instrument; karma — action; karteti — kartā — agent + iti — thus; trividhaḥ — three; karmasaṁgrahaḥ = karma — action + saṁgrahaḥ — parts

Experience, the item of research, and the experiencer are the three aspects which serve as the impetus for action. The instruction, the action itself, and the agent are three parts of an action. (18.18)

ज्ञानं कर्म च कर्ता च
त्रिधैव गुणभेदतः ।
प्रोच्यते गुणसंख्याने
यथावच्छृणु तान्यपि ॥ १८.१९ ॥

jñānaṁ karma ca kartā ca
tridhaiva guṇabhedataḥ
procyate guṇasaṁkhyāne
yathāvacchṛṇu tānyapi (18.19)

jñānaṁ — experience; karma — action; ca — and; kartā — agent; ca — and; tridhaiva = tridha — three types + eva — indeed; guṇabhedataḥ — categorized by the influences of material nature; procyate — is stated; guṇasaṁkhyāne — in the Sāṁkhya analysis of the influences of material nature; yathāvat — correctly; śṛṇu — hear; tāni — these; api — as well

In the Sāṁkhya analysis of the influence of material nature, it is stated that experience, action, and the agent are of three types as categorized by the influence of material nature. Hear correctly of these as well. (18.19)

सर्वभूतेषु येनैकं
भावमव्ययमीक्षते ।
अविभक्तं विभक्तेषु
तज्ज्ञानं विद्धि सात्त्विकम् ॥ १८.२० ॥

sarvabhūteṣu yenaikaṁ
bhāvamavyayamīkṣate
avibhaktaṁ vibhakteṣu
tajjñānaṁ viddhi sāttvikam (18.20)

sarvabhūteṣu — in all beings; yenaikaṁ = yena — by which + ekam — one; bhāvam — being; avyayam — imperishable; īksate — one perceives; avibhaktaṁ — undivided; vibhakteṣu — in the divided; tat — that; jñānaṁ — experience; viddhi — know; sāttvikaṁ — clarifying

That experience by which one perceives one imperishable being in all beings, undivided in the divided, know it to be an experience in clarity. (18.20)

पृथक्त्वेन तु यज्ज्ञानं
नानाभावान्पृथग्विधान् ।
वेत्ति सर्वेषु भूतेषु
तज्ज्ञानं विद्धि राजसम् ॥ १८.२१ ॥

pṛthaktvena tu yajjñānaṁ
nānābhāvānpṛthagvidhān
vetti sarveṣu bhūteṣu
tajjñānaṁ viddhi rājasam (18.21)

pṛthaktvena — with difference; tu — but; yat — which; jñānaṁ — experience; nānābhāvān = nānā — different + bhāvān — beings; pṛthagvidhān — of different kinds: vetti — realises; sarveṣu — in all; bhūteṣu — in beings; tat — that; jñānaṁ — experience; viddhi — know; rājasam — of the impulsive mode

But that experience by which one realizes different beings of different kinds with differences in all beings, should be known as experience in the impulsive mode. (18.21)

यत्तु कृत्स्नवदेकस्मिन्
कार्ये सक्तमहैतुकम् ।
अतत्त्वार्थवदल्पं च
तत्तामसमुदाहृतम् ॥ १८.२२ ॥

yattu kṛtsnavadekasmin
kārye saktamahaitukam
atattvārthavadalpaṁ ca
tattāmasamudāhṛtam (18.22)

yat — yad — which; tu — but; kṛtsnavat — appears as the whole; ekasmin — in one; kārye — in order of action; saktam — attached; ahaitukam — without due cause; atattvārthavat — without a valid purpose; alpaṁ — petty; ca — and; tat = tad — that; tāmasam — of the depressive influence; udāhṛtam — is said to be

But that experience which appears to be the whole vision, being attached to one procedure without due cause, without a valid purpose, being petty, that is said to be of the depressive influence. (18.22)

नियतं सङ्गरहितम्
अरागद्वेषतः कृतम् ।
अफलप्रेप्सुना कर्म
यत्तत्सात्त्विकमुच्यते ॥ १८.२३ ॥

niyataṁ saṅgarahitam
arāgadveṣataḥ kṛtam
aphalaprepsunā karma
yattatsāttvikamucyate (18.23)

niyatam — controlled; saṅgarahitam = saṅga — attachment + rahitam — free from; arāgadveṣataḥ — without craving or repulsion; kṛtam — performed; aphalaprepsunā = aphala — without result + prepsunā — desire to get; karma — action; yat = yad — which; tat = tad —such; sāttvikaṁ — of the clarifying influence; ucyate — is said

Action which is controlled, which is free from attachment, which is performed without craving or repulsion, without desire for results, such action is said to be of the clarifying influence. (18.23)

यत्तु कामेप्सुना कर्म
साहंकारेण वा पुनः ।
क्रियते बहुलायासं
तद्राजसमुदाहृतम् ॥ १८.२४ ॥

yattu kāmepsunā karma
sāhaṁkāreṇa vā punaḥ
kriyate bahulāyāsaṁ
tadrājasamudāhṛtam (18.24)

yat — yad — which; tu — but; kāmepsunā = kāma — craving + ipsunā — desiring to get; karma — action; sāhaṁkāreṇa — with false assertion; vā — or; punaḥ = punar — alternatively; kriyate — is performed; bahulāyāsaṁ =

bahula — much + āyāsaṁ effort; tat — that; rājasam — of the impulsive influence; udāhṛtam — is said to be

But that action which is performed with a wish for cravings, with false assertion or alternately with much effort, that is said to be of the impulsive influence. (18.24)

अनुबन्धं क्षयं हिंसाम्
अनपेक्ष्य च पौरुषम् ।
मोहादारभ्यते कर्म
यत्तत्तामसमुच्यते ॥१८.२५॥

anubandhaṁ kṣayaṁ hiṁsām
anapekṣya ca pauruṣam
mohādārabhyate karma
yattattāmasamucyate (18.25)

anubandhaṁ — consequence; kṣayaṁ — damage; hiṁsām — violence; anapekṣya — regardless of: ca — and; pauruṣam — practical power; mohāt — from misconception; ārabhyate — is undertaken; karma — action: yat — which; tat — that; tāmasam — of the depressive mode: ucyate — is said to be

That action which is undertaken from a misconception, regardless of the consequence, the damage and the violence, and without considering one's practical power, is said to be of the depressive mode. (18.25)

मुक्तसङ्गोऽनहंवादी
धृत्युत्साहसमन्वितः ।
सिद्ध्यसिद्ध्योर्निर्विकारः
कर्ता सात्त्विक उच्यते ॥१८.२६॥

muktasaṅgo'nahaṁvādī
dhṛtyutsāhasamanvitaḥ
siddhyasiddhyornirvikāraḥ
kartā sāttvika ucyate (18.26)

muktasaṅgo = muktasaṅgaḥ — freed from attachment; 'nahaṁvādi = anahaṁvādi — free from self praise, free from vanity; dhṛtyutsāhasamanvitaḥ — dhṛty (dhṛti) — consistence + utsāha — perseverance + samanvitaḥ — possessed with; siddhyasiddhyoḥ — in success or failure; nirvikāraḥ — unaffected; kartā — performer: sāttvika — in the clarifying mode; ucyate — is rated to be

A performer who is free from attachment, free from vanity, who is consistent and perseverant, and who is unaffected in success or failure, is rated to be in the clarifying mode. (18.26)

रागी कर्मफलप्रेप्सुर्
लुब्धो हिंसात्मकोऽशुचिः ।
हर्षशोकान्वितः कर्ता
राजसः परिकीर्तितः ॥१८.२७॥

rāgī karmaphalaprepsur
lubdho hiṁsātmako'śuciḥ
harṣaśokānvitaḥ kartā
rājasaḥ parikīrtitaḥ (18.27)

Rāgī — prone to impulsiveness; karmaphalaprepsuḥ — karma — action + phala — result + prepsuḥ — craving; lubdho = lubdhaḥ — greedy; hiṁsāmako hiṁsāmakaḥ — violent nature; 'śuciḥ = aśuciḥ — unclean;

harṣaśokānvitaḥ — harṣa — joy + śoka — sorrow + anvitaḥ — prone to; kartā — performer; rājasaḥ — of the impulsive mode; parikīrtitaḥ — is declared

A performer who is prone to impulsiveness, who craves the results of action, who is greedy, violent by nature, unclean and who is prone to joy or sorrow, is declared to be under the impulsive mode. (18.27)

अयुक्तः प्राकृतः स्तब्धः
शठो नैकृतिकोऽलसः ।
विषादी दीर्घसूत्री च
कर्ता तामस उच्यते ॥ १८.२८ ॥

ayuktaḥ prākṛtaḥ stabdhaḥ
śaṭho naikṛtiko'lasaḥ
viṣādī dīrghasūtrī ca
kartā tāmasa ucyate (18.28)

ayuktaḥ — undisciplined; prākṛtaḥ — vulgar; stabdhaḥ — stubborn; śaṭho = śaṭhaḥ — wicked; naiṣkṛtiko = naiṣkṛtikaḥ — deceitful; 'lasaḥ = alasaḥ — lazy; viṣādī — depressed; dīrghasūtrī — neglectful; ca —and; kartā — performer; tāmasa — in the depressive mood; ucyate — is said to be

A performer who is undisciplined, vulgar, stubborn, wicked, deceitful, lazy, depressed and neglectful, is said to be in the depressive mode. (18.28)

बुद्धेर्भेदं धृतेश्चैव
गुणतस्त्रिविधं श‍ृणु ।
प्रोच्यमानमशेषेण
पृथक्त्वेन धनंजय ॥ १८.२९ ॥

buddherbhedaṁ dhṛteścaiva
guṇatastrividhaṁ śṛṇu
procyamānamaśeṣeṇa
pṛthaktvena dhanaṁjaya (18.29)

buddheḥ — intellect; bhedaṁ — difference; dhṛteḥ — determination; caiva — and indeed; guṇataḥ — according to the influences of material nature; trividham — three types; śṛṇu —hear; procyamānam — explained; aśeṣena — thoroughly; pṛthaktvena — distinctly; dhanaṁjaya — conqueror of wealthy countries

Now, O conqueror of wealthy countries, hear of the three types of intellect and also of determination, explained thoroughly and distinctly, according to their distinctions under the influences of material nature. (18.29)

प्रवृत्तिं च निवृत्तिं च
कार्याकार्ये भयाभये ।
बन्धं मोक्षं च या वेत्ति
बुद्धिः सा पार्थ सात्त्विकी ॥ १८.३० ॥

pravṛttiṁ ca nivṛttiṁ ca
kāryākārye bhayābhaye
bandhaṁ mokṣaṁ ca yā vetti
buddhiḥ sā pārtha sāttvikī (18.30)

pravṛttiṁ — endeavor; ca — and; nivṛttiṁ — non-endeavor; ca — and; kāryākārye = kārya — what should be done + akārya — what should not be done; bhayābhaye — what is dangerous and what is safe; bandhaṁ — restriction; mokṣaṁ — freedom; ca — and; yā — which; vetti — discerns;

buddhiḥ — intellectual insight; sā — if, partha — son of Pṛthā; sāttvikī — in the clarifying mode

That intellectual insight which discerns when to endeavor and when not to strive, what should be done and what should not be done, what is dangerous and what is safe, what brings restrictions and what gives freedom, that O son of Pṛthā, is in the clarifying mode. (18.30)

यया धर्ममधर्मं च
कार्यं चाकार्यमेव च ।
अयथावत्प्रजानाति
बुद्धिः सा पार्थ राजसी ॥१८.३१॥

yayā dharmamadharmaṁ ca
kāryaṁ cākāryameva ca
ayathāvatprajānāti
buddhiḥ sā pārtha rājasī (18.31)

yayā — by which; dharmam — right; adharmaṁ — wrong; ca — and; kāryam — duty; cākāryam = ca — and + akāryam — neglect; eva — indeed; ca — and; ayathāvat — miṣṭakenly; prajānāti — is identified; buddhiḥ — intellectual insight; sā — it; pārtha — son of Pṛthā; rājasī — in the impulsive mode

That intellectual insight by which right and wrong, duty and neglect are mistakenly identified, is, O son of Pṛthā, in the impulsive mode. (18.31)

अधर्मं धर्ममिति या
मन्यते तमसावृता ।
सर्वार्थान्विपरीतांश्च
बुद्धिः सा पार्थ तामसी ॥१८.३२॥

adharmaṁ dharmamiti yā
manyate tamasāvṛtā
sarvārthānviparītāṁśca
buddhiḥ sā pārtha tāmasī (18.32)

adharmaṁ — wrong method; dharmam — right method; iti — thus; yā — which; manyate — it considered; tamasāvṛtā = tamasa — ignorance + āvṛtā — absorbed by; sarvārthān — all values; viparītāṁśca = viparītān — perverted + ca — and; buddhiḥ — intellectual insight; sā — it; pārtha — son of Pṛthā; tāmasī — in the depressive mode

That intellectual insight which is absorbed by ignorance, which considers the wrong method as the right one and perceives all values in a perverted way, is O son of Pṛthā, of the depressive mode. (18.32)

धृत्या यया धारयते
मनःप्राणेन्द्रियक्रियाः ।
योगेनाव्यभिचारिण्या
धृतिः सा पार्थ सात्त्विकी ॥१८.३३॥

dhṛtyā yayā dhārayate
manaḥprāṇendriyakriyāḥ
yogenāvyabhicāriṇyā
dhṛtiḥ sā pārtha sāttvikī (18.33)

dhṛtyā — by determination; yayā — by which; dhārayate — it holds; manaḥprāṇendriyakriyāḥ — manaḥ — mind + prāna — energizing breath + indriyakriyāḥ — senses; yogenāvyabhicāriṇyā = yogena — by yoga practices +

avyabhicāriṇyā — unwavering, constant; dhṛtiḥ — determination; sā — it; pārtha — son of Pṛthā: sāttvikī — of the clarifying influence

The determination which holds the mind, the energizing breath, and the senses by constant yoga expertise, that O son of Pṛthā, is of the clarifying influence. (18.33)

यया तु धर्मकामार्थान् धृत्या धारयतेऽर्जुन । प्रसङ्गेन फलाकाङ्क्षी धृतिः सा पार्थ राजसी ॥ १८.३४ ॥	yayā tu dharmakāmārthān dhṛtyā dhārayate'rjuna prasaṅgena phalākāṅkṣī dhṛtiḥ sā pārtha rājasī (18.34)

yayā — by which; tu — but; dharmakāmārthān = dharma — duty + kāma — pleasure + arthān — wealthy; dhṛtyā — with determination; dhārayate — it holds; 'rjuna = arjuna — Arjuna; prasaṅgena — with attachment; phalākāṅkṣī — desiring results: dhṛtiḥ — determination; sā — it; pārtha — son of Pṛthā; rājasī — impulsion

But the determination by which one holds duty, pleasure, and wealth with attachment and with desire for results, is an impulsion, O son of Pṛthā. (18.34)

यया स्वप्नं भयं शोकं विषादं मदमेव च । न विमुञ्चति दुर्मेधा धृतिः सा पार्थ तामसी ॥ १८.३५ ॥	yayā svapnaṁ bhayaṁ śokaṁ viṣādaṁ madameva ca na vimuñcati durmedhā dhṛtiḥ sā pārtha tāmasī (18.35)

yayā — by which: svapnaṁ — sleep: bhayaṁ — fear; śokaṁ — sorrow; viṣādaṁ — despair; madam — pride; eva — indeed; ca — and; na — not; vimuñcati — abandons; durmedhā — idiot: dhṛtiḥ — determination; sā — it; pārtha — son of Pṛthā; tāmasī — of the depressive mode

That determination by which an idiot does not abandon sleep, fear, sorrow, despair and pride, is of the depressing mode. (18.35)

सुखं त्विदानीं त्रिविधं श्रृणु मे भरतर्षभ । अभ्यासाद्रमते यत्र दुःखान्तं च निगच्छति ॥ १८.३६ ॥	sukhaṁ tvidānīṁ trividhaṁ śṛṇu me bharatarṣabha abhyāsādramate yatra duḥkhāntaṁ ca nigacchati (18.36)

sukhaṁ — happiness; tu — but; idānīṁ — now; trividhaṁ — types; śṛṇu — hear; me — from me; — O strong man of the Bharatas; abhyāsāt — from habit; ramate — enjoys; yatra — where, through which; duḥkhāntaṁ— end of sorrow; ca — and, or; nigacchati — one comes to

But now hear from Me, O strong man of the Bharatas, regarding the three types of happiness which one either enjoys from habit or through which one comes to the end of sorrow. (18.36)

यत्तदग्रे विषमिव
परिणामेऽमृतोपमम् ।
तत्सुखं सात्त्विकं प्रोक्तम्
आत्मबुद्धिप्रसादजम् ॥ १८.३७॥

yattadagre viṣamiva
pariṇāme'mṛtopamam
tatsukhaṁ sāttvikaṁ proktam
ātmabuddhiprasādajam (18.37)

yat = yad — which; tat — that; agre — initially; viṣam — poison; iva — like; pariṇāme — in changing; 'mṛtopamam = amṛtopamam — amṛta — nectar + upamam — likeness; tat = tad — that: sukham — happiness; sāttvikaṁ — of the clarifying mode; proktam — is said to be; ātmabuddhiprasādajam = ātmabuddhi — spiritual discernment + prasāda — clarity + jam — produced by

That which initially is like poison but which changes into an experience like nectar, and which is felt through the clarity of spiritual discernment, is said to be happiness in the clarifying mode. (18.37)

विषयेन्द्रियसंयोगाद्
यत्तदग्रेऽमृतोपमम् ।
परिणामे विषमिव
तत्सुखं राजसं स्मृतम् ॥ १८.३८॥

viṣayendriyasaṁyogād
yattadagre'mṛtopamam
pariṇāme viṣamiva
tatsukhaṁ rājasaṁ smṛtam (18.38)

viṣayendriyasaṁyogāt = viṣaya — attractive objects + indriya — sense organs + saṁyogāt — from contact: yat — which; tat — that; agre — in the beginning; 'mṛtopamam – amṛtopamam = amṛta — nectar + upamam — likeness; pariṇāme — changes into; viṣam — poison; ivā — like; tat— that; sukham — happiness; rājasaṁ — impulsion; smṛtam — recognized as

That happiness which in the beginning seems like nectar and which comes from the contact between the sense organs and attractive objects, which changes as if it were poison is recognized as an impulsion. (18.38)

यदग्रे चानुबन्धे च
सुखं मोहनमात्मनः ।
निद्रालस्यप्रमादोत्थं
तत्तामसमुदाहृतम् ॥ १८.३९॥

yadagre cānubandhe ca
sukhaṁ mohanamātmanaḥ
nidrālasyapramādotthaṁ
tattāmasamudāhṛtam (18.39)

yat — which; agre — in the beginning: cānubandhe — ca — and + anubandhe — in consequence; ca — and; sukham — happiness; mohanam — bewildering; ātmanaḥ — of the person: nidrālasyapramādotthaṁ = nidrā — sleep + ālasya

— laziness + pramāda — confusion + uttham — comes from; tat = tad — that; tāmasam — depressive mode; udāhṛtam — said to be

And that happiness which in the beginning and in consequence is bewildering to the person, which comes from sleep, laziness and confusion, is said to be of the depressive mode. (18.39)

न तदस्ति पृथिव्यां वा	na tadasti pṛthivyāṁ vā
दिवि देवेषु वा पुनः ।	divi deveṣu vā punaḥ
सत्त्वं प्रकृतिजैर्मुक्तं	sattvaṁ prakṛtijairmuktaṁ
यदेभिः स्यात्त्रिभिर्गुणैः ॥ १८.४० ॥	yadebhiḥ syāttribhirguṇaiḥ (18.40)

na — not; tat — that; asti — there is; pṛthivyāṁ — on earth; vā — or; divi — in the supernatural world; deveṣu — among the supernatural rulers; vā — or; punaḥ = punar — even; sattvaṁ — something substantial; prakṛtijaiḥ — produced by material nature; muktaṁ — freed, without; yat — which; ebhiḥ — by these; syāt — it can exist; tribhiḥ — by three; guṇaiḥ — by influence

There is no object on earth nor even in the subtle mundane domains, that can exist without these three modes which were produced from material nature. (18.40)

ब्राह्मणक्षत्रियविशां	brāhmaṇakṣatriyaviśāṁ
शूद्राणां च परंतप ।	śūdrāṇāṁ ca paraṁtapa
कर्माणि प्रविभक्तानि	karmāṇi pravibhaktāni
स्वभावप्रभवैर्गुणैः ॥ १८.४१ ॥	svabhāvaprabhavairguṇaiḥ (18.41)

brāhmaṇakṣatriyaviśāṁ = brāhmaṇa — priestly teacher + kṣatriya — ruling sector + viśāṁ — productive managers; śudrāṇāṁ — of the working class; ca — and; paraṁtapa — scorcher of the enemy; karmāṇi — activities; pravibhaktāni — allotted; svabhāvaprabhavaiḥ = svabhāva — own nature + prabhavaiḥ — by being produced; guṇaiḥ — by the modes of material nature

The activities of the priestly teachers, the ruling sector, the productive managers and the working class, are allotted by the modes of material nature which arise from natural tendencies. (18.41)

शमो दमस्तपः शौचं	śamo damastapaḥ śaucaṁ
क्षान्तिरार्जवमेव च ।	kṣāntirārjavameva ca
ज्ञानं विज्ञानमास्तिक्यं	jñānaṁ vijñānamāstikyaṁ
ब्रह्मकर्म स्वभावजम् ॥ १८.४२ ॥	brahmakarma svabhāvajam (18.42)

śamo = śamaḥ — tranquility; damaḥ — restraint; tapaḥ — austerity; śaucaṁ— cleanliness; kṣāntiḥ — patience; ārjavam — straightforwardness; eva — indeed; ca — and; jñānaṁ — knowledge: vijñānaṁ — discrimination; āstikyaṁ — a belief in God; brahmakarma — work of a priestly teacher; svabhāvajam — based on natural tendencies

Tranquility, restraint, austerity, cleanliness, patience, straightforwardness, knowledge, discrimination and a belief in God, are the work of a priestly teacher based on his natural tendencies. (18.42)

शौर्यं तेजो धृतिर्दाक्ष्यं
युद्धे चाप्यपलायनम् ।
दानमीश्वरभावश्च
क्षात्रंकर्म स्वभावजम् ॥ १८.४३ ॥

śauryaṁ tejo dhṛtirdākṣyaṁ
yuddhe cāpyapalāyanam
dānamīśvarabhāvaśca
kṣātraṁkarma svabhāvajam (18.43)

śauryaṁ — heroism; tejo = tejaḥ — majesty; dhṛtiḥ — determination; — expertise; yuddhe — in battle; cāpi — and also; apalāyanam — lack of cowardice; dānam — charitable disposition; īśvarabhāvaśca — īśvarabhāvaḥ — governing tendency + ca — and; kṣātraṁ — of the ruling human being; karma — action; svabhāvajam — based on natural tendency

Heroism, majesty, determination, expertise, lack of cowardice in battle, charitable disposition, and governing tendency are the actions of a ruling human being, based on natural tendency. (18.43)

कृषिगोरक्ष्यवाणिज्यं
वैश्यकर्म स्वभावजम् ।
परिचर्यात्मकं कर्म
शूद्रस्यापि स्वभावजम् ॥ १८.४४ ॥

kṛṣigorakṣyavāṇijyaṁ
vaiśyakarma svabhāvajam
paricaryātmakaṁ karma
śūdrasyāpi svabhāvajam (18.44)

kṛṣigaurakṣyavāṇijyaṁ = kṛṣi — agriculture + gaurakṣya — cow tending + vāṇijyaṁ — trading; vaiśyakarma — action of the productive manager; svabhāvajam — based on natural tendency; paricaryātmakaṁ — paricaryā — service + ātmakaṁ — of natural tendency; karma — action; śudrasyāpi — śudrasya — working class + api — also; svabhāvajam — based on natural tendency

Agriculture, cow-tending and trading are the productive manager's activity based on natural tendency. Service actions are produced of a working class person based on natural tendency. (18.44)

स्वे स्वे कर्मण्यभिरतः
संसिद्धिं लभते नरः ।
स्वकर्मनिरतः सिद्धिं
यथा विन्दति तच्छृणु ॥ १८.४५ ॥

sve sve karmaṇyabhirataḥ
saṁsiddhiṁ labhate naraḥ
svakarmanirataḥ siddhiṁ
yathā vindati tacchṛṇu (18.45)

sve sve — his own, his own, consistent; karmaṇi — in action; abhirataḥ — content; saṁsiddhiṁ — perfection; labhate — attain; naraḥ — human being; svakarmanirataḥ = svakarma — own duty + nirataḥ — satisfied; siddhiṁ — perfection; yathā — as the means; vindati — finds; tat — that; śṛṇu — hear

A human being attains perfection by being content in the consistent execution of his duty. Hear of the means through which a duty-satisfied person finds perfection. (18.45)

यतः प्रवृत्तिर्भूतानां येन सर्वमिदं ततम् । स्वकर्मणा तमभ्यर्च्य सिद्धिं विन्दति मानवः ॥ १८.४६ ॥	yataḥ pravṛttirbhūtānāṁ yena sarvamidaṁ tatam svakarmaṇā tamabhyarcya siddhiṁ vindati mānavaḥ (18.46)

yataḥ — from whom; pravṛttiḥ — origin; bhūtānāṁ — of beings; yena — by whom; sarvam — all; idam — this; tatam — is pervaded; svakarmaṇā — through his duly; tam — his; abhyarcya — worshipping; siddhiṁ — perfection; vindati — he finds; mānavaḥ — human being

Through the performance of his own duty, a human being finds perfection by worshipping the Person from Whom the beings originate and by Whom all this is pervaded. (18.46)

श्रेयान्स्वधर्मो विगुणः परधर्मात्स्वनुष्ठितात् । स्वभावनियतं कर्म कुर्वन्नाप्नोति किल्बिषम् ॥ १८.४७ ॥	śreyānsvadharmo viguṇaḥ paradharmātsvanuṣṭhitāt svabhāvaniyataṁ karma kurvannāpnoti kilbiṣam (18.47)

śreyān — better; svadharmo = svadharmaḥ — own duty; viguṇāḥ — imperfectly; paradharmāt — then another's duty; svanuṣṭhitāt = su + anuṣṭhitāt — well performed, perfectly; svabhāvaniyataṁ = svabhāva — own nature + niyatam — restricted; karma — action; kurvan — performing; nāpnoti — na — not + āpnoti — he acquires; kilbiṣam – sin, fault

Better to attend to one's own duty imperfectly than to heed another's perfectly. By performing actions which are restricted by one's own nature, one does not acquire fault. (18.47)

सहजं कर्म कौन्तेय सदोषमपि न त्यजेत् । सर्वारम्भा हि दोषेण धूमेनाग्निरिवावृताः ॥ १८.४८ ॥	sahajaṁ karma kaunteya sadoṣamapi na tyajet sarvārambhā hi doṣeṇa dhūmenāgnirivāvṛtāḥ(18.48)

sahajaṁ — inborn; karma — action; kaunteya — son of Kuntl; sadoṣam — with fault; api — even; na —not; tyajet — should abandon; sarvārambhā — all undertakings; hi — indeed; doṣeṇa — with defect; dhumenāgniḥ — dhumena — with smoke + āgniḥ — fire; ivāvṛtaḥ iva — like + āvṛtaḥ — is shrouded

One should not abandon inborn duty, O son of Kuntī, even if it is faulty. Indeed, all undertakings are with defect, even as fire is shrouded with smoke. (18.48)

असक्तबुद्धिः सर्वत्र
जितात्मा विगतस्पृहः ।
नैष्कर्म्यसिद्धिं परमां
संन्यासेनाधिगच्छति ॥ १८.४९ ॥

asaktabuddhiḥ sarvatra
jitātmā vigataspṛhaḥ
naiṣkarmyasiddhiṁ paramāṁ
saṁnyāsenādhigacchati (18.49)

asakta — unattached; buddhiḥ — intellect; sarvatra — in all applications; jitātmā — self-conquered; vigataspṛhah = vigata — disappeared + spṛhaḥ — yearnings; naiṣkarmyasiddhiṁ — naiṣkarmya — exemption from activities + siddhim — perfection; paramāṁ — supreme; saṁnyāsenādhigacchati = saṁnyāsena — by renunciation of opportunities + adhigacchati — he attains

He whose intellect is unattached in every application, who is self-controlled, whose yearnings disappeared, by the renunciation of opportunities, attains supreme perfection of being exempt from action. (18.49)

सिद्धिं प्राप्तो यथा ब्रह्म
तथाप्नोति निबोध मे ।
समासेनैव कौन्तेय
निष्ठा ज्ञानस्य या परा ॥ १८.५० ॥

siddhiṁ prāpto yathā brahma
tathāpnoti nibodha me
samāsenaiva kaunteya
niṣṭhā jñānasya yā parā (18.50)

siddhiṁ — perfection; prāpto = prāptaḥ — attained; yathā — as; brahma — spirituality; tathāpnoti = tathā — thus + āpnoti — attains; nibodha — learn; me — from me; samāsenaiva = samāsena — in brief + eva — indeed; kaunteya — son of Kuntī ; niṣṭhā — state; jñānasya — of experience; yā — which; parā — highest

Learn from Me briefly, O son of Kuntī, how a person who attained perfection, also reaches a spirituality which is the highest. (18.50)

बुद्ध्या विशुद्धया युक्तो
धृत्यात्मानं नियम्य च ।
शब्दादीन्विषयांस्त्यक्त्वा
रागद्वेषौ व्युदस्य च ॥ १८.५१ ॥

buddhyā viśuddhayā yukto
dhṛtyātmānaṁ niyamya ca
śabdādīnviṣayāṁstyaktvā
rāgadveṣau vyudasya ca (18.51)

buddhayā — with intellect; viśuddhyā — with purified; yukto = yuktaḥ — yogically disciplined; dhṛtyātmānaṁ = dhṛtyā — with firmness + ātmānaṁ— self; niyamya — controlling; ca — and; śabdādīn — śabda — sound + ādīn— beginning with, and others; viṣayān — attractive sensations; tyaktvā — abandoning; rāgadveṣau= rāga — craving + dveṣau — hatred; vyudasya — rejecting; ca — and

Being yogically-disciplined with purified intelligence and controlling the soul, firmly abandoning sound and other attractive sensations, rejecting craving and hatred, (18.51)

विविक्तसेवी लघ्वाशी
यतवाक्कायमानसः ।
ध्यानयोगपरो नित्यं
वैराग्यं समुपाश्रितः ॥ १८.५२ ॥

viviktasevī laghvāśī
yatavākkāyamānasaḥ
dhyānayogaparo nityaṁ
vairāgyaṁ samupāśritaḥ (18.52)

viviktasevī = vivikta — is isolated + sevī — living at; laghvasi = laghv (laghu) — lightly + āsī — eating; yatavākkāyamānasaḥ = yata — controlled + vāk (vāc) — speech + kāya — body + mānasaḥ — mind; dhyānayogaparo — dhyāna — meditation + yoga — yoga + paro (paraḥ) — devoted to; nityam — always; vairāgyam — dispassion; samupāśritaḥ — resorting to

...living in isolation, eating lightly, controlling speech, body and mind, always being devoted to yogic meditation, resorting to dispassion, (18.52)

अहंकारं बलं दर्पं
कामं क्रोधं परिग्रहम् ।
विमुच्य निर्ममः शान्तो
ब्रह्मभूयाय कल्पते ॥ १८.५३ ॥

ahaṁkāraṁ balaṁ darpaṁ
kāmaṁ krodhaṁ parigraham
vimucya nirmamaḥ śānto
brahmabhūyāya kalpate (18.53)

ahaṁkāraṁ — without a misplaced initiative, without a false assertion; balaṁ — brute force; darpaṁ — arrogance; kāmaṁ — cravings; krodhaṁ — anger; parigraham — possessions; vimucya — freeing oneself; nirmamaḥ — unselfish; śānto = śāntaḥ — peaceful; brahmabhūyāya = brahma — spirit + bhūyāyā — to that level, existential; kalpate — is suited

...freeing oneself from a false assertion, from the application of brute force, from arrogance, from craving and from possessiveness, being unselfish and peaceful, one is suited to the spiritual level. (18.53)

ब्रह्मभूतः प्रसन्नात्मा
न शोचति न काङ्क्षति ।
समः सर्वेषु भूतेषु
मद्भक्तिं लभते पराम् ॥ १८.५४ ॥

brahmabhūtaḥ prasannātmā
na śocati na kāṅkṣati
samaḥ sarveṣu bhūteṣu
madbhaktiṁ labhate parām (18.54)

brabmabhūtaḥ — being absorbed in spiritual existence; prasannātmā = prasanna — peaceful + ātmā — self, spirit: na — not; śocati — laments; na — no; kāṅkṣati — hankers for something; samaḥ — impartial; sarveṣu — in all; bhūteṣu — in the beings; madbhaktiṁ — devotion to me; labhate — attains; parām — supreme

One who is absorbed in the spiritual existence, who has a peaceful spirit, who does not lament nor hanker for anything, who is impartial to all beings, attains the supreme devotion to Me. (18.54)

भक्त्या मामभिजानाति
यावान्यश्चास्मि तत्त्वतः ।
ततो मां तत्त्वतो ज्ञात्वा
विशते तदनन्तरम् ॥ १८.५५॥

bhaktyā māmabhijānāti
yāvānyaścāsmi tattvataḥ
tato māṁ tattvato jñātvā
viśate tadanantaram (18.55)

Bhaktyā — by devotion; mām — to me; abhijānāti — he realizes; yāvān — how great: yaścāsmi = yaḥ — who + ca — and + asmi — I am; tattvataḥ — in reality; tato = tataḥ — then; mām — me; tattvato = tattvataḥ — in truth; jñātvā — having known; viśate — enters; tadanantaram — immediately

By devotion to Me, he realises how great I am and who I am in reality. Then having known Me in truth, he enters My association immediately.(18.55)

सर्वकर्माण्यपि सदा
कुर्वाणो मद्व्यपाश्रयः ।
मत्प्रसादादवाप्नोति
शाश्वतं पदमव्ययम् ॥ १८.५६ ॥

sarvakarmāṇyapi sadā
kurvāṇo madvyapāśrayaḥ
matprasādādavāpnoti
śāśvataṁ padamavyayam (18.56)

sarvakarmāṇi — in all actions; api — furthermore; sadā — always; kurvāṇo = kurvāṇaḥ — performing; madvyapāśrayaḥ — taking reliance in me; matprasādāt — from my grace; avāpnoti — gets; śāśvataṁ — eternal; padam — abode; avyayam — imperishable

Furthermore, know that while performing all actions, he whose reliance is always on Me, gets by My grace, the eternal imperishable abode. (18.56)

चेतसा सर्वकर्माणि
मयि संन्यस्य मत्परः ।
बुद्धियोगमुपाश्रित्य
मच्चित्तः सततं भव ॥ १८.५७॥

cetasā sarvakarmāṇi
mayi saṁnyasya matparaḥ
buddhiyogamupāśritya
maccittaḥ satataṁ bhava (18.57)

cetasā — by thought; sarvakarmāṇi — all actions; mayi — on Me; saṁnyasya — devoted to me; matparaḥ — devoted to Me; buddhiyogam — disciplining the intellect by yoga practice; upāśritya — relying on; maccittaḥ — thinking of Me; satataṁ — constantly; bhava — be

Renouncing by thought, all actions to Me, being devoted to Me, relying on the process of disciplining the intellect by yoga, be constantly thinking of Me. (18.57)

मच्चित्तः सर्वदुर्गाणि
मत्प्रसादात्तरिष्यसि ।
अथ चेत्त्वमहंकारान्
न श्रोष्यसि विनङ्क्ष्यसि ॥ १८.५८॥

maccittaḥ sarvadurgāṇi
matprasādāttariṣyasi
atha cettvamahaṁkārān
na śroṣyasi vinaṅkṣyasi (18.58)

maccittaḥ — thinking of Me: sarvadurgāṇi — all difficulties; matprasādāt — from my grace; tariṣyasi — you will surpass; atha — but; cet = ced — if; tvam — you; ahaṁkārān — false assertion; na — not; śroṣyasi — you will listen; vinaṅkṣyasi — you will be lost

Thinking of Me, you will, by My grace, surpass all difficulties. But if by false assertion, you do not listen, you will be lost. (18.58)

यदहंकारमाश्रित्य
न योत्स्य इति मन्यसे ।
मिथ्यैष व्यवसायस्ते
प्रकृतिस्त्वां नियोक्ष्यति ॥ १८.५९ ॥

yadahaṁkāramāśritya
na yotsya iti manyase
mithyaiṣa vyavasāyaste
prakṛtistvāṁ niyokṣyati (18.59)

yat — which; ahaṁkāram — false assertive attitude; āśritya — relying on; na —not; yotsya — I will fight; iti — thus; manyase — you thing; mithyaiṣa = mithya — mistaken + eṣa — this; vyavasāyaḥ — determination; te — your; prakṛtiḥ — material nature; tvāṁ — you; niyokṣyāti — you will be forced

While relying on a false assertive attitude, you may think, "I will not fight." But that determination is mistaken. Your material nature will force you. (18.59)

स्वभावजेन कौन्तेय
निबद्धः स्वेन कर्मणा ।
कर्तुं नेच्छसि यन्मोहात्
करिष्यस्यवशोऽपि तत् ॥ १८.६० ॥

svabhāvajena kaunteya
nibaddhaḥ svena karmaṇā
kartuṁ necchasi yanmohāt
kariṣyasyavaśo'pi tat (18.60)

svabhāvajena — of your own natural tendencies; kaunteya — son of Kuntī ; nibaddhaḥ — bound; svena — by your own; karmāṇa — obligation; kartuṁ — to perform; necchasi — na — not + icchasi — you want; yan = yad — which; mohāt — from delusion; kariṣyasi — you will do; avaśo — avaśaḥ — against your own will; 'pi = api — also, even; tat — tad — that

By your natural tendencies, being bound by obligations, O son of Kuntī, that which you do not want to perform due to delusion, you will do even if it is against your will. (18.60)

ईश्वरः सर्वभूतानां
हृद्देशेऽर्जुन तिष्ठति ।
भ्रामयन्सर्वभूतानि
यन्त्रारूढानि मायया ॥ १८.६१ ॥

īśvaraḥ sarvabhūtānāṁ
hṛddeśe'rjuna tiṣṭhati
bhrāmayansarvabhūtāni
yantrārūḍhāni māyayā (18.61)

īśvaraḥ — Lord; sarvabhūtānām — of all beings; hṛddeśe = hṛd — central psyche + deśe — in the place; 'rjuna — arjuna — Arjuna; tiṣṭhati — is situated; bhrāmayan — cause to transmigrate; sarvabhūtāni — all beings;

yantrārūḍhāni = yantra — machine + ārūḍhāni — fixed to; māyayā — by mystic power

The Lord of all beings is situated in the central psyche, O Arjuna, causing all beings to transmigrate by His mystic power, just as if they were fixed to a spinning machine. (18.61)

तमेव शरणं गच्छ
सर्वभावेन भारत ।
तत्प्रसादात्परां शान्तिं
स्थानं प्राप्स्यसि शाश्वतम् ॥१८.६२॥

tameva śaraṇaṁ gaccha
sarvabhāvena bhārata
tatprasādātparāṁ śāntiṁ
sthānaṁ prāpsyasi śāśvatam (18.62)

tam — to him; eva — only; śaraṇaṁ — shelter; gaccha — go; sarvabhāvena — with all your being; bhārata — O descendant of Bharata: tatprasādāt — from that grace; parāṁ — supreme; śāntiṁ — security; sthānaṁ — place; prāpyasi — you will attain: śāśvatam — eternal

With your whole being, go only to Him for shelter, O descendant of Bharata. You will attain the supreme security and the eternal place by His grace. (18.62)

इति ते ज्ञानमाख्यातं
गुह्याद्गुह्यतरं मया ।
विमृश्यैतदशेषेण
यथेच्छसि तथा कुरु ॥१८.६३॥

iti te jñānamākhyātaṁ
guhyādguhyataraṁ mayā
vimṛśyaitadaśeṣeṇa
yathecchasi tathā kuru (18.63)

iti — thus; te — to you; jñānam — information; ākhyātaṁ— was explained; guhyāt — than secret; guhyataraṁ — more secret; mayā— by me; vimṛśyaitat = vimṛśya — having considered + etat — this; aśeṣena — fully; yathecchasi = yathā — as + icchasi — you desire, you please; tathā — in the way; kuru — act

The information that is more secret than secret was explained by Me to you. Having considered this fully, you may act as you please. (18.63)

सर्वगुह्यतमं भूयः
शृणु मे परमं वचः ।
इष्टोऽसि मे दृढमिति
ततो वक्ष्यामि ते हितम् ॥१८.६४॥

sarvaguhyatamaṁ bhūyaḥ
śṛṇu me paramaṁ vacaḥ
iṣṭo'si me dṛḍhamiti
tato vakṣyāmi te hitam (18.64)

sarvaguhyatamaṁ — of all, the most secret; bhūyaḥ — again; śṛṇu — hear; me — of me; paramaṁ — supreme; vacaḥ — discourse; iṣṭo = iṣṭaḥ — loved; 'si = asi — you are; me — of me; dṛḍham — surely; iti — this; tato — tataḥ — hence; vakṣyāmi — I will speak; te — your; hitam — benefit

Hear again of My supreme discourse, the most secret of all information. You are surely loved by Me. Hence I speak for your benefit. (18.64)

मन्मना भव मद्भक्तो
मद्याजी मां नमस्कुरु ।
मामेवैष्यसि सत्यं ते
प्रतिजाने प्रियोऽसि मे ॥१८.६५॥

manmanā bhava madbhakto
madyājī māṁ namaskuru
māmevaiṣyasi satyaṁ te
pratijāne priyo'si me (18.65)

manmanā — be mindful of me; bhava — be; madbhakto = madbhaktaḥ — be devoted to me; madyājī — sacrifice to Me; māṁ — to me; namaskuru — do bow; mām — to me; evaiṣyasi — eva — in this way + eṣyasi — you will come: satyaṁ — in truth; te — to you; pratijāne — I promise; priyo — priyaḥ— dear; 'si — asi — you are ; me — of me

Be mindful of Me, be devoted to Me. Sacrifice to Me. Do bow to Me. In this way you will in truth come to Me. I promise for you are dear to Me. (18.65)

सर्वधर्मान्परित्यज्य
मामेकं शरणं व्रज ।
अहं त्वा सर्वपापेभ्यो
मोक्षयिष्यामि मा शुचः ॥१८.६६॥

sarvadharmānparityajya
māmekaṁ śaraṇaṁ vraja
ahaṁ tvā sarvapāpebhyo
mokṣayiṣyāmi mā śucaḥ (18.66)

sarvadharmān — all traditional conduct; parityajya — abandoning; mām — in me; ekam — alone; śaraṇaṁ — refuge; vraja — lake; aham — I; tvā — you; sarvapāpebhyo = sarvapāpebhyaḥ — from all sins; mokṣayiṣyāmi — I will cause you to be freed; mā — not; śucaḥ — worry

Abandoning all traditional conduct, take refuge in Me alone. I will cause you to be free.of faults Do not worry. (18.66)

इदं ते नातपस्काय
नाभक्ताय कदाचन ।
न चाशुश्रूषवे वाच्यं
न च मां योऽभ्यसूयति ॥१८.६७॥

idaṁ te nātapaskāya
nābhaktāya kadācana
na cāśuśrūṣave vācyaṁ
na ca māṁ yo'bhyasūyati (18.67)

idaṁ — this; te — of you; nātapaskāya — na — not + atapaskāya — to one who does not perform austerity; nābhaktāya = na — not + abhaktāya — to one who is not devoted: kadācana — at any time; na — not; cāśuśrūṣave — ca — and + aśuśrūṣave — one who does not desire to hear; vācyaṁ — what is to be said; na — not; ca — and: mām — me; yo — yaḥ — who; 'bhyasūyati = abhyasūyati — lie is critical

This should not be told by you to anyone who does not perform austerity or is not devoted at anytime, or does not desire to hear what is said or is critical of Me. (18.67)

य इदं परमं गुह्यं
मद्भक्तेष्वभिधास्यति ।
भक्तिं मयि परां कृत्वा
मामेवैष्यत्यसंशयः ॥ १८.६८॥

ya idaṁ paramaṁ guhyaṁ
madbhakteṣvabhidhāsyati
bhaktiṁ mayi parāṁ kṛtvā
māmevaiṣyatyasaṁśayaḥ (18.68)

ya — who; idam — this; paramam — supreme; guhyam —secret; madbhakteṣu — to my devotees; abhidhāsyati — he will explain; bhaktiṁ — devotion; mayi — to me; parām — highest: kṛtvā — having performed; mām — me; evaiṣyati = eva — indeed + eṣyati — he will come: asaṁśayaḥ — without a doubt, certainly

Whosoever, having performed the highest devotion to Me, will explain this supreme secret to My devotees, will certainly come to Me. (18.68)

न च तस्मान्मनुष्येषु
कश्चिन्मे प्रियकृत्तमः ।
भविता न च मे तस्माद्
अन्यः प्रियतरो भुवि ॥ १८.६९॥

na ca tasmānmanuṣyeṣu
kaścinme priyakṛttamaḥ
bhavitā na ca me tasmād
anyaḥ priyataro bhuvi (18.69)

na — not; ca — and; tasmān — than this person; manuṣyeṣu — among human beings; kaścit — anyone; me — of me; priyakṛttamaḥ = priyaḥ — pleasing + kṛttamaḥ — more in performance; bhavitā — he will be; na — not; ca — and; me — to me; tasmāt — than this person; anyaḥ — other; priyataro = priyataraḥ — more dear; bhuvi — on earth

And no one among human beings is more pleasing to Me in performance than he. And no one on earth will be more dear to Me than he, (18.69)

अध्येष्यते च य इमं
धर्म्यं संवादमावयोः ।
ज्ञानयज्ञेन तेनाहम्
इष्टः स्यामिति मे मतिः ॥ १८.७०॥

adhyeṣyate ca ya imaṁ
dharmyaṁ saṁvādamāvayoḥ
jñānayajñena tenāham
iṣṭaḥ syāmiti me matiḥ (18.70)

adhyeṣyate — he will study; ca — and; ya — who; imaṁ — this; dharmyaṁ — sacred; samvādam — conversation; āvayoḥ — of ours; jñānayajñena — by the sacrifice of his knowledge; tenāham — tena — by him + aham — I; iṣṭaḥ — loved; syām — I should be; iti — thus; me — my; matiḥ — opinion

I would be loved by the devotee who by sacrifice of his knowledge, will study this sacred conversation of ours. This is My opinion. (18.70)

श्रद्धावाननसूयश्च
श्रृणुयादपि यो नरः ।
सोऽपि मुक्तः शुभाँल्लोकान्
प्राप्नुयात्पुण्यकर्मणाम् ॥ १८.७१॥

śraddhāvānanasūyaśca
śṛṇuyādapi yo naraḥ
so'pi muktaḥ śubhām̐llokān
prāpnuyātpuṇyakarmaṇām (18.71)

śraddhāvān — with confidence; anasūyaśca — anasūyaḥ — without ridiculing + ca — and; śṛṇuyāt— he should hear; api — even; yo — yaḥ— who; naraḥ— the person; so = saḥ — he; 'pi = api — also; muktaḥ — freed; śubhān — happy; lokān — worlds; prāpnuyāt — he should attain; puṇyakarmaṇām — punya — pious + karmaṇām — of actions

Even the person who hears with confidence, without ridiculing is freed. He should attain the happy worlds where persons of pious actions reside. (18.71)

कच्चिदेतच्छ्रुतं पार्थ
त्वयैकाग्रेण चेतसा ।
कच्चिदज्ञानसंमोहः
प्रनष्टस्ते धनंजय ॥ १८.७२ ॥

kaccidetacchrutaṁ pārtha
tvayaikāgreṇa cetasā
kaccidajñānasaṁmohaḥ
pranaṣṭaste dhanaṁjaya (18.72)

kaccit — has it?; etat — this; śrutaṁ — was heard; pārtha — son of Pṛthā; tvayaikāgreṇa = tvayā — by you + ekāgreṇa — by one-pointed; cetasā — by mind; kaccit — has it?; ajñānasaṁmohaḥ — ajnāna — ignorance + saṁmohaḥ — confusion; pranaṣṭaḥ — removed; te — your; dhanaṁjaya — conqueror of wealthy countries

Was this heard by you, O son of Pṛthā, with a one-pointed mind? Was your ignorance and confusion removed, O conqueror of wealthy countries? (18.72)

अर्जुन उवाच
नष्टो मोहः स्मृतिर्लब्धा
त्वत्प्रसादान्मयाच्युत ।
स्थितोऽस्मि गतसंदेहः
करिष्ये वचनं तव ॥ १८.७३ ॥

arjuna uvāca
naṣṭo mohaḥ smṛtirlabdhā
tvatprasādānmayācyuta
sthito'smi gatasaṁdehaḥ
kariṣye vacanaṁ tava (18.73)

arjuna — Arjuna ; uvāca — said; naṣṭo = naṣṭaḥ — removed; mohaḥ — confusion; smṛtiḥ — memory; labdhā — retrieved; tvatprasādān = tvat — your + prasādān (prasādāt) — from grace; mayācyuta = mayā— by me + acyuta — O unaffected one; sthito — sthitāḥ—standing; 'smi = asmi — I am; gatasaṁdehaḥ = gatā — gone, cleared away + saṁdehaḥ — doubt; kariṣye — I will execute; vacanaṁ — instruction; tava — your

Arjuna said: Through Your grace, the confusion is removed, memory is retrieved by Me, O unaffected one. I stand clear of doubts. I will execute Your instruction. (18.73)

संजय उवाच
इत्यहं वासुदेवस्य
पार्थस्य च महात्मनः ।
संवादमिममश्रौषम्
अद्भुतं रोमहर्षणम् ॥ १८.७४ ॥

saṁjaya uvāca
ityahaṁ vāsudevasya
pārthasya ca mahātmanaḥ
saṁvādamimamaśrauṣam
adbhutaṁ romaharṣaṇam (18.74)

saṁjaya — Sanjaya: uvāca — said; iti —thus; aham — I; vāsudevasya — of the son of Vasudeva; pārthasya — of the son of Pṛthā; ca — and; mahātmanaḥ — great souled one; saṁvādam — talk; imam — this; aśroṣam — I heard; adbhutaṁ — amazing; romaharṣaṇam — causing hair to stand on end

Sanjaya said: In this way, I heard this talk of the son of Vasudeva and the great-souled son of Pṛthā. It is amazing. It causes the hairs to stand on end. (18.74)

व्यासप्रसादाच्छ्रुतवान्
एतद्गुह्यमहं परम् ।
योगं योगेश्वरात्कृष्णात्
साक्षात्कथयतः स्वयम् ॥ १८.७५ ॥

vyāsaprasādācchrutavān
etadguhyamahaṁ param
yogaṁ yogeśvarātkṛṣṇāt
sākṣātkathayataḥ svayam (18.75)

vyāsaprasādāt = vyāsa — Vyasa + prasādāt — from grace; śrutavān — one who heard; etad — this; guhyam — secret; aham — I; param — supreme; yogaṁ — yoga; yogeśvarāt = yoga —yoga + īśvarāt — from the Lord; kṛṣṇāt — from Krishna ; sākṣāt — directly; kathayataḥ — explaining; svayam — himself

By the grace of Vyasa, I am the one who heard this secret information of the supreme yoga from the Lord of yoga, Krishna, who Himself explained it directly. (18.75)

राजन्संस्मृत्य संस्मृत्य
संवादमिममद्भुतम् ।
केशवार्जुनयोः पुण्यं
हृष्यामि च मुहुर्मुहुः ॥ १८.७६ ॥

rājansaṁsmṛtya saṁsmṛtya
saṁvādamimamadbhutam
keśavārjunayoḥ puṇyaṁ
hṛṣyāmi ca muhurmuhuḥ (18.76)

rājan — king; saṁsmṛtya saṁsmṛtya — remembering repeatedly; saṁvādam — talk; imam — this; adbhutam — amazing; keśavārjunayoḥ — of Keśava and Arjuna; puṇyaṁ — holy; hṛṣyāmi — I rejoice; ca — and; muhuḥ muhuḥ — again and again

O King, remembering repeatedly, this amazing and holy talk between Keśava and Arjuna, I rejoice again and again. (18.76)

तच्च संस्मृत्य संस्मृत्य
रूपमत्यद्भुतं हरेः ।
विस्मयो मे महान्राजन्
हृष्यामि च पुनः पुनः ॥१८.७७॥

tacca saṁsmṛtya saṁsmṛtya
rūpamatyadbhutaṁ hareḥ
vismayo me mahānrājan
hṛṣyāmi ca punaḥ punaḥ (18.77)

tat — this; ca — and: saṁsmṛtya saṁsmṛtya — remembering repeatedly;rūpam— form; atyadbhutaṁ — super-fantastic; hareḥ — of Hari: vismayo = vismayaḥ — astonished; me — my; malum — great; rājan — O King; hṛṣyāmi — I excitedly rejoice; ca — and; punaḥ punaḥ — again and again

And remembering repeatedly that super-fantastic form of Hari, my astonishment is great, O King, and I excitedly rejoice again and again. (18.77)

यत्र योगेश्वरः कृष्णो
यत्र पार्थो धनुर्धरः ।
तत्र श्रीर्विजयो भूतिर्
ध्रुवा नीतिर्मतिर्मम ॥१८.७८॥

yatra yogeśvaraḥ kṛṣṇo
yatra pārtho dhanurdharaḥ
tatra śrīrvijayo bhūtir
dhruvā nītirmatirmama (18.78)

yatra — wherever; yogeśvaraḥ — the Lord of yoga; kṛṣṇo = kṛṣṇaḥ — Kṛṣṇa; yatra — wherever; pārtho = pārthaḥ — son of Pṛthā; dhanurdharaḥ — bowman; tatra — there; śrīḥ — splendor; vijayo — vijayaḥ — victory; bhūtiḥ — prosperity; dhruvā — surely; nītiḥ — morality; matiḥ — opinion; mama — my

Wherever there exists the Lord of yoga, Krishna, wherever there is the son of Pṛthā, the bowman, there would surely be splendor, victory, prosperity and morality. This is my opinion. (18.78)

OM TAT SAT

END

Indexed Names of Arjuna

anagha — blameless one, good man, 3.3
anagha — sinless one, 14.6
Arjuna -- third son of King Pandu and Queen Kuntī, cousin of Lord Krishna, 1.4; 2.1,4,54; 2.68; 3.1,7,36; 4.4,5,9,37; 5.1; 6.16,32,33,37; 6.46; 7.16; 8.1,16; 10.32,37,39,42; 11.1,36,50,51,54; 13.1; 18.73,76
bhaktaḥ — devoted person, 4.3
bhārata — man of the Bharata family, descendant of Bharata, 2.18,30; 3.25; 4.7,42; 7.27; 11.6; 13.3,34; 14.3,8,9,10; 15.19,20; 16.3; 17.3; 18.36,62
bharatarṣabha — powerful son (strong man) of the Bharatas, bullish man of the Bharata family, 7.11,16; 8.23; 13.27; 14.12
bharataśreṣṭha — best of the Bharatas, 17.12
dehabhṛtām vara — best of the embodied souls, 8.4
dhanaṁjayaḥ — conqueror of wealthy countries, 1.15; 7.7;.11.14; 18.29,72
dhanurdharaḥ — bowman, 18.78
guḍākeśa — the thick-haired baron, conqueror of sleep, 1.24, 11.7
kapidhvajaḥ — the man with a monkey insignia (Hanuman), 1.20
kaunteya — son of Kuntī (Pṛthā),1.27; 2.14,21,60; 3.37; 5.22; 6.35; 7.8; 8.16; 9.7,10,23,27,31; 13.2; 14.4; 16.20,22; 18.50,60
kurunandana — dear son of the Kurus,2.41,48; 6.43, 14.13
kurupravīra — great hero of the Kurus, 11.48kurusattama — best of the Kurus., 4.31
kuruśreṣṭha — best of the Kuru clan, 10.19
mahābāho — powerful man, 3.28,43; 5.3; 10.1; 14.5; 18.13
pāṇḍava — son of Pandu, 1.14; 4.35; 6.2; 11.13,55; 12.1; 14.21,22; 16.5; 17.1, 18.1,9,34,61
paraṁtapa — burner of enemy forces, scorcher of enemies, 4.2,5; 11.51
pārtha — son of Pṛthā (Kuntī), 1.25,26; 2.3,32,39,42,55,72; 3.16,22,23; 4.11,33; 6.40; 7.1,10; 8.8,14,19,22,27; 9.32; 10.24; 11.5,9; 12.7; 16.4,6; 17.26,28; 18.6,31,33,72,78
puruṣarṣabha — bull among men, 2.15
puruṣavyāghra — tiger among men, 18.4
sakhā — friend, 4.3
savyasācin — ambidextrous archer, 11.33
tāta — ideal one, 6.40

Indexed Names of Krishna

hṛṣīkeśa, Master of the sense organs, 1.15,18,24; 18.1
īśam īḍyam, Lord who is to be praised, 11.44
īśvaraḥ, Lord, 4.6
jagannivāsa (jagat-nivāsa),
refuge of the worlds, 11.25
resort of the world, 11.37
shelter of the world, 11.45
jagatpate, Lord of the universe, 10.15
janārdana, motivator of human beings, 1.38;43; 3.1; 11.51
kālo (kālah), time-limit, 11.32
kamalapatrākṣa, Person whose eyes are shaped like lotus petals,11.2
keśava, pretty-haired one, 2.54; 10.14; 11.35; 13.29; 15.17;18.61,75,76
keśiniṣūdāna, slayer of Keshi, 18.1
kṛṣṇa, person with blackish complexion 1.28,31; 6.34,37,39;
11.35,41; 17.1; 18.75,78
kṣetrajñam (sarva), experiencer of all living spaces, 13.3
mādhava, descendant of Madhu, 1.36
madhusūdana, slayer of Madhu,1.34; 2.1; 6.33; 8.2
mahābāho, mighty-armed Person, 11.23
mahātman, great personality, 11.20,37
mahātmanaḥ, great personality, 11.12
mahāyogeśvaro, the great master of yoga, 11.9
maheśvaraḥ, Supreme Lord, 5.29;13.23
mahīpate, Lord of the earth 1.21
paraṁ brahma, supreme reality, 10.12
paraṁ dhāma,
supreme refuge, 10.12
ultimate sanctuary, 11.38
paraṁ nidhānam, ultimate shelter, 11.18
paramātmā, Supreme Soul, Supreme Spirit, 13.32,15.17
parameśvara, Supreme Lord, 11.3; 13.28
pavitraṁ paramaṁ, 10.12
prabho (prabhuḥ), respected Lord, 5.14; 11.4; 14.21
prapitāmahaḥ, father of Brahmā, 11.39
pūjyaḥ guruḥ garīyān, gravest spiritual master, 11.43
puruṣaḥ paraḥ, highest spirit, 13.23
puruṣaḥ purāṇaḥ, most ancient spirit, 11.38
puruṣaṁ śāśvataṁ divyam, eternal divine person, 10.12
puruṣottama, Supreme Person, 11.3; 10.15; 15.18,19
rūpaṁ, God-form, 11.45
sahasrabāho, O thousand-armed person, 11.46
sanātanas puruṣo, most ancient person,11.18

Names, Places and things

Index To Verses: Selected Sanskrit Words

A

B

C

D

E

G

H

I

J

N

O

P

R

S

T

Index to Translation

B

E

F

G

H

I

L

M

Q,R

S

W

Y

LIST OF TEACHERS

Gaudiya Vaishnava teacher: Srila Bhaktivedanta Swami Prabhupada

Hatha yoga teacher: Swami Vishnudevananda

Kundalini yoga teacher: Yogi Harbhajan Singh

Celibacy yoga teachers: Swami Shivananda, Srila Yogiraj Yogeshwarananda

Purity-of-the-psyche yoga teacher: Srila Yogiraj Yogeshwarananda

Kriya yoga teachers: Srila Babaji Mahasaya, Siddha Swami Muktananda

Brahma yoga teacher: Siddha Swami Nityananda

About the Author

Michael Beloved (Madhvāchārya dās) took his current body in 1951 in Guyana. In 1965, while living in Trinidad, he instinctively began doing yoga postures and trying to make sense of the supernatural side of life.

Later on, in 1970, in the Philippines, he approached a Martial Arts Master named Mr. Arthur Beverford, explaining to the teacher that he was seeking a yoga instructor; Mr. Beverford identified himself as an advanced disciple of Sri Rishi Singh Gherwal, an astanga yoga master.

Mr. Beverford taught the traditional Astanga Yoga with stress on postures, attentive breathing and brow chakra centering meditation. In 1972, Madhvāchārya entered the Denver Colorado Ashram of Kundalini Yoga Master Sri Harbhajan Singh. There he took instruction in Bhastrika Pranayama and its application to yoga postures. He was supervised mostly by Yogi Bhajan's disciple named Prem Kaur.

In 1979 Madhvāchārya formally entered the disciplic succession of the Brahma-Madhava Gaudiya Sampradaya through Swami Kirtanananda, who was a prominent sannyasi disciple of the Great Vaishnava Authority Sri Swami Bhaktivedanta Prabhupada, the exponent of devotion to Sri Krishna.

After carefully studying and practicing the devotional process introduced by Sri Swami Bhaktivedanta Prabhupada, Madhvacharya was inspired to do a translation of the Bhagavad-gītā. At the time, his personal Deities were a small marble set of Sri Sri Krishna-Balaram Murtis. Lord Balaram encouraged him to take a closer look at what Sri Krishna actually said in the Gītā and to consider its relevance to the history which became known as the Mahābhārata. It was under that energy of Lord Balarama that this translation was produced.

This translation does not concern religious affiliation. It is designed to give readers insight to what Sri Krishna and Arjuna discussed in the discourse, without any effort to convince or convert the reader. It is free of missionary overtones.

Krishna said this about those who study the Bhagavad-gītā:

adhyeṣyate ca ya imaṁ dharmyaṁ saṁvādamāvayoḥ
jñānayajñena tenāham iṣṭaḥ syāmiti me matiḥ (18.70)

I would be loved by the devotee who by sacrifice of his knowledge, will study this sacred conversation of ours. This is My opinion. (18.70)

Publications

English Series

Bhagavad Gita English

Anu Gita English

Markandeya Samasya English

Yoga Sutras English

Uddhava Gita English

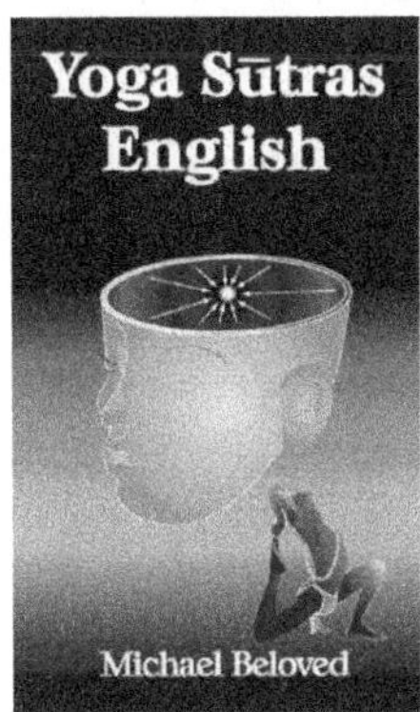

These are in 21st Century English, very precise and exacting. Many Sanskrit words which were considered untranslatable into a Western language are rendered in precise, expressive and modern

English, due to the English language becoming the world's universal means of concept conveyance.

Three of these books are instructions from Krishna. **In Bhagavad Gita English** and **Anu Gita English**, the instructions were for Arjuna. In the **Uddhava Gita English,** it was for Uddhava. Bhagavad Gita and Anu Gita are extracted from the Mahabharata. Uddhava Gita was extracted from the 11th Canto of the Srimad Bhagavatam (Bhagavata Purana). One of these books, the **Markandeya Samasya English** is about Krishna, as described by Yogi Markandeya, who survived the cosmic collapse and reached a divine child in whose transcendental body, the collapsed world was existing. Another of these books, the **Yoga Sutras English,** is the detailed syllabus about yoga practice.

My suggestion is that you read **Bhagavad Gita English**, the **Anu Gita English, the Markandeya Samasya English,** the **Yoga Sutras English** and lastly the **Uddhava Gita English**, which is much more complicated and detailed.

For each of these books we have at least one commentary, which is published separately. Thus your particular interest can be researched further in the commentaries.

The smallest of these commentaries and perhaps the simplest is the one for the Anu Gita. We published its commentary as the Anu Gita Explained. The Bhagavad Gita explanations were published in three distinct targeted commentaries. The first is Bhagavad Gita Explained, which sheds lights on how people in the time of Krishna and Arjuna regarded the information and applied it. Bhagavad Gita is an exposition of the application of yoga practice to cultural activities, which is known in the Sanskrit language as karma yoga.

Interestingly, Bhagavad Gita was spoken on a battlefield just before one of the greatest battles in the ancient world. A warrior, Arjuna, lost his wits and had no idea that he could apply his training in yoga to political dealings. Krishna, his charioteer, lectured on the spur of the moment to give Arjuna the skill of using yoga proficiency in cultural dealings including how to deal with corrupt officials on a battlefield.

The second commentary is the Kriya Yoga Bhagavad Gita. This clears the air about Krishna's information on the science of kriya yoga, showing that its techniques are clearly described free of charge to anyone who takes the time to read Bhagavad Gita. Kriya yoga concerns the battlefield which is the psyche of the living being. The internal war and the mental and emotional forces which are hostile to self-realization are dealt with in the kriya yoga practice.

The third commentary is the Brahma Yoga Bhagavad Gita. This shows what Krishna had to say outright and what he hinted about which concerns the brahma yoga practice, a mystic process for those who mastered kriya yoga.

There is one commentary for the **Markandeya Samasya English**. The title of that publication is Krishna Cosmic Body.

There are two commentaries to the Yoga Sutras. One is the Yoga Sutras of Patanjali and the other is the Meditation Expertise. These give detailed explanations of the process of Yoga.

For the Uddhava Gita, we published the Uddhava Gita Explained. This is a large book and requires concentration and study for integration of the information. Of the books which deal with transcendental topics, my opinion is that the discourse between Krishna and Uddhava has the complete information about the realities in existence. This book is the one which removes massive existential ignorance.

Meditation Series

Meditation Pictorial

Meditation Expertise

Core-Self Discovery

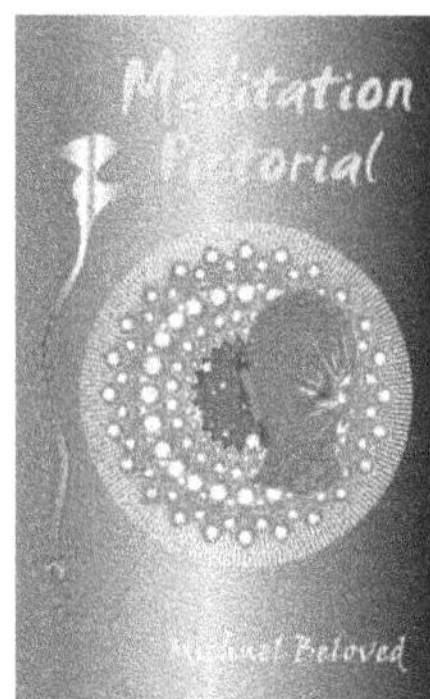

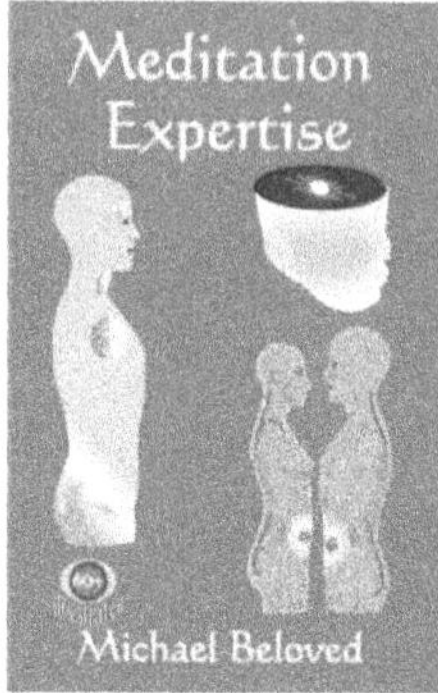

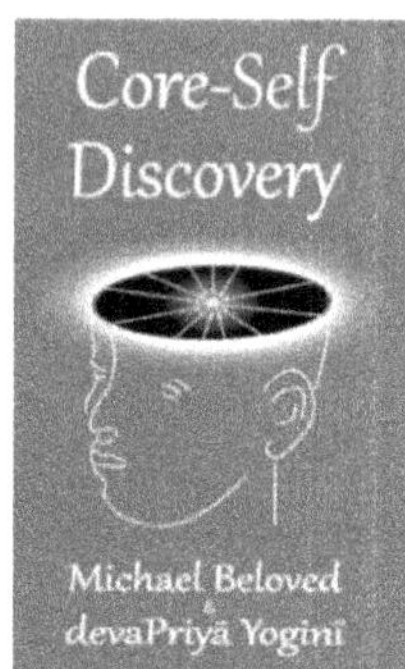

The specialty of these books is the mind diagrams which profusely illustrate what is written. This shows exactly what one has to do mentally to develop and then sustain a meditation practice.

In the **Meditation Pictorial**, one is shown how to develop psychic insight, a feature without which meditation is imagination and visualization, without any mystic experience per se.

In the **Meditation Experti**se, one is shown how to corral one's practice to bring it in line with the classic syllabus of yoga which Patanjali lays out as the ashtanga yoga eight-staged practice.

In **Core-Self Discovery**, one is taken though the course of pratyahar sensual energy withdrawal which is the 5th stage of yoga in the Patanjali ashtanga eight-process complete system of yoga practice. These events lead to the discovery of a core-self which is surrounded by psychic organs in the head of the subtle body. This product has a DVD component for teachers and self-teaching students.

These books are profusely illustrated with mind diagrams showing the components of psychic consciousness and the inner design of the subtle body.

Explained Series

Bhagavad Gita Explained

Uddhava Gita Explained

Anu Gita Explained

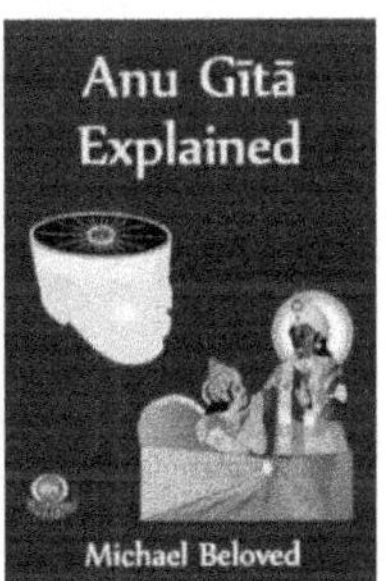

The specialty of these books is that they are free of missionary intentions, cult tactics and philosophical distortion. Instead of using these books to add credence to a philosophy, meditation process, belief or plea for followers, I spread the information out so that a reader can look through this literature and freely take or leave anything as desired.

When Krishna stressed himself as God, I stated that. When Krishna laid no claims for supremacy, I showed that. The reader is left to form an independent opinion about the validity of the information and the credibility of Krishna.

There is a difference in the discourse with Arjuna in the Bhagavad Gita and the one with Uddhava in the Uddhava Gita. In fact these two books may appear to contradict each other. In the Bhagavad

Gita, Krishna pressured Arjuna to complete social duties. In the Uddhava Gita, Krishna insisted that Uddhava should abandon the same.

The Anu Gita is not as popular as the Bhagavad Gita but it is the conclusion of that text. Anu means what is to follow, what proceeds. In this discourse, an anxious Arjuna request that Krishna should repeat the Bhagavad Gita and again show His supernatural and divine forms.

However Krishna refuses to do so and chastises Arjuna for being a disappointment in forgetting what was revealed. Krishna then cites a celestial yogi, a near-perfected being, who explained the process of transmigration in vivid detail.

Commentaries

Yoga Sutras of Patanjali

Meditation Expertise

Krishna Cosmic Body

Anu Gita Explained

Bhagavad Gita Explained

Kriya Yoga Bhagavad Gita

Brahma Yoga Bhagavad Gita

Uddhava Gita Explained

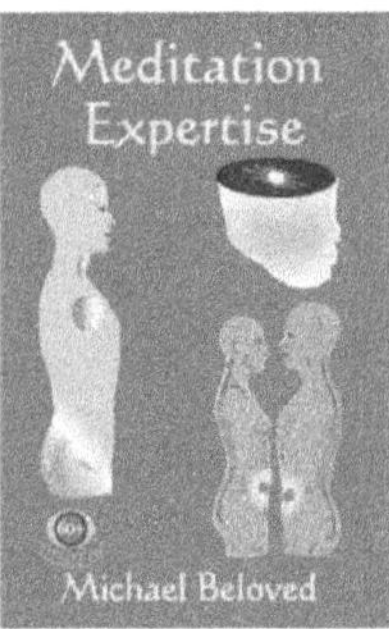

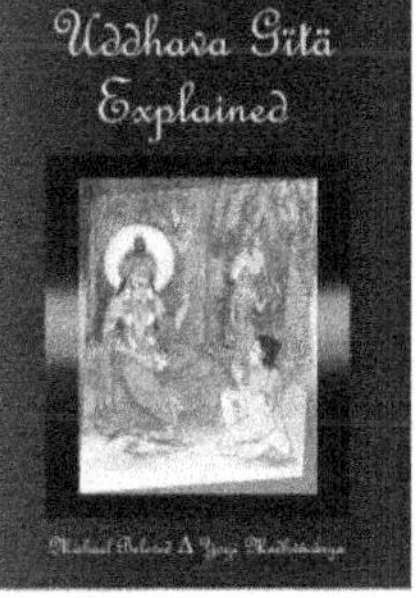

Yoga Sutras of Patanjali is the globally acclaimed text book of yoga. This has detailed expositions of yoga techniques. Many kriya techniques are vividly described in the commentary.

Meditation Expertise is an analysis and application of the Yoga Sutras. This book is loaded with illustrations and has detailed explanations of secretive advanced meditation techniques which are called kriyas in the Sanskrit language.

Krishna Cosmic Body is a narrative commentary on the Markandeya Samasya portion of the Aranyaka Parva of the Mahabharata. This is the detailed description of the dissolution of the world, as experienced by the great yogin Markandeya who transcended the cosmic deity, Brahma, and reached Brahma's source who is the divine infant, Krishna.

Anu Gita Explained is a detailed explanation of how we endure many material bodies in the course of transmigrating through various life-forms. This is a discourse between Krishna and Arjuna. Arjuna requested of Krishna a display of the Universal Form and a repeat narration of the Bhagavad Gita but Krishna declined and explained what a siddha perfected being told the Yadu family about the sequence of existences one endures and the systematic flow of those lives at the convenience of material nature.

Bhagavad Gita Explained shows what was said in the Gita without religious overtones and sectarian biases.

Kriya Yoga Bhagavad Gita shows the instructions for those who are doing kriya yoga.

Brahma Yoga Bhagavad Gita shows the instructions for those who are doing brahma yoga.

Uddhava Gita Explained shows the instructions to Uddhava which are more advanced than the ones given to Arjuna.

Bhagavad Gita is an instruction for applying the expertise of yoga in the cultural field. This is why the process taught to Arjuna is called karma yoga which means karma + yoga or cultural activities done with a yogic demeanor.

Uddhava Gita is an instruction for apply the expertise of yoga to attaining spiritual status. This is why it is explains jnana yoga and bhakti yoga in detail. Jnana yoga is using mystic skill for knowing the spiritual part of existence. Bhakti yoga is for developing affectionate relationships with divine beings.

Karma yoga is for negotiating the social concerns in the material world and therefore it is inferior to bhakti yoga which concerns negotiating the social concerns in the spiritual world.

This world has a social environment and the spiritual world has one too.

Right now Uddhava Gita is the most advanced informative spiritual book on the planet. There is nothing anywhere which is superior to it or which goes into so much detail as it. It verified that historically Krishna is the most advanced human being to ever have left literary instructions on this planet. Even Patanjali Yoga Sutras which I translated and gave an application for in my book, **Meditation Expertise**, does not go as far as the Uddhava Gita.

Some of the information of these two books is identical but while the Yoga Sutras are concerned with the personal spiritual emancipation (kaivalyam) of the individual spirits, the Uddhava Gita explains that and also explains the situations in the spiritual universes.

Bhagavad Gita is from the Mahabharata which is the history of the Pandavas. Arjuna, the student of the Gita, is one of the Pandavas brothers. He was in a social hassle and did not know how to apply yoga expertise to solve it. Krishna gave him a crash-course on the battlefield about that.

Uddhava Gita is from the Srimad Bhagavatam (Bhagavata Purana), which is a history of the incarnations of Krishna. Uddhava was a relative of Krishna. He was concerned about the situation of the deaths of many of his relatives but Krishna diverted Uddhava's attention to the practice of yoga for the purpose of successfully migrating to the spiritual environment.

Specialty

These books are based on the author's experiences in meditation, yoga practice and participation in spiritual groups:

Spiritual Master

sex you!

Sleep **Paralysis**

Astral Projection

Masturbation Psychic Details

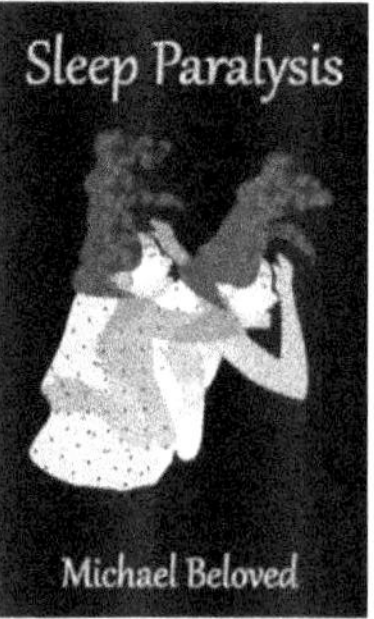

In **Spiritual Master**, Michael draws from experience with gurus or with their senior students. His contact with astral gurus is rated. He walks you through the avenue of gurus showing what you should do and what you should not do, so as to gain proficiency in whatever area of spirituality the guru has proficiency.

sex you! is a masterpiece about the adventures of an individual spirit's passage through the parents' psyches. The conversion of a departed soul into a sexual urge is described. The transit from the afterlife to residency in the emotions of the parents is detailed. This is about sex and you; learn about how much of you comprises the romantic energy of your would-be parents!

Sleep Paralysis clears misconceptions so that one can see what sleep paralysis is and what frightening astral experience occurs while the paralysis is being experienced. This disempowerment has great value in giving you confidence that you can and do exist even if you are unable to operate the physical body. The implication is that one can exist apart from and will survive the loss of the material body.

Astral Projection details experiences Michael had even in childhood, where he assumed incorrectly that everyone was astrally conversant. He discusses the life force psychic mechanism which operates the sleep-wake cycle of the physical form, and which budgets energy into the separated astral form which determines if the individual will have dream recall or no objective awareness during the projections. Astral travel happens on every occasion when the physical body sleeps. What is missing in awareness is the observer status while the astral body is separated.

Masturbation Psychic Details is a surprise presentation which relates what happens on the psychic plane during a masturbation event. This does not tackle moral issues or even addictions but shows the involvement of memory and the sure but hidden subconscious mind which operates many features of the psyche irrespective of the desire or approval of the self-conscious personality.

Online Resources

Visit The Website And Forum

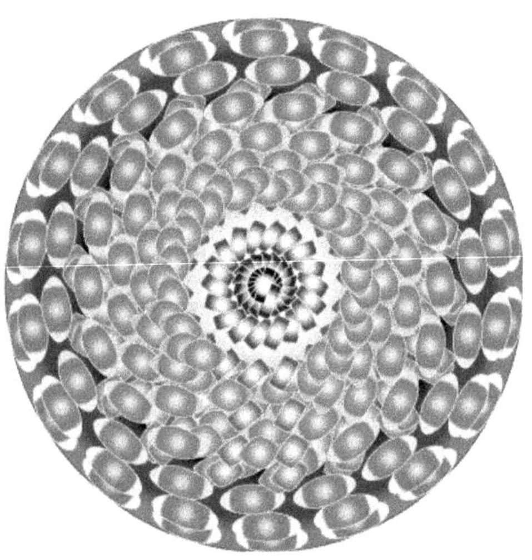

Email:	michaelbelovedbooks@gmail.com axisnexus@gmail.com
Website Forum:	michaelbeloved.com inselfyoga.com

www.ingramcontent.com/pod-product-compliance
Lightning Source LLC
Chambersburg PA
CBHW072338090426
42741CB00012B/2831

* 9 7 8 0 9 7 9 3 9 1 6 2 0 *